CENTURY IN BLACK

100 Years of All Black Test Rugby

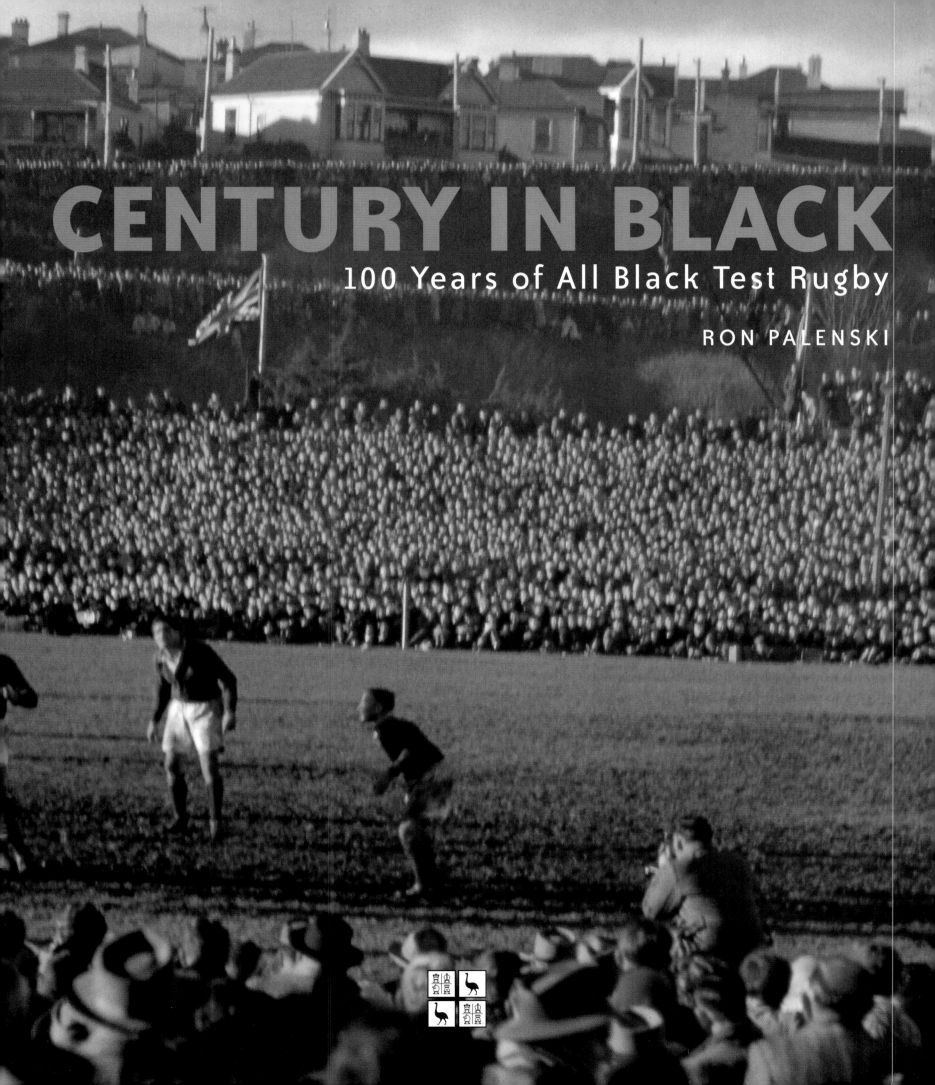

CENTURY IN BLACK

100 Years of All Black Test Rugby

RON PALENSKI

Photographic Credits

Ron Palenski Collection: Endpapers, 4–5, 14, 15, 17, 20, 21, 22, 23, 26, 27, 28–29, 33, 37, 48–49, 57, 63, 67, 75, 80, 81, 84–85, 91, 93, 94, 96–97, 107 (inset), 110, 112–113, 114, 116, 118, 121, 124–125, 126–127, 143, 144, 146, 154, 156, 157, 158–159, 172, 179, 180, 181, 184, 185, 191, 192, 193, 195, 196, 197, 198 (bottom), 200, 201, 205, 226, 227.

Fotopress: 19, 36, 38–39, 42, 43, 55, 56, 58, 60, 70, 71, 79, 82–83, 86–87, 89, 102–103, 108–109, 128–129, 131, 132–133, 137, 138, 142, 155, 166, 168–169, 170, 178, 183, 186, 190, 203, 207, 208–209, 210, 214, 215, 216–217, 218, 219, 220–221, 224–225, 229, 230–231, 232, 233, 235, 237, 238–239.

Peter Bush: 34, 40, 47, 59, 64, 73, 78, 88, 98, 100, 101, 105, 107, 119, 122, 123, 130, 134, 140–141, 145, 148–149, 150–151, 152, 160, 164, 165, 167, 171, 174–175, 175, 176–177, 182, 187, 189, 198 (top), 202, 213, 223, 228.

NZ Rugby Museum: 25, 30, 35, 41, 53, 65, 76, 77, 92, 95, 104, 161.

John Selkirk: 68–69, 153.

R. A. White Collection: 2–3, 199.

NZRFU: 11.

The Rugby Football Union: 45.

L'Equipe: 50.

Morrie Hill: 52.

Otago Daily Times: 99.

Endpapers: The multitude celebrates. Lancaster Park in 1956 after the third test against South Africa was won. Note the celebrants on the crossbar.

Pages 2–3: A city and a nation is riveted. The first test against South Africa in 1956. Carisbrook is crowded, so too the railway embankment and the road beyond, the famed 'Scotsman's grandstand' of days long gone.

This page: The final challenge. Bob Stuart's All Blacks of 1953–54 at the climax of the haka before their last match, against France at Colombes Stadium in Paris.

National Library of New Zealand Cataloguing-in-Publication Data

Palenski, Ron.
Century in black: 100 years of All Black test rugby/Ron Palenski.
Includes bibliographical references.
ISBN 1-86958-937-8
1. All Blacks (Rugby team) — History. 2. Rugby Union football — New Zealand—History. I. Title.
796.3330993 — dc21

ISBN 1-86958-937-8

© 2003 Original text Fernlea Trust
The moral rights of the author have been asserted.

© 2003 Design and format — Hodder Moa Beckett Publishers Limited

First published in 2003 by Hodder Moa Beckett Publishers Limited
[a member of the Hodder Headline Group],
4 Whetu Place, Mairangi Bay, Auckland, New Zealand

Reprinted 2003

Designed and produced by Hodder Moa Beckett Publishers Limited
Prepress by Microdot, Auckland
Printed through Imago Productions, Singapore

Contents

Acknowledgements

The photographs in this book come from many sources other than Ron Palenski's own collection of photos and rugby ephemera. The author and publishers also thank Peter Bush of Wellington, Ross Land and his staff at Fotopress in Auckland, Graeme Brown in Palmerston North, Delly Carr in Sydney, Sharon Bennett in Dunedin, and Bob Luxford, the tireless and ever-helpful curator of the New Zealand Rugby Museum.

Special thanks are extended by the author and publishers to Dave McLaren of Dunedin, Peter Crittle of Sydney and Peter Rack of Auckland for making their invaluable test programme collections available for photographing.

The author and publishers would also like to acknowledge the assistance of the New Zealand Rugby Football Union, with special thanks to the Union's chairman, Jock Hobbs, for agreeing to write the Foreword.

The author thanks the staff of the Invercargill City Libraries for so efficiently finding and copying Billy Stead's unique record of the Originals' tour.

Foreword

The New Zealand Rugby Football Union is rightly proud of the traditions and heritage of its flagship team, the All Blacks. I don't think it's boasting to say that at times the All Blacks have been world leaders in rugby and I believe that all of New Zealand, not just the game itself, can take great pride and joy in that.

The history of test matches shows that the All Blacks have a better win-loss ratio than any other national rugby team and it has been this enduring standard of excellence that has shaped and sustained all of New Zealand rugby over the past 100 years.

Rugby has changed enormously, almost out of sight, since New Zealand first played a test match in 1903 and there is neither the time nor the room here to catalogue even a fraction of those changes. But there have been some things that have not changed: the passion that New Zealanders have for their national sport and for the pride they have in the All Blacks, and the commitment and determination that the players bring to every test match. I can imagine that those pioneers who went to Sydney for the first test in 1903 had pretty much the same attitude as the players who are wearing the black jersey with the silver fern in tests in 2003: a will to win, a burning desire to do their best, and a commitment to let neither their team-mates nor their country down.

As someone who was fortunate enough to be an All Black, and who was even more fortunate to be captain, I know that contemporary players do not dwell on the past.

They're aware in a general sense of the tradition of course, and they know the All Blacks have a record and a heritage to maintain and improve on, but they do not have the time or, being young men, the inclination, to study thoroughly the lessons and examples that history provides us. Such is their single-minded pursuit of their goals, they need to seize their days rather than reflect on someone else's yesterdays.

But I also know that as players come to the end of their careers, and as they settle into rugby's long afterlife, the past takes on a greater meaning and their knowledge of what has been is more appreciated.

It is thanks to people such as Ron Palenski, who, in addition to being a keen student of the modern game, is able to value, research and record the rich history of the All Blacks and of rugby in general. He does this out of interest and passion, but he does it too for all of New Zealand. The All Blacks who have played test rugby are a select band, but I'd like to think there's a little bit of the All Blacks in every New Zealander.

This book records the passing of 100 years of rugby since the first test. It also celebrates what test rugby means to each and every one of us.

Jock Hobbs
Chairman
New Zealand Rugby Football Union

Preface

It seems like an aeon or two ago that I first saw a rugby test. I remember who played — Australia — and who won — New Zealand! — but the details of how that outcome was achieved have been left behind, if indeed they were ever with me. What remained were impressions: the sense of occasion, the collective anticipation of the crowd before the match, the thrill of the match itself and the warm nationalistic afterglow of another victory. There were also memories of sights: of people wearing black and white rosettes with long black and white ribbons attached to their lapels; sometimes it was just a simple black ribbon with the words 'New Zealand' in white on it, with the ribbon hanging from a small metal rugby ball. There may also, though I don't recall noticing them at the time, have been similar displays of allegiance in the green and gold of Australia. But this was in the age before large supporters' parties followed their teams and, anyway, it was also in the days when Australia were not considered a serious threat to New Zealand — not like the Springboks or the Lions and not, alas, like now.

To young New Zealand boys of the 1950s, or at least this young New Zealand boy, the All Blacks were as gods. The black of their jerseys and shorts seemed formidably blacker than the coal we shovelled onto the fire at nights; the white of their collars, the silver ferns and the two hoops on their socks were impossibly white, 'whiter than white' as the Persil ads used to have it.

It wasn't so much their size, though they were big men to a young boy, but their bearing and their attitude that made them seem like giants. It was only in later years I realised that the burden of history and tradition they carried on their broad shoulders, and behind them the ghostly unheard sound of a thousand trampling boots of footballers who had gone before, added to the impression of size. A reputation forged by victories, a trail of excellence, had to be upheld.

Many test matches were to follow, in New Zealand and elsewhere, and the boy became a man and the All Black gods were reduced to mortals; but still the apprehension, the anticipation, the thrill and the afterglow of tests has remained.

They are a special part of the New Zealand sporting pysche, and maybe the qualifying adjective isn't needed. While it may be true that the frequency of tests in recent years, and the quality of some opponents, may have diminished in some eyes the status of all tests, matches by the national rugby team against a team from another country, remain the centrepiece of the New Zealand sporting landscape. Other sports, other events, have their days in the sun, or under lights, but it is rugby tests which underpin the soul of the sporting nation because it is in rugby tests that New Zealand has been so continually successful.

The record of the All Blacks in tests in anyone's language is astonishing and must represent an achievement barely able to be matched, if at all, in any sport. Since the first quiet beginning on a Saturday afternoon in Sydney on August 15, 1903, the All Blacks have played 367 tests and have won almost 72 per cent of them. Think of the superlative sporting teams of 100 years, think of Manchester United or Brazil in soccer, of the Yankees in American baseball or of the Australians in cricket, and wonder if their records over the same period stand comparison.

The All Blacks, like it or not, and a great deal of New Zealanders certainly do like it, are the flagship of not just New Zealand rugby, but of New Zealand as a whole. In our isolationist islands in a corner of the world, it's important to us as a country that we're noticed by others, that we achieve where others don't, that though we're small and though we barely register on the radar of the great countries of Europe, Asia and North America, we can and do make a difference. We contribute. Many New Zealanders have done so but none so often and none so enduringly as the All Blacks.

The All Blacks are many. About 700 New Zealanders, plus the odd foreigner, have been admitted to that most exclusive of clubs that is made up of those who have played rugby tests for New Zealand. While it is the record of the All Blacks as a collective that is extolled, while it is the national team that has fashioned such an impressive and enviable record in the rugby world, it is the players — the parts that make up the whole — who take the credit. Rugby to many is the ultimate team game, but it is the skills, commitment, pride and passion of the individuals which have made it so. Some of the great names of New Zealand sport — of the great names of New Zealand — have had greatness thrust upon them because of their contributions as rugby players. And each of them will have known that, but for their team-mates, and but for the caprices of sport, such greatness may have passed them by.

There are names that signpost rugby eras: Billy Wallace and Dave Gallaher of the Originals; Bert Cooke, Mark Nicholls and the incomparable George Nepia of the Invincibles; Bob Scott and Fred Allen of the wartime Kiwis and the All Black teams that followed; the men of the 1950s and 60s such as Don Clarke, Wilson Whineray, Kel Tremain, Brian Lochore and the mighty Pinetree himself, Colin Meads; the 70s men such as Bryan Williams, Graham Mourie, Grant Batty, Andy Haden; and so on into the 80s, the 90s and a new century. Even singling out such giants of the game leaves too many unnamed.

It is self-evident that rugby has changed almost beyond recognition from the time New Zealand rugby players — not even the All Blacks then — played their first official test, this against Australia at the Sydney Cricket Ground in 1903. It had changed within 10 years of their playing and has changed gradually and often since. To Billy Wallace, today's game would seem an entirely different game. To Anton Oliver, rugby in Wallace's day would not look like the game he plays. But as a Frenchman once wrote, before an oval ball had been kicked in France in earnest, *Plus ça change, plus c'est la même chose* — the more things change, the more they remain the same. And what is the same for the All Blacks in tests is their commitment and their attitude and their collective will to play as best as they're able so they can score more points certainly, but also so they maintain the record of excellence that has been established and continued by their forebears. There is a desire not to let themselves down, not to let their supporters down and not to let their jersey down. Their jersey is not just a piece of cloth that over the years has represented changing fashions and fabrics, but is in a sense the essence of their being, their reason for playing.

The All Blacks in 1903 and for the next 90 or so years were amateurs, in name and in fact. Since 1995, the All Blacks have been professionals and by comparison with the average in New Zealand, they have been well paid. Rugby players were among the last of sportsmen to be freed of the amateur shackles fastened by 19th century England. Money and market value are now factors in New Zealand rugby, as in rugby elsewhere, and sometimes, perhaps too many times, more money elsewhere takes New Zealanders out of the New Zealand game. But for those who stay to remain as All Blacks, or for those who aspire to be All Blacks, the lure of the jersey is a more powerful magnet than riches available elsewhere. They want to be All Blacks first. In that respect they're no different from any one of their predecessors who were amateurs. It is 100 years of achievement; it is winning 72 per cent of tests played, not the span of a contemporary playing career, that has created that lure. The riches of All Black rugby are not built on sponsorship or endorsement contracts or television rights — they are a by-product. The richness of All Black rugby is built on the sustained excellence of the teams that played, and mostly won, tests from 1903. Every so often a player from an earlier era might lament that when he played he struggled for a quid and how he'd love to be playing now when he could set himself up for life. It is a lament deserving of a sympathetic ear because it was through the efforts of those players that the platform of today was established, just as it is through the efforts of players today that the future should be assured.

The centennial of New Zealand rugby's 100 years of tests was a milestone that had to be marked. Too much of rugby history, too much of New Zealand history, is encompassed in the 100 years of tests for it not to be. The idea of this book was grasped with typical enthusiasm and wholeheartedness by managing director Kevin Chapman and executive editor Warren Adler of Hodder Moa Beckett, the publishing company that has done so much to chronicle rugby and other sports in New Zealand. Their passion for publishing books is matched only by their passion for the game that is represented so well in their list.

It was thanks to them that early in 2001 I revisited some scenes of a well-spent youth and spoke again to players who were great in their times and who, in the memory, shall forever remain great. Men such as Gareth Edwards and Phil Bennett in Wales, Ian McLauchlan, Andy Irvine and Ian McGeechan in Scotland, Will Carling in England, Tony Ward of Ireland, Philippe Sella in France . . . and many more welcomed me warmly and relived their memories, revelling in the brotherhood of rugby.

A contemporary All Black who, to spare his blushes, shall remain nameless, asked what these 'old buggers' were like and how co-operative they were. They were like, I told him, any rugby player of a high level anywhere at any time, and they were as co-operative as he was and many other All Blacks, young and old, whom I approached.

If there was one overwhelming impression gained from talking to overseas stars of the past, it was the huge respect they had for the All Blacks, both in their playing days and since. If I heard the line 'There's no such thing as a weak All Black team' once, I heard it dozens of times. These men with their glory unfaded had stayed in touch with the game; they knew the talk about a gap between New Zealand and the rest being smaller now than it was, perhaps even non-existent; they knew and understood that in a wholly professional environment New Zealand did not have the financial muscle to be on equal terms with an England or a France, but still their faith in the All Blacks was unqualified, their respect undiminished, their regard unflagging. They had seen the All Blacks from across the divide. Those of us who are on the New Zealand side, who have lived through the emotions of following the All Blacks at home and away, who have devoured millions of words about All Blacks of the past, can feel no less. A little of the All Blacks resides in all New Zealanders.

I thank all those players to whom I spoke for sharing their experiences. Some were interviewed specifically for this book, others have been interviewed at various times in various places over many years. The New Zealand Rugby Football Union also provided at different times scrapbooks and other assistance.

I particularly thank Kevin Chapman and Warren Adler of Hodder Moa Beckett for their faith, their enthusiasm and their company and may all three in equal parts be continued.

Writing colleagues helped me along the way, particularly Steve Bale, Richard Bath, Norman Harris and Bill Lothian in Britain, and Jean-Roger Delsaud in France, who acted as chauffeur and interpreter as well.

As always, I thank my family for their usual forbearance when I either had my nose stuck in some rugby material or was peering past it at a computer screen that thankfully didn't remain blank.

Ron Palenski
Dunedin, February 2003

Introduction

It is August, 1903. Two men are driving a five-horsepower Locomobile on their way to completing the first trip by a motor car between Auckland and Wellington. Joe Warbrick, captain of the Natives rugby team that made an epic tour of Britain in 1888, dies in an eruption of Waimangu geyser. Cornwall Park in Auckland, named for the Duke and Duchess of Cornwall who had visited New Zealand two years earlier, is opened to the public. The city of Wanganui has the only motorised fire engine in New Zealand.

The rugby players from New Zealand are in the Metropolitan Hotel in Sydney. It is early Friday evening. It's raining and most of the players are sitting around playing cards in the parlour of the hotel. A fire flickers in the grate. Tobacco smoke from pipes and cigarettes hangs in the air. Someone is playing the piano in the corner of the parlour. They'd spent the morning at a brewery, where they briefly sampled the product, and in the afternoon they were given a tour of the Sydney docks, Australia's shop window to the world.

None of the players has played a test before for the very good reason that the match on the morrow is New Zealand's first. But all are talented footballers, some very experienced, some less so, and all know the importance of the game that's now fewer than 24 hours away. For the first time, New Zealanders are preparing to play a rugby match against Australia.

It started to rain while they were down at the docks and it's still raining. It's what keeps the players cooped up in their hotel, though a few go for a brief walk after the team meal that began at 6 p.m.

It is a quiet night. A team of footballers from Melbourne who play the Victorian rules game is also in the hotel and there has been some friendly joshing between the two groups. But now the Victorians leave the Maorilanders alone; they know they are beginning to concentrate on what lies ahead.

Jimmy Duncan, bald and stocky, sits with some of the players, talking quietly about how the rain, if it continues, may affect the surface of the Sydney Cricket Ground. You may need to keep the ball at toe, he will have said. A football gets idly passed from one player to the next. It's more round than oval, it's a dark brown leather and its laces protrude where they conceal the valve.

There are other New Zealanders in the hotel. They approach the players and exchange a few words of greeting and best wishes. They too can feel the tension rising, like the buildup of magma far underground, waiting to unleash itself the next day. Tom Pauling, who played for New Zealand and is now a referee in Sydney, is among them.

Singly or in twos or threes the rugby players leave their cards and cribbage boards on the small, round wine tables and head off up the stairs. See you in the morning. Yeah, get a good night's sleep. Duncan is among the last to leave, perhaps because he's the oldest, perhaps because he wants to make sure none of his players is still about. He might stroll out of the hotel's imposing front entrance, just to check if it's still raining. It is.

It is morning. It is January 3, 1925 and the All Blacks are in London. Back home, the *Wahine* has just a few days before completed a record crossing from Wellington to Lyttelton in eight hours 21 minutes. Sir Charles Fergusson has taken over as the chief resident of Government House in Wellington. William Ferguson Massey doesn't know it, but he's entering his last year as premier.

It is unlikely that Cliff Porter, as dear to him as Wellington is, will have thought of such things if he knows of them. He is the captain of the New Zealand rugby team and for 27 matches in England, Wales and Ireland they have gone unbeaten. One match remains. One match alone will decide whether they will end with a record equal to that of the Original All Blacks of 20 years before or whether they will finish their tour unbeaten. Porter is the

The Union Steam Ship Company's first — and fast — *Wahine*.

captain, but not the captain today. Nevertheless, like outdoor sportsmen of any generation, he gets out of bed and pads over to the window and pulls the heavy drapes aside to check on the weather. A grey overcast hangs so low it seems to rest on the chimney pots that sprout from the roofs. The hotel, one of the grandest in London, is typical of its type and of its time. Porter's room has a washbasin on one wall with a small face towel hanging from a rail underneath. He splashes cold water on his face, dresses and walks down the broad staircase to the dining room.

They only arrived at Berner's Hotel the day before by train from Deal on the Kent coast, where they had spent Christmas. They'd had a free afternoon and most players strolled around the shops of Oxford and Regent Streets, buying presents and souvenirs for home.

All Blacks relax by an open fire at their hotel in Deal on the Kent coast during Christmas 1924. Above, the well-organised and well-dressed Invincibles' manager, Stan Dean.

Other players are already gathered, though there is no set time for breakfast on test match morning. Each player eats in his own time and the obliging hotel staff has been alerted to differing needs at differing times. The captain for the day, big Jock Richardson, is already there. So, too, is another senior player, Mark Nicholls. The Brownlie brothers are there, inseparable as always. The manager, Stan Dean, who seems never to sleep and who seems never to be seen in public in anything other than a suit and tie, is reading *The Times*. 'Morning Tugboat, morning boys,' Porter says. (Tugboat because Dean's initials were S.S.) 'Good night?' Nods and grunts of assent. Test match morning is the worst of times to expect idle chat among the players. Dean knows better than to tell his charges what *The Times* man is saying in his preview of the match against England. Complimentary of the All Blacks or not, it's irrelevant. The time for words is almost done; the time for action is approaching. If the players aren't ready now, Dean knows, they never will be.

He hands them a cablegram received from the New Zealand union in Wellington: 'WE ARE ALL WITH YOU ON THIRD STOP WISH YOU A FINE DAY DRY GROUND AND LUCK FIFTY-FIFTY STOP HAPPY NEW YEAR TO YOU ALL STOP.'

Conversation is mostly confined to the necessities determined by hunger and politeness. Pass the salt please. The milk please. Sleep well? You feeling all right? There are inquiries, though, about the state of Bert Cooke's knee. He's had what the doctor said was synovitis, but to the players it's known as water on the knee. He's all right and will play.

Breakfast comes, plates go. Players drift in and drift out. Some pick up odd pages of *The Times* or the *Daily Telegraph* and look without seeing, read without comprehending. Minds are a few hours distant.

After breakfast, some players go for a stroll along Piccadilly, thankful the wintry showers of the past few days are gone. The skies remain leaden; London's infamous smog hangs in the chilly air, but at least it's dry. Players head for their rooms to get their gear ready, maybe clean their boots, maybe fiddle with other chores, anything while they think about the pending game and try to keep the nervousness at bay.

Bill Gray lies on his bed and idly picks away at his guitar, a constant companion. Room-mate Ron Jarden doesn't mind. He's heard it many times before but Gray is a good guitarist, the music isn't intrusive, and it helps them both relax. It's late in the morning in Christchurch on Saturday, August 18, 1956. For New Zealand rugby, it is the day of days. The All Blacks have to beat the Springboks. They know it, the selectors demand it, the country cries out for it. A test each and two to go. A win today, the series can't be lost. A simple equation, a Herculean task.

The tour, this match, is riveting, thrilling, chilling New Zealand like no other event of 1956. Not the Prime Minister, Sid Holland, laying the foundation stone for the Auckland Harbour Bridge. Not the death, sad as it was, of Opo the dolphin at Opononi. Not the noisy exit of diesel buses and the quiet entry of trolley buses in

Christchurch. Not the first cricket test win earlier. Not the two New Zealand gold medals at the Melbourne Olympics later.

Breakfast for those who wanted it is long gone. Brunch for those who had it is just gone. The signposts of the day get ticked off as the match approaches. Kickoff is at 2.30 and the aim is to get there about an hour before. All going to plan, the second half of the third curtain-raiser will have just started. It's between Christchurch Boys High and Otago Boys High. The All Black captain, Bob Duff, played for the CBHS first XV 13 years before, but he'll have more things on his mind than watching his old school. The first of the three curtain-raisers started at 10 a.m. and, in between, the Band of the Third Armoured Regiment kept the growing crowd entertained. But the players know none of this.

They're mostly in their rooms. Radios may be playing in some but, for most, it is the quiet before battle commences. It is the time of contemplation, of going over in the mind what has been talked about over the last few days — the All Blacks assembled in Christchurch on the Tuesday, which was unusually early — and what is to come. Boots get given another unnecessary polish, other gear is checked and checked again. The time for the second-last talk approaches. This will be from the chairman of selectors, Tom

Morrison, and the coach of the forwards, Bob Stuart.

The players know what happened after the second test was lost, how the Rugby Union council had a special meeting, how the selectors were carpeted at that meeting, how changes were made. But they put such things from their minds. They think about what's to come and what they can control, not what's been and what they can't.

Two among them are new. One is completely new. Don Clarke, the big-kicking fullback from Waikato, brought in to stiffen the All Blacks' defence, missed a couple of the trainings in Christchurch because of a cold. But when he's asked on the morning of the match how he is, he says he's as right as rain, as good as gold.

The other is not so much new as an older one brought back in time of crisis. Kevin Skinner is relaxed, laconic. He had also been retired until Morrison went in search of him. He's been a little taken aback by the intense feelings in Christchurch, the tense atmosphere. It's like being in a kamikaze pilots' training camp, he says. But he's there to do a job, to shore up the front row.

The players dress in their uniform of grey serge slacks with turned up cuffs, heavy black blazer, white shirt and narrow black tie with silver stripes and the letters, 'NZRFU'. It is time for the team talk. It is time to file into one of the hotel lounges, a room that will

CAST IN BLACK

Myths are the Old Man's Beard of history and, like the pesky vine, their reach is insidious and enduring. Rugby, like all sports, has its myths and none better — or worse, depending on how romantic the beholder is — than that about William Webb Ellis.

The most enduring myth specific to the All Blacks is how they acquired their name. While researching an earlier book, *The Jersey*, I found that the 1905 Originals had been referred to as the All Blacks in a report of their first match.

The *Express and Echo* in Devon recorded the day after the Originals beat Devon 55–4: 'The All Blacks, as they are styled by reason of their sable and unrelieved costume . . .'

This in 15 words — an apposite number in the circumstances — put the lie to the hoary old story about how a reporter later in the tour wrote of the team as 'all backs' but some interfering intermediary, copytaker, sub-editor or linotype operator, thought he knew better and inserted an 'l'.

This story gained currency because it was believed by one of the Originals, Billy Wallace, and he often related it. Since he was the last of the Originals to die (in 1972), his word was taken as gospel.

Further research has shown that the All Blacks were indeed referred to as 'all backs', but the context was a complete reversal of the myth.

Around the time the Originals were in Scotland for their first test, vice-

captain Billy Stead reflected on the tour so far in his weekly column in the *Southland Times*. Stead was a prolific chronicler of the team's doings and not much, it seemed, escaped his notice.

Stead wrote about the All Blacks' unbeaten record to that point and told how British writers were trying to work out why the team was so good.

'The nearest guess to the secret of our success,' he wrote, 'was by a well-known army officer who suggested the altering of the name All Blacks to "all backs". For, he said, the moment the ball is secured or lost in the scrum then the whole fifteen "Sweeps" seem to be backs.'

Stead did not name the army officer but two were regular writers about the tour. One was Captain the Hon Southwell FitzGerald, who wrote for *The Sporting Life*, and the other was Major Philip Trevor, who wrote for *The Sportsman*.

Of the two, Trevor probably qualified for the description 'well known' since he seemed to have been a man about the sporting town early in the 20th century. He didn't just confine himself to rugby, either. He was also manager of an MCC tour of Australia in 1907–08, covered the matches during the tour for

until the speaking starts be as quiet as any tomb. The first step of the final journey to the match is taken.

Brian Lochore talks quietly. He doesn't raise his voice. He doesn't need to. Every pair of ears is attuned to what he is saying. Every mind has shut out everything but what the coach is saying. They're at the Poenamo on the North Shore, a home away from home for a generation of All Blacks. The bus waits outside, its motor running already. It's a part of the ritual. A bus having to start up while the players are on board delays the transition from hotel to ground and there's always a chance it won't start. Nothing can be left to chance. So the motor runs while Lochore talks.

It is June 20, 1987. It is final day. World Cup final. There has been no other. It is the most important match in the lives of the 15 players who will take the field and of the other 11 who are as much a part of the playing team as a piston is part of an engine.

The All Blacks have not had a good couple of years. Losses on the field yes, but also losses off it: a loss of public support because of the attempt to send a team to South Africa in 1985, then a split in the ranks when the unofficial team went in 1986. That's past in the players' minds, but the public — the general public, not the committed rugby supporters — took longer to win over.

Lochore tells his players they represent all of New Zealand. Divisions are of the past. He talks about France and how they played the previous week against Australia, how France showed then how good they could be, how they can deliver the unexpected when it is least expected. But that was a week ago. Perhaps they showed their hand a week early but Lochore doesn't say that. And in any case, if they hadn't shown their hand it would be Australia in Auckland now. But it's not. It's France.

Lochore, like coaches before him, goes over the broad outline

The start of an epic voyage . . . an invitation to the Originals' farewell.

the *Daily Telegraph* and later wrote a book on the tour.

I could find no record of either of them referring to the team as 'all backs' though the phrase did appear in another newspaper that gave copious coverage to the tour, the *Daily Chronicle*.

In a report of the Originals' 47–0 victory against Oxford University, the paper's writer — who was not identified — looked ahead to the next match, which was against the other great English university, Cambridge.

'I see that Cambridge,' he wrote, 'are to employ the device of five three-quarters and seven forwards in tomorrow's match and this seems to be a move in the right direction for the scrummage is the merest detail in New Zealand football.

'At the same time, even five three-quarters, plus the two halves, cannot be regarded as possessed of the capacity to cope with a team who, ignoring all the traditional theories, convert themselves into all backs.'

As was previously known, teams at the time were often referred to by their colours — Wellington were 'the Blacks' a century before they became the Lions — and the Originals' manager, George Dixon, referred to his players as 'the Blacks' when recording their daily activities in his diary on board ship on the way to Britain.

And why black?

There's no definitive answer. It's well enough known that the New Zealand union decided at its first annual general meeting in 1893 that the national team's uniform would be a black jersey with a silver fern and white knickerbockers. The white knickerbockers became black shorts before the end of the 19th century. That still doesn't answer the 'why'.

The man who moved the successful motion on the uniform at the 1893 meeting was one of the Wellington delegates, Tom Ellison, a man of considerable achievement who, among other things, was the dominant forward in the 1888 New Zealand Native team that toured Britain and Australia. Its jersey had been black with a silver fern while the jersey worn by the first New Zealand team, in

1884, had been blue with a gold fern.

It is presumed that Ellison felt that the national team continuing to wear the colours worn by the Native team was an appropriate way to go. The Feilding club must have thought the same. It had adopted an all black uniform, complete with silver fern, in 1889 but changed to black and gold in deference to New Zealand.

Why the Native team chose black has not been recorded, but the reasons may have been prosaic. One of the promoters of the Natives' odyssey, Tom Eyton, had been born in Britain and would have known the national colours of the teams the Natives would face. The Natives playing in white, blue, red or green would therefore have made no sense. The range of colours available in imported bolts of cloth in the 1880s would not have been great, either, so perhaps the Natives' decision on dress came down to the Henry Ford maxim: you can have any colour as long as it's black.

of the game plan again. But it is not a time for detail; that time has gone. It is a time for complete and utter dedication and commitment to a task.

He mentions a few players by name: Andy Dalton, the captain who never played but who has been invaluable; David Kirk, the captain who did play and who has been equally valuable. The players who are not playing today and who never played in the cup.

Lochore mentions the weeks that have gone, the five cup matches that preceded today. All would be for nought if today is not seized. He talks about the eyes of the world, the eyes of New Zealand, the eyes of families and friends and mates, on what they do today.

He could quote from Shakespeare's rendering of Henry V before Agincourt: 'He that lives this day and comes safe home will stand a-tiptoe when the day is named.'

But he doesn't. That is not the Lochore style. He conveys the same feeling with different words.

Then it is done. It is time for the bus. The players walk out of their meeting room, faces immobile, voices mute. Each with his own thoughts but none with thoughts to share. They pick up their bags on the way and file out to the bus. On their way, outside the hotel on the street, they're greeted by an extraordinary sight, a level of spontaneous public support not seen since the dark days of 1981. There's about 1000 people there — clearly not going to the game, just wanting to be a part of the occasion and to wish the All Blacks well. Applause breaks out, supportive comments are shouted. It's a moving scene and the All Blacks can't help but notice it, can't help but be buoyed by it. Lochore, too, is touched by it.

When all are on the bus, Lochore, sitting behind the driver, utters a quiet 'Let's go'.

Along the motorway and over the bridge, the bus is recognised. Some people give a cheery wave, some roll down windows and shout good wishes, some toot their horns.

When the bus goes up Cook Street and waits at the lights for the swing right, more people recognise them. More waves and cheers. Comments such as 'Go, All Blacks!', 'We're with you, boys!' When the bus gets on to Sandringham Road, it has to slow, such is the density of traffic and of people criss-crossing the road. The players in their silent reverie still see the people and appreciate what they see. What they see is that New Zealand is with them. Unlike some times of the recent past, these are a group of young New Zealand men on their way to do their country's bidding. The country is with them and wills them on.

The bus pulls to a halt in Reimers Avenue, alongside the back of the main stand. It is almost time.

The players file from the bus, some chewing, some with headphones on, all silent. It is night. It is Sydney, 2002. The bus pulls in under the main stand of the huge stadium that in its brief

life has seen sporting drama run its gamut from delight to despair, celebration to desolation. Here, the All Blacks are shielded from the public. The supporters, those in black and white and waving New Zealand flags, and those in gold scarfs and waving various flags depicting their Australianness, see the bus only briefly before it glides down a ramp into the bowels of the stadium.

The players pick up their gearbags and head for the dressing room; various management people pick up what's left — the bigger bags of spare gear, the folded massage table, other equipment. The manager, Andrew Martin, ever vigilant, ever industrious, ensures nothing is left behind and somehow contrives to get to the dressing room in time to ensure no interlopers are there. There are none. Players walk in where jerseys lie neatly folded in their designated places, numbers uppermost. Socks are folded alongside. They drop their bags at their places; some sit, some seek out the toilet, but most head down the long sloping tunnel to the arena.

Players do this; they have always done this. They arrive at a ground, they walk out onto the ground. They sniff the air, they throw up bits of grass to test the wind, they stand in pockets and that's where their hands are, too. They gaze at the curtain-raiser without really seeing it. They have what soldiers in Vietnam used to call the 1000-yard stare, a gaze that goes beyond the immediate into the future. Some players wander away on their own. Andrew Mehrtens talks to one of the television people on the touchline. Then he chats to someone else. Then he ventures out onto the field, testing the wind, looking up at the night sky as if wondering what the stars foretell for him tonight.

The dressing room door opens. Martin, ball in hand, says, 'It's time, Reuben.'

John Mayhew, the doctor who first went to Australia with the All Blacks in 1988, is just as apprehensive as the players. All associated with the team feel the tension. They take deeper breaths than usual. Some idly chuck a ball around. Some, to use the apt Australian vernacular, have just chucked.

John Mitchell and Robbie Deans walk from player to player with words of encouragement or words of advice. Whatever they are, they're lost on the night breeze.

Mitchell gives a signal and they start returning to the dressing room. Some have a massage, others would have had one back at the hotel which is just 150 metres or so away. Some strap their own ankles or other parts of their bodies that need support, others line up to have it done for them. They change into shorts, socks, T-shirts and runners. Some put on tracksuit tops. It's time for the warm-up out on the ground. No idleness this time, no thoughts in which to be lost. It's a time for the grids that All Blacks first did in 1986; it's time for the whole range of loosening-up exercises.

The crowd is building but the players barely notice. Their opponents are down the other end of the field but there's no thought for them.

Another signal from Mitchell and back under the stand. Reuben

Introduction

Thorne joins referee André Watson and Australian captain George Gregan for the toss. Gregan wins. The two shake hands but it's perfunctory and there's no eye contact.

Thorne returns to the dressing room and calls his players together. All but the players have left by now. He talks briefly. The players form a tight circle, arms around each other.

The dressing room door opens. Martin, ball in hand, says, 'It's time, Reuben.'

He walks out, takes the ball, starts to trot as he reaches the turf and an ear-splitting noise comes from the New Zealanders in the crowd.

Out in the middle, they get together again as the Australians come out to an even greater wall of sound.

The captains tell their teams to line up for the anthems. As has become the norm, the visiting team's anthem is first. 'E Ihoa Atua, O nga Iwi! Matoura, Ata whaka rongona; Me aroha noa . . .'

Some players grip each other tightly. Some sing the whole anthem, some just the words in English. Some tears slip down unshaven cheeks. Hearts thud. Knees tremble.

Then it's the Australians' turn and the crowd belts it out: 'Australians all let us rejoice, for we are young and free . . .'

The All Blacks have their own thoughts, trying to blot out the overt nationalism from a country that is not theirs, a country they are there to beat.

The anthems over, the All Blacks assemble for the haka. The Australians line up opposite, and the referee and his touch judges are alongside . . . just in case. Caleb Ralph leads the haka. 'Ka rita!' he shouts as he faces the All Blacks, urging them to be ready. Then he faces his enemy of the night.

'Ka mate! Ka mate! . . .'

It is done.

John Williamson sings 'Waltzing Matilda' from the touchline just in front of the Australian reserves and the crowd joins in. It's intended to be the Australian answer to the haka. The All Blacks ignore it.

Andrew Mehrtens places the ball at halfway. Watson looks over at Thorne. 'Okay?' he asks. Thorne raises a hand. Watson searches out Gregan. 'All right?' Gregan nods. The whistle blows.

It is Sydney, 2002. It could have been Sydney, 1903.

Everything has changed but nothing has changed.

Head to head. Opposing captains Reuben Thorne and George Gregan during the Bledisloe Cup test in Sydney in 2002.

Genesis – the First Test

They were young men on an adventure, those New Zealand footballers who went to Australia in 1903. Three times before, New Zealand teams had gone to Australia but this visit was different; this visit heralded not just change, but the beginning of a century in black of test matches. Great were the expectations of the New Zealanders in Sydney and they fulfilled them when they played their first international match, fulfilled them so well that the Australians were left wondering if they would ever beat their opponents from across the Tasman. The New Zealanders left for Australia with the hopes and pride of a young nation; and they left to the words of the Premier, Richard John Seddon: '. . . it behoves you footballers . . . to uphold your country's high reputation on the football field.' Over 100 years of playing tests against allcomers, they're words that echo still in the ears of all succeeding teams.

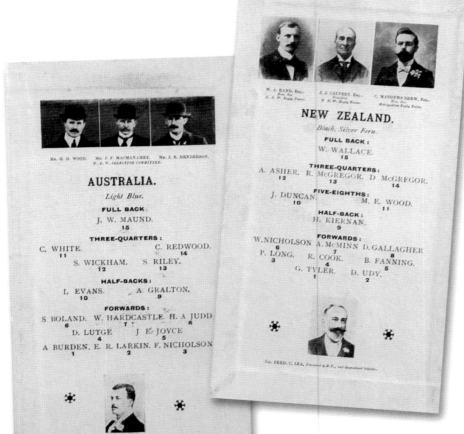

These were the men who started it all. The first New Zealanders to play a rugby test, captain Jimmy Duncan (middle row, centre) wearing his trademark beanie.

The New Zealand rugby players who lined the rails of the Union Steam Ship Company's liner *Moeraki* as it bobbed through the Sydney Heads on Wednesday, July 15, 1903 could hardly have imagined they would find immortality in the display case of history.

They were young men on the adventure of a lifetime and only their captain, 33-year-old Jimmy Duncan, and halfback 'Skinny' Humphries had been to Sydney before. They were not just young men, they were young footballers. Like young men of any generation, they wouldn't have wondered how posterity might regard them; they were there to live their moments and seize their days.

Three times had New Zealand rugby teams previously gone to Australia and three times they had returned across the Tasman victorious — 28 matches for just two losses, both of them to New

South Wales. But on none of those visits had they played the combined force of Australia.

This trip would be different. They were not All Blacks yet (they wouldn't be called that for another two years when they were in Britain), and they were not test players yet, but they soon would be.

For the first time, they who were variously called the New Zealanders, the Maorilanders or the Men from the Land of the Moa would be playing a true international match.

But not even that historic prospect would have been on their minds as the year-old *Moeraki*, with its distinctive green hull and single orange and green funnel, steamed into Sydney Harbour between South and North Heads, past Watson's Bay to port and Manly off to a distant starboard.

The magnificence of the harbour and the imminent landfall would have been enough on their own to attract the footballers to the rails. It was only just over 100 years before that Arthur Philip had commanded the First Fleet through the same heads and described what he saw as 'one of the finest harbours in the world, in which a thousand sail of line might ride in perfect security'.

Philip had had with him his cargo of convicts, but by 1903 Sydney, a city born in misery, was showing already that it was instead a city endowed with riches.

Sydney then was still harbour-dependent. Its maritime association was inescapable; the urban sprawl was yet to begin and the majority of the population lived and worked in close proximity to the harbour.

The footballers saw this for themselves. 'I well remember our arrival in Sydney,' one of the players, Billy Wallace, later wrote. 'We had a record trip across with beautiful weather the whole way and as we entered that wonderful harbour on which Sydney stands, crowds of ferry boats filled with people going to work came alongside our ship and cheered us to the echo. It was a rousing welcome.'

Crowds lined the wharf at Circular Quay when the *Moeraki* glided into its berth, its sleek lines blending into the bustle of seaborne commerce; forests of masts and rigging marking a terminus for steamers from over the seas, for colliers from Newcastle, grain lighters from the Hawkesbury River waiting to transfer their cargo, coastal packets from Victoria and Queensland.

Circular Quay, its berths numbered from the seaward side reflecting the importance of the harbour, was thronged with people, many of them there to greet the footballers. When the ship bearing the first New Zealand team arrived in Sydney in 1884, a football was slung from its rigging to show who its passengers were. There was no need of such contrivance when the 1903 team arrived.

It had been described (as have many others since) as the finest body of footballers to leave New Zealand. They'd been beaten 14–5 by Wellington in a warm-up game the day they left New Zealand, but as government minister Sir Joseph Ward said at a farewell function for the team, the game that day should not be taken as a criterion of the team's ability. He was confident, he said,

T.S.S. MOERAKI.

they would at least equal the record of their predecessors.

They would do more than that.

The Premier, Richard John Seddon, laid a burden squarely on the footballers' shoulders, one that's seldom left any New Zealand team. 'I believe,' he said, 'that athletic sports in reasonable limits tend to improve the stability of a country. It is only a question of degree . . . it behoves you footballers all the more to uphold your country's high reputation on the football field.'

But a former footballer of note, William McKenzie, better known as 'Offside Mac' because of his wing forward play, was dismissive of the New Zealanders' chances. 'There are too many has-beens in the team,' he wrote in the Sydney *Bulletin*. 'Jimmy Duncan has outlived his usefulness. There is not enough devil about some of the forwards, who are on the slow side, while, as regards the backs, they are great in attack but poor in defence. I am afraid the team will not come back with a clean sheet.'

The *Moeraki* had left Wellington in a southerly that howled as only Wellingtonians know it can, but once into the Tasman the weather settled down and the players got to plotting.

They knew from a New South Wales tour of two years before that Australia had adopted the 3-2-3 scrum formation introduced to them by the English and much of the shipboard talk was about how New Zealand's 2-3-2 would combat this.

'This matter was very fully discussed in our team talks,' Wallace wrote, 'both on the boat going over and after we had arrived in Sydney. Jimmy Duncan was captain and was the presiding genius in our discussions. He had a great wealth of football knowledge and was a great tactician and so when we stepped out for our first match our plan of campaign had been fully mapped out. We knew exactly how we were going to pack against their eight-man scrum, who was to take the kicks and so on.'

A hundred years later, the names of the 1903 All Blacks may be just data from the past, names that fill out the roll call of 100 years of test rugby, a few of them known still but most of them the bones of history without the flesh of personal recollection. Among them were Wallace, the 'Carbine' of the Originals of 1905 and a back without peer; diminutive Auckland wing Albert Asher who was nicknamed Opai after a Great Northern Hurdles winner because he had the extraordinary ability to leap over his opponents; Jimmy Duncan, the master of tricks, feints and dodges

Crowds lined the wharf at Circular Quay when the *Moeraki* glided into its berth, its sleek lines blending into the bustle of seaborne commerce.

The Great Rugby Football Match.

AUSTRALIA v. NEW ZEALAND.

BY WANDERER.

A new era—Australia v New Zealand at football—Australia, that is, Queensland and New South Wales, the two Australian States out of the six that play Rugby. The title is rather ambitious, perhaps, and possibly New South Wales and Queensland combined would have better suited the circumstances. Will we ever be able to put a genuine Australian team in the field, whether Rugby, Australian, or "Soccer?" I am sure never at Rugby, never against England at Australian, and apparently hopeless at British Association. Saturday was the first occasion in the history of football that Queensland and New South Wales have joined forces against New Zealand. It is, however, doubtful whether the combination resulted in a better side being pitted against the visitors than New South Wales single handed could have placed in the field. The methods of the two State teams are dissimilar, the combination had no practice together, therefore it was a combination in title only. Perhaps we would have seen more combination from a team of N.S.W. players. There was no unanimity of opinion as to how the Australian team would shape. But it was generally thought the New Zealanders were too good for any fifteen we could place in the field, though it was considered that the home side would play a harder game than any that had hitherto met the visitors, and that the margin of victory would be comparatively small. The contrary was the result. The combined fifteen fairly well held their opponents up to half time, but afterwards it was simply a succession of scores for New Zealand.

Most of us have observed that in all the matches played by the New Zealanders in Sydney, they do not appear to begin to play until the second half, and then they run clean over every one who would block their progress. It matters not to them whether a pass be off side or whether there be a knock-on, they go right on, forgetting all about the existence of the referee until they hear his whistle sound. There is no deliberation about them at all. A system apparently without a thought. They think afterwards. With the Australians it is different. In the case of something occurring which is palpably illegal there is a momentary and frequently a fatal pause. If the whistle sounds it is all right, if it do not, then points follow to the visitors. This was painfully brought home to us on Saturday when we saw the Australian team "lining" out at the touch line while R. M'Gregor was running behind the home goal. M'Gregor went on until the whistle sounded, and then it was the acknowledgment that a try had been secured. That couple of seconds' deliberation by the home fifteen cost five points. The visitors play a game altogether different to the Australians. In their forward rushes they bump an opponent to the ground and walk over him or to the side, and so do some of them when running with the ball in possession. It is simply the survival of the fittest, but brute strength has rather too much to do with the game. The New Zealanders are sufficiently clever in working the scrums, in catching, line and goal kicking, in beating the tackle with smart passes, and in toe work, to defeat Australia with a good margin, in a sportsmanlike game instead of depending so much upon a force which carries with it considerable, if unchecked, illegal interference.

Everything was in favour of a brilliant game. There were fears on the Friday evening that rain would spoil the contest, indeed some fairly heavy showers fell in the city up to 11 o'clock, but, fortunately, the morning broke bright and cheerful, the ground was dry, and everything surrounding the scene looked lovely. A great crowd, there were over 30,000 present, assembled to witness the first contest of its kind, and among the interested spectators were his Excellency the Governor-General, Lord Tennyson, his Excellency the State Governor, Sir Harry Rawson, and parties from the respective Government Houses. Everything worked up to a great contest, and everyone expected a brilliant exhibition of Rugby. The game was a great one, as before mentioned, the visitors won easily, by 22 to 3, but

J. R. Henderson, Selector.   S. Boland.   A. Burdon.   E. R. Larkin.   F. C. Lea, Selector.   L. Evans.   F. Nicholson.   D. Lutge.   H. D. Wood, Selector.

J. E. Joyce.   H. A. Judd.   S. Wickham, Captain.   C. White.   J. W. Maund.
O. Redwood.   S. Riley.   W. Hardcastle.   A. Graitot.

AUSTRALIAN FOOTBALL TEAM, 1903.

COLLAPSE OF A "SCRUM."

A TOUCH-LINE STRUGGLE.

How the *Sydney Mail* told its readers about the first test played between New Zealand and Australia. The *Mail* was a weekly paper that served mainly a rural readership. It was the only Sydney paper at the time that regularly ran photographs and was the only one to illustrate such a historic moment in rugby history.

'NOT WANTED ON VOYAGE' — JIMMY DUNCAN'S JOURNEY

The place of Jimmy Duncan in New Zealand rugby history is assured. Captaining New Zealand in the first test should have been assurance enough that Duncan's name would linger long on rugby's honour roll. There were other notable entries on his rugby CV: he captained the South Island in the first interisland match in 1897, he played 48 games for Otago over a 14-year period, he was regarded as a master tactician — credited with inventing the distinctive New Zealand five-eighth positions — and he refereed a test match.

Yet his name bears with it still a constant shadow, an asterisk of doubt that stems from his role as coach of the Original All Blacks of 1905–06.

His playing background and what appears to have been an innovative, inquiring rugby brain should on the face of it have made him an ideal coach. The success of the Originals, losing just the match to Wales, should have made him as lauded as a coach as he was as a player.

But not so. Duncan's name barely figures in any of the books and reports on the Originals' tour and when he was mentioned in newspaper accounts in New Zealand, kindness was not uppermost in the writers' minds.

The captain and vice-captain of the Originals, Dave Gallaher and Billy Stead, did not even mention Duncan in their 322-page tome, *The Complete Rugby Footballer*, published after the tour and which became one of the great early classics of rugby literature.

It was the procedure on long sea voyages to tag bags that would not be needed during the passage as 'not wanted on voyage'. Duncan himself could have carried such a tag when the Originals boarded the *Rimutaka* in Wellington for the voyage to Britain.

He had been appointed coach by the New Zealand union early in 1905 but several provincial unions, notably Auckland and Southland, complained that taking Duncan would be at the expense of another player and on such a tour, long and into the unknown, they'd need all the players they could get. In the event, another player was added, Auckland lock Bill Cunningham, but Duncan remained.

A story has appeared down the years that when the Originals began their first training at Newton Abbot in Devon, Gallaher decided he'd take the forwards and Stead the backs. Duncan was shut out and, so it seems, shut out for the rest of the tour.

It may have happened even before that. Billy Wallace, in extensive memoirs he wrote for the *New Zealand Sportsman*, said Gallaher put Cunningham, who Wallace said had an invaluable knowledge of scrummaging, in charge of the forwards almost as soon as their ship had cleared the Wellington heads.

Significantly perhaps, Gallaher was from Auckland and Stead from Southland. Stead was a prolific writer throughout the tour but never once publicly mentioned the man who was ostensibly the coach.

The first public signs of discontent among the players came when the New Zealand union dispatched a team to Australia in July 1905, a tour arranged in part to raise enough money to dispatch the team to Britain a month or so later.

While in Sydney, the captain — Taranaki five-eighth Jimmy Hunter — told manager Neil Galbraith that choosing Duncan to go to Britain as coach had caused general dissatisfaction among the players.

Galbraith, who was also treasurer of the New Zealand union, lobbed this hot potato immediately to his bosses in Wellington. In a letter that had been approved by Hunter and other players, he wrote if Duncan went there would be considerable friction within the touring party.

The New Zealand union, stubbornly impenitent in the face of this player power, sent a letter to all provincial unions explaining why Duncan had been appointed. It pointed out, none too subtly, that there had been no objection when Duncan had been made coach against the British team of the year before and that no voices had been raised in protest in April when the union's annual meeting heard of Duncan's appointment.

The union also laid the blame for not taking more players on the provinces. It had appealed for more money to finance the British tour and it had offered debentures to the provincial unions. Very little assistance had been offered and only a few of the debentures had been taken up.

'The committee,' the union said, 'regretted to find . . . that owing to the very small amount taken up in debentures since the annual meeting they were reluctantly compelled to send only 25 players instead of 26 and also to send the team to Sydney purely and simply for the purpose of raising funds. The committee would be very pleased to send 30 players if they received financial support strong enough to enable them prudently to do so.'

It said it deemed the appointment of Duncan as essential — 'Mr Duncan will not only be a coach but he will be at the manager's call to assist generally in looking after the interests of the members of the team and in any other capacity that the manager may direct.'

Cunningham was added to the team after the return from Australia but Duncan remained. The provinces forced a special general meeting of the national union, at which Duncan's appointment was reconfirmed.

Discontent during the tour surfaced in a newspaper account on December 19, 1905, when the Originals were in the last third of their tour (reports were shipped home and could appear up to two months after they were written).

Relations between certain sections of the New Zealand team were very much strained, the report based on letters from players said. 'The trouble has apparently arisen out of the old sore feeling over the appointment of Jimmy

Genesis — the First Test

Duncan as coach. The letters indicate that from the first the Auckland members set themselves up in sharp opposition to Duncan and then to the Otago members in general. A number of others, including Stead, had sided with the Auckland contingent and the general result had been that every attempt by Duncan to assert authority had been met with open hostility at meetings of the team while, on the field, he has been simply ignored.'

'He is just nobody,' one of the letter writers was quoted as saying.

Such was the ill feeling within the camp that, according to the letter writer, 'a well-known Otago player gave one of the Aucklanders a good thrashing'.

In the news media of the 21st century, such assertions would be given sensational treatment. A coach being openly ignored, one player giving another a thrashing would be the stuff of big headlines, breathless television reporting, endless talkback and revelatory books. But in the newspaper world of 1905 most events were given the same understated treatment. The report of dissension in the *Southland Times* (the paper for which Stead wrote) was single column and simply headed, 'Unpleasant Statements'. In the column alongside was a similarly understated heading, 'Russia's Internal Affairs', which was all about an army mutiny in Russia and fighting in the streets as Russia was on the verge of bankruptcy.

Four days later, a reader of the *Southland Times* leapt to Stead's defence. In a letter to the editor, 'Fair Play' said if Stead had sided with the Auckland contingent, 'I have no doubt he did so thinking it in the best interests of the team as a whole and not from any personal motive or desire to slight any members of the combination.'

The affronted writer was no doubt a friend of Stead's because he then quoted from a letter from Stead: 'You need to be on a voyage like this to find the way of your chums and I can now say that they are a fine lot, not one whom I would not take into my confidence as a brother.'

Perhaps Duncan had taken too many of the team into his confidence. Being a good southern man, he had taken on the ship with him a crate of Speight's. Some players knew about it and raided and drained the supply when Duncan was elsewhere. They filled the just-emptied bottles with water and carefully recapped them. It was apparently when the ship was in the heat of Montevideo that Duncan decided to slake his thirst with some of the comforts of home. How he reacted to his nectar being turned into water was not recorded.

Wallace, whose memoirs were published 26 years after the tour in 1932, was kinder towards Duncan than some of the contemporary reports had been. 'Another man [after manager George Dixon] who put in a lot of hard work behind the scenes was Jimmy Duncan. Not only had he been a clever player, but he was able to impart his knowledge to others . . . his coaching, especially in the early part of the tour, when we were working out our plans of campaign, [was] of very great value to us and helped to weld us into a very powerful attacking combination,' Wallace wrote.

He also added, without additional comment: 'In addition to his coaching, Jimmy put in a lot of time with the injured players and assisted with the baggage.'

Duncan's All Black coaching career therefore was not a resounding success, despite the success of the team of which he nominally had charge. His playing career, however, and his service to rugby, certainly held no such question marks.

Five years after the tour, a team-mate of Duncan's in the first test in 1903, Canterbury lock Bernard Fanning, was asked by his author brother Leo to name the greatest players he had seen.

'Great players?' the elder Fanning began. 'Jimmy Duncan. I place him on top as a footballer. He knew how to get every ounce and every breath out of his men without nigger-driving them. He was plucky, too. He was as cool as the South Pole. His coolness was terrible to the other side.'

Duncan was a stocky inside back with a listed playing weight of 12 stone 4 pound (78 kg), heavier than the average for backs at the time. His most distinctive physical feature was that from an early age he was as bald as a billiard ball. He often played wearing a tweed cloth cap or a knitted cap that today would be called a beanie. This was not just out of vanity.

Another early writer, R.A. Stone, recorded that a favourite Duncan trick was to pass his cap instead of the ball, confusing his opponents in the speed and heat of the moment. He once used the ploy against Auckland and as the cap flew through the air, the Aucklanders followed it and Duncan went for the goal-line.

In Sydney, where Duncan captained New Zealand in the first test, his bald pate was exposed in a match against New South Wales.

An Australian writer recorded it thus: 'Do you remember the day a New South Wales player snatched from Jimmy Duncan's head the pointed woollen cap which the famous captain of New Zealand teams wore to hide his bald head? It was remarkable how seldom this feat was performed upon a man who threw himself so fervently, yet skilfully, into the fray. What a roar of delight went up from "the Hill" when his cunning bald pate was so blatantly exposed to public gaze and ridicule.'

Duncan also played during the Originals' tour, a fact not often recorded. He and five of the All Blacks played for a hastily assembled New York team which was beaten 46–13 by the rest of the touring team. The referee was the All Blacks' manager, George Dixon.

Jimmy Duncan

and the tactician supreme; Billy Stead, the Southlander who was one of the great thinkers of the game; the lanky George Nicholson who began his rugby life as a wing and carried his speed into the loose forwards; and Dave Gallaher, upon whom history looks fondly for his leadership of the Originals and his commanding roles in Auckland rugby until the First World War when he became a battlefield casualty.

No fullback had been picked for the team, and as Wallace matter of factly recorded, '. . . it was generally anticipated that I would fill that position and Davy Gage, who was fullback for the Native team of 1888, had coached me thoroughly in the duties of a fullback and so I found the job easy.'

Sydney was then a rugby town or, as Australians would now say, a 'union' town. The game had been played in Sydney for more than 20 years and the forerunner of the New South Wales union (and therefore of the Australian union), the Southern Rugby Union, had been formed in 1874. As the game developed, its opposition came from what was then known as the Victorian rules game that later became

An official souvenir of the New Zealand team's tour of Australia in 1903 and (below) Dave Gallaher breaks from a scrum in the first test with Opai Asher (12) and Jimmy Duncan (10) in support.

Australian rules. Early rugby authorities in Sydney evidently spent a lot of time and effort in ensuring that the distinctively Australian game that originated in Melbourne did not establish itself in Sydney.

Melbourne missionaries were still trying to spread their word in 1903 and two Victorian rules teams were resident in the Metropolitan Hotel in Sydney when the New Zealand footballers arrived. Footballers being footballers and young men being young men, the two groups got together and the merits of their games were top of the discussion list.

'They reckoned we couldn't kick,' Wallace recalled.

Duncan, as argumentative off the field as he was combative on it, invited the Aussies out to the next match to show them a kid who could kick.

As Wallace wrote, 'The kid Jimmy referred to was myself. They came out to the match and during the game Skinny Humphries (his given names were Arthur Larwill but he was Skinny to all) took a mark on the halfway line.'

In those days, marks could be claimed anywhere on the field and anyone could take the resulting kick.

'Jimmy called me up to take the shot at goal,' Wallace said. 'I protested that the distance was too great but Jimmy insisted and told me to show the Victorians what New Zealanders could do. There was no escape and so I came back about 11 yards behind the halfway line and placed the ball. The ball sailed straight and true, clean between the posts at a great height, right over the dead ball line, over the heads of the crowd and landed behind them. It was the finest goal I ever

kicked. The crowd gasped and I think the Victorians were satisfied.'

Satisfied, too, were Duncan and his team-mates with the way the tour progressed. Their first eight games in Australia were all won, the closest being the two against New South Wales, the first won 12–0 and the second 3–0. All were but entrées to the main course, the first test against Australia.

If the *Sydney Morning Herald* was any guide, and there's no reason to suppose it was not, the test match was keenly anticipated but no great hopes were held for the Australians.

'This match will mark a new era in this branch of winter sport,' it said, 'for though there have been engagements between the states and New Zealand . . . Queensland and New South Wales have not furnished a combined team until now to meet the visitors from Maoriland.

'The present New Zealand team have shown form so far in advance of every fifteen opposed to them that it seems almost impossible for Australia to put a side into the field with any hope of victory unless wet weather makes it a forward game.'

Whether this was also the prevailing view in the Australian team is doubtful. The Australians at least had had the experience of playing full test matches before. They'd played four in 1899 against a Great Britain team that, unusually, did not also go on to New Zealand.

> **'It seems almost impossible for Australia to put a side into the field with any hope of victory . . .'**

The advantage the Australians had was that they had seen more recently than the New Zealanders British developments in the game such as passing and interplay between backs and forwards. The New Zealanders, though, had developed a style of game to their own liking which, as was to be proved in two years, was vastly superior to the British style.

The British captain in 1899 had been Mathew Mullineaux, who didn't like what he saw in Australia. He thought the Aussies were introducing unbecoming habits to the game and he mentioned holding opponents back when they didn't have the ball, pushing in lineouts and calling for the ball when an opponent had it. 'Please blot these things from your football,' he said, 'for instead of developing all that is manly they bring forth all that is unmanly.'

Mullineaux, incidentally, was the only British captain never to play a test for his own country, England. A small man even by the standards of the day, he was also a schoolteacher and church curate and was listed wherever he went as the Reverend Mullineaux. He even attracted the attention of the revered Australian bard, Banjo Paterson:

New Zealanders and Australians vie for the ball in the first test between the two countries.

I'd reckon his weight at eight-stun-eight,
And his height at five-foot-two,
With a face as plain as an eight-day clock
And a walk as brisk as a bantam-cock —
Game as a bantam too,
Hard and wiry and full of steam,
That's the boss of the English team,
Reverend Mullineaux!

Though Mullineaux's team never played in New Zealand, he developed an affection for the country. He was living in San Francisco when the 1913 All Blacks were there and refereed their third match, against the Barbarians (or Barbs, as the American papers called them). When the First World War began, Mullineaux took ship to New Zealand, enlisted in the New Zealand Expeditionary Force, was designated captain-chaplain, and served throughout the war, winning the Military Cross.

In Sydney, the Australian hopes of wet weather as a leveller first rose then disappeared. It rained the afternoon and night before the match when the New Zealanders did what touring teams used to do: they were given a tour of Tooth's Brewery in the morning and of the Sydney docks in the afternoon.

By the Saturday morning, however, the rain had cleared, the sky was a duck-egg blue, there was just the gentlest of breezes and trans-Tasman rugby hostilities were set to commence.

The Australians, who wore the light blue jerseys of New South Wales, included three New Zealanders: three-quarters Sid Riley and Charlie Redwood and forward Bill Hardcastle, a Wellingtonian who had played for New Zealand in 1897.

They also included several players who later became prominent in league when it was introduced to Sydney by the New Zealand All Golds in 1907. Among them was prop Alex Burdon, a catalyst in the split from rugby when he was refused compensation for lost wages while nursing a broken jaw sustained in a rugby match.

That was all in the future, though, when Duncan won the toss in front of a crowd of 30,000 at the Sydney Cricket Ground and Australian forward Jim Joyce kicked off the first test between New Zealand and Australia.

Genesis — the First Test

The *Sydney Morning Herald*'s gloomy forecast proved to be prophetic. New Zealand led 7–3 at halftime, a penalty goal and a goal from a mark to a penalty from Australian captain Stan Wickham, but took control in the second half and won 22–3. 'The combined fifteen fairly well held their opponents up to halftime,' the *Sydney Mail* noted, 'but afterwards it was simply a succession of scores for New Zealand.'

If there was one lesson the Australians learnt from the match, it was the need to play to the whistle. The Australian habit apparently was to stop when there was a knock-on or forward pass. That was not the New Zealand way.

'It matters not to them whether a pass be offside or whether there be a knock-on,' the *Mail* said, 'they go right on, forgetting all about the existence of the referee until they hear the whistle sound. There is no deliberation about them at all. A system apparently without a thought. They think afterwards. With the Australians it is different. In the case of something occurring which is palpably illegal there is a momentary and frequently a fatal pause.'

There was evidence of this when Dick McGregor scored New Zealand's final try. There was a thought that he put a foot into touch and the Australians stopped and started to assemble for the lineout, but McGregor, hearing no whistle, ran happily on and scored under the crossbar. The referee, like a line umpire on the clay at Roland Garros, went and looked for a footprint on or over the touchline. Finding none, he signalled the try.

The *Mail* held little hope for the future of Australian rugby against New Zealand. 'It seems hopeless to expect to ever score a substantial victory over the Maorilanders,' it said. '. . . A suitable climate and a longer season have made New Zealand the headquarters of rugby in the Southern Hemisphere and though we may never be able to inflict defeat upon them, as they have upon us, we could with, say, annual meetings look forward to considerable improvement in our method of playing rugby.'

The considerable improvement, as no New Zealander needs telling, eventually came.

A panoramic shot of a corner of the Sydney Cricket Ground — complete with cycling track — during the first test.

LONG LOST ALL BLACK

Several All Blacks through the years, especially in the early days, have been given the tag 'mystery'. They're the players about whom little was written at the time and about whom even less is known now.

But the champion of all the mystery All Blacks was Paddy Long, who played in the first test against Australia in 1903. He's listed in All Black and Auckland records as 'A.J. Long' and in terms of life data, that's about all that's known. It's clear he was known as Paddy, perhaps indicating an Irish ancestry, and it's been well enough documented that he was one of the outstanding forwards of his day, but that's when the Long story becomes very short indeed. His full name is not known, his birth and death dates are question marks and what happened to him after rugby has also escaped the attention of those who would dearly love to know.

Tracking down the Long facts defeated even the indefatigable Rod Chester who, with Neville McMillan, chronicled New Zealand rugby in ways it had never been chronicled before with books such as *Men In Black*, *Centenary*, *The Visitors* and *The Encyclopedia of New Zealand Rugby*.

The bare bones of the Long career were that he first played for Auckland in 1902 and in the same year played in the interisland match in Wellington, scoring one of the North Island's four tries. He went to Australia with the All Blacks — though they weren't known as All Blacks then — in 1903 and played in 10 of the 11 matches, including the first test. His four tries on the tour were the best by a forward. Back home, he again played for Auckland and the North Island.

His fame turned to infamy in 1904. He was found guilty by an Auckland Rugby Union judicial committee of being involved in an incident in which a City club player had been offered a bribe by a bookmaker to fix the result of a club match. (Such occurrences were not all that uncommon in rugby's first 40 or so years.) Long was suspended for 10 years for his role, whatever that may have been. He applied two years later for the suspension to be lifted but was unsuccessful. It was finally dropped in 1911, which just happened to be the year in which bookies in New Zealand were declared illegal.

Long, as far as Chester and other rugby historians were concerned, disappeared from the rugby radar after that. The only other sighting was in 1951 when he appeared in a photo in the *New Zealand Herald* with Opai Asher and George Nicholson, the three of them at a reunion of the 1903 team.

Chester could not find Long's details anywhere. Not in Wise's directories, not in electoral rolls, not in birth or death registrations, not in obituary files, not in defence nominal rolls . . . nowhere.

He once heard that someone called Paddy Long had died in Auckland Hospital in 1960 or 1961 but a check at the hospital's records showed no one of that name dying on its premises around that time. He also heard that Long may have died at a Catholic home in Ponsonby. Chester checked the only likely establishment and staff at the Little Sisters of the Poor checked thoroughly but could come up with nothing.

A mystery man he remains, but there's not much doubt about his calibre as a player.

R.A. Stone, in his 1937 book, *Rugby Players Who Have Made New Zealand Famous*, called Long great.

'I say "great" because he knew just what it meant to his team for a forward to put every ounce into the scrum at the right time, and he also excelled in the loose,' Stone wrote.

'He played in the days when forwards could be seen rushing down the field with the ball at toe in dribbling rushes — a form of attack which tested the defence of the opposing backs and, mark you, a back was not considered good in defence unless he could handle this mode of attack.

'. . . the forwards of Paddy Long's class could not only tear down the field in devastating, dribbling rushes, but they could handle the ball brilliantly in the open.'

Stone said Long, had he still been playing in 1905, would undoubtedly have been selected for the Originals' tour of 1905–06.

Paddy Long . . . the All Blacks' mystery man.

ENGLAND RUGBY

FFR

SCOTLAND

IRFU

WRU

The Old Order

This was the part of the world where rugby began and it was where the far-flung disciples returned to show how well they'd learnt the game. The British countries and Ireland are the rump of the old eight-member International Rugby Board, the masters who more often than not have been shown up on the playing field by their pupils. The French developed their rugby at a different tack. The All Blacks, when they first played France, literally showed the French what to do — but that didn't last long. The French have been, and can be, the most exciting side in world rugby — and the most difficult to beat.

ENGLAND

There is, it must be said, a strange relationship in rugby between England and New Zealand. It may take a learned social historian or even a psychologist to explain adequately why this is so. Results between the two take on a significance beyond that applying to other internationals.

There's no trophy at stake when New Zealand and England play outside of World Cups; there are no points towards some mythical crown, no prize beyond the game itself. Yet in their meetings there is invested an emotional energy rarely matched by other opponents.

Such a phenomenon is not restricted to New Zealand playing England. Every national team, it seems, sees England as the foe beyond all others that must be beaten. The Celtic nations have their own historic reasons for this wrapped up in their rugby reasons. The Australians and New Zealanders have different motivation and not all of it is to do with the simple act of playing a rugby match.

When Andrew Mehrtens at the start of the All Blacks' brief European trip in 2002 said that All Blacks hate losing to England more than they do to any other side, he might have been speaking for generations of All Blacks, as well as other rugby-playing countries.

Mehrtens' comments naturally enough were highlighted and reacted to but he was saying nothing new. Gareth Edwards, the great Welsh halfback, once said it was inbred in Welsh players that England beyond all others had to be beaten. 'Losing to England was unthinkable,' he said. The Scots have made the desire to beat England at anything almost a national industry. And the Irish, well, every meeting seems to be motivated by paying back for all the ills and wrongs, real or imagined, the English visited upon the Irish.

The loss to England in 1993 festered and rankled with the All Blacks for two years to the extent that before they next met, in the World Cup semifinal in Cape Town in 1995, some of the All Blacks worried about the intensity of feeling. Josh Kronfeld, who was playing against England for the first time in that match, said he had not known such a feeling before a match, either before or since.

For that game, though, the motivation was revenge, pure and simple. The All Blacks had been stunned by their loss at Twickenham in 1993 and they wanted in Cape Town to purge the lingering memory. One win, no matter how magnificent (and in Cape Town it was inspiring), cannot wipe out a previous loss but it is satisfying to the soul.

But what is it about England that evokes such attitudes? A loss to any other country, even Australia, seldom seems as bad. All Blacks — and New Zealanders generally — never take their losses easily, no matter what the circumstances, but some are easier to live with than others. Against the French, for example, a loss can always be explained away as just another example of the unexpectedness of the way France play their rugby (and there have been no better examples of that than the Auckland loss in 1994 and the World Cup semifinal loss in 1999, no matter how much it hurt).

Perhaps, at the risk of getting deeply philosophical about it, there is still something buried within the New Zealand pysche about wanting to show 'the Mother Country' that her furthest-flung son has learnt his lessons well; how the servant became the master. Perhaps there is still some of the independence of spirit that drove the English settlers in New Zealand in the 19th century. Perhaps rugby between New Zealand and England is still a battle between egalitarianism on the one hand and elitism on the other. Perhaps there is resentment lurking deep within the New Zealand soul that England still aspires to a lofty place in world rugby even though we have been demonstrably better at the game than they have for a century or so. Perhaps there is resentment at the overtly Anglocentric view of the world the English have.

Maybe these factors lie within New Zealanders without realisation and without expression. But maybe the reasons for the

Dave Gallaher leads the All Blacks onto the field at Crystal Palace for the first New Zealand test against England. At left, the programme for that historic encounter.

antipathy towards England are much more prosaic. The English effect an attitude that goes against the New Zealand grain; witness the England players' extraordinary behaviour of jogging a victory lap at Old Trafford in 1997 after they had lost — lost! — the test match by 25 points to eight. Or a fortnight after that when the second test was drawn at Twickenham and England saw it as victory. To All Blacks, a draw might as well be a loss.

Maybe Twickenham itself engenders some of the feeling. New Zealanders can be bemused, thrilled, irritated, flabbergasted by the crowd reaction at Twickenham. Bemused that the level of knowledge of rugby is sometimes so questionable that the crowd still applauds a kick into touch or even, as happened in the test in 2002, applauded when captain Martin Johnson instructed Johnny Wilkinson to kick at goal. But thrilled at the majesty of the stadium and the wall of noise, even though Jeff Wilson once dismissed the cathedral of grounds as just another patch of grass with goalposts at either end. Irritated by the recent trend towards drowning out the haka with a lusty rendition of 'Swing Low Sweet Chariot' that somehow made the journey from the cotton belt of the United States of 150 years ago to the unlikely setting of the sheepskin jackets, Rolls-Royces and BMWs of Twickenham. Flabbergasted when a loss gets turned into a glorious defeat.

Then there is the British press that creates the environment in which, in England, the matches are played. The newspaper system in England is vastly different from what it is in New Zealand, where generally each city has its own newspaper and few are distributed far beyond their bases. Papers in New Zealand (with the exceptions of the *Dominion-Post* in Wellington and the *New Zealand Herald* in Auckland) are the equivalent of what in Britain are called the

England halfback Nigel Melville attempts to get the ball away at Athletic Park in the second test, 1985, in the face of attention from David Kirk and Mark Shaw and under the eyes of referee Kerry Fitzgerald.

provincial press. The layer above that in Britain is the national press, all distributed from London. They fall into two categories, the tabloids and what are sometimes called the quality press, the broadsheets. Though Britain is soccer-sated, the coverage of rugby has increased over the past 30 or so years, more or less in line with rises (and falls) in England's fortunes. With that increase has come a greater willingness to go beyond mere reportage to strident calls for action on this or that front or condemnation of this or that action.

All Blacks first noticed this change in 1972 when Ian Kirkpatrick's All Blacks were painted as unsmiling giants and when Keith Murdoch gave the papers a ready-made villain. It has continued on subsequent tours, incidents signposting the years: the Andy Haden lineout dive and the battle of Bridgend and the 'maiming' of J.P.R. Williams in 1978; the 'sending off' of Graeme Higginson against Llanelli in 1980; Wayne Shelford and the All Blacks generally supposedly flouting amateur regulations in 1989 . . . the list goes on. Welsh incidents in the main, but English-dominated coverage.

Wise All Blacks don't read newspapers. But the public do and if the English public is told day after day that the All Blacks are dirty cheats who will stop at nothing to win matches, that in the end is what the public will believe.

This was the climate in which the All Blacks played England in 1993. Even the England captain, Will Carling, wrote a column at the end of that tour saying the All Blacks will be remembered as a dirty side.

Colin Welland, a playwright with a fondness for league, wrote a damning piece about New Zealand rugby generally. After the All Blacks had been beaten by England, he wrote: 'The beating of a bully is always great theatre and the bashing of the All Black brutes was in the Palladium class. It was a wonderful occasion, alongside Great Britain's rugby league win in Melbourne last year [1992] in my tales of the unexpected. That was sweet, but Twickenham, with the element of good versus evil, shades it by a whisker.'

CYRIL'S NOT SO LONELY WALK

For all the passing of the years (and of the participants), for all the words which have been written and spoken about the sending off of Cyril Brownlie in the test against England at Twickenham in 1925, it's still possible for something new to emerge.

Brownlie, whose brother Maurice scored one of the tries in the All Blacks' 17–11 defeat of England, became the first player to be dismissed from the field in a rugby international.

It happened seven minutes after the start and Welsh referee Albert Freethy took the action after a fiery beginning and after giving a general warning. Brownlie was singled out supposedly for kicking, though he and his team-mates forever questioned that.

Entreaties to Freethy to not take such drastic and unprecedented action fell on unresponsive ears. Even the Prince of Wales, the later King Edward VIII and still later Duke of Windsor, wondered aloud at halftime whether 'Mr Brownlie' might be allowed to resume.

But no dice, not even in the face of the royal query.

Photographs show Freethy pointing ominously and finally, and Brownlie, head bowed, beginning his long walk.

It wasn't altogether a lonely walk, it's now possible to learn.

As the crowd of 60,000 hushed — team-mate Read Masters called it a weird silence — a slightly built 57-year-old New Zealander made his way down from the official seats in the main stand to provide some company and comfort for the distraught Brownlie.

They must have looked an odd couple as they disappeared under the stand:

'This great bear of a man was in tears, absolutely inconsolable...'

the six foot three inches and 15 stone Brownlie, and Sir Arthur Myers, about five foot seven and about 10 stone. The one in the forbidding garb of an All Black, the other dapper in suit and overcoat.

The story has come to light from Sir Arthur's grandson, Douglas Myers, a man who habitually is prefixed with the description of beer baron.

'This great bear of a man was in tears, absolutely inconsolable, while my rather diminutive grandfather was placed in the position of cheering him up,' the younger Myers says. 'The thought of the sight of the two of them walking off together has always amused me.'

Sir Arthur was living in London, having moved there permanently in 1921 after a life of industry and endeavour for his company, city and country. He had been managing director and guiding force of the company founded by an uncle, Campbell and Ehrenfried, which later formed the basis of brewing giant Lion Nathan; he had been Mayor of Auckland for five years during which he had built the Auckland Town Hall and, in the face of criticism, forged ahead with the construction of the Grafton bridge; and he had been a Member of Parliament for 11 years, holding various portfolios including finance.

As an influential New Zealander in London, Sir Arthur followed the Invincible All Blacks avidly and so impressed was he by their record and their demeanour that after the England match, and while they were away in France, he had gold medals made to give to each of the team.

The medals, engraved with a kiwi, a fernleaf and the name of each player, were presented to the All Blacks when they returned from France.

'I always thought my grandfather's move to strike a medal for the All Blacks was highly romantic,' Douglas Myers recalls. 'He was a great patron of sport and was involved in a comprehensive range of sporting activity when he lived in Auckland, both during his commercial career and later when he became Mayor and later still Minister of Finance.'

The gold medal (top) presented by Sir Arthur Myers to each of the Invincible All Blacks. This particular medal was George Nepia's.
Left: Albert Freethy tells Cyril Brownlie to go.

RACISTS? NEVER!

Much was made in the days after England beat the All Blacks in 1993 that during the game Sean Fitzpatrick had made racist jibes at England's Nigerian-descended prop, Victor Ubogu.

The accusation was made initially by England hooker Brian Moore and picked up by journalists. When Moore's comments first surfaced, the day after the game when the All Blacks were by then in Devonport, Fitzpatrick laughed them off. Nearly a decade later, he's still laughing.

'I was in England recently with Will Carling and he reminded me of the fuss in 1993,' Fitzpatrick says. 'I finally told Will the truth. What neither he nor Moore realised was that I wasn't talking to Victor at all, I was talking to Jamie Joseph. The English don't have a great sense of humour and they don't understand the way we talk to our brown brothers.'

Victor Ubogu ploughs into Arran Pene during the 1993 test at Twickenham. The referee is South African Freek Burger. Stu Forster is in the background.

Welland clearly thought New Zealand put too much emphasis on rugby. 'New Zealand, you must reweigh your values,' he said. 'A national disaster, [Ian] Kirkpatrick called your defeat. Codswallop! If that's what you think, what your country thinks, it's time you both grew up. What we all cheered at Twickers was not just the winning of a test but the defeat of an attitude . . . an archaic, unsavoury attitude which somehow has survived and festered in the dark bottom right-hand corner of the globe. The world is maturing around you. Get with it, mend your ways, take another look at yourselves . . . or you won't be invited again.'

It was not always thus and the world has much to thank England and, specifically, English rugby for. Though the Webb Ellis myth needs to be disposed of (and the English union gives it no

credence anymore), England's role as the birthplace of rugby and the regulation and codifying of it and other sports has been profound. English attitudes to sport, if watered down and made more practical, have permeated the globe.

The Original All Blacks of 1905–06, aside from some raised eyebrows at the play of the wing forward, were feted in England and acknowledged as taking rugby to a higher plane, adding new dimensions to a game that hitherto had been played by bunches of heaving forwards and mostly idle backs.

The popularity of the All Blacks was what led to their first test in England being played at Crystal Palace in south London because of its greater capacity rather than any of the grounds then used for tests such as Richmond or Blackheath (Twickenham was

FLOWER BEDS . . .

It wasn't a room with much of a view, but it was a room with a message.

When the All Blacks checked into their hotel in rural Surrey before the test against England in 1993, they found that their rooms were not numbered in the normal way, but had names instead.

The flora of southern England served as their room identification.

The assistant coach, Earle Kirton, for example, was in a room called Pear Tree, which occasioned some mirth among the players.

Marty Berry was in, appropriately, Juniper, and new All Black John Mitchell, bald even then, was in Elder.

Sean Fitzpatrick's room, befitting the captain, carried an exotic title, Buddleia — an ornamental shrub that attracts butterflies, so that may not have been very appropriate.

Manager Neil Gray, among whose functions was to soothe and charm, was in Camellia.

But the most apt room name surely went to the test lock, Steve Gordon. Every time he went to his room he was confronted with the bold sign: Pine Tree.

not a test match venue until 1910).

'We found great interest centred in our match with England at Crystal Palace and seats were at a premium,' Originals vice-captain Billy Stead wrote home, 'one duke offering £10 for a half-guinea seat and he would have taken four at that price.'

Crystal Palace was no Twickenham, no ordinary rugby ground. A complex of buildings almost entirely built of glass (hence crystal), it had originally been part of an exposition in Hyde Park in London's West End extolling the industrial virtues of England. It was then moved piece by piece to Sydenham in south London and reconstructed as London's playground, as it was popularly known. The Crystal Palace of today, the home of British athletics, stands on the site.

'The immense size of the buildings,' Stead wrote, '. . . is the first thing that struck us. Under one roof a circus was performing, hundreds were indulging in roller skating, many were listening to an organ recital while, besides many other sideshows, you could not help noticing the beautiful selections rendered by one of England's most famous military bands. All this time trains had been pouring their living freight into the Palace and there was a continual stampede and rush for the playing area.'

The rugby test was the main event of the day but it fell short of expectations. 'I think our speculations as to the size of the gate and our anticipations as to how the huge crowd would appeal to our eye engaged our thoughts more than the result of the game,' Stead wrote, 'for I think I may say without being egotistical that we had every confidence in our ability to beat the representatives of the Rose.'

> **'I may say without being egotistical that we had every confidence in our ability to beat the representatives of the Rose.'**

Stead called the game, won by the All Blacks 15–0 and with wing Duncan McGregor scoring four tries, a tiresome, disappointing one. 'Unfortunately, there had been a lot of rain during the week and fog had prevented the ground (which was formerly a lake) from drying, so that the playing pitch was in a terrible state, so much so that good hand-to-hand passing was well nigh impossible.'

It was a match in which mostly the forwards had the ball and Stead remarked 'that on all four occasions on which McGregor hopped over the line were the only attempts we made on the short side of the scrum.'

Though the All Blacks preserved their unbeaten record, Stead worried that it wasn't much of a spectacle. 'I am afraid that the great number of soccer spectators (and there were many there) would not go away with a very good idea of rugby,' he wrote.

SPOOKY STUFF

Who said the All Blacks were unsmiling giants, uncouth and with all the personal charm of a piece of granite?

The Gimmerburn Ghost: Ian (Spooky) Smith.

Certainly not Queen Elizabeth, the Queen Mother.

Meeting royalty is one of the highlights of an All Black tour of Britain and for the past 50 years the hosts have usually been the Queen and Prince Philip. But when the All Blacks were there in 1963–64, the Queen was pregnant with, as it turned out, Prince Edward, and her mother stepped in to receive the All Blacks.

As the All Blacks, so forbidding on the field but awkward in the refined surrounds of Clarence House, readied for the royal presence, they were told to chat to Her Majesty so she wouldn't have to do all the talking.

The Queen Mother was scheduled to visit New Zealand and one of the All Blacks, Ian (Spooky) Smith, chose this as his topic when he was introduced.

'Ma'am,' he said in his most refined voice, 'are you by chance going to Gimmerburn?' (Among other things, Smith was also known as the Gimmerburn Ghost).

'I don't think I know where Gimmerburn is,' the Queen Mother replied to the surprise of no one within earshot.

'Don't worry, Ma'am,' replied another All Black in on the conversation, 'not many of us know where it is, either.'

Smith warmed to his theme. 'Ma'am, actually, I understand you will not be going to Gimmerburn . . . you will be leaving Cromwell and thence to Dunedin . . .' He then proceeded to rattle off the next two days of her itinerary.

'You're very well informed,' the Queen Mother told the unruffled Smith.

'Yes, Ma'am,' he said, 'it pays to be informed on such important matters.'

Pressing the conversational advantage he had gained, Smith then pointed to a pen and ink drawing in an exquisite gold frame. The drawing was of a young woman.

'Please help me, Ma'am,' he said, 'I've been looking at this extraordinarily beautiful young woman and couldn't help wondering who she was.'

'Oh, you gorgeous young man,' she replied, 'that was me at the age of 23.'

At this, the Queen Mother held up an arm to be taken (which Smith did) and she told him with a mischievous gleam in her eyes, 'Come and have a drink with me.'

They got a better idea the next time the All Blacks and England met. That was in 1925, a match made memorable by the sending off of All Black flanker Cyril Brownlie, the first dismissal in an international rugby match. The 17–11 victory was the final match of the tour and gave the All Blacks the Invincibles tag they carried into history.

Brownlie's lonely walk was the catalyst for the outcome, the All Blacks agreed. 'I wonder, though,' fullback George Nepia wrote, 'does England know, will she ever agree, that she lost the game in that very moment?'

The Invincibles' tour, coupled with the record of the Originals 20 years earlier, cemented in British minds the calibre of the All Blacks and laid the foundation of the tradition of excellence that has, with occasional hiccups, endured. The All Blacks played 60 matches in Britain on the first two tours and lost just one of them, the 3–0 loss to Wales in Cardiff in 1905.

Just as All Blacks always want to beat England, so does England — and anyone else — want to beat the All Blacks because to them, beating New Zealand is beating the best. 'Playing the All Blacks,' Will Carling said 70 years after the Invincibles' tour, 'was always very special. They were unique games and they had a certain edge to them. You knew each time against New Zealand you were up against the very best.'

Imagine then the ecstasy in Britain, and the despair in New Zealand, when the All Blacks were beaten by England for the first time — thanks to an exiled Russian prince with the wind at his heels.

Alex Obolensky was of noble birth and had the speed of gods. The All Blacks had first seen him when they played Oxford University two months before. He'd scored a try then through sheer speed and it was that performance that led the England selectors to choose him for the test, even though there were some published murmurs about him not being English. That was okay, though, he had a British passport and, anyway, the England fullback, 'Tuppy' Owen-Smith, was a South African. He later captained England and he also played test cricket for South Africa.

Contemporary accounts show that the All Blacks did not play as

England

well against England as they had in the other tests and that Obolensky was the undoubted star of the show.

One of the All Black loose forwards, Hugh McLean, later said that Obolensky would never again tread the heights he did that day. 'Everything went right for him,' McLean wrote in a review of the tour. 'His second try, when he turned infield, might not come off again in 100 years. [Peter] Candler had thrown a pass into the blue, a despairing effort, and there was Obolensky, running infield because he had nowhere else to go and miraculously finding the way open to him.'

Obolensky's first try was an orthodox move made unorthodox by his speed. He was in the backline as an extra man and 'he turned on remarkable speed that left [Mike] Gilbert standing and he was over like a shot out of a gun,' one report said. 'It was not a sidestep or a swerve that beat Gilbert, but sheer speed.'

New Zealanders lamented that the All Black wing, George Hart — the national 100 yards champion in 1931 — would have had the pace to match Obolensky but he'd been replaced by Nelson Ball

after playing the other tests in Britain. His form, it was said, had fallen away towards the end of the tour.

'Obolensky has had several days of continuous praise in the papers,' the *Free Lance* reported, 'and rightly so after his spirited game. He has been hailed as the saviour of English rugby and the greatest winger since the war. But although Hart would have had to play on his unaccustomed wing to mark the flying prince, I still maintain that in speed alone he would have been a match for the Russian.'

The history of rugby is riddled with such might-have-beens and what-ifs and England was left to rejoice in their first victory against the All Blacks. It was to be more than 30 years before they had another.

Bob Stuart's All Blacks of 1953–54 were the next to play against England, winning 5–0 in what appeared to be a tight, dour encounter, with Nelson Dalzell scoring the only try after 19 minutes of the first half and it was converted by one of the British crowd favourites, Bob Scott.

Scott had been a key member of the Second New Zealand

Has there been a more memorable, career-enhancing try than this one? Jonah Lomu is captured as he scores his first try against England in the World Cup semifinal in Cape Town in 1995, having trampled over Mike Catt along the way. It helped the All Blacks to a notable win and launched Lomu into his super-celebrity status.

Expeditionary Force team in the months after the Second World War, the famed Kiwis who did so much to restore international rugby after six years of war. Many of the players on both sides on January 30, 1954 had, like Scott, fought in the war and perhaps this shared experience was a major factor in the climate of tours until the late 60s and early 70s.

Stuart's All Blacks, in the manner of the time, still referred to England as 'the Mother Country' and when the team became the first to fly into England, manager Norm Millard said at a welcome at Heathrow that his players were keen to be as popular with the people 'at Home' as the Lions had been in New Zealand in 1950.

Evidently they were and in newsreel footage of the England test, the commentator remarks as New Zealand and England players swap jerseys that they have been 'a very popular and well-liked touring side'. It was at the end of this tour, after the match against the Barbarians in Cardiff, that the players from both sides linked arms out on the field and they and the crowd sang

'Auld Lang Syne'. Scott, with the ball stuffed up his jersey and wearing a hat he'd been given by someone, was carried from the field on the shoulders of team-mates Kevin Skinner and Rom Hemi.

It was a simpler age, an age of innocence and tolerance and rugby then was the product of its times. In England, rugby then was still firmly rooted in the great universities and the public schools and armed services. The game was the thing and if English rugby could have played internationals purely for the sake of the game and away from the prying eyes of the public, it probably would have done. Rugby in England, deeply entrenched in its amateurism ethic, was not for the masses. Soccer was their game.

This attitude continued through the 1960s when Wilson Whineray's All Blacks beat England 14–0 at Twickenham and, early in 1963, England toured New Zealand for the first time, losing both tests. The 1967 team, led by Brian Lochore, coached by Fred Allen and managed by Charlie Saxton, was the last of the old tours; not in length, because the 1972–73 tour was longer, but in mood and style. Saxton had been captain of the post-war Kiwis and Allen had been a faithful ally in that team, and English rugby was ruled still by men who had served during the war. The 1967 team played a brand of attacking, entertaining rugby that was redolent of the Kiwis' style and even 30 years later, older people in English rugby

Wayne Smith finds some space in the 1983 test against England at Twickenham, the All Blacks' first test loss in Britain for 30 years. Murray Davie and Gary Braid are behind Smith, and Brian McGrattan and Andy Donald to the left. The referee is Scot Alan Hosie.

FROM THE COURT OF TSAR NICHOLAS

Alexander Obolensky has an undying fame in England rugby. It's a fame based on two facts: one that he introduced a touch of the exotic to English rugby and the other that he scored two tries against the All Blacks in 1936 and thus was the most significant contributor — certainly the most publicised — to England's first win against New Zealand.

England prized the victory highly and prized it even more because Obolensky was a Russian prince.

His nephew, British businessman Nick Obolensky, is nicely pragmatic about his uncle's fame.

'He is a legend,' Nick says. 'I draw the conclusion that to be a legend you need two things: firstly good performance in a field which is popular and secondly (maybe just as important) pathetic performance in the same field for many years after. So my uncle's fame owes as much to the English failure to defeat the All Blacks as it does to his speed and agility. Put it another way, his fame owes much to the All Blacks' performance since.'

England did not beat the All Blacks again until 1973.

Obolensky's rugby fame endured, perhaps for the reason his nephew advanced, but his career was fleeting. The match against the All Blacks was his England debut, and his only other matches were later the same season in the 'four nations' championship against Wales, Ireland and Scotland. (France had been banned since 1931 for supposedly paying players and did not reappear to restore the four to five until 1947.)

His only subsequent rugby of note, if noted it was, was on a tour of South America later in 1936 with an English team. He scored what was held to be a record 17 tries against a Brazilian XV, which may say more for Brazil's obsession with soccer than it does for Obolensky's ability at rugby.

Prince Alexander Obolensky

Obolensky played three times for Oxford in the annual match against Cambridge and, at university, he was also an accomplished sprinter and was said to have experimented with rugby boots that were a cross between running shoes and the more orthodox heavy rugby boot of the day.

His family background was rooted deeply in the Russian imperial court. His father was Prince Sergei Alexandrovich Obolensky, an *aide-de-camp* to the Moscow governor-general and captain in the Tsar's Horse Guards. Prince Sergei was said to have been a confidant of the last Tsar, Nicholas, who spoke warmly of him in letters that have survived to his wife, the Tsarina Alexandra.

The family's nobility did not rest solely on the patronage of the Tsar. The Obolenskys could trace their ancestry back to Saint Vladimir, the ruler who introduced Christianity to Russia in the 10th century, and before that to the 9th century founder of Kiev, Rurik the Viking chief of the Russ tribe (who literally put the 'Russ' into Russia).

The younger Obolensky was a child of the revolution, born in St Petersburg in 1916. He did not see much of his homeland. When the revolution dawned, Mum and the kids, plus uncles and aunts, were sent off to the haven of the Alupka Palace in the Crimea (later to be Winston Churchill's residence during the 1944 Yalta conference). A year after that, they were spirited out of Murmansk on a British warship and taken to France.

They were joined there by Dad, Prince Sergei, who had escaped via Odessa. Sergei landed a job in England and the family then tagged along.

Young Alex went to Trent College in Nottingham (where he was a member of the college's unbeaten first XV in 1932 — points for 539, against 22) and then on to Oxford where he gained his rugby 'blue' in 1935.

Obolensky was still not a British citizen (though demonstrably a resident) when he was chosen to play for England against New Zealand and there were some murmurings about the selection of a foreigner. He eventually was issued with a British passport though (No 10637 in the name of Mr A. Obolensky) and it is now on display in the museum at Twickenham.

Obolensky joined the British Royal Air Force in 1939 and in 1940 went on a training course in piloting Hawker Hurricanes. He was killed when his aircraft flipped and burned on landing in Norfolk in March 1940.

His nephew Nick ruefully recalled his own rugby exploits as a halfback or first five-eighth. 'My rugby career was a bit of a disaster,' he says. 'Whenever I was on the pitch I would be squashed by the opposite wing forwards [flankers] as they feared I was about to perform as well as my uncle. After the match, I was squashed by my own wing forwards because I never did!'

WILL AND DETERMINATION

**Will Carling remembers very clearly saying to Rob Andrew before England played the All Blacks at Twickenham in 1993:
'We're going to get these bastards.' Get them England did.**

It was a strange match, not so much because of the way in which it was played, but because of the moods and attitudes that surrounded it. Twickenham was the centre of the stage and the curtain was up. But in the wings, much had happened that created the mood of the day.

For a start, the Lions had been beaten 2–1 in New Zealand earlier in the year and Carling, the darling and almost the personification of English rugby, had been dropped after playing only the first test. He felt he had something to prove against New Zealand — for himself, if not for New Zealanders who wondered why people made a fuss about him.

The All Blacks' third match of their tour in England had been against a south-west combined team in Cornwall and the England centre, Phil de Glanville, had emerged from a ruck with a flesh wound below an eye. Not for the first time, the All Blacks were vilified in England for rucking. De Glanville's wound became 'Scarred for life!' in newspaper headlines, his father shouted his son could have been blinded, and the president of the august Rugby Football Union (the only national union whose name does not include its country), demanded a meeting there and then with the All Black management to stamp out rucking (bad choice of words, that).

A campaign of hate was whipped up among the British tabloid newspapers, salivating that one of their favourite targets, the All Blacks, were back.

'There was a bit of an edge to that tour,' Carling remembers. 'It's hard sometimes to keep everything in perspective. We didn't have a problem with the All Blacks rucking because we as players understood it was a part of the New Zealand game. But we objected to stomping and we felt the All Blacks were guilty of that.'

There was a bit of an edge to the game as well. Carling remembers being told by Sean Fitzpatrick at some stage during it, 'You're finished. Why don't you just give up?'

The England hooker, Brian Moore, accused the All Blacks of making racial taunts toward the England prop, Victor Ubogu, who was of Nigerian ancestry.

'I thought before the game that we could beat them,' Carling says, 'even though they'd given Scotland a bit of a hiding the week before and we had several new players. But they seemed a little disrupted — they'd brought Eroni Clarke into the centres [second five-eighth], they had to use young Jeff Wilson as the goalkicker and they had Zinzan Brooke at openside, which we didn't think suited him.'

In the dressing room before the match, Carling spoke quietly about what was needed to be done. Not for him the pounding of a fist into a hand, or ranting and raving. 'There was some mention of the Lions, about getting revenge, but that was more in the background,' he says.

'It's an honour to play for England and that was the sort of point I would have made.'

England won 15–9 through four penalty goals by fullback Jonathan Callard and a dropped goal by Andrew, and Carling never felt secure.

'I never felt during the game we had total control,' he says. 'If we'd scored a try, I might have but there was always the possibility of a breakout by them with players like Timu and Tuigamala. There was one moment like that, when Timu nearly scored but he put a foot in touch and I remember thinking, "Oh, there is a God".'

The mood between the teams didn't improve much after the game. Carling said there was a feeling within the England camp of, 'To hell with you lot, we've beaten you.'

The next week, a column by Carling appeared in the *Mail on Sunday*, headlined, 'Rugby Image Was Wrecked by All Blacks'.

'There is a special bond that comes with beating New Zealand and we shall thoroughly enjoy basking in the glory a little longer,' Carling wrote. '. . . our win will change the whole perception of these All Blacks. They have a tremendous tradition and the game never has a higher profile than when they tour.

'. . . if they had beaten England, they would have been remembered as an all-conquering team. Now they will be remembered mostly as a dirty side. That is sad for them but I think they deserve it.'

Years later, with the heat of the moment well and truly dissipated, I asked Carling if he really meant what he wrote.

'Oh, I probably over-reacted a bit,' he says, 'but there was a bit of edge at the time. There was a lot of goading from our media to get those sorts of quotes.'

Will Carling

still looked back on the 1967 team as among the finest of sides to ever play in England.

Lochore's team beat England 23–11 and hymns of praise were sung for them. Vivian Jenkins, the former Welsh and Lions fullback, called the win one of the finest displays of rugby seen in the British Isles.

'I have seen All Black packs give outstanding displays before,' he wrote, 'and I have seen their backs score fine tries, too, but never have I seen both pack and backs blending in such perfect unison and bringing off movements with beautiful handling and running after perfect heeling from the rucks such as brought the 75,000 crowd at Twickenham to its feet.

'This was rugby I had to admire, even though it meant the end of England's hopes.'

Touring England then, as it had been since the Originals, was as much a social whirl as it was about training and preparing for 80 minutes of hard test rugby. In 1967, the All Blacks arrived in London on the Thursday for the England test on the Saturday. On the Thursday night, they had a reception by the New Zealand High Commissioner, Sir Thomas MacDonald, followed by a dinner put on by the British rugby writers. On the Friday, the day before, there was no training so they were allowed to go shopping. After the test on the Saturday night, there was first the formal dinner at the London Hilton then back round the corner to the team's headquarters at the Park Lane Hotel for a dance. On the Sunday, the team had its normal court session in the morning then several of the players went with Allen to a champagne lunch at the home of one of the English officials, after which they returned to the Park Lane, packed and caught a train to Cardiff, eating dinner on the train.

It was a gentler way of rugby life that was coming to an end.

Peter Cranmer, who had played for England in the Obolensky test, lamented the changing of ways in a story he wrote in the 1967 match programme. He reflected that people were taking the game seriously these days with coaching schemes and what he described as new expressions such as good ball and bad ball. 'I think there are still a very great many people who still do not treat the game as a business,' he wrote, 'and long may they continue to do so.'

But not for much longer.

Respect for the next All Blacks, Ian Kirkpatrick's team of 1972–73, was grudging. Though they went within a whisker of being the first All Blacks to achieve the grand slam in Britain, and they outclassed England 9–0 with players such as Kirkpatrick himself and Sid Going in commanding form, praise was sparse.

Veteran *Daily Mirror* columnist Peter Wilson said the All Blacks had been written off as no-hopers before the England test because of their lack of friendliness off the field. By that yardstick, the All Blacks' playing efforts were judged by their perceived behaviour off the field rather than on it, and most of those judgements were

Christian Cullen working up to top gear against England in the World Cup pool match at Twickenham in 1999.

A TUNE FOR TWICKENHAM

**For those who think about such matters, it's always been a bit of a mystery why the crowd at Twickenham,
so English in so many ways, roars out an old African American spiritual in support of its team.**

'Swing Low Sweet Chariot' is a relatively modern phenomenon. It got its first big airing during the World Cup final against Australia in 1991 and now it's the venerable old ground's signature tune. When the All Blacks played there in 1993, the crowd sang it to drown out the haka. They repeated the dose when the All Blacks were there in 1997 and in 2002.

Will Carling, when he captained England, used to detest it.

He envies the Scots their singing of 'Flower of Scotland' and the Welsh a whole repertoire of stirring nationalistic tunes. He ruefully recalls that in 1990 at Murrayfield, the crowd's singing and the Scots' players' inspired reaction cost England the Calcutta Cup and the grand slam.

Carling once had a campaign to rid Twickenham of the echoes of the old south of the United States, redolent of racism and slavery, and instead inject a bit more appropriate English patriotism.

The song he came up with was 'I Vow to Thee My Country', from Gustav Holst's 'The Planets', the piece of music that also gave the World Cup its theme song, 'World in Union'.

'I tried to pursue it at committee level but they weren't interested. They were more interested in the New Year honours,' Carling says. This was the committee of the English union that Carling had famously dubbed '57 old farts' so a fair hearing was probably not very likely.

He also says he mentioned it 'to a few people at the palace' — Buckingham Palace, that is. No, it wasn't through his well-publicised association with the Princess of Wales; he'd been to the palace for a reception with the Lions.

The Queen would surely have agreed with the opening lines of 'I Vow to Thee My Country' —

All earthly things above,
Entire and whole and perfect,
In service of my love . . .

The tune by Holst, who was English despite the Swedish surname, is stirring and the words of the first verse could be seen as patriotic. But the second belies that, being about 'another country I've heard of long ago' and its ending hardly fits in with the characteristics of a rugby test, 'And her ways are ways of gentleness and all her paths are peace'.

Carling concedes the crowd has less difficulty remembering the only two lines of its No 1 hit that it seems to know, 'Swing low sweet chariot, coming for to carry me home . . .'

Another uniquely English song, 'Land of Hope and Glory', has been sung occasionally at Twickenham but for some reason never caught on despite its patriotic fizz and echoes of Empire.

Twickenham crowds have also occasionally sung one that seems ideally suited, William Blake's 'Jerusalem', a tune that took on a whole new life when it was sung at the beginning of the movie, 'Chariots of Fire'.

'It didn't take me very long to realise that I was chasing a lost cause,' Carling says.

---

coloured by writers' beliefs about what had happened at the Angel Hotel in Cardiff after the Welsh test.

For All Blacks in England, the gloves were off.

The success of the Lions in New Zealand in 1971, though it was a success based largely on Welsh influence, raised the bar for British rugby and England seemed to have benefited when it had away wins against South Africa in 1972 and against New Zealand at Eden Park in 1973. For all England's success, it proved a false dawn, if just a temporary one. England's second win against the All Blacks came about more through the circumstances of New Zealand rugby at the time rather than through any resurgence of spirit by England. They'd beaten Fiji by only a point on their way to New Zealand then they promptly lost their three provincial games leading up to the test. No one gave England a show at Eden Park. But the All Blacks were in something of a hiatus after the British tour and coach J.J. Stewart made experiments which, frankly, did not work and he did not settle on a winning team until the following year. England scored three tries to two at Eden Park for the most unlikely of wins and two of those could be attributed directly to New Zealand

mistakes. The year was not a vintage one for the All Blacks. They lost to the New Zealand under 23 side, they lost to a President's team that was captained by Colin Meads and they lost to an England team that, for all the glory attached to beating the All Blacks, does not rank among history's finest.

Ian Kirkpatrick's All Blacks had gone close to achieving the grand slam in Britain; the next team to make a full tour, Graham Mourie's in 1978, did achieve it. The England test, won 16–6 by the All Blacks, was the most convincing win of the four tests. Wales, Ireland and Scotland each had chances to stop the slam. England had none and indeed, could have lost by more than the 10 points they did had the All Blacks been more adventurous.

It was a similar story a year later when again Graham Mourie led the All Blacks, this time on a twin tour of England and Scotland. They were beaten comprehensively by a North of England team but, inexplicably, the England selectors ignored key northerners such as flanker Tony Neary and first five-eighth Alan Old for the test. The All Blacks won by a point and England must have rued missed chances. The All Blacks' manager, Russ Thomas, frankly told English rugby where it was going wrong. At the test dinner, he said too much emphasis was being placed on big, ball-winning forwards and not enough on what to do with the ball once it was won. English rugby, he said, was obsessed with the unlovely 'pileup', a style of the day that held echoes of children's 'stacks on the mill and more on still', and until they learned how to create space for backs (and give them the ball), they would continue to suffer. Thomas said that if England could ever get their organisation and coaching right, they could lead the world in rugby.

It wasn't only Thomas who realised this and gradually the English rugby giant was beginning to wake. They had been the great wasters of world rugby. They had the biggest pool of players but had results that were inferior to countries with just a fraction of their number.

England had a flurry of success in the early 1980s when Bill Beaumont was captain and among those successes was another win against New Zealand, in 1983, against an All Black side that contained no Aucklanders and was demonstrably understrength. By the first World Cup in 1987, England were back in a slump and their cup quarterfinal against Wales in Brisbane, won 6–3 by the Welsh, would go close to topping the list of stinkers to be played in top-level world rugby.

It was after that that England introduced a national competition — what is quaintly called in England, a league structure. Playing for league points, that is, playing meaningful games instead of interminable 'friendlies', helped to hone player awareness of the implications of success and failure. At around the same time, they introduced a manager-coach, Geoff Cooke, who overhauled the national squad structure and injected edge into the international competition. With Will Carling as captain, he took England to successive grand slams in the Five Nations and to a World Cup final (1991), as well as the win against the All Blacks in 1993.

Professionalism was introduced a year after he stood down and though England struggled administratively because players were contracted, soccer-style, to clubs (a problem demonstrated by the low quality of the team that was beaten twice in New Zealand in 1998), the extra money in the game helped provide the players and a framework that has seen England rise to being consistently among the top three or four countries.

'EYEBALLS-OUT AGGRESSION'

The All Blacks make England players sick. Literally. The All Blacks of 2002 who played England at Twickenham might have been surprised to learn they can have such an effect on the opposition.

It is true. It came from none other than Lawrence Dallaglio, the England loose forward and one-time captain.

He wrote a column for *The Times* ahead of the 2002 match against the All Blacks, which England won, saying what it's like to play against the best-known rugby team in the world.

'Here's what playing the All Blacks means,' he wrote. 'Eyeballs-out aggression from start to finish, underpinned by peak fitness and huge motivation to live up to the jersey.

'Be prepared for players who think on their feet and react to what is in front of them, instead of looking to the sidelines or to one or two team-mates for a lead.'

There is no respite when you play the All Blacks, he said, and they generate immense intensity.

'In the 26–26 game at Twickenham in 1997, half of the England players were physically sick at halftime because of the exertion.'

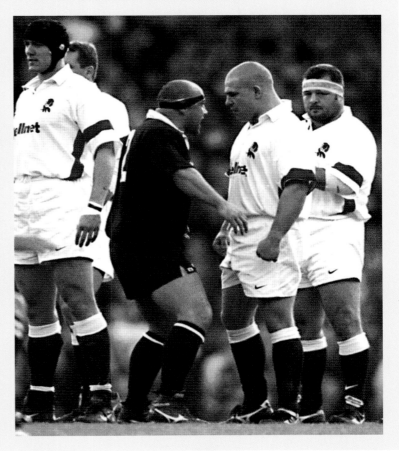

'Puhuru, huru . . .' Norm Hewitt lays down the face-to-face challenge to England hooker Richard Cockerill in 1997.

FRANCE

In a word association test, one of those little psychological games in which a word is given and the subject has to react with the first words that come to mind, France would be an easy topic. In a rugby context, France would be even easier. The reactive words would be fired out like the ball from an attacking scrum. Champagne. Temperamental. Unpredictable. Flair.

All apply. French rugby is many things and has been many things. It's been up and it's been down — possibly on the same day — it's sometimes gone its own way, not knowing or caring what the rest of the rugby world may be doing or saying. It's flirted with playing the New Zealand style, or what coaches from time to time have perceived the New Zealand style-to-be, but always it's gone back to doing what it does best: being French.

It can be the most innovative, enterprising, entertaining rugby; and it can be infuriatingly frustrating. The French make a habit of losing matches they should have won, and winning matches they should have lost.

Much of French rugby is foreign to New Zealand. Only those New Zealanders who have lived and played there and mastered the language could say they understood the French, but perhaps only those born French could truly understand. For other New Zealanders, those whose knowledge of French rugby comes from seeing them play and of hearing tales of players of long ago, it is something akin to a mystery.

Some of the mystery is because of the language. New Zealanders get their news in English and there is a natural emphasis on news that is in English elsewhere. Most New Zealanders speak and read only English but there is a great deal about France that is never translated, especially much about French rugby.

New Zealanders who pride themselves on their rugby knowledge would be able to name the great French players of the past, would even be able to name whole teams, and they would know the importance and significance the French attach to their club championship. Few, however, would be able to name more than half a dozen French clubs.

Rugby also is a remarkably insular sport. While British soccer results are fully reported in New Zealand and avidly followed, few New Zealanders it seems care much for any rugby results beyond test matches. If the results of the English rugby premiership mean little in New Zealand, results of the French championship mean even less. There is no constant information flow reaching New Zealand about French rugby. The only time there is, and even then it's selective, is when France are about to tour New Zealand or the All Blacks are there.

Part of the mystery is also because of attitude. The French way of doing things and looking at things, especially in rugby, can be quite different from the inherently conservative ways of New Zealanders. Anglo-Saxons versus Latins.

Cultural differences are to be savoured rather than criticised but there's many a tale from All Black tours of France when the differences have led to acrimony, when All Blacks or their managers can get paranoid about the motivation that lies behind their hosts' actions. Many underdone French steaks have been sent back to the kitchen — or tipped on the table in protest — as New Zealanders have wanted things their way and not the French way. A French liaison officer touring with the All Blacks was once ejected from the team bus and told to walk. Another walked out of his own volition, but that was welcomed by the All Blacks because he wasn't much use anyway. Appointed interpreters have had only a passing knowledge of English; promised transport either hasn't run on time or not run at all. Teams have been booked on non-existent flights and waited for non-existent buses. Such is France. French culture is all very well, but All Blacks like things their way, just as the French do when they take wine with breakfast and lunch when they're in New Zealand.

When the French were in New Zealand in 1989, there was an unusual incident to New Zealand eyes that to the French was quite normal. Or so they said at the time. It happened in Christchurch at the hotel that used to be run by the former test referee, Tom Doocey. It was a couple of nights before the first test and the French players and management were in a partitioned-off section of the dining room. They appeared not to be aware, but the partition was not complete and other diners could see some of the players and hear them all. The other diners, unfortunately for the French, included a table of journalists. At some point during the meal, it might have been before the main course — it could even have been the main course — a woman joined the players. It was said she worked at an establishment that was not generally regarded as an ideal career path for young women. The diners could see, willingly or otherwise, that the woman and her top layer of clothing parted company as she moved around the players' tables, sitting on laps.

The New Zealand union's liaison man with the French, Neil Gray, was dining in the main part of the restaurant and, not being in a position to see for himself, was told what was happening. He moved in and told the French coach and general factotum, Jacques Fouroux, that such activities may be all right in the private confines of a hotel room but surely not in partial view of the public. The warning was too late because the journalists had seen all — and reported as much as they decently could.

When the stories appeared the following day, Fouroux remonstrated with the journalists and even French journalists criticised their New Zealand colleagues for writing what they had seen.

The point they made was that there was nothing unusual in such behaviour and the fault lay with those who reported it rather than with those who took part. *Vive la différence*, yet again.

It was on an earlier tour, and in the same city, that the French manager, Yves Noe, Fouroux and the captain, Daniel Dubroca, took time out from their test preparation to visit the French saboteur, Dominique Prieur, in prison

John Schuster and Serge Blanco dispute possession during the 1989 series in New Zealand.

for her part in the bombing of the *Rainbow Warrior* in Auckland. As laudable as their fraternal greetings to one of their own may have been, it's difficult to imagine an All Black manager visiting a convicted New Zealand criminal, government employee or not, in a French prison.

The French, as always, are full of surprises, as the All Blacks discovered from their first contact with France when they found that the French players had rather more enthusiasm than they had talent or even understanding of the game. That was when the Originals played in Paris in 1906 in what amounted to more of an exhibition match than a serious test, though it remains one in the record books. The Invincibles also went to France in 1925 and played a test in Toulouse which was won well enough, but the French by then had a far better idea of rugby than they had had in 1906.

Rugby by then was firmly established, especially in the south of France with Toulouse its unofficial capital. Just one point needs to be made to illustrate the extraordinary hold rugby had: in 1920 France had 173 clubs; by 1930, there were 784. France could even lay claim to having erected the first statue in the world of a rugby player. The first five-eighth who played against the All Blacks in 1925, Yves du Manoir, was killed in an air crash in 1928 and a statue of him was erected at the gates to Colombes Stadium in Paris. The only other known full-size statue of a rugby player came much later — it is of Gareth Edwards and stands in the centre of a shopping mall in Cardiff.

France

The 1920s were a period of huge growth for French rugby, but with the growth and the rise in popularity of the club championship came a burning need to be successful at all costs. Players were openly wooed from one club to another and some happily lived off their earnings, a state of affairs that didn't impress the conservatives in Britain who guarded jealously the game's amateur code. French rugby was also rough — brawls were commonplace and such niceties as eye-gouging and testicle-squeezing are not modern innovations. Clubs argued among each other and some split to form the French Amateur Rugby Union, a move that prompted the British unions to cry enough. They wrote a letter complaining about the 'unsatisfactory state of rugby football in France' and delivered a wounding blow when they said: 'The unions would be unable to arrange or fulfil fixtures with France or French clubs at home or away . . . unless and until we are satisfied that the control and conduct of the game has been placed on a satisfactory basis in all essentials.'

It was nearly a mortal wound and, naturally enough, was not well received in France. One newspaper commented: 'They burnt our Joan of Arc; that's enough from them.' Peace was declared not long before war took over and while the British unions said in 1939 that France could come back and play, it didn't happen until the Five Nations resumed in 1947. Even then, the British were still not happy and they warned France in 1947 that if professionalism in rugby was not wiped out they would risk being suspended again. Nothing much in France seemed to change and warnings were again issued in 1952, 1953 and 1958, all with little or no effect. By 1978, France was finally admitted to the International Rugby Board.

France's period of suspension was of little moment in New

Neat and efficient on and off the field. The Invincibles resplendent in their No 1s in Toulouse at the end of their epic tour.

FROM THE ENDS OF THE EARTH

Jean-Luc Sadourny is known among French journalists as a personable, friendly man but not one given to lengthy interviews. His reticence is unusual among French players.

Sadourny plays for the Colomiers club on the outskirts of Toulouse, France's second city and the home of its hugely successful aviation industry. He's been a loyal club man for more than a decade, spurning offers to go to wealthier or more fashionable clubs. He is, not surprisingly, the toast of Colomiers.

On the drive to the club one training night, my French colleague, Jean-Roger Dalsaud of the weekly rugby paper, *Midi-Olympique*, told me not to expect much from Sadourny. He's a lovely man, he explained, but he just doesn't like talking to rugby writers.

We'll see, I thought. It's a hell of a long way to go to listen to silence.

Training was winding down when we got there. Some of the lights had been turned off and fog swirled around those still lit. In the outer darkness, voices and the occasional unmistakable sound of a boot hitting a rugby ball could still be heard.

We walked out onto the park to determine who it was. It was David Skrela, another French international and the son of the national coach and former great player, Jean-Claude, practising goalkicking.

Jean-Luc, he told us, was in the dressing room.

When we knocked, a head appeared and asked what we wanted. And who wants Jean-Luc? A couple of minutes later, the man himself appeared, draped only in a towel.

We were introduced and I told him of my mission. Five minutes, he said, and he would see us in the bar.

French clubs do not skimp on the niceties of life. The bar was worthy of any found in the best of hotels, the smell of food wafted from the kitchen and the lounge could have seated a couple of hundred.

When Jean-Luc appeared, he indulged in the mandatory French courtesy of approaching all in the bar — and there would have been 30 or so — and shook hands, all the while exchanging phrases such as, '*Ça va?*' and '*Tres bien, merci*'.

He returned to us with a beer for each while he had a juice, and led us to a table away from the immediate noise of the bar.

Sadourny sat and looked expectantly at me. I would like first, I said, to talk about the try you scored at Eden Park in 1994.

It was the key to his soul. His eyes lit up, he leaned forward and began talking . . . and talking.

An hour later, we left. Sadourny talked for most of the time, animatedly. It all came out. The French joy. The respect for the All Blacks. The fear of losing in Auckland after winning in Christchurch. How hard the All Black forwards were in Auckland. The importance to French rugby of beating the All Blacks not once, but twice. How the All Blacks are the yardstick for French rugby, for world rugby.

This was not Sadourny the silent, this was Sadourny the eloquent.

The Sadourny try that won the Eden Park test for France was described in the immediate aftermath as the try from the ends of the earth. He didn't know who used that expressive phrase, but said it was a phrase often heard in France to describe something unexpected, something that comes from nowhere.

And it did.

'The phrase,' he said, 'reflected what we felt — it was the final act of a great occasion, it was the end of a long tour, it was a try from France scored in New Zealand . . . from one side of the world to the other.'

At what point in that mad scramble up the field, when French player after French player kept the ball alive and All Blacks tackled and tackled again only to see another French jersey disappearing, did Sadourny think the winning try was 'on'?

Never, he said. 'I only knew for sure the try would be scored when I scored it. For me before then, there was hope and just the concentration by me and by all the French players to keep the ball and not to make a mistake.

'But even before that move, we were very confident we could win the match because the All Blacks did not capitalise on the dominance they had. After Christchurch, we thought the All Blacks would be hell in Auckland. The All Black forwards that day were very strong, much more than they had been in Christchurch, yet still they didn't score as much as they should have. We knew that we needed only one more score to beat them and we thought we could get it.'

That win was the middle of a trio of successive wins by France against New Zealand, something only Australia had achieved.

Did the French think then that they somehow had a mental edge over New Zealand, that the aura had gone?

No, not at all. The French were not arrogant. 'Before we were in New Zealand we lost to Canada and we knew we had to atone for that,' he said. 'We shouldn't have lost to Canada and so winning in New Zealand became very important to us personally for our self-belief and our credibility.

'Then the next year, 1995, the All Blacks were the best team at the World Cup. We thought they would win the final and perhaps they should have. They were a very strong team, very spectacular. So when the All Blacks came to Toulouse, we remembered how good they were and we feared we could get beaten by a big score. It made us all the more determined, to prove ourselves worthy of playing such a mighty team.'

The try from the ends of the earth . . . and one that broke New Zealand hearts. Jean-Luc Sadourny scores, Guy Accoceberry celebrates and John Timu tackles.

Zealand but it did mean that Jack Manchester's All Blacks, who toured Britain and Ireland in 1935–36, didn't go on to France as their predecessors had. There was thus a gap of nearly 30 years until the All Blacks next played in France and far from the frolic of the first match and the near-frolic of the second, the All Blacks were beaten 3–0.

History is a harsh and exacting judge in rugby. The Originals lost just to Wales on their grand tour and the Invincibles lost none, so all succeeding All Black tours become judged by comparison with those outstanding records. Manchester's team sits below the highest pedestal because it lost to Wales and England and so does Bob Stuart's team of 1953–54 because it lost to Wales and France. The French win came about through resolute defence, especially against continual attacks by the All Black fullback Bob Scott, in his final test, but also through a passage of play that came to be known as typical of French rugby. All Black halfback Keith Davis fumbled as the ball emerged from a scrum about 40 metres out and the French No 8, Robert Baulon, grabbed it and ran down the touchline. Two players, hooker Paul Labadie and captain and flanker Jean Prat, were with him and he feinted to pass to both as the initial defence was breached. A few metres out from the line, he finally passed to Prat who went over with three All Blacks clinging to bits of his body.

The French daily sports paper, *L'Equipe*, was ecstatic the next morning. '*Le rugby Français a montré, a Colombes, qu'il avait atteint les hauts sommets internationaux.*' ('French rugby showed at Colombes that it has reached the very top international standard,' or words to that effect).

The All Blacks' manager, Norman Millard, must have thought so too because while the team was in Paris he formally invited the French to send a team to New Zealand in 1957. As often happens with such things, the tour didn't eventuate then but it did four years later, in 1961, when New Zealanders for the first time came to grips with what French rugby was like. It said much for the French that they decided to tour New Zealand before any of the British Isles countries individually mounted such a venture.

It was the tour that introduced a touch of the exotic to New Zealand rugby after a constant home diet of Brits, Australians and South Africans. It introduced men such as the captain, François Moncla, flanker Michel Crauste, No 8 Michel Celaya, the brothers Boniface, André and Guy, in the midfield and at first five-eighth, Pierre Albaladejo. Albaladejo began his test career as a fullback at the age of 20 but for six years wasn't required again. Then he returned in the No 10 jersey and a new career was born. In France, where he was a favourite, the crowds called him 'Bala' but in New Zealand, where the crowds soon got to know him, he became 'Monsieur Le Drop'. He kicked 12 dropped goals in his 30-test career and two of them were in the first test against the All Blacks at Eden Park. The match was all New Zealand's, though, with Don McKay and Terry O'Sullivan scoring tries and Don Clarke converting both and showing that he could do anything the French could do by kicking a dropped goal as well.

In his rugby afterlife, Albaladejo was a restaurateur and worked also as a television comments man, and he was frequently around All Black teams in France. On a recent tour he was introduced to a young New Zealander who probably wasn't born in 1961. 'Ah,' said the New Zealander, 'Monsieur Le Drop!'

The second test was memorable not so much for anything but the weather, which was among the worst experienced at Athletic Park in Wellington. The southerly gale during the morning was so high that the passenger liner *Canberra*, then on its maiden voyage, wouldn't risk the passage through the Wellington Heads. Consideration was given to postponing the match but rugby officials, for neither the first nor last time, decided the game could go on. France played the first half with the gale at their backs but could make no headway in the face of tight All Black defence. They scored first into the gale and for a time, France looked headed for an upset win but then Kel Tremain charged down a clearing kick and fell gratefully onto the ball over the French line. The difference in the test was Don Clarke's extraordinary conversion, a kick said to be one of the greatest in his long and illustrious career. He took the ball back to the 22 and aimed almost parallel to the goal-line, gambling on the wind picking it up and taking it in the required direction. It did.

Strangely, 'The Boot' was on the other foot when France and New Zealand next met, in Paris in 1964. Clarke had a rare off day with his kicking and Mac Herewini kicked the only penalty in the All Blacks' 12–3 win. Ralph Caulton and Ken

Both known the world over. The 1963–64 All Blacks pose with the Eiffel Tower as an imposing backdrop.

Gray scored tries and test debutant Chris Laidlaw adopted the maxim of 'When in France . . .' and dropkicked a goal. Albaladejo didn't respond in kind, but he did kick a penalty goal.

The French connection well and truly established, the All Blacks were back there again in 1967, the fabled side coached by Fred Allen and captained by Brian Lochore winning 21–15, and France were again in New Zealand the following year.

This was the period when the All Blacks were at unstoppable heights. They hadn't lost a test match since 1965 and wouldn't lose one until 1970. It was to France's great credit that they stayed within reasonable touch in each of the three tests in New Zealand — the first was 12–9, the second 9–3 and the third 19–12. In the third, at Eden Park, France scored three tries to the All Blacks' two. But for all the solidity of their play, it was once again a kicker who made the most impression. Their fullback was Pierre Villepreux, a name revered still in French rugby, and in the second test he kicked an enormous penalty goal. Records of the length of successful kicks are sketchy and incomplete, but there's no doubt Villepreux's, from eight metres inside the French half and 15 metres in from touch, was one of the biggest.

The French can be eloquent and expressive and Walter Spanghero was both when he talked of leading France to beat the All Blacks in Paris in 1973. 'Beating the All Blacks was extraordinary,' he said. 'Succeeding in Paris against the All Blacks was all I could hope for.'

FUNNY HA-HA, FUNNY PECULIAR

All Blacks over the years will have used a variety of descriptions for matches against France: hard, gruelling, fast among them; confusing, frustrating and no doubt words which have stayed in the dressing rooms.

But funny? It's not a word often associated with rugby tests, yet that's the word All Black vice-captain Billy Stead used after the All Blacks had played France for the first time, in Paris on New Year's Day in 1906.

'Much comment on the game is not necessary,' he wrote in his regular column for the *Southland Times*, 'except to say that it was voted by all of us to be the funniest match we had ever played in.'

Funny peculiar and funny ha-ha.

It was funny peculiar because the French had only the most rudimentary ideas of international rugby and wouldn't even go down for the first scrum until they could see how the All Blacks did it.

And funny ha-ha because a scrum once had to be delayed when lock Fred Newton literally fell about laughing. The cause of his mirth had been two of the French forwards having beards and after some comments on the merits of footballers and beards, All Blacks at the next scrum tried to avoid contact with the hirsute Frenchmen. Two All Black forwards both trying to claim the loosehead side is what caused Newton's fit of laughter.

Stead wrote that it was difficult to play seriously against such opponents.

'Time and again we hoisted the slippery oval high into the air and it was laughable to watch the antics of the Frenchmen as to who should attempt to catch it.'

The All Blacks won by a record score, 38–8, but it could have been much, much higher if the game had been played with more seriousness.

Billy Wallace recorded that captain Dave Gallaher had struck up an instant rapport with his French counterpart, Henri Amand, and shortly after halftime sent the word around his players to let the French score a try or two, which they were happy to do.

The All Blacks during their pioneering tour had guarded their line jealously and only once previously in 32 matches

Billy Wallace

had any side scored twice against them. Yet here were the All Blacks happily conceding tries to encourage the French.

Both Stead and Wallace remarked on the courtesy of their French opponents, who were mostly soldiers (though they did include an Englishman, William Crichton, and an American, Alan Muhr). The French were willing tacklers and each time they knocked an All Black over, they stood by and gave their victims a helping hand back up.

The All Blacks had not had the most rigorous of preparations for their only match in France. They'd beaten Swansea two days before and travelled through the night to London, arriving at 4 a.m. They had a few hours sleep before changing trains for the trip to Folkestone, then a cross-channel ferry to Boulogne, then another train to Paris, arriving at 6 p.m. on the eve of the test.

'All very tired and sore,' Stead noted, 'we retired to bed early and most of us (for the first time in our lives) missed seeing the New Year in.'

Even then their travails were not over. They travelled the 20 kilometres from the centre of Paris to the stadium in a fleet of private cars, the drivers of which seemed to regard it as a point of honour to get there first.

'There were no speed limits in Paris,' Wallace recalled, 'and off they went like the wind. People were ducking and diving out of the way and the horns were tooting at every corner and we wondered if we would get to the ground alive. "General" Booth was sitting in the front seat of one car and the speed was so great that his hat blew off his head and through a hole in the celluloid window behind.

'One car got a puncture on the way and so arrived at the ground just as we were about to take the field. They had a great job trying to get through the crush at the gates and the police had to come to their aid.'

DESPERATELY SEEKING SELLA

To the French, *Agen* means prunes. It's the prunes capital of France. Another phrase that could also have a marked and even quicker effect on one's health came more to mind. Cold. Damn cold. *Froid. Très froid*.

I was in Agen looking for Philippe Sella. He is to Agen what Colin Meads is to Te Kuiti; Brian Lochore to Eketahuna. But neither Te Kuiti nor Eketahuna could ever have been as cold as Agen the morning of my mission. Taumarunui could, though. The icy mist that hung over and through Agen that morning was similar to mornings I recalled in Taumarunui on some rugby tour in the middle of winter. This was the middle of winter, to be fair to Agen, but it was the south-west of France, which to an Antipodean mind is supposed to be relatively warm.

Not this day. I'd been in Toulouse, an hour and 10 minutes away on the TER (*trains express régionaux*), part of the wonderful French rail network on which it's sometimes possible to get on a train at one end of France and get off it at the other without having had to produce a ticket. A friend in Toulouse had told me everyone in Agen knew Sella and his house was impossible to miss. Just in case I didn't achieve the impossible, he helpfully drew me a map tracing the route from the *gare* to *chez* Sella.

For all the hour and 10 minutes as the TER whisked me through the frostscape, I studied the map, trying to decipher the handwritten name of the street in which Sella lived. It was only as the train slowed that the cramped writing translated into Richard Coeur de Lyon, Richard the Lionheart, the mad, bad son of Eleanor of Aquitaine, who once ruled in these parts and whose marriage to King Henry II precipitated a couple of hundred years of war between England and France. Richard the Lionheart was best known in history for trying to capture Jerusalem. Sella captured all of the rugby world.

Just to check the veracity of the map, and to stay in the warmth a moment longer, I asked someone at the station how to get to *rue Richard Coeur de Lyon. Bonjour*, I said in my best French. *Comment allez-vous?* After an exchange of *bons* and *très bons*, I said, '*Où est Richard Coeur de Lyon s'il vous plaît?*'

This brought forth a volume of French quicker than the TER. *Je ne comprends pas*. Ah, play it again Sam. And then the ultimate line of defeat, *Parlez-vous anglais?*

Non.

Great.

After a *droite* here and a *gauche* there accompanied by much pointing, I set off. Two hundred metres, *tournez à droite. Ici la Bourse. Cent metres, tournez à gauche*. And so on. Since it was early in the morning, most shops were closed. I lurked in doorways to get out of the light mist or snow or whatever it was that was chilling my bare head. I stopped at every café, demanding an espresso *grande* and a place by the heaters. I filled in the time by running through my

knowledge of Agen. It didn't take long. The *Monsieur* Big of French rugby for so long, Albert Ferrasse, came from Agen. I'd been there before, with the All Blacks in 1977, and somehow I remembered it had a special place in Tour de France history. The great bike race doesn't often reach Agen but when it does, something special seems to happen. It was there that the great Swiss rider, Hugo Koblet, won a stage towards winning the tour in 1951 and it was on the stage from Agen in 1996 that the Dane, Bjarne Riis, ended the five-year domination of the Spaniard, Miguel Indurain.

Enough mental meanderings. Back on the road. A lingerie shop had just opened. I idled my way past racks of bras and unmentionables to gain a little more warmth. I left feeling like a voyeuristic Captain Oates.

A few more *gauches* and *droites* later, there was the blessed street sign: *rue Richard Coeur de* etc., etc.

Another café was strategically placed on the corner and in I dived so my face would thaw enough to be able to talk to Sella and my hands enough to write. The barman, *soigner* or whatever, had more English than I did French. He didn't have much. He wanted to know what a nice guy like me was doing in a place like that. I uttered the magic word, 'Sella'. This sent the man into a frenzy, both voluble and physical. His speech was faster than the TER's; it was up to TGV pace. And all the while, he rummaged furiously through a pile of magazines and newspapers behind the bar. He emerged triumphant with a dog-eared copy of what I recognised as the Toulouse weekly rugby paper, *Midi-Olympique*. He thrashed through the pages and thrust his find under my defrosting nose. '*Voilà! Sella!*'

It was indeed. That centenarian prince of centres, there in the blue of *l'équipe de France*, stepping out of what I happily noticed was an attempted English tackle.

Then even more rapid French, which I learned slowly was my friend the barman's *coup de triomphe*. He not only had a photo of Sella, he not only knew where Sella lived, he was married to Sella's sister's cousin (or something like that). Tossing his apron aside, he beckoned me to follow. Out into the street we went, *á gauche* we went, at a fair clip along *rue Richard* etc., etc. until we came to a solid wooden door in a wall that looked as if it had once been attached to the Bastille.

'*Ici*,' he proudly announced. 'Sella!'

And sure enough, there alongside a little push-button was the indication, P Sella. It said *poussez* so I pushed. When a distinctly female '*Oui?*' filtered down, my new-found friend went back into TGV mode, slapped me cheerfully

> '*Ici*,' he proudly announced. 'Sella!'

Charm, grace, talent — they all add up to Philippe Sella.

on the back and took off back to his café.

A few seconds later, a woman who introduced herself as Josie opened the door, bade me a warm welcome, and told me Philippe was not home but would be soon. Would I mind waiting? No, I wouldn't, especially if you've got a heater. I was ushered into what in English would be called a study or den. I preferred study because I studied the Sella memorabilia on the mantelpiece and around the walls. A French jersey there, a ball here, a few photos, a bronze rooster . . . a rugby man's place.

It had been a few years since I'd met Sella and I couldn't remember how good his English was. I need not have worried. The front door opened and shut again, there was the sound of greetings, and in strode the man I was there to see.

'Ron,' he said, extending a hand, 'good to see you again. How are you? Enjoying our weather?'

Coffee materialised, questions were asked, memories flowed. As smooth and as full of charm behind his desk as he ever was on the rugby fields of the world. The sun was out for the walk back to the station. But the warmth came from the camaraderie of rugby.

France won 13–6 and Spanghero's memory was that his team could have won by a lot more against a New Zealand team that he thought was obviously tired of being on tour. He was right about the latter point — it had been a long and mentally wearing tour by the All Blacks and it would have been no surprise if by the time they got to the second week in February that they'd had enough. For all that, the All Blacks had gone close to a grand slam, just drawing with Ireland, and if only in a results sense, it had been a successful tour. Until they got to Paris, that is.

Well established by then in international rugby, if not yet admitted to the inner sanctum of the International Rugby Board, France by the early 70s had begun flexing its administrative muscle. The French had tired of hosting the All Blacks only at the end of tours of Britain and Ireland and pressed for a separate tour by New Zealand. The prospect was discussed in 1973 when Ces Blazey, then the deputy chairman of the New Zealand union, and the president of the French federation, Albert Ferrasse, met in Edinburgh. Blazey said he had no objection in principle to a separate tour, but didn't know when it could be fitted in. Ferrasse's response was blunt. If it didn't happen, he said, France wouldn't tour New Zealand. *Impasse* is, after all, a French word.

New Zealand bowed to the inevitable, even the overdue, and the All Blacks made their first full tour of France in 1977. They lost the first test in Toulouse — when Brian McKechnie played his first game of rugby at any level at fullback — but won the second in Paris, a noted comeback test in which the brains trust of coach Jack Gleeson, captain Graham Mourie and senior forward Andy Haden dissected and destroyed the French tactical plan.

Politics were still bubbling away in the background. Ferrasse, who ruled French rugby in a similar dominant way to Danie Craven's rule in South Africa, insisted that neutral referees be appointed for the French tour of New Zealand in 1979. In the blunt way in which he argued, Ferrasse said there would be no tour unless referees came from a third country. The French had been unimpressed with the refereeing of New Zealanders Dave Millar, John Pring and Pat Murphy — three referees of high standing — in 1968.

Again, New Zealand bent to the will of the French and, again, it was inevitable that they did. Neutral referees had been used in the Five Nations for the best part of 100 years and it seemed illogical, and long overdue, that the same principle wasn't applied in test matches in other parts of the world. One argument against their use was the cost and the travel factor. It was simple for a Scottish referee, for example, to zip down to Cardiff for a match between England and Wales, but less simple for someone to travel halfway round the world for 80 minutes of action. It was a losing argument and Irishman John West, a referee well known to the All Blacks as much for his sense of humour as his refereeing, went to New Zealand for the two tests of 1979. Only once since has a New Zealander refereed the All Blacks in a test — Dave Bishop in the second of the centenary tests in 1992.

The French celebrate their rugby victories and most of all they celebrate their victories over New Zealand, and especially they

STRIKING OUT IN '95

A tour of France, generations of All Blacks have found, is seldom dull. There's always something to keep minds occupied and tongues wagging. Rugby tours in other countries follow similar patterns which have been laid down over the years. In France? The unexpected is bound to happen.

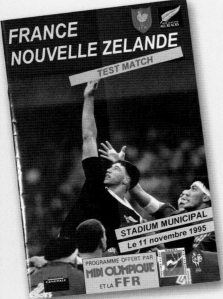

In 1995, it happened in Toulouse, the venue of the first test. As the All Blacks prepared for the match in the manner that All Blacks do, all seriousness and much talk of focus and concentration, the French were in a state of anguish.

On the Thursday, some of the players threatened to strike — they said they wouldn't play on the Saturday.

There were two issues. One was that after the World Cup three months before, three of the French players, Olivier Roumat, Laurent Cabannes and Thierry Lacroix, went against the explicit orders of the French federation and returned to South Africa to play in the Currie Cup.

As a punishment, they were declared ineligible for selection in the team to play the All Blacks in Toulouse.

The other issue was money. The dawn of professionalism had just broken and the French were not happy with their pay deal (not that they'd always been happy with their pay deals in the amateur days either).

Several of the players told manager André Herrero, an uncomfortable mediator between players and federation, that they would go on strike unless the three players were reinstated and unless more money was forthcoming.

They got some more money, but the federation was unbending on the banned trio. The refusal to play was downgraded to a refusal to attend a reception for the team being hosted by the mayor of Toulouse.

As a side issue, the French were also upset at their ticket allocation for the test — something that has often been a source of friction between players and union, especially in home tests.

All this unrest was played out in public in the two days before the test.

Such dissension in an All Black camp 48 or 72 hours before a test is scarcely imaginable. Even the ramifications of the return of the rebels in 1986 for the Australian series was put in the background for the greater good of winning the final test (which was lost anyway).

One of the principals in the negotiations was the French fullback, Jean-Luc Sadourny. He recalled the Toulouse buildup with a smile.

'That is our Latin temperament, is it not?' he said. 'Not for Anglo-Saxons. I can understand how it could be a distraction for other teams and affect the way they played, but for us it was motivation.

'It was part of the pride of playing rugby for France. We wanted the best and we wanted to be the best. We didn't get our own way in the arguments but we decided to play in Toulouse in a manner that would show the federation we deserved what we asked for.'

And they did. France won 22–15, three tries to none.

The contrast, Sadourny said, was the following week in Paris when the All Blacks won the second test. 'We had proved our point,' he said, 'so perhaps in Paris our motivation wasn't as great as it had been in Toulouse.

'But, in Paris, the All Blacks had the motivation. They needed to play well because they'd lost the previous week and they wanted to play well as a tribute to their coach, Laurie Mains. [The Paris test was Mains' last as the All Blacks' coach.]

'So, you see, the team with the better motivation should always win.'

The All Blacks won the second test 37–12.

From disaster to triumph. All Blacks carry coach Laurie Mains from the field after his last test, victory against France in Paris.

C'EST LA VIE, WALTER

Walter Spanghero, the hulking No 8 who toured New Zealand in 1968 and captained France against the All Blacks in 1973, says he doesn't like to criticise referees.

When a player says that, almost always a 'but' will follow.

Spanghero, who now owns a car hire company in Toulouse, was ready with his 'but'.

'France would have won the three-test series in New Zealand in 1968 if there had been neutral referees,' he says emphatically.

The series was tight, of that there was no doubt, and it was something of a surprise that France could run a formidable All Black team, in Fred Allen's last year of coaching, so close. Spanghero has not mellowed with the passing of the years.

'The standard of the refereeing destabilised France,' Spanghero says.

The first test in Christchurch, won 12–9 by the All Blacks, was refereed by Dave Millar of Otago. The second test, 9–3 to the All Blacks, was refereed by John Pring of Auckland and veteran North Aucklander Pat Murphy refereed the third, won 19–12.

'We should have won the first and the third tests', Spanghero says, 'and if there had been neutral referees I'm sure we would have. I'm not suggesting the New Zealand referees favoured the All Blacks but the problem was they refereed in a New Zealand style, not an international style, and it was that which favoured the All Blacks.'

He says there were particular difficulties at rucks where, he felt, the All Blacks were allowed to ruck illegally, judging by the standards applying elsewhere.

'Our style and rhythm was upset by the refereeing and, as a result, we couldn't play the way we wanted,' Spanghero says. 'It was a difference in interpretation, nothing more, but we felt that if you play international rugby you must play to a universal set of laws that are applied uniformly but that didn't happen. We were surprised and angry with what we discovered in the tests, especially in the first and third tests.

'The All Blacks then were a great side and I still have the greatest admiration for New Zealand rugby, but I do think the All Blacks benefited from having their own referees for so long.'

Within five years, the French Rugby Federation president, Albert Ferrasse, told New Zealand administrator Ces Blazey that France would only tour New Zealand on two conditions: that the All Blacks reciprocate with a tour of France and that neutral referees must be used in New Zealand.

France got their way on both.

This is the way we play it here. Referee John Pring lays down his law to French captain Marcel Puget in the second test in 1968. Brian Lochore seems to agree.

celebrated their first win in New Zealand, which happened to fall on the most revered day in France, Bastille Day. It was a surprising win because the All Blacks had won the first test well enough at 23–9 and, in between the two tests, Southland had beaten the French. But not for nothing are the French regarded as unpredictable. They were compelling in the second test in Auckland, even from early in the match when they trailed 7–3. Their standard bearer was Jean-Pierre Rives, the flanker whose mane of blond hair earned him the nickname of Casque d'Or (helmet of gold). He was, in inspiration, in thought and in deed, to the French what Graham Mourie was to

The face of defeat. Craig Dowd after leaving the field in the World Cup semifinal against France in 1999.

the All Blacks. The All Blacks had been beaten by France before but they were all in France — this was a victory on enemy soil and one to be savoured all the more because of that. It also gave New Zealand a healthier respect for a French team when it can get its forwards and backs playing together in a united purpose.

The politics and the referees sorted out, and with France admitted to the IRB in 1978, touring took on a more settled nature. The days of add-on matches in France were at an end and the All Blacks toured there again in 1981, 1986 and 1990, with France being such a frequent visitor in the 80s they could almost have gained residence status. France was in New Zealand in 1984, 1986, 1987 (for the World Cup) and in 1989.

There was the dogged persistence of Jean-Patrick Lescarboura in the first test of 1984, trying and trying again and again to kick a winning dropped goal when his side trailed 10–9. There was the great Serge Blanco, whom the All Blacks of 1977 had first seen as a promising teenager but who through the 80s was fashioning a career that ranks him at or near the top of all French players. There was Fouroux's successor, Pierre Berbizier, leading France against the All Blacks in Christchurch in 1986 — the game celebrated as the vindication of the Baby Blacks for their 18–9 victory. There were the tests in France at the end of 1986 and most of all the French win in

BOLLOCKS!

One of Welsh referee Derek Bevan's record 16 tests involving New Zealand was the second test loss to France at Eden Park in 1994.

It was the test won by France with the try that came, as the French said, from the ends of the earth. Bevan was impressed.

'It was magnificent to be standing there to award what was an outstanding try,' Bevan wrote in his book, *The Man in the Middle*. 'The New Zealand players were trudging back, with their heads bowed because they were now losing after this wonder try.

'Sean Fitzpatrick looked up at me and I said, "Wasn't that a brilliant try?"

'"Bollocks" was his reply. Perhaps my comment to Fitzpatrick was somewhat naive. It was made on the spur of the moment. He gave me eye contact and I thought I had to say something. But perhaps he didn't like the grin on my face either.'

From out of the mouths of babes . . . it was an upset victory when the All Blacks — the Baby Blacks — beat France in 1986. Andy Earl and Gordon Macpherson ready themselves for lineout ball, and Brian McGrattan and Kevin Boroevich are poised to lend a hand. The French are Francis Haget, Jean Condom and Jean-Patrick Garuet.

Nantes, which became a rallying call for the All Blacks the following year as they headed towards the World Cup. There was the cup final itself against a France that had perhaps played out its magnificence the week before in the semifinal against Australia.

There was the extraordinary run by France in the 90s — three test victories in a row over the All Blacks, something that only Australia had previously managed. For the two tests in 1994, there was the epiphanic appearance of Jonah Lomu, a player with impact like no other. There have been French teams in New Zealand since

Out of my way. Tana Umaga in the pose New Zealanders love to see. The dismissed Frenchman is Imanol Harinordoquy. This was against France in 2002.

then that have looked and played like shadows of a great rugby country, but then with a change or two here and there can then go and beat the All Blacks, most notably in the World Cup semifinal in 1999 and then in Marseilles in 2000.

They are a contradiction; they are an enigma. They can play like a disorganised rabble on one day and like champions on the next. Even their players are at a loss to explain it. It depends on temperament, they say. It depends on preceding results. If they've had a couple of good wins, they're less anxious about proving themselves. If they've had a couple of losses or just one bad loss — like they did to Canada on the way to New Zealand in 1994 — they become infused with a will to win that is just about unbreakable.

PUNTING ON BRIAN

Toulouse in 1977 was when the All Blacks were party to a lie — all in the national interests of course.

It was when the All Blacks were going through a lean time at fullback. Six different fullbacks had been fielded in the previous 10 tests, a stark contrast to the time when Don Clarke had the job to himself for the best part of a decade.

Heading for the first test against France in 1977, coach Jack Gleeson's problems were obvious. The only fullback chosen for the tour, Bevan Wilson, had a damaged thigh muscle that eventually forced his early return home. Before Toulouse, it was clear he couldn't play.

One option for fullback was Bryan Williams, but if he wore No 15, that meant the only other wing, Brian Ford, would have to play and he had a strained achilles tendon.

So when Gleeson named his first test team, the first name he read out was that of Brian McKechnie, selected for the tour as a first five-eighth.

It stunned the reporters who were dutifully jotting the team down. 'You weren't the only guys who were stunned,' McKechnie says. 'Jack came to me in the dressing room before training and said I would be playing at fullback. I might have gulped. He told me the reporters would ask me about my experience at fullback and that I would have to give the impression I was quite experienced in the role.

'The fact was I'd never played there in a proper game. I think I might have been fullback in a social game at some stage but that was it. My first real game at fullback was a test.'

McKechnie says Gleeson's entreaty to mislead wasn't directed at New Zealand but at France. 'He wanted to get the message across to the French team that I wasn't a beginner in the role,' he says, 'but they knew or if they didn't, they found out fairly quickly.'

He says he was more nervous before that test than any other. And it showed on the field. McKechnie readily concedes that the test in Toulouse was not one of his shining moments.

'They had a good tactical kicker, Jean-Pierre Romeu, and he put the ball all over the place and I ran around like a headless chook all day. I always remember not being where the ball was. I think because of that, because I was thinking of other things, my goalkicking suffered as well. I got one from in

front but I missed one from in front as well. It was not a great day. We lost and I blamed myself for it. I was pretty distraught afterwards; I felt as if I let the team down.'

McKechnie remembers looking at the French papers the next day and asking the best French speaker in the team, Andy Haden, to tell him what they were saying. 'Andy told me, "You don't want to know".'

One headline in the rugby paper, *Midi Olympique*, needed no translation: *McKechnie débute mal, Romeu finit bien . . .*

The bad for McKechnie soon turned to good, though.

Gleeson kept him at fullback for the midweek match on a rainswept night in the southern provincial town of Angoulême and, there, McKechnie fared much better. 'We played a French selection team on a dirty night and the guys in that team obviously had seen the test and they peppered me with up and unders, but this time I was under them. We'd also had a team meeting after the test and I told the guys that when they supported me, they needed to get behind me rather than in front. They had to give me the space to get to the ball. This worked and I was much happier with my game.'

The heightened confidence showed early in the second test in Paris. Eight minutes into the game, French centre Roland Bertranne kicked for touch and McKechnie was in position, taking it on the full as he slid near the touchline. He steadied himself, turned and dropkicked a 35-metre goal.

'I've got no idea why I did that,' he says. 'I was nearly in touch, it was quite a way out for me, but it just happened. All of a sudden, I felt good about myself. That kick brought the confidence back and the rest of the game went well.'

That was also the game in which lock Gary Seear — nicknamed Milk Bottle for his fair looks and shape — kicked a 45-metre penalty goal.

'Gary had kicked the round-the-corner stuff at training and he put one over in one of the midweek matches,' McKechnie says. 'When we were given that penalty in Paris, Graham Mourie looked at me and I thought it was too far for me, but I said to him, "If Gary wants to have a go, let him".'

The triumph in Paris was a turnaround not just for the team, but for McKechnie as well.

IRELAND

To the men of Munster, a debt. If Munster, a team of men possessed, hadn't beaten the All Blacks of 1978, the test against Ireland four days later may have been lost. History wouldn't have a grand slam to record for the All Blacks, and Ireland would not be among the sides never to have beaten New Zealand.

If — a small word with large implications. May — a weasel word that lacks commitment.

The facts and their less reliable companions, impressions, lead to the conclusion, though, that the All Blacks won the first leg of their grand slam — with Wales, England and Scotland still to come — because they had been beaten 12–0 by Munster on a day that will never be forgotten by the rugby-mad people of Limerick.

Until Munster, the All Blacks, coached by Jack Gleeson and captained by Graham Mourie, were expansive. They won the first four games of their tour well by moving the ball as often and as quickly as they could to the wings and, as a result, 13 of the 16 tries scored in those games were scored by wings. There was even talk, at that early stage, of an unbeaten tour.

After Munster, the All Blacks became more cautious, more prudent. They moved the ball when it was convenient to do so, rather than when it was possible to do so. They concentrated more on retaining possession and gaining territory.

Munster, coached by one former Irish and Lions player, Tom Kiernan, and helped by another, Noel Murphy — who at the time was also the Ireland coach — had but one aim in their match against the All Blacks. That was to tackle, tackle, tackle and then to tackle some more. Stu Wilson reckons he has never been tackled as hard or as often, either before or after.

In Wales, songs have been sung about defeats of the All Blacks. In Ireland, Munster's win — still the only loss by the All Blacks to any Irish side — became a play, 'Alone it Stands'. In it there's a passage about one of the Munster players who's almost concussed — or he might have been concussed — after he went down in an All Black tackle. The play depicts him groggily rising and tearing

back into it, looking for something in black to lay low. It's true. That's the way it was.

Thomond Park on October 31, 1978 was electric with the intensity of the Munster players' will. It was almost a tangible thing and New Zealanders could only watch aghast, and with grudging admiration.

The next morning, as Gleeson sat at breakfast and ruminated over the events of the day before, he talked about kamikaze tackles. He said no side would have beaten Munster that day. Munster could have beaten anyone. They beat the All Blacks. What more could an Irish side want?

But as Munster's first five-eighth, Tony Ward, went back to his Limerick sports shop and ordered bumper stickers saying 'Munster 12, New Zealand 0', and as printers pressed the button to run off hundreds more of the match programme, and as a great many people in Limerick nursed gigantic hangovers or continued celebrating, the All Blacks headed off by bus for Dublin to prepare for the test.

And they thought and they plotted. From now on, they decided, things would be different. The idea of expansive, entertaining rugby went the way of the unbeaten tour.

For Gleeson, Mourie and all the players the loss to Munster was a lesson not just in how the tour should proceed, but in how all previous All Black visits to Ireland had been.

Ireland is not and never has been the greatest rugby country. It is not a Wales where rugby is the ruling passion; it is not an England where vast numbers of players can be called upon. Rugby is a sport of significance in Ireland but their own brand of football, the Gaelic variety that seems a close relative of Australian rules, and soccer are of greater significance.

But if there is one thing that All Blacks have learnt in nearly 100 years of playing in Ireland or against Ireland, it's that there is

Just the ticket — the Irish snapped these up for their first test against New Zealand.

no such thing as an easy game; there's no such thing as an Ireland team that does not take the field with passion oozing from players' pores. It may sound trite to say, but what they lack in talent or player depth, they make up in heart.

So the All Blacks of 1978 went to Lansdowne Road for their first test and they won, but they won by only a point. It was 10–9 and it was thanks to halfback Mark Donaldson shooting round the front of a lineout with time almost up and flicking the ball into the waiting and grateful arms of his hooker, Andy Dalton. It was thanks also to stupendous efforts by the All Black forwards and especially Andy Haden, whose display that day was one of his greatest in an All Black jersey, perhaps the greatest (though he disputes that, putting higher the two unofficial tests in 1976 against Argentina).

It was thanks, too, to what Mourie called the educated left boot and well-mannered right boot of first five-eighth Doug Bruce. He dropkicked two goals but it was his tactical kicking, forcing Ireland back and gaining territory for the All Blacks, that was as crucial. After Munster, these were the percentage All Blacks and Bruce was the man with the calculator.

All Blacks of whatever generation have loved playing in Ireland and Ireland generally have loved having them there. It's an enjoyable country to tour, the people are friendly and there's none of the intensity of Wales, for example, where people live for the

day that the All Blacks will be beaten. There are, of course, the Irish jokes, the Irish music, the Irish bars, and none is told better, sung better or run better than by the Irish themselves.

There is one rugby story that surely could have happened only in Ireland. It was in 1989 and the Irish team played in its typical fiery fashion until finally Wayne Shelford's champion side, then at its peak, was able to subdue them. This was the test that was preceded by the Irish players advancing on the All Blacks during the haka, going almost nose to nose and with eyes afire, as Shelford climaxed with 'whiti te ra'. The Irish captain was Willie Anderson, a big raw-boned lock to whom the word 'niceties' might have applied only to a shop selling Irish lace. It certainly didn't apply to his manner of playing, especially not against the All Blacks. After he'd showered and changed, he walked along the front of the main grandstand at Lansdowne Road heading towards a clubrooms where the press conference was held. He took a silver flask from his blazer pocket and had a swig. 'What's that?' he was asked by a nosy New Zealander. 'Here, try it,' Anderson said. It was poteen, the illicit Irish whiskey distilled from potatoes. As Anderson left the press conference, Shelford arrived. Out came the flask again, 'Here,' he said, 'have some of this.' It might have been the only time on the tour that Shelford's eyes watered.

For the All Blacks in Ireland, it was ever thus. Hard rugby, but the living was easy.

Billy Wallace, the nonpareil of the Originals, caught the mood when his team arrived in Ireland from Scotland, where they had been given the cold shoulder by Scottish officialdom.

'After our treatment at the hands of the Scottish union', he wrote, 'how different it was in Ireland . . . The Irish people took us to their hearts right away and hundreds of them came in to have a yarn.'

One newspaper account of the first test against Ireland, won 15–0 by the Originals with Bob Deans scoring two tries, could have related to any number of Ireland-New Zealand encounters.

'That the Irishmen showed dash and pluck in plenty goes without saying', it said, 'but these found more than their match in Colonial skill and resource. For the first half hour, however, the New Zealanders were hard put to stop the brilliant rushes of the Irish forwards who, worked up to a fine pitch of frenzy by the fiery Celtic crowd, swept down on the Colonial defence time after time in an impetuous wave that seemed certain to carry all before it. But there was always one All Black at least to finally bar the way; however imminent the breach, always some grim, dark figure to arrest the tide of green jerseys that threatened to surge over the New Zealand line.'

The theme continued in 1924 when the Invincible All Blacks were in Dublin, though since it was their first test, the All Blacks' first for three years in fact, they were not yet invincible.

George Nepia, the celebrated fullback who played in every match, captured the mood of the test in memoirs he wrote for *Truth* in 1937. 'That game was one of the hardest of the tour,' he wrote. 'In fact, I give it pride of place for if ever 15 men met 15 other men on a rugby field and knocked each other so hard for so long without ever a suspicion of anything unsporting, I'd like to hear of it.'

The All Blacks won by a try to Snowy Svenson — he scored in each of the Invincibles' tests — and a penalty goal to Mark Nicholls, to nothing, but to say the Irish came out of the test with nothing does them a disservice.

It was a horrible day, made more horrible for the All Blacks by a wind shift around halftime that had them playing into wind and rain in both halves. Nepia said Ireland should have trailed by just a point had their Belfast centre, George Stephenson, not slipped over when heading for a probable try.

'I just had time to get to the ball before the Irish pack tore down on it but if ever I was glad of anything, it was the sight of Stephenson falling,' Nepia wrote.

It was one of the few days, possibly the only one, on that tour when Nepia was outplayed. Newspaper writers said so and

TIKI MARKS THE SPOT

A little bit of New Zealand lies buried forever beneath the sod in dear old Ireland. Lansdowne Road sod, to be precise.

The All Blacks beat Ireland there 10–9 in 1978, an Andy Dalton try in the last minute just saving the All Blacks and putting them on the road to the Grand Slam. History would record the victory well, the All Blacks knew, but they decided later the night of the match to add their own little footnote.

After the festivities and frivolities that mark post-match celebrations in Ireland, where they're often more boisterous than in other places, Mourie and a few players thought it would be a good idea to mark the spot of Dalton's try with something distinctly New Zealand.

All the players had been issued with pocketfuls of plastic tikis to hand out to the locals during the tour (which they did with gusto, delightedly pointing out to female recipients the tiki's fertility properties).

The tiki seemed an appropriate gift from the All Black gods to leave implanted in the Irish soil. Mourie, Andy Haden and a few others made their way back out to Lansdowne Road from central Dublin late in the night and scaled a fence to get into the ground, hoping to alert neither guard dogs nor alarm bells.

If there were such, they remained silent as the players crept out onto the ground, found the appropriate spot and dug with their hands until the hole was deemed sufficiently deep. The tiki was then placed reverently in its resting place and the visitors stole back into the Dublin night.

First leg in. Andy Dalton scores to clinch victory against Ireland and the first leg of the grand slam.

GALLAHER'S TEST OF NERVES

Imagine this. You're the captain of the All Blacks on a nation-defining tour and you're injured. Not just injured but advised to be immobile. And your team is playing Ireland in a test match.

You're in bed. There's no radio, no television, just a runner with a promise to bring the score as quick as he can at halftime and again at the end of the match.

Such was the lot of Dave Gallaher when the All Blacks went to Dublin for the first time.

He'd been kicked in his right shin in the test against Scotland a week before and when the team arrived in Dublin after a steamer trip across the Irish Sea to Belfast, then train from Belfast to Dublin, the leg had swollen alarmingly.

A doctor, Burke Savage by name, took firm control when the team checked into the Imperial Hotel. Gallaher, he diagnosed, was suffering from cellulitis, inflammation of the skin and the underlying tissue. Anyone could see that without necessarily being able to put a name to it.

The good doctor explained what had happened. The kick at Inverleith had broken the surface of Gallaher's skin and the wound had become infected. A lack of prompt and proper treatment could lead to blood poisoning and even to death.

These days, such a condition would be treated with penicillin or some other antibiotic. But alas for Gallaher, the discovery of the healing properties of penicillin was still 23 years away.

So hot compresses or poultices were the order of the day and the wound, according to the *Irish Times*, required constant fomentation.

So there was Gallaher with his swollen leg, propped up in bed, book and smokes handy, while his team-mates played.

'I shall never forget the Irish match,' he later recalled. 'It was one of the most anxious times I lived through. I was in bed in Dublin and after I heard the halftime score [5–0] I could neither smoke nor read. In fact, I hardly kept still until I heard the result and knew my boys were safe.'

This story had a happy ending.

The All Blacks won 15–0 and Gallaher recovered in time to play in the next test, against England.

Leaders of men. The Originals' captain and vice-captain, Dave Gallaher and Billy Stead.

MUNSTER MEN IMMORTALISED

Munster's defeat of the All Blacks in 1978 could have cost Ireland the chance of winning the test that was played four days later, the first five-eighth for Munster and Ireland, Tony Ward, believes.

He was one of five Munster players who confronted the All Blacks on both the Tuesday and the Saturday.

'The fact we'd won in Limerick gave us all an inner confidence that we could do it,' Ward says. 'And perhaps subsconsciously we just expected it to happen. We were on the verge of something special, but for the Munster players at least, we'd already done something special. What we didn't think about was the collective hunger for the All Blacks that comes with the pride of wearing the All Black jersey, an inner belief that mattered.

'We were good enough to beat the All Blacks, I don't doubt that, but when push came to shove late in the second half the All Blacks had the greater hunger, or the greater pride, whatever it is that pushes rugby teams on.

'That Irish test made their tour and they knew it. They knew the success of their tour depended on that match at Lansdowne Road.'

Ward, a mercurial first five-eighth who ranks among Ireland's best, never toured New Zealand but his regard for All Black rugby is of the highest.

'We were a bit worried after we'd beaten them in Limerick,' Ward says. 'We were waiting around in the carpark at the Limerick Inn for the dinner after the game and wondered what the All Blacks would be like. We'd heard they were bad losers.'

Then the All Blacks arrived in their bus and walked into the inn in single file, hand on the shoulder of the player in front, singing the work song from 'Snow White and the Seven Dwarfs'. 'Hi ho, hi ho, it's off to work we go . . .'.

The Scots in New Zealand in 1975 performed the same act, but no matter. It was a gesture that was greatly appreciated.

'They marched up the stairs, then back down again and right round the dining room singing this song before they sat down,' Ward says. 'They were magic. They set the tone for the night.'

It was far from the end of the singing. Late in the night, the Munster players sang 'The Isle', actually a Scottish song, that is the Shannon club's victory song, Shannon being one of the two dominant clubs in Limerick with Garryowen. In that song lay the title that Limerick man John Breen later gave the play

A flyer for a London production of the play that celebrates Munster's greatest rugby day.

he wrote about Munster's most noted victory, 'Alone it Stands'. The lyrics go: 'There is an isle, a bonnie isle, stands proudly from, stands proudly from the sea, and dearer far than all this world, is that dear isle to me. It is not that alone it stands, where all around is fresh and fair, but because it is my native land . . .'

While the singing went on far into the Limerick night, it continued in the morning, too, when the All Blacks were at breakfast. Andy Haden trooped into the dining room singing, to the tune of Boney M's 'Brown Girl in the Ring': 'All Blacks a load of shit, tra la la la la . . .'

Nepia agreed. The man who outplayed him was the Irish fullback, Ernie Crawford and, according to Nepia, without him the All Blacks could have won by more than 6–0.

Though Jack Manchester's 1935 All Blacks won by the superficially comfortable margin of 17–9, all was not as the scoreline may indicate. The forwards, their pluck undaunted and their courage fiery hot, to use Banjo Paterson's words in a rugby context, attacked and attacked the All Black line and captain Jack Siggins got across to score, but the referee didn't acknowledge it. That was when Ireland trailed by only two points and a score to them then could have made all the difference.

While Nepia may have been outplayed in 1924, it was the All Black fullback this time, Mike Gilbert, who was held to have been the critical factor for the All Blacks. He stopped several Irish forward rushes in a hectic second half by the simple but effective

expedient of going down on the ball, hoping his loose forwards would get there in time to give him some assistance. Generally they did. Gilbert also kicked two penalty goals late in the game that inflated the margin and made it safe for New Zealand.

Again it was a fullback, this time Bob Scott, who made the difference when Bob Stuart's All Blacks played in Dublin in January 1954. The All Blacks had lost the first test of their tour, against Wales, and in the match before the Irish test they'd been held to a draw by Ulster. So these were desperate times. Five new All Blacks were introduced, among them Wellington first five-eighth Guy Bowers who displaced the touring vice-captain, Laurie Haig. The Irish had what many people called the greatest player of his

All Black entrance. Jock Richardson leads his team onto Lansdowne Road for the opening test by the Invincibles. He's followed by Les Cupples and Maurice Brownlie.

Ireland

generation, Jack Kyle, at first five-eighth, and New Zealanders knew well his capabilities after the 1950 Lions tour.

The match in the end was a more comfortable victory than the All Blacks had expected, even though they were reduced effectively to 14 men after Ron Jarden was injured and Stuart had to put flanker Des Oliver out onto the wing to cover for him. Two tries to none was a telling enough factor in the 14–3 scoreline and Scott was in the type of form that made him one of the great fullbacks of any All Black era, whether his kicking (one penalty goal from in the mud on halfway and a 30-metre dropped goal), his defence or his innovative running into the backline.

On the night of December 7, 1963, the All Blacks would have been a relieved bunch as they celebrated their 6–5 victory against Ireland that afternoon. To the vanquished went the plaudits, to the victors a grudging respect and a wish, as expressed in the *Daily Express*, that they lift their game beyond the crude and unimaginative.

It was not, evidently, entertaining rugby, but as any All Black of any era would say, the first task is to win. If they can win by playing crowd-pleasing rugby, then all well and good, but first and foremost the job is to win.

This is what the All Blacks did, despite robust Irish forward play that bordered on the illegal for much of the game and what captain Wilson Whineray called 'unsettling, to say the least'. They won despite the All Blacks' inside back pairing of Kevin Briscoe and Mac Herewini kicking away more possession than the rest of the backs would have liked. And they won because Ireland missed a try through flanker Eamonn Maguire knocking on when the line was open and first five-eighth Mick English missing a dropped goal attempt late in the game.

But the All Blacks won also because they had more power, strength and knowledge in the forwards and because they could withstand whatever Ireland threw at them, including the first — and apparently only — punch that Willie John McBride flung in the direction of Colin Meads.

Terry McLean, the constant companion of All Black teams through the 1950s and 60s and a good part of the 70s, too, covered the tour for the *New Zealand Herald*. But he also wrote about the test for the *Irish Independent* and did not stint at his disappointment with the All Blacks.

McLean recalled that the All Blacks the week before had been at Rugby School where William Webb Ellis supposedly (not McLean's word) 'first picked up the ball and ran with it, thus originating the distinctive feature of the rugby game'.

McLean lamented the absence of this distinctive feature when the All Blacks played Ireland. 'Unhappily, all too unhappily I am afraid,' he wrote, 'the All Blacks kicked.'

He said Briscoe kicked too often and he gave as an instance a try-scoring chance that was kicked away: 'Herewini kicked, too, and at that moment of the second half when he was running the blind with Don Clarke roaring along beside him, the best tryscorer in the team, Malcolm Dick, panting for a pass, his kick, I must reluctantly admit, aroused total dismay.'

The All Blacks of 1978 went to Lansdowne Road for the first match of their grand slam. Their predecessors of 1972–73 were in Dublin for the last leg. They'd beaten Wales, Scotland and England and now only Ireland stood between them and a first grand slam for a New Zealand team, something the South Africans had achieved four times. Ian Kirkpatrick's All Blacks, so derided and criticised, sometimes fairly, sometimes unfairly, were a much better side than retrospective judgements have determined. Opinions on their worth have been coloured by incidents off the field such as the sending home of Keith Murdoch and others, plus losses in midweek matches, rather than their results in the tests being the sole yardsticks. Even a photo taken in mirth of three of the players, Alex Wyllie, Tane Norton and Sid Going, trying to look like sinister gangsters, has coloured the perception of the team. Each one of them would make unlikely gangsters: sour cream on the outside sometimes, but the milk of human kindness inside. If Kirkpatrick's side had achieved the grand slam, and it was only a kick and chase away, it would be regarded, like Mourie's team of 1978, as one of the most illustrious in New Zealand rugby history. But instead it is a side which, in a phrase perpetuated in McLean's tour book title, missed the bus.

Sid Going scored for the All Blacks in the first half after a typically cheeky move in which he robbed the Irish halfback, John Moloney, of the ball and Joe Karam's conversion gave the All Blacks a 6–3 lead at halftime, Barry McGann having kicked a penalty goal for Ireland. A stiff wind blew down the ground and the Irish had to play into it in the second half, raising the prospects of an All Black win and, therefore, the grand slam. The All Blacks went further ahead when Wyllie crashed through an attempted tackle by Tom Kiernan to score. But McGann, against the odds and the wind, kicked another penalty goal after Going was again accused of doing what he was accused of doing a lot on that tour, putting the ball in crooked.

McGann was in the thick of it again when he put a short kick through, the Irish forwards swooped on the ball and Moloney raced around the blindside. He got the ball to wing Tom Grace and when he was confronted by Karam, he kicked into the All Blacks' in-goal area. It became a footrace between Grace and the All Blacks' first five-eighth Bob Burgess and Grace won. McGann's conversion attempt would have won the match for Ireland but it was wide. A victory that could have given the All Blacks the grand

Up and over. Ian Kirkpatrick about to score against Ireland in 1976 despite the attentions of Barry McGann. Wing Wallace McMaster can only stand and stare.

slam could also have been a loss but instead it became a draw.

It was a mark of the mutual respect between New Zealand and Irish rugby — and of the pulling power of the All Blacks — that the All Blacks were back in Dublin in 1974 to mark the centenary of the Irish union.

For all the changes wrought by the new All Black coach, J.J. Stewart, earlier in 1974 for a tour of Australia, the All Blacks were still a remarkably similar side to that which drew in 1973. In the backs, Joe Morgan was at second five-eighth instead of Ian Hurst and Duncan Robertson inside him instead of Bob Burgess. In the forwards, captain Andy Leslie was at No 8 instead of Alan Sutherland; Ken Stewart was on the open side of the scrum instead of Wyllie and the only change in the front row was at loosehead, where Kerry Tanner was there instead of Graham Whiting.

This time the All Blacks were more convincing, with Karam scoring all the points from a converted try and three penalty goals.

Oddly enough, the All Blacks played only one more test — against Scotland in Auckland — before again playing Ireland, this

time at Athletic Park in Wellington, a match intended as much as a shakedown test before a tour of South Africa as it was a formal international against an enduring foe. The All Blacks never looked like losing the match and eventually won 11–3 but it wasn't a test that would live long in the annals of matches that need to be seen again and again.

Two years later the grand slam All Blacks were in Dublin but it was another 11 years before the two sides met again, the encounter between Wayne Shelford's All Blacks and Willie Anderson's Irish. By this time, the Four Home Unions had embarked on a concept of twin tours and the prospect of a grand slam withered away, the Australians being the last to gain one in 1984. It meant some fine Irish players, and none finer than the red-haired first five-eighth, Ollie Campbell, never played for their own country against the All Blacks. Campbell played all four tests for the Lions in 1983 but he

Right: Jeff Wilson in acrobatic mode in the World Cup pool match against Ireland in 1995.
Below: Arran Pene against Ireland in 1992.

never once donned his beloved emerald green against the black of New Zealand. He was retired when the All Blacks were in Dublin in 1989, and sitting over coffee one day at a rugby club the All Blacks were visiting, he remarked, 'Ah, I wish I could have played for Ireland against you boys.'

It meant, too, that some fine All Blacks were fated never to meet Ireland, among them the best halfback of his generation, Dave Loveridge, and the fullback who stopped just six short of Don Clarke's record tally then of 207 points for New Zealand, Allan Hewson.

The Irish were back in New Zealand in 1992 in the first year of Laurie Mains' tenure as coach of the All Blacks and he and the players were still in the process of building towards a consistent team when the first test was played in Dunedin. It was yet another example of Ireland going so close to their breakthrough win, but

DOUBLE BOOKED IN DUBLIN

Only in Ireland . . . When the All Blacks arrived in Dublin for their test against Ireland in 1978, the first of their grand slam tests, they found to their horror that the Irish team was staying in the same hotel.

The All Blacks checked into the imposing Shelbourne, a home away from home for rugby teams for generations, on the Wednesday and the Irish the next day.

The All Blacks' manager, Russ Thomas, queried the arrangement and when told it couldn't be avoided, he was assured the Irish were on a different floor and meals for the teams were scheduled at different times.

Remarkably, the two teams remained separate, though on the afternoon before the test a group of All Blacks sat in one corner of a large lounge on the ground floor while two of the Irish players sat with relatives in another corner.

Captain Graham Mourie left breakfast one morning and just avoided running into his opposite number, Shay Deering, who was on his way into the dining room.

One of the Irishmen, Tony Ward, said many of his team-mates avoided taking the Shelbourne's lifts for fear of an unscheduled stop on the All Blacks' floor.

He recalled being in the Shelbourne when Ireland were playing Wales and, again, the Welsh were also in the hotel.

'The Welsh were on the top floor,' he said. 'I got in the lift one morning to go to breakfast or training or something and it was full of Welshmen. I squeezed in and studied the arrow that marked the descent of the lift, trying not to acknowledge the presence of these hulking blokes. Not a word was spoken. But when the lift got to the bottom and I walked out, I heard Gareth Edwards say from within the lift, "Good luck to you, Tony". I felt 10 feet tall.'

just failing at 24–21. It was a much different story in the second test a week later when the All Blacks thumped their visitors 59–6, the highest score recorded by New Zealand against any of the established rugby countries.

Mains was well on top of his coaching and selection the next time they met, during the World Cup in 1995, and the All Blacks won 43–19. It was a measure of what the All Blacks expected of themselves, and of how good they were at that World Cup, that they were dissatisfied with the margin and the manner of their win. Any other rugby country would be proud of such a result against Ireland, but not the All Blacks.

It was also an early sign of the gap developing between what might be called the top tier of rugby countries and those, including Ireland, aspiring to that level. The All Blacks in 1995 were professional in all but decree from the International Rugby Board, while the Irish were as they always had been — a collection of university students and graduates with the odd manual worker thrown in. Rugby to them was still their weekend activity; for the All Blacks it was the purpose of their being.

When John Hart took his team to Dublin in 1997 on the tour that marked the end of the stupendous career of Sean Fitzpatrick, the gap was even more noticeable. Ireland still had extremely talented players, but they were beaten 63–15.

Under a succession of coaches, though, including New Zealander Warren Gatland who had been on Shelford's tour in 1989, Ireland made progress in its attempt to bridge the gap from the first division of international rugby to the premier league which comprised, in no particular order, New Zealand, Australia, South Africa, England and France.

Led by hooker Keith Wood, one of the finest tight forwards in the world, and with Brian O'Driscoll one of the finest midfielders, Ireland led the All Blacks 16–7 at halftime in a test in Dublin in 2001 but eventually lost 40–19. In 2002, when Ireland again toured New Zealand, the Irish could have won the first test in Dunedin had they had a goalkicker in form. For reasons best known to coach Eddie O'Sullivan, the kicking was entrusted to Munster first five-eighth Ronan O'Gara, and he had a hapless night with the boot. There's no way of knowing, but it could have been yet another Irish chance gone begging.

By the second test, the All Blacks were far more composed and won 40–8.

While the International Rugby Board rightly spends much time and money in trying to develop rugby in the unlikeliest corners of the world, even if there is sometimes an overemphasis on sevens, world rugby's interests would be equally well served by more competitive matches at the top of the tree. Scotland, Ireland and Wales, in their times among the best sides in the world, have slipped down a league from the big five and show only occasional signs of climbing back up again.

It will become a cloistered, even boring, rugby world if the same sides win all the time. And as the history of their matches against the All Blacks show, the Irish are overdue for some wins.

WHEN PINEY MET WILLIE

Colin Meads and Willie John McBride were as peas in a pod. Both were locks, both were the hard men of their packs and their careers more or less went along parallel paths.

McBride, who enjoyed great battles for Ireland and the Lions with Meads, recalls clearly the first time they confronted each other.

It was at Lansdowne Road in Dublin on December 7, 1963. The All Blacks had won all 13 matches of their tour so far and the 14th, the test against Ireland, was expected to be a formality. But the Irish players, McBride among them, had other ideas. The All Blacks won by a single point, with much of the credit going to Ireland.

McBride recalls the match had hardly started before he, in his words, felt the full extent of Meads' experience and psychology.

'In the first lineout of the game, I found myself fired three or four yards out of the line,' he told biographer Sean Diffley. 'I did not have to exercise my mind to any great degree to know how that came about. I immediately said to myself, "Now I either live or die today". I intended to go on living . . . The next lineout, I hit Meads as hard as I could and he went down . . . He did not stay down very long. Almost immediately, there was a ruck and I got a punch in the jaw. I did not see it delivered but I had no doubt of its origin. I freely admit I was dazed, yet from that moment, I never again had any physical trouble with Meads.'

Curiously, that was the only time McBride and Meads met in an Irish test. The 1967 All Blacks did not play Ireland because of a foot and mouth disease outbreak in Britain. Their other test confrontations were all when McBride was in the Lions — three tests in 1966 and four in 1971.

'Meads was as hard a man as I ever encountered,' McBride said. 'There are some who will tell you he was a dirty player. I cannot subscribe to that view. He was the best, most aggressive and perhaps the most totally committed player that I have opposed.'

Hard men together. Old foes Willie John McBride and Colin Meads during the Lions series in 1971.

SCOTLAND

For two countries that got off on such a wrong foot, there's a remarkable affinity and mutual respect between Scotland and New Zealand. The Scots like being in New Zealand; the All Blacks like being in Scotland.

The affinity can be partly explained because of ancestral links, at least from the New Zealand side to the Scottish, but if that was the whole reason, there'd be a greater affinity with England and, on the evidence of tours here and there, there's not.

When the All Blacks travelled by bus in 1993 from Gateshead in northern England to Peebles in Scotland, they raised a cheer as they crossed the border into Scotland; England was behind them temporarily and Scotland was ahead of them. Most of the players on that tour had not been to Scotland before and knew little about the country.

By the end of 2002, 16 New Zealanders had played rugby for Scotland, more than for any other country except Australia. The first of those was in just the second rugby test, in 1872, and just two years after rugby was introduced into New Zealand.

If the affinity can be explained away by blood links, by a similarity of character and by parts of the New Zealand topography bearing a remarkable resemblance to that of Scotland, why the mutual respect?

It is something that the great Scottish fullback, Gavin Hastings, ponders over. 'It's strange that they respect us,' he says. 'Of course the ancestry is a factor, but it's slightly curious because they still smash us on a regular basis.'

Scotland joins Ireland as another of the only well-established rugby countries never to beat the All Blacks.

Relations between New Zealand and Scotland could hardly have got off on a less cordial note. It's been written often enough that the Scots refused to pay the Original All Blacks the gate guarantee of

£200 they sought (and which all other host unions had paid) on the grounds they didn't think the gate for the test in Edinburgh would justify such a sum. Instead, the Scots offered the All Blacks the entire gate receipts (less match expenses). The popular story goes that the Scots, who were already mightily miffed at the All Blacks for being paid three shillings a day expenses, were so put out at losing money in 1905 they refused to play New Zealand when they were next there in 1924. It's also been recorded that the Scottish union, which was then led by an arch conservative, James Aikman Smith, got in such a huff at losing money it refused to entertain the All Blacks after the match.

It's been a good story over the years, but as with a lot of good stories, it never let a few facts get in the way.

The poor Scots were not as parsimonious as they had been painted and neither did they turn all churlish because they lost both the money and the match.

It's true the Originals were not met at Waverley Station in Edinburgh by anyone from the Scottish union; it's true they hardly saw anyone from Scottish rugby except on the field at Inverleith; it's true the All Blacks were left after the match to entertain themselves (something which All Blacks historically are well capable of doing) and it's true that the Scottish union did not initially deem the match a full international (though it later did so).

But the reasons were not as they have often been stated.

The most compelling fact when the Scots first heard that the All Blacks were coming their way was that they had a bit of a money problem. They couldn't afford the £200 asking price. They'd been developing the Inverleith ground in what is now suburban Edinburgh to international standard (though it proved in time to be inadequate and the

Scotland joins Ireland as another of the only well-established rugby countries never to beat the All Blacks.

Scots moved to Murrayfield in 1925) and had debts of £6600. They didn't want to add to the debt by offering the guarantee so instead offered the All Blacks the net receipts (and since Aikman Smith was a chartered accountant, it's reasonable to assume he got his sums right and knew that in all likelihood the net receipts would be greater than the guarantee).

The contention the Scots didn't realise how good and how popular the All Blacks were is hard to fathom. Scots could read newspaper accounts like anyone else, and all were positively glowing in their praise of the All Blacks, and the Scottish captain was Darkie Bedell-Sivright, who'd led a British team in New Zealand in 1904 and knew well how good New Zealand rugby was.

As to the supposed ignoring of the All Blacks off the field, that was true — but also partly because the All Blacks wanted it that way. Resting in the Scottish Rugby Union archives is a letter from the New Zealand union's man in London at the time, Cecil Wray Palliser, saying that the team did not want to be entertained after matches. (New Zealand was not allowed to join the International Rugby Board until 1948 and Palliser was New Zealand's man on the English union, to which the New Zealand union was affiliated.) The Scots decided instead to offer the All Blacks theatre tickets for the night before the match — but the offer was not accepted.

The Scots may have taken the All Blacks' Garbo stance a little too far, though, by failing to show up at the station when the Flying Scotsman express brought the team into Edinburgh. The failure of the common courtesy of greeting and farewelling visitors did not go unnoticed by the All Blacks.

The Scottish decision not to treat the match as an official international also meant, according to All Black vice-captain Billy Stead, that Inverleith was not properly prepared. Despite clinging low fog and persistent frosts in the week of the match, the ground surface was not covered with straw the night before the game and, as a result, was frozen solid the next morning.

'It was frozen so hard that the matter of postponement was freely discussed,' Stead said. 'However, we visited the ground and knowing that we had been very discourteously treated by their union, we decided to play though it was taking on a great risk.'

In the event, the All Blacks won 12–7 after trailing for much of the match and gaining the benefit of a couple of late tries. The All Blacks won the fight as well. Billy Wallace had been late tackled and retaliation was swift.

'The local papers admitted that their men started the foul play first by deliberately knocking out Wallace after he had found touch,' Stead wrote, 'and after all, we are only human and I think better able to play rough than they — at least we can do it scientifically.'

One newspaper's view of the non-appearance of the Invincibles in Scotland.

"ALL BLACKS" TABOO ACROSS THE SCOTTISH BORDER.

PURITAN UNION BECOMES MORE STIFF-NECKED THAN EVER.

RUGBY'S STRENGTH.

By SCRUM-HALF.

A POET, of sorts, once wrote to the effect that:

Man wants but little here below,
As someone said before,
And when he's got it, don't you know,
He wants a little more?

This explains in a nutshell why a good many Rugby football enthusiasts are grumbling to-day about the arrangement of the fixture card for the New Zealand touring team.

Each of the most important Rugby centres in England, Wales, and Ireland has been given at least one opportunity of welcoming the "All Blacks," but, in general, we are a greedy, impatient lot of people, and already such questions are being asked as, "Why should London have to wait so long?" "What about Sussex?" and "Why is puir auld Scotland left out in the cold?"

It is certainly tantalising for stay-at-home Londoners that they will have no opportunity of seeing the tourists till the middle of November, but as for the Scots, they have made their own boycott in submitting tamely to the stiff-necked Puritanism of their home Union, whose officials seem to take a positive delight in quarrelling with their neighbours, and to smell professionalism where none exists.

G. Nepia.

COMPLICATIONS.

The Scottish Union, in short, will have nothing to do with the New Zealand tour, though I do not suppose that, followi...

THE MURRAYFIELD MARCH

On the Friday night before the 1967 All Blacks played Scotland, their final test, coach Fred Allen and the All Black dirt-trackers went to a ball. They were dressed in their best bib and tucker, the silver fern hand-embroidered on the breast pockets of their jackets.

An Irish farewell. Kevin Kelleher tells Colin Meads to go.

It should have been, in the permissible language of the time, a gay affair. Going to a ball without a partner had wallflower potential but these were the mighty All Blacks, sporting celebrities, and according to one of their number, Grahame Thorne, they didn't lack for dances. The women were happy to leave their partners to be with the All Blacks; the partners, it can be imagined, were less happy.

While it was an enjoyable night, Allen was not comfortable and he confided to Thorne that he had a nagging feeling something was going to go wrong the next day. Given the locale, Allen was what Robbie Burns might have called 'fey'.

The feeling persisted with Allen when the party returned to their hotel, the imposing North British in the lee of Edinburgh Castle and with the most desirable address in Scotland, No 1 Princes Street.

The 'NB', as it was popularly known, was home to many All Black teams and its head waiter, Hugh Macdonald, who began there as a 16-year-old page boy in 1929, was almost an honorary All Black. He was known to all simply as 'Mac'. When the All Blacks were staying, Mac was at his post all hours of the day and night. But not even his ministrations could have quelled the unease that Allen felt.

The All Blacks had beaten England, Wales and France; they hadn't lost a match; they were feted wherever they went as one of the finest of visiting international teams and they had a manager, Charlie Saxton, and coach, Allen, regarded still as one of the best combinations any rugby team could have. So what possibly could go wrong?

What went wrong, as the rugby world knows only too well, was that shortly before the end of the test at Murrayfield, with the Scots beaten, Colin Meads was sent off. Nearly 40 years on, the impact of that singular event has dimmed. Red cards and the fateful finger of the referee pointing towards the dressing rooms have become more commonplace. Meads' celebrity has grown not because of his dismissal in that match, but because of the totality of his 14-year career with the All Blacks and because of his image that somehow typified a rugged, more simple, age of rugby.

But the impact of the events at Murrayfield on December 2, 1967 was immense at the time. Only once before had a player been sent from the field in an international — and that was another All Black, Cyril Brownlie, against England in 1925.

Meads had lunged at the ball emerging from a ruck and lashed out a kick at it. The Scottish first five-eighth, David Chisholm, was in the way of both ball and boot. Referee Kevin Kelleher of Ireland, who had warned Meads earlier for the heinous New Zealand offence of rucking, unhesitatingly blew his whistle and told Meads he was off. Entreaties from the All Black captain, Brian Lochore, even a gesture of sympathy towards Meads from Chisholm, were to no avail. Meads walked. Disbelievingly. Hands on his hips, headgeared head bowed, he walked, the No 5 on his back the last sight as he disappeared through the crowd and into the dressing room, escorted for the last few steps by Maori administrator Ralph Love and by the team's baggageman, Richard Walker.

The moment was not without light relief. A couple of Scottish bandsmen hovered near the All Blacks' dressing room, clearly having enjoyed the national drink of Scotland more than they had the rugby. One inquired of Meads if he had been hurt. The other observed aloud that Meads must have been injured. Since they were blocking the way, Meads in his best King Country vernacular told them they'd best move out of the way. Only two words were necessary.

Up in the stand, Grahame Thorne was as aghast as every New Zealander in the crowd, and as many Scots were, too. While in New York on the way to Britain, he'd bought a Super 8 movie camera and he clutched it in his hands. But he was so shocked by Kelleher's decision and the sight of Meads' intensely personal but public *Via Dolorosa* that he forgot to use the camera. 'I was so gobsmacked at the sending off that I never raised it to my eye,' he recalls.

Allen, whose premonition proved horribly prescient, wrote in his diary that night: 'Whole party very upset as it was completely unjustified as was shown when Charlie and I watched it on television shortly after game and had them slow it down, play it back three times during the so-called incident.'

Saxton, scrupulously fair-minded and honest, described Kelleher's decision as unfair on Meads and on the reputation of the All Blacks generally.

He wrote a report to the New Zealand union in Wellington. 'I am quite sure the referee didn't see it and was carried away by the booing of a section of the crowd in close proximity to him,' Saxton wrote.

He said he watched the film with Allen and wrote: 'The second time it was stopped, you could see Colin's boot, the ball and Chisholm's hands so plainly that it left no doubt in our minds that Colin had definitely shot his foot out at the ball.'

After the formal test dinner at the North British — where most of the local guests wore kilts and where a haggis was piped in and addressed before being ceremonially distributed and sprinkled with whisky — Saxton had an informal meeting with a few British rugby luminaries.

Under the terms of the tours agreement between New Zealand and what are known as the Four Home Unions, a disciplinary hearing had to be convened. The panel to hear the case was required to comprise two representatives of the Four Home Unions plus the manager. It was decided the Four Home Unions would be represented by Cyril Gadney, a former international referee and president of the (England) Rugby Football Union, and Glynn Morgan, president of the Welsh union.

They met in Cardiff on the following Tuesday with the secretary of the International Rugby Board, Eddie Kirwan, also there. They decided, by two votes to one, that Meads would be suspended for two matches.

'This was particularly hard for me,' Saxton said in his report to the New Zealand union, 'as I said I would accept the referee's statement along with the others. I had to anyway, but I fought hard for no further penalty or suspension. Unfortunately, I was on my own and eventually had to compromise for a penalty of a suspension for the next two games.

The whistle Kevin Kelleher used in the test against Scotland.

'The consensus . . . was that Colin was very unlucky but the referee had to be backed up for the future of rugby football. The IRB, if you remember, gave strict instructions about this at their last meeting. You have no idea of the amount of sympathy that has been extended to Colin by letter, telephone and personal conversation.'

Kelleher was able to give his evidence to the Cardiff hearing but Meads was not. This denial of natural justice was remarked upon at the time but appeared to receive little sympathy in Wellington from the chairman of the New Zealand union, Tom Morrison, who had been kept informed of events in phone calls with Saxton.

'The decision reached by the committee is final,' Morrison said. 'There is no right of appeal.'

Meads' All Black team-mates had conducted their own hearing on the Sunday morning in Edinburgh at their regular court session, a rugby team ritual that has survived professionalism and the advent of dietitians.

Allen was instructed to appear in front of the court dressed as Kelleher in a green jersey, white shorts and football boots. Saxton had to appear in All Black gear wearing size 12 boots which, with Saxton's diminutive status, made him look like Puss in Boots.

The judge, Brian ('Jazz') Muller, was dressed in a kilt. He ordered that Allen and Saxton be tied together by rope and thus joined together, they shuffled into the court to the accompaniment of a piper hired for the occasion. Allen was given a whistle which he blew shrilly as he pointed to Meads and told him he was off.

While there was evident sympathy from New Zealanders and British alike for Meads, there was none from prop Alister Hopkinson. He told Meads he was a dumb bastard.

When asked why, Hopkinson explained that he'd been sent off in a game at Cheviot in North Canterbury the year before for fighting. Hopkinson's opponent left the field immediately but Hopkinson slumped to the ground, gesturing that he needed the assistance of a St John Ambulance man. 'I pretended I had an injured leg, got some treatment and limped off with the Zambuck,' Hopkinson said. 'The crowd thought I had to go off because of the injury and they applauded me all the way.'

Kelleher and Meads didn't meet the night of the test, though both were at the dinner, but they got to know each other later and exchanged Christmas cards for a few years.

Kelleher perhaps should not even have refereed the test. He was invited to do so by the all-powerful Four Home Unions but did not seek the necessary permission from the Irish Rugby Union. A foot and mouth disease outbreak in Britain at the time limited contact between Ireland and the British mainland and the All Blacks had to call off their planned visit to Ireland. Kelleher feared that if he sought permission from the Irish union to go to Edinburgh, it might be refused so he stayed mum. After the test, he left his boots, shorts and jersey in Edinburgh to avoid any risk of carrying contaminants back to Ireland.

Kelleher refereed another five tests in his 23-test career, but the 1967 match was his only international involving New Zealand.

Scots wha hae? Joe Stanley has Craig Chalmers guessing at Eden Park in 1990. Walter Little is the All Black at left and Mike Brewer on the right.

Instead of the normal post-match dinner, the All Blacks were entertained by the Edinburgh Australasian Club, whose members were mainly students and academics from New Zealand and Australia. (Among the former was Nolan Fell, who was studying medicine at Edinburgh University and had played seven tests for Scotland. He'd been chosen to play against the All Blacks, but withdrew because he didn't want to oppose his compatriots. Coincidence or not, he was never asked to play for the Scotland national side again.)

The All Blacks left Edinburgh to the same silence from the Scottish union that had greeted them. 'Nine of our playing team were of Scottish parentage', Stead wrote, 'and we were not at all proud of the treatment meted out to us.'

For all the Scots' dislike of the amateur All Blacks' expenses payments and for the regret that the All Blacks took money and match in 1905, that had nothing to do with the two countries not meeting in 1924.

Research by the Scottish union's historian, John Davidson, in 2001 shows that it was all to do with the English, upon whom Scots don't often look kindly. The genesis of the 1924 disagreement was an International Rugby Board meeting in 1911, at which the British countries agreed various terms and conditions that would apply for future tours by 'colonial' teams. One of the conditions was that any such tour would need to be agreed to by all countries. But, alas, the English union went ahead in 1923 and invited the All Blacks without any consultation with their northern neighbours. It so happened that at the time, the Scottish union was yet again in a financial bind, this time with the building of Murrayfield (which

opened in March 1925). It had borrowed £75,000 (about £2.1 million in today's terms) by the issue of debentures of £100 each and was in no position to pay the £750 guarantee agreed at the 1911 conference.

Using the attraction of touring teams to raise the money to pay off capital works, the trend in stadium development in Britain in the 1990s, when television rights were also a lucrative factor, was clearly not seen as an option 70 years before.

The Scottish union, financially strapped and incensed by England's unilateral decision to go ahead with the tour, sent a statement to all of its clubs. 'In July 1923 your committee were more than surprised to be advised that the RFU were bringing over a New Zealand team in 1924 and were asked if they wanted fixtures,' the statement read. 'This arrangement was so absolutely opposed to the agreement formally come to . . . and would naturally open the way to any of the four countries having the right to entertain a touring team for their own profit, that they [the SRU] promptly declined to entertain the proposal and, in any case, no fixtures would have been arranged by your union, even if willing, under the financial arrangements which they understood were laid down by the RFU.'

As history knows well, the All Blacks were unbeaten on their tour and became the Invincibles. The Scots, ironically enough, had a strong team in the 1924–25 season and won what was grandly known as the international championship, later to be more commonly known as the Five Nations. That season may have been the Scots' first realistic chance of beating New Zealand. They had a side that is still revered in Scotland and included in it was a three-quarter line regarded as the best Scotland has ever had. All four players were from Oxford University — Johnny Wallace, Ian Smith, George Macpherson and George Aitken.

Ironically enough, Aitken was a New Zealander who had captained the All Blacks against South Africa in 1921 and Wallace was an Australian.

The strength of Scottish national teams, then or now, had seldom matched the strength of club rugby in Scotland until the advent of professional teams, especially Edinburgh and Glasgow. Scottish teams have regularly been peppered with players based in England or Wales or even further afield.

By the time the All Blacks eventually played Scotland again, in November 1935, the Scottish union was again putting money into Murrayfield, this time adding wings to the main stand in time for the New Zealand match. The All Blacks won the match 18–8 with second five-eighth Harcourt Caughey scoring three tries and though Scottish papers acknowledged the better team won, there were laments that the score didn't well enough reflect the Scottish efforts. That's a lament that's often been played after New Zealand matches against Scotland.

It was there again when they next met, in 1954, and the All Blacks won 3–0 by a solitary Bob Scott penalty goal. It was greeted as a victory for Scottish grit as much as it was for the play of Scott, who was reported to have had one of his finest games on the muddy, slippery Murrayfield surface. 'Scott Beat Great Scots' was the headline in the Edinburgh Saturday night sports paper, the *Evening Dispatch*. The All Blacks' captain, Bob Stuart, knew well the significance of the result for Scotland and, ever the diplomat, he said at the test dinner that night, 'We have been present at the renaissance of Scottish rugby.' This was just a couple of seasons after Scotland had been beaten 44–0 by South Africa, a match that first raised the hoary old line about 'being bloody lucky to get nil'.

And it was there yet again in January 1964 when New Zealand and Scotland played out a scoreless draw, but the laments were not just played for the Scots. They were for New Zealand, too, because the draw deprived New Zealand of the grand slam, something the All Blacks for all their dominance had never achieved in Britain (and wouldn't until 14 years later). And most galling of all, the South Africans had five times toured Britain and four times won the

SCOTS CAN'T WIN — IRVINE

Andy Irvine, voted in 2001 as Scotland's greatest player, reckons his country will never beat the All Blacks.

He was in sides that went close, especially in 1972 and 1981, but he believes Scotland have now missed the bus.

'The match in 1972 was a very special one because it was my first test,' he says, 'and because we went so very close to beating the All Blacks. It was 10–9 until Sid Going scored that try in the last minute. That was our greatest chance.

'If Scotland went down 14–9 to the All Blacks now,' he says, 'it would be regarded as a moral victory to the Scots. I don't think Scotland will ever beat the All Blacks. The gulf has just got bigger and bigger. We'd struggle now against New Zealand provinces. When you're talking about New Zealand and Scotland in international rugby, you're not comparing like with like.'

Irvine, now a successful property consultant based in Glasgow, has lost none of his fondness or respect for New Zealand since quitting his illustrious career.

'I always loved playing the All Blacks and I loved playing in New Zealand,' Irvine says. 'It was a rugby player's dream come true. I just love the New Zealand attitude towards rugby — not just the attitude of the All Blacks, but of New Zealand people. I always support the All Blacks whoever they're playing — unless it's Scotland of course.'

One of his long-held ambitions is to spend a few months in New Zealand during a summer. 'I've only ever been there in the winter as a rugby player or something to do with rugby so I've mostly seen airports, hotel rooms and rugby grounds. I've got this ambition to take my family there for a long holiday during the summer and catch up with some of the All Blacks who've become friends and see more of the country than I have.'

Great Scot. Andy Irvine, voted Scotland's greatest player of the 20th century.

The boys on the bus. Some of the 1963–64 All Blacks seem to be taking delight in a little reversing error by their bus in Scotland.

grand slam. It was unfinished business writ large for the All Blacks.

Surely the 1963–64 All Blacks, captained so well by Wilson Whineray, should have beaten Scotland and should have claimed the grand slam. In the previous tests against Ireland, Wales and England, they'd conceded only one score, a converted try to Ireland. It could have been a victory to New Zealand because there were chances aplenty, but equally it could have been a victory to Scotland because they had their chances, too. One of the Scottish flankers, Jim Telfer, later to have such an enduring influence on Scottish rugby, seemingly had the line open until he was felled somehow by the All Black fullback, Don Clarke. But then John Graham of the All Blacks nearly scored, too, and somehow Telfer got hold of the ball on the ground and wrapped his body around it and refused to let go. He knows he should have been penalised but instead, he recalls with a smile, Colin Meads was penalised for trying to ruck the ball back.

In 1967, Meads was the centrepiece and his sending off

Purchasers of this ticket saw the All Blacks win — just.

overshadowed the quality of the All Blacks' performance, a 14–3 victory that was well deserved and could have been more. In that respect, the 1967 match was an exception because when the two sides next met, in 1972, again Scotland left the field wondering how they had lost a game they could have won. Could have? Ian McGeechan, the inside back who later followed Telfer's coaching path, made his debut at Murrayfield in 1972 and reckons that was Scotland's best chance of beating New Zealand. But they didn't. It has been a characteristic of the All Blacks that they have taken their chances better than their opponents' and that was the case in 1972. With 10 minutes to play, the All Blacks led 10–9 and the Scots threw everything they had into attack — and they had plenty with props such as Ian McLauchlan and Sandy Carmichael, locks Gordon Brown and Alastair McHarg and at No 8 Peter Brown, a veteran of the 1964 match. Also making his debut among the Scottish backs was Andy Irvine, voted in 2001 as Scotland's greatest player. But they couldn't breach the All Blacks' defence and neither could they counter Sid Going who scored in the last minute after he gleefully fastened on to an in-pass from McHarg.

It was a valiant effort by the Scots, but valiant, too, by the All Blacks. They'd struggled in their midweek games in the lead-up to the test; they were handicapped by injuries and illnesses and had the mental baggage of having lost Keith Murdoch after the Welsh test. And after just five minutes at Murrayfield, they also lost prop Jeff Matheson, which meant a test debut for his replacement, 21-year-old Kent Lambert, who had to pack down against McLauchlan, then the finest loosehead in the world.

Scotland toured New Zealand for the first time in 1975 and though they'd lost in successive matches to Otago and Canterbury, they had barely spoken hopes of beating New Zealand for the first time in the one test. Whatever hopes they had were washed away with the first rain that began on the Friday night and continued

THRIFTY MAYBE, BUT MEAN? NEVER!

The stereotypical image of Scots and their money being difficult to part is about as accurate as the theme that runs through most Irish jokes. And just as the Irish love telling jokes against themselves, the Scots have often encouraged the notion that they have moths in their sporrans and gorse in their pockets.

An All Black forward, Frank Glasgow, souvenired the ball at the end of the Originals' first test against Scotland and spirited it off to the dressing room.

The Scottish union secretary, James Aikman Smith, descended from the committee box to secure the ball and, not being able to find it, made urgent inquiries and was pointed in the direction of the New Zealand dressing room.

In he strode, found the prized McKenzie-brand ball, tucked it under an arm and departed.

Most Scottish players, then and now, can tell similar tales of Scottish thrift. Even stories that may have been upsetting at the time have entered into rugby folklore as hilarious illustrations of a supposed national characteristic.

One concerned a great Scottish player, Jock Wemyss, who played either side of the First World War. When he returned from the war, minus an eye left on the battlefield, he was solemnly charged seven shillings and sixpence when put into his first post-war team for a jersey he was said not to have sent back after a test match before the war.

A goalkicking forward and captain of the 1960s and 70s, Peter Brown (the brother of lock Gordon) used to tell the story of how one of his blue Scottish socks developed a hole in the leg. Upon asking for a new pair, he was told players were entitled to only one pair. Brown sat in the dressing room before a test assiduously applying boot polish to his bare leg so the white skin would not show through the hole.

Bill Dickinson was Scotland's first official coach, though such a title was frowned upon in conservative Scotland and he toured New Zealand in 1975 with the title of adviser to the captain. Three years after that tour, in 1978, Dickinson was banned from the Scottish team's bus because he had dared to appear on a television programme about rugby.

The Scots were the last of the main rugby countries to adopt the 'novel' aid to crowds of having numbers on their backs. 'It is a rugby match, not a cattle sale,' Aikman Smith said when the outrageous idea was first put to him. The Scots eventually adopted numbering in 1936.

THE GREAT FLOOD TEST OF '75

Fears were held for players' lives when the All Blacks played Scotland on a flooded Eden Park in 1975.

Ian McGeechan, the Scottish first five-eighth that day, recalls there wasn't the usual intensity of a test match because players were well aware of the dangers.

'Both teams handled it really well,' he says. 'Players were sympathetic to each other because they realised there was a very real danger that someone could drown. There was a lot of self-discipline in both teams to ensure that none of us were left in dangerous circumstances.'

Referee Peter McDavitt told players before the game that he would not allow any prolonged rucking because there was so much water on the field and someone could drown.

Andy Irvine, who began on a wing for Scotland and finished at fullback, says the conditions were the most dangerous in which he played.

He makes no bones about it. The game shouldn't have been played, he says.

'We didn't realise how bad it was until we ran out onto the field,' he says. 'The Eden Park people had put down duckboards for us to run out on and one of the boys got the fright of his life when he stepped off the boards and he felt like he was stepping into a lake.'

McGeechan laughs that Scots are no strangers to rain but he couldn't recall anything as sustained as the rain that fell in Auckland the night before and during the test day. 'It was just unbelievable,' he says.

McGeechan, Irvine and captain Ian McLauchlan all believe the Scots had a genuine chance of beating the All Blacks — until Eden Park was flooded.

'Years later I'm not making excuses,' McGeechan says. 'The fact is the All Blacks handled the conditions much better than we did. They had four opportunities and took them all. We had only two or three and couldn't take them. Poor Andy couldn't even have a shot at goal because he couldn't place the ball.'

McLauchlan is emphatic, if philosophical. 'Of the times I played for Scotland against the All Blacks,' he says, 'the one time I thought we had a genuine chance before the game was 1975. On a dry day, we could have given them a good run for their money because we had experienced forwards and a good set of backs. When I got up in the morning and saw the rain, I thought, "God's smiling on New Zealand today". They got four chances and they took them all.'

While players joked after the game with black humour about the dangers in the game, there were genuine fears that lives could have been lost. Sandy Carmichael, who propped the other side of the scrum from McLauchlan, said at the time he could scarcely believe it when he set himself for a scrum and noticed that the water was up to his shins.

'I don't doubt that if someone had been caught at the bottom of a ruck they could have drowned,' he said.

Water polo rugby. All Blacks and Scots go for a paddle on Eden Park in 1975.

through most of Saturday. Eden Park was awash, so much so that the Scottish manager, George Burrell, and the New Zealand union chairman, Jack Sullivan, stood at the players' entrance half an hour before kickoff and considered postponing the match. No one could remember conditions as bad for any test though Ces Blazey, Sullivan's deputy, recalled being taken as a 12-year-old to the drawn test against South Africa in Wellington in 1921 when a southerly drenched the ground and made rugby all but impossible to play.

If Scottish expectations were dealt a blow by the weather, things got only worse when they lost fullback Bruce Hay in the first half when he had an arm broken in a tackle. But the story of the match, which the All Blacks won by four converted tries to nothing, was the big wet. The All Blacks adapted and handled it better. The Scots were beaten by it.

The wind and rain eased around halftime and the Scots, expecting some advantage in the second half, gained none. It prompted the All Black wing, Grant Batty, to shout over to his friend and team-mate, Joe Karam: 'Hey "Clock", it's an ill wind that blows no bastard any good!'

Tests against Scotland seem fated to produce unusual conditions more often than in any other tests. The Scottish vocabulary has words seldom if ever used in English as it is spoken elsewhere. One of them is *gloaming*, the word given to twilight, and another is *dreich*, which when applied to the weather means dreary. Both applied when the All Blacks went to Murrayfield in 1978 in search, like their predecessors of 1964, of not just a win against Scotland, but of the grand slam.

On the Friday afternoon, a few of the All Blacks walked down Princes Street (it was originally Prince's Street but somehow the apostrophe got lopped off along the way) for some shopping and remarked on the way back at around 4 p.m. how dark it was. Street lights and car lights were on; the castle could barely be seen in the murky distance. 'Hope it's not like this tomorrow,' one remarked. It was. It was, as the Scots would say, a *dreich* day and towards the end of the test the Scots and the All Blacks were roaming in the gloaming. It was so dark when the score was 12–9 to the All Blacks that some of the crowd in the more distant confines of Murrayfield may not have even seen McGeechan's dropped goal attempt that, if successful, would have tied the scores. People in the stand, with the best view of all, saw it but could barely identify that it was Doug Bruce who charged the kick down and it was Bill Osborne who flykicked the ball away downfield. And it was Bruce Robertson who chased after it and scored to ensure the All Blacks at last had been able to beat Ireland, Wales, England and Scotland on the one tour — something that no All Black team before it had been able to do.

The All Blacks were back at Murrayfield the following year and though the test was memorable for a remarkable try scored by Murray Mexted on his debut, it wasn't memorable for much else. The All Blacks, far from being at full strength because of the

Flying Scot. Wing Chris Elliot starts to hare off downfield after team-mate John Rodd had drawn Kevin Briscoe (left) and Ralph Caulton in the 1964 match at Murrayfield.

increasing demands on players' time, won 20–6. It was the last of 43 tests for Scotland played by their captain, Ian McLauchlan, and the day before there was an example of the bond that exists between New Zealander and Scot.

McLauchlan rang a New Zealand friend at the All Blacks' hotel on the Thursday night and asked if a couple of the All Blacks could go to the school where he was teaching on the Friday. 'It won't be long,' he said, 'just talk to the kids and then have a cup of tea and then they'll be gone . . . and if Graham Mourie could be one of the players, that would be great.'

The proposition was put to Mourie and he readily agreed so there on the day before a test, one captain spoke to a class taught by the other captain then the pair of them sat down and had a cup of tea together and chatted away. It was an example of not just the kinship between the two teams, but of a far more flexible though no less rigorous preparation for a test match than applies now.

There had been an example the year before, too, of the close links between Scotland and New Zealand. A Scottish newspaper, the *Daily Record*, came up with the novel idea of putting kilts on all the All Blacks who had Scottish ancestry. The idea was put to manager Russ Thomas, who saw no harm in it, and photographer Andrew Hosie went off and hired the kilts and the resulting photo appeared across the centrespread of the paper under the heading 'The All Mighty All Macs'. The genealogy wasn't subject to too much scrutiny, but the All Blacks who paraded their Scottish blood were Billy Bush, Andy Dalton, Doug Bruce, Eddie Dunn, John Black, John Fleming, Dave Loveridge, Stu Wilson, Brad Johnstone, Robert Kururangi, Richard Wilson, Brian McKechnie, Barry Ashworth, Ash McGregor and Mourie.

That period also marked the beginning of a continuing era of increased contact between New Zealand and Scotland. The Scots, it would seem, are more ready to tour than any of the other 'home' countries and readily acknowledge that, though they've always been beaten by New Zealand, they see value in learning experiences outside their own classroom. And while the Scots seem always ready to go to New Zealand, they've also been fated to meet the All Blacks in each of the World Cups — they've been the one constant in All Black cup campaigns, though their meeting in the 1991 cup in Cardiff was a match that neither was seeking. That was for the unloved playoff match, a game that should be pensioned off because it serves no one's interests.

Concomitant with the increased contact has been the fact the Scots have been left with more chances to rue. The first test in Dunedin in 1981, won by the All Blacks 11–4, was another chapter in the Scottish rugby history of 'could haves' and 'should haves'. It was another game when the All Blacks took their chances and the Scots contrived somehow not to take theirs. It was the same in 1983 at Murrayfield when there was a 25–25 draw and there was even more for the Scots to rue when they were beaten 21–18 at Eden Park in 1990. This was when the All Blacks were at their best,

Fullback on attack. Gavin Hastings against the All Blacks in the
World Cup third place match in 1991.

GEECH'S HIT AND HOPE

Amid the intensity and speed of a rugby test, Ian McGeechan remembers looking up and noticing how brightly the lights in the press box in the stand at Murrayfield shone. He turned and beyond the ground he could see the headlights of cars out in the street.

Mutual admirers. Graham Mourie and Ian McGeechan after Mourie's All Blacks had sealed the grand slam.

'I remember thinking how different it was, how dark it was,' McGeechan says of the last 10 or 15 minutes of the test against the All Blacks at Murrayfield in 1978.

Not long after, with the score at 12–9 to the All Blacks, he tried for a dropped goal from just beyond the 22. Success would have tied the scores, perhaps could have denied the All Blacks their first grand slam.

'In those conditions, and playing a team wearing black, it was very difficult seeing anything,' he says. 'I kicked more in hope I suppose. And as luck would have it, a black jersey emerged and the ball was charged down. There was a flurry of movement and the All Blacks scored at the other end.'

The charger was Doug Bruce and the flurry came from Bill Osborne and Bruce Robertson. End of game.

The test had begun at 2.15 to get it in before Scotland's early winter darkness, but it wasn't early enough. The All Blacks knew that. They'd noticed the previous day how dark it was at the time they'd still be playing.

'The Scottish union learnt its lesson from that day,' McGeechan says. 'Every international after that until lights were installed at Murrayfield began at two o'clock.'

McGeechan doesn't think Scotland could have won that day, however. 'We might have drawn it,' he says, 'but the All Blacks deserved to win, there's no doubt about that.

'The closest I felt to beating the All Blacks was in my debut match, in 1972. But for Sid Going intercepting a pass from Alastair McHarg we could have won it. We had the ball and we were doing all the attacking and I felt we were the better team. I was inexperienced at test level then and it was only later, looking back on it, that I realised how close we were to beating the All Blacks.'

DRESSING DOWN FOR REF

It's an essential element of the oft-told story about the Bob Deans non-try against Wales in 1905 that the referee, John Dallas, wore ordinary street clothes and boots and was so far behind play that he couldn't possibly have seen Deans pulled back over the line after apparently scoring.

It should be pointed out in fairness that referees then were not required to be as fit as they later were and that, in any case, even the fittest referee would have struggled to keep up with Billy Wallace when he ran to set up Deans for his 'try'.

What's perhaps less well known was that Dallas was far from the only referee the Originals struck whose dress was better suited to the office than to the rugby field.

Irishman William Kennedy who refereed the Originals' first test of their tour, against Scotland, not only turned out in the *de rigeur* street clothes, but was also one-eyed, according to the All Blacks' vice-captain, Billy Stead.

Stead had no qualms in his excellent series of articles in the *Southland Times*

about saying precisely what he thought of the referee.

He got straight to the point: 'The referee, an Irishman, appointed without our approval in direct opposition to one of the rugby rules, which says "The referee shall be mutually agreed upon", came on in ordinary dress and had only one eye.'

Kennedy was often 20 yards or more behind the play, Stead wrote, and disallowed the All Blacks at least twice when they knew they had scored.

'It was, to my thinking,' Stead wrote, 'entirely his one-eyedness that made us, six minutes from time, look a beaten team.'

Despite the referee, the All Blacks still managed to win their first test against Scotland 12–7.

Scotland

among the finest of All Black teams, but they were lucky to win and probably wouldn't have but for a mistake by the Welsh referee, Derek Bevan. He penalised Gavin Hastings for not releasing and appeared not to have realised that Hastings' tackler, Mike Brewer, arrived from within the 10-metre circle. Grant Fox kicked the penalty goal and in the context of the match, it was a critical decision. In the context of several lifetimes of trying to beat the All Blacks, it was even more critical for the Scots.

There have been times when the Scots haven't even been in the hunt and one of those was in the first test in 1996 in Dunedin, the second test of John Hart's coaching career and the second test for Christian Cullen. It was a remarkable display of attacking rugby by the All Blacks and momentous finishing by Cullen, who scored four tries, one of them seemingly by evading all the Scottish backs and a couple of forwards as well. The Scottish captain then, Rob Wainwright, when asked afterwards what would remain his lasting memory of the match, said: 'The sight of No 15 disappearing into the distance.' The match prompted Ian McGeechan to wonder why Scottish backs, for all the talent they've been able to muster over the years, have not been consistently good finishers.

Among the spectators that day at Carisbrook was a future Scot who could be a good finisher, Brendan Laney, though playing for Scotland would have been far from his thoughts. It was an unlikely circumstance still far from his thoughts when he left Dunedin within days of the NPC final in 2001 for his new career with Edinburgh. But he'd barely overcome jetlag before he was whisked into the Scotland A team to play the All Blacks and then a week later into the test team, there to confront his team-mates of just 21 days before. Laney became the 16th of what Scots call the 'kilted kiwis' to play for Scotland. He was joined at the Edinburgh club by the former All Black captain, Todd Blackadder, and within a few months his former coach at Otago and of the Highlanders, Tony Gilbert, was coaching the new Borders club and a former Waikato coach, Kiwi Searancke, was in charge of the third Scottish professional team, Glasgow.

Though a vastly different era and in hugely different circumstances, each was extending the close links between the two countries begun in 1872 by John Anderson, the first New Zealander to play for Scotland.

John Kirwan and Michael Jones in the World Cup playoff match in 1991.

WALES

It's not possible to be in Wales and not feel the rugby, not feel the passion there is for a game that once they played better than just about anyone else, a game they made their own almost as soon as rules were drawn up to differentiate one ball game from another.

It's not possible to speak to Welsh people, to hear Welsh people, and not be imbued with their deep love of the game.

It's not possible to hear Welsh people sing songs such as 'Sospan Fach' and 'Calon Lân' and 'Cwm Rhondda' and that relative newcomer, 'Hymns and Arias', without memories being conjured up of great players with their dark Celtic-Iberian looks, their red jerseys with the white Prince of Wales feathers on them; of epic matches, especially against New Zealand.

It's not possible to be at the start of a match and hear the Welsh sing with such fervour that most stirring of national anthems and not be moved.

Rugby is a part of the Welsh soul, a part of their being, a part of their reason for being.

Dave Gallaher and his team of Originals would have seen and sensed the passion for rugby when they were in Wales in 1905; so, too, would Taine Randell and his latest team of All Blacks to visit Wales in 2002; so, too, all the All Blacks in between. And if any of the latest All Blacks, none of them alive in an era of Welsh dominance, might have wondered what all the fuss was about, they needed to wander only five minutes from their hotel and there gaze at a bronze statue of the man voted Wales' greatest player, halfback Gareth Edwards. That alone expresses the depth of feeling for rugby in Wales.

Rugby is a common bond between two countries that are so diverse in so many other ways. Social historians might argue that it was through rugby that each country chose to define themselves in their own terms, to establish their own identities. It would be an argument with some merit but there can be no argument that what was defined in December 1905 when the Originals played Wales was an international rivalry that has waned more than waxed in recent years but has nevertheless been enduring.

That first meeting was far from being the first international, but it laid down a template that was followed for the next 100 years. It both shattered and created the aura of the All Blacks and if that sounds like a contradiction, that's because it is. The shattering bit was because the All Blacks on their pioneering tour beat everyone but Wales and how the Welsh loved that; the aura came from the knowledge in Britain that New Zealand had taken rugby to new, previously unimaginable heights. The All Blacks became the touchstone of rugby, regardless of the result in Wales.

The match in Cardiff introduced ritual that has endured in all manner of sport: the singing of national anthems. The Welsh had sent spies around Britain to follow the progress of the Originals and among their reports they noted the ferocity and psychological value of the haka, which they described as a war dance. How, the Welsh officials wondered, could they counter that? Their most influential selector, Tom Williams, came up with the idea of the Welsh players singing 'Hen Wlad fy Nhadau' ('Land of my Fathers'), an air composed nearly 50 years before by a pair of Pontypridd publicans.

Williams' idea was taken up by the local morning paper, the *Western Mail*, and the Welsh union agreed, saying the players would sing it and it hoped the spectators would join in.

Dave Gallaher led the All Blacks out onto the Arms Park and, according to the *South Wales Daily News*, 'amidst a silence that could almost be felt, the Colonials stood in the centre of the field and sang their weird warcry'.

Then the Welsh players, faintly at first but then with more gusto, began their anthem. Its strains were picked up by the crowd and the All Blacks must have felt as if they were being assailed by a wall of sound. Gallaher said afterwards he had never been more impressed in his life.

The *Lyttelton Times*, then an influential paper in New Zealand, recorded a few days later: 'It was the most impressive incident I have ever witnessed on a football field. It gave a semi-religious

George Nepia leads the All Blacks in their haka in Swansea before their 19–0 victory against Wales.

solemnity to this memorable contest . . . was intensely thrilling, even awe-inspiring. It was a wonderful revelation of the serious spirit in which the Welsh take their football.'

It wasn't just the ceremony that endured. So, too, did the unique circumstances of the result, the solitary try by Teddy Morgan and the protestations by New Zealand that Bob Deans had scored, but had been pulled back over the line before the referee, John Dallas, could get close enough to see what was going on.

So began one of the great pieces of folklore of the game, the first tie to bind Wales and New Zealand together in competitive rivalry. It's well known how Morgan believed Deans did score and wrote his affirmation on a dinner menu when the All Blacks were in Wales in 1924. That was good enough for New Zealanders but the Welsh had ears only for the views of Rhys Gabe, who tackled Deans: 'If the man who collared Deans says he scored that's the end of the argument,' he once said. 'But it was me, not Morgan, made that tackle. I confess that, just for a moment, I thought Deans had made it. Then he started to try to wriggle forward. I knew the truth. He had grounded the ball short of the line. I hung on.'

Robbie Deans, a great-nephew of Bob's and a fine All Black himself, once said that if his great uncle Bob had said he had scored, his word had to be accepted.

In the wider rugby scheme of things, it's all an irrelevance anyway. Dallas didn't award a try and that's where the matter, for all practical purposes, ended. But rugby is more than an 80-minute game; it is conversations and recollections, opinions and facts, discussions in bars and learned dissertations. The Deans non-try and other incidents gave flesh to the bones of the results.

There have been numerous such incidents in matches between New Zealand and Wales and they've kept the rivalry healthy and alive, even if nearly 50 years have passed since Wales last beat the All Blacks. There have been controversial moments in tests against

IN PRAISE OF FERGIE

There can't be many individual All Blacks who have had to suffer the embarrassment — and the ribbing of their mates — of having had a song written about them. There've been any number of songs that have celebrated the All Blacks collectively, most of which had fleeting success before being consigned to musical history, but not many about individuals.

Some of the Originals, Dave Gallaher, Duncan McGregor and Billy Wallace, were the subject of poems during their tour. It seemed to be a newspaper stock-in-trade in Britain at the time that poets were employed almost as much as rugby writers.

Colin Meads surely had a song or two written about him (and if he didn't, he should have), and Jeff Wilson was the subject of a specially written song in 2000 to coincide with the publication of his book.

There may have been others.

Fergie McCormick may not have been too thrilled to learn that he was celebrated in song after he scored 24 points, which was then a world record, against Wales in Auckland in 1969.

It was written and recorded by Lew Pryme, who was then one of New Zealand's noted pop singers and who was later a music promoter and, in a fitting finale to his career given his 1969 interest, chief executive of the Auckland Rugby Union.

Many were the mutterings when Pryme gained the top job in Auckland rugby in 1986, but he proved to be an able administrator and he was a godsend when he was given just a few weeks to organise the opening ceremony for the 1987 World Cup at Eden Park.

Pryme's paean of praise to McCormick in 1969 was called 'The Feat of Fantastic Fergie' and sung to the tune of the Johnny Horton hit 'Sink the *Bismarck*!', a jingoistic celebration of the British navy's hunting down of the German battleship, *Bismarck*, in 1941.

Interspersed through Pryme's lyrics were the voice of commentator Winston McCarthy (though he'd retired 10 years before) and the sound, it is assumed, of the crowd at Eden Park the day the All Blacks beat Wales 33–12.

This was how Pryme remembered it:

And again. Fergie McCormick goals another against Wales in Auckland in 1969.

McCarthy: New Zealand has scored!

In June of 1969 McCormick made his name
He played against the touring Welsh and kicked his way to fame
McCormick is an All Black back who has made history
And the way in which he did it, boys, was a sight to see

That day at Eden Park he played a rugged touring team
The way he scored his record points no one e'er could dream
The All Blacks fought the Welsh and won by adding to their score
McCormick made the day for us, scoring twenty-four

The All Blacks are a breed apart, a mighty football team
The All Blacks are a massive bunch who e'er rule supreme
They hit the field a-running and they spun the ball around
The All Blacks o'er the ragged Welsh, they really cut 'em down

McCarthy: New Zealand has scored!

Pinetree Meads, Lochore and Gray played mighty games that day
Along with fullback Fergie, they stormed into the fray
Kirkpatrick, Smith and Lister, McLeod and Hopkinson
Combined in strength to race away for yet another win
Behind the pack was Going, Kirton and MacRae
Sharing play was Fergie, making breaks all day
Skudder, Dick and Davis, and what about poor Thorne
Behind them all stood Fergie, and so a star was born!

The All Blacks are a breed apart, a mighty football team
The All Blacks are a massive bunch who e'er rule supreme
They hit the field a-running and they spin the ball around
Fergie's kicked it all for us, he made the Welshmen frown

McCarthy: It's a goal!

With kicks so true he beat the Welsh and raced
    ahead to fame
McCormick is a giant and we shan't forget
    his name
He joins the hallowed Kiwi race as All
    Black back supreme
Fergie is our hero and a must for any
    team

The All Blacks are a breed apart, a
    mighty football team
The All Blacks are a mighty bunch
    fore'er will rule supreme
They hit the field a-running and they
    spin the ball around
The Welsh, the French, the Springboks,
    too, we'll cut them to the ground

The All Blacks are a breed apart, a
    mighty football team etc., etc.

McCarthy: He has kicked . . . Listen . . .
It's a goal! . . . Goodness gracious me,
it was twice as high as the posts!

**Man of many talents. Entertainer
Lew Pryme who later became chief
executive of the Auckland Rugby Union.**

other All Black opponents, too, but none is debated in so lively a fashion, or for so long, as any of those involving Wales. It is because of the passion that each country has for the game, a far greater national passion than in any other country.

It is not solely controversy that has fuelled that passion. There's respect there, too. Until relatively recent years, the All Blacks in Wales were a rarity and for anyone in Wales, watching the All Blacks play was a life's highlight. As mature men become ever more mature, their boyhood memories of watching the All Blacks acquire the glow of nostalgia. The men in black from their memories become larger, the matches, Homeric struggles.

Phil Bennett recalled being taken to Stradey Park to see Wilson Whineray's All Blacks in 1963. 'They were like giants,' Bennett recalled. 'I remember thinking how the boys in Llanelli would have no chance against such huge men.'

Another great Welsh player, Ieuan Evans, took different strength and inspiration from his earliest memory of watching the All Blacks. His was an example of how the great sporting deeds of a nation can inspire the youth. 'My baptism as a spectator in the Arms Park was as an eight-year-old where I witnessed the game between the 1973 Barbarians and the All Blacks,' he wrote in a foreword to a book recording the statistical history of Welsh rugby. 'What impression do you imagine it left on me to watch Phil Bennett, Gareth Edwards, Tommy David, J.P.R., John Dawes, Derek Quinnell and John Bevan in those famous black and white hoops? It was profound.'

The careful reader will note that Evans mentioned only the Welshmen in the Barbarians team that day.

It was Edwards who wrote in his biography, 'There's something about an All Black jersey that sends a shudder through your heart.'

Such feelings were a part of the aura of the All Blacks, an air of invincibility, fuelled by the deeds of the Originals and those that followed, especially the 1924–25 team that was unbeaten and came to be known as the Invincibles. It wasn't just in Wales where the power of the All Blacks was appreciated, but it was where it was understood better and appreciated all the more because of that understanding. It remains a blemish on the golden era of Welsh rugby through the 1970s, the era of the men Evans revered, that they beat everyone but the All Blacks.

The fervour and passion for rugby is not something that is deep-seated in the Welsh, probed and teased to the surface only occasionally. It is always there for all to see and hear. Every All Black who's ever toured Wales will know that after a win against Swansea, or Llanelli or Newport or Cardiff, that Welsh supporters will have told them long and often, 'Ah, but wait till you get to Swansea [or Llanelli or Newport etc.].' And then the line delivered with utter conviction in the soft, lilting south Wales accent, 'Wales will beat you, boy.'

The passion is used and channelled for it to be expressed on the rugby field. When the All Blacks of 1989, World Cup winners and one of the best teams fielded by New Zealand, played Neath, the All Blacks were astounded and taken aback by the ferocity of

NEPIA'S CROWNING MOMENT

No serious student of rugby needs telling that the 19-year-old fullback, George Nepia, played every game of the Invincibles' epic tour in 1924–25 — 28 matches in Britain and Ireland and 10 before and after in Australia, France and North America.

Almost as well known as Nepia's feat of endurance and sustained brilliance was that, of all those games, his best was in the test against Wales — a match that the All Blacks were desperate to win beyond all others because of the loss in 1905.

Nepia's feats illuminated New Zealand rugby history and his light has not dimmed with the passing of the years. Even today, when sage judges rank the best of All Black fullbacks, Nepia still stands among them, even though none saw him play.

Years after the Welsh test, Nepia's finest moment, he revealed that before the match he shook with nervousness and fear.

The Welsh test came a week after the All Blacks had beaten Cardiff. The test players and manager Stan Dean went off to Tenby, a 13th-century seaside village on the rugged Pembrokeshire coast in the far west of Wales. The rest of the touring party went to Swansea to wait for the supreme test of the tour.

Separating the touring party is unusual in All Black history. John Hart did it with the All Blacks in South Africa in 1996 and the mission they were on then was of no less significance than the mission Cliff Porter's team was on in 1924.

The fact the test players went to Tenby for light trainings each morning and sightseeing and relaxing each afternoon was indicative of the importance they had given the Welsh match. Nothing could be left to chance. It was a match they had to win. A loss, even just the one loss on tour, would have meant failure.

The players felt that 20 matches into the tour, they didn't need more hard training. What they needed, more even than the light runs they had, was the isolation and freedom in which they could concentrate their minds on the task that

The guardian of the gate. The incomparable George Nepia against Wales in 1924.

awaited them at the St Helen's ground in Swansea on the following Saturday.

There is a danger, modern players know, of the potential for disaster if a mental buildup for a match starts too soon. Players, to use their phraseology, can get too wound up, with the effect that they're mentally spent by the time the great day arrives.

Perhaps there was an element of that affecting Nepia when the test All Blacks joined their team-mates in Swansea on the Friday afternoon.

'On the Saturday morning I was really nervous,' Nepia recalled in an interview 40 years after the event. 'I couldn't keep still. A short distance away thousands were pouring into the St Helen's ground. I was bottled up, tense, excited. I could only eat two slices of toast with a cup of tea for lunch.

'Then we were off in the bus. By this time I was so jumpy I didn't want anyone to talk with me.

'In the dressing room I felt a little better. Once I had changed and had my boots on, my nerves turned to cold fear. I went through agony walking, sitting, standing, going out for photographs or to the toilet.

'My kneecaps shook. I couldn't stop them. Then I was taking the field. Once on the field I was cool, calm, relaxed, ready.'

So was everyone else for this epic match. It was the habit for the players to go out onto the field shortly before the start for a team photo, following a simple formula of one row of players sitting on a form and the rest standing behind. After the photo, they'd disappear back into the dressing rooms.

When Wales appeared for their photo, the crowd broke into a spontaneous version of 'Land of My Fathers' — the moving anthem boomed from 50,000 throats and the *South Wales Evening Express* remarked that never before, not even for the 1905 match between these two opponents, had there been such a spectacle on the rugby field.

When the British Prime Minister, Ramsay MacDonald, took his place in the St Helen's stand, the crowd serenaded him with their third or fourth rendition of 'Cwm Rhondda', no one could quite remember how many times they'd pleaded in song, 'Feed me till I want no more . . .'. The noise and the air of expectation could unnerve the hardest of players.

There was more before this encounter of the ages could get under way. Halfback Jimmy Mill led the All Blacks in their haka and, bizarrely, Welsh flanker David Hiddlestone then led his players in a parody of a reply, with Welsh arms and legs flapping in various directions.

But even after that the match couldn't get started. Nepia must have been ready to burst. The Welsh captain, Jack Wetter, rejected four balls, disdainfully tossing them towards the touchline, before finally the referee plonked one on halfway in a clear message that said play with that or else.

And play they did, and none better than Nepia, the man whom the New Zealand High Commissioner in London, William Pember Reeves, had called the 'guardian of the gate'.

Bert Cooke, the All Black centre and one of the undoubted stars of the tour, later wrote that no one in New Zealand saw Nepia play as he did on that tour and that he touched his greatest heights in the Welsh test.

Another team-mate, Read Masters, wrote that the All Black backs all played exceptionally well 'but the palm must go to Nepia'.

'There were times when the hopes of the great crowd were aroused by the sight of the scarlet jerseys sweeping down the field taking the ball at toe, but Nepia invariably dashed their hopes,' Masters wrote.

'One marvellous effort by Nepia resulted in Wetter getting his injury — three Welshmen were dribbling the ball in a dangerous position with only our fullback to beat when he, rushing up the field at full speed, took a flying leap at their toes and after securing the ball, turned a couple of somersaults, landing on his feet, and raced up the field leaving two of the Welshmen knocked out.'

It wasn't just New Zealanders who put Nepia up on the pedestal. 'Observer' in the Cardiff *Western Mail* said Nepia never played better than he did that day at St Helen's.

'There were times when it appeared that nothing would stay the fierce rushes of the Welsh pack,' he wrote.

'By sheer strength they barged their way through with the ball and there stood Nepia alone between them and the desired objective . . . Nepia creeps forward and unexpectedly dives at the ball . . . his judgement is uncanny and his pluck magnificent . . .'

The man himself bore the marks of his excellence. 'I was sore for days after that match from kicks and bruises,' he said. 'It was one of the proudest moments I have known.'

The All Blacks won 19–0.

Nepia made a triumphal return to the St Helen's ground almost sixty years later when the New Zealand Maori were there. Before the match, this slight figure, dressed in a long overcoat, was introduced to the crowd and given a tremendous reception.

the Welsh play. It became something more than a rugby match, more a nation fighting for its rugby life, which perhaps it was.

No All Blacks were privy to what went on in the Neath dressing room but it's not difficult to imagine the intensity of the parochial and nationalistic feelings roused before battle commenced.

Ray Gravell, a fine centre for Llanelli and Wales, could have been born in a leek field. Passion oozed from his pores. Not just for rugby, though that was near and dear to his heart, but also for Wales. He was a Welsh nationalist and Phil Bennett recalls that in some of Gravell's team talks, the delivery was so excited and quick that it was sometimes difficult to tell whether he was speaking English or Welsh and no one could see him because of the tears streaming out of their eyes.

Bennett recalls the team talks before Llanelli played the All Blacks in 1980. It was a vastly different Llanelli team from the one

that had beaten the All Blacks in 1972 and no one seriously expected them to win, but the buildup was intense.

Carwyn James, the mastermind of the 1972 win, dropped in to give what Bennett called an inspiring monologue. The captain from 1972, Delme Thomas, also spoke and the coach of the day, John McLean, even got a word in. By the time the players got to Stradey Park, the talking was still not done.

The final words were left to their skipper, Gravell. The players were on an emotional rack, most of them crying, some trembling, all ready to explode out onto the field. Just as they were about to go, Gravell finished up, according to Bennett's recollection: 'Boys! . . . Boys! I've got a telegram here I want to read to you. "Best wishes to my son", it says, boys. "All my love". And do you know who signed it? "Best wishes from Mam and Shamrock". *Chi'n gwbod pwy yw Shamrock bois? Y gath?* Do you know who Shamrock is, boys?

Wales

The fucking cat. The fucking cat sent us a telegram!'

Graham Mourie's All Blacks, perplexed as they may have been by saucepans sitting on top of the Llanelli goalposts, would have been more mystified had they known Gravell used a cat as his parting shot before the game.

The saucepans, emblematic of Llanelli's past tinplate industry, are a part of the Welsh fervour. 'Sospan Fach', the song that is Llanelli's own but which is borrowed by the pretenders from east Wales for the crowd to sing at test matches, is all about a saucepan. It is as much a part of the Welsh tradition as the coalmines and the valleys, the coalmines also just about a thing of the past.

There is much of the past in Wales and there are those who say that one of the reasons for the decline of Welsh rugby is that there is too much dwelling in the past and not enough planning for the future. It's natural enough to reach behind for past glories if there are none immediately in front, and it's commendable to remember the great deeds of the past and glory in them, but it's

necessary also to look forwards and shuck off some of the ways of the past if they've served their time.

Welsh rugby has been reluctant to adapt to the changing rugby world, preferring to keep its multiplicity of professional clubs in a relatively small pocket of Britain of about 8000 square kilometres and with a population of about three million. Protecting patches and power sometimes seems more important to rugby in Wales than working towards the country regaining the international esteem it once had.

Those concerned about Welsh rugby know that something has to be done; the question is what. The appointment of the former New Zealand rugby chief executive, David Moffett, late in 2002, to run the Welsh union may have been the catalyst that was needed. He's no stranger to challenging entrenched positions but only time

Judgement uncanny and pluck magnificent,
George Nepia poised to defend in the Invincibles' test against Wales.

Excuse me. Nicky Allen fends off Gareth Davies during the 1980 centenary test. Stu Wilson is anxious to lend a hand.

can tell if he holds rugby's Rosetta stone.

Gerald Davies, the great wing of the era of dominance, recalled how he ran into Jonathan Davies, the gifted first five-eighth, after the humiliation of Wales losing to Romania. The pair met in semi-darkness under the old Arms Park and Jonathan looked sadly at Gerald and said, 'I've had enough. I'm going.' And go he did, to league, as so many other fine Welsh players did; the money was part of the attraction there's no doubt, but so, too, some disillusionment.

Jonathan Davies was one of the few players of genuine flair of the old Welsh style in New Zealand with Wales in 1988. That team was a sad echo of the great days of the past and they were thumped in two tests by the All Blacks. Even the All Blacks could see sadness in the size of their victories. 'Doesn't it make you sad to see a score like that against Wales?' asked Sean Fitzpatrick, whose father Brian was in the last All Black team to lose to Wales.

It was a far cry from the days when Wales were the team to beat, when on a tour of Britain the All Blacks would look at Wales as the ultimate test of their tour, a plane above England, Scotland and Ireland.

The Invincibles of 1924 made no bones about beating Wales as the main mission of their tour. Whatever else they achieved would be as nothing if they didn't beat Wales. It was the match in which George Nepia excelled — he played in all of the Invincibles' 32 matches in Britain and North America, but the Welsh match was where his talents were demonstrated to the full.

The All Blacks' outstanding centre, Bert Cooke, wrote of Nepia: 'He touched his greatest heights in the Welsh match, the game we were most anxious of all to win. We felt that the eyes of New Zealand were on us. In that game George would repeatedly sweep the ball up from the toes of the Welsh forwards and charge backwards through them, and in one of these daring and spectacular exploits he skittled no less than three of them, including the Welsh skipper, Jack Wetter.'

It wasn't just New Zealanders who marvelled at Nepia. The Welsh union's centenary book, *Fields of Praise*, quoted 'an admirer': 'He has snatched the ball away from the very toes of the men, and his bullet-like rush carries him through the mass. By a miracle he has kept his feet and with the kick which comes in his stride he has cleared. There is a gasp from the crowd, which has been in a frenzy because a score seemed so certain. Occasionally a Welsh three-quarter eluded the vigilant outside men, but always there was Nepia. The embrace of man and ball was like that of an octopus.'

That match, won by the All Blacks 19–0 — a point for every

JUSTICE — THE MEADS WAY

When Wales toured New Zealand for the first time in 1969, great were the expectations. The Welsh, dauntless foe of the All Blacks since their first infamous encounter in 1905, were the best team in Europe and the All Blacks, well, at the time they were demonstrably the best in the world. They hadn't lost a test since 1965 and they had players whose greatness even now hasn't been dimmed by time or their successors.

It was an unofficial championship of the world.

The Welsh had players whose stars were in the ascendant and chief among them were names that also have stood the test of uncompromising time, including Gareth Edwards, Barry John, John Dawes, J.P.R. Williams and Gerald Davies.

A clash of titans was anticipated, but anticipation sometimes fails to be matched by the event itself.

The Welsh were thrashed. No other word for it. They lost the first test in Christchurch 19–0 and lost the second in Auckland 33–12, with All Black fullback Fergie McCormick scoring 24 points, which was then a world record.

The All Blacks were too strong, too talented and too ruthless.

Welsh manager Handel Rogers, one of the great men of Welsh rugby, summed up the tour thus: 'Where we failed was in the first place because the All Blacks were decisively the superior team — no question whatever about that. But we also failed because we could not get enough ball. I think there is no question our backs came off well, extremely well, but the best backs can't come off when you can't get the ball.'

In the case of Welsh hooker Jeff Young, it wasn't for want of trying that his backs didn't get the ball.

Young, a 25-year-old schoolteacher who had been on the Lions' tour of South Africa the year before, found himself the central character in the enduring drama of the first test in Christchurch.

Young, with the combativeness characteristic of his position, did his best in lineouts to harass the All Blacks and spoil their possession. The code among rugby players then was it was up to them to sort it out.

And they did. Newspaper reporting of the incident was cautious. One said Young was felled 'and C.E. Meads was in the vicinity'. Another said Young was lowered by an All Black forward but there was no hint of who it could possibly have been. What happened on the field stayed on the field in those days.

Even while Young was being tended in Burwood Hospital in Christchurch and his team-mates had moved on to their next match, the Welsh management acted like the three wise monkeys. They saw no evil, they heard no evil and they spoke none.

Coach Clive Rowlands, another Welsh rugby figure who seemed to have been around as long as the Welsh dragon, was told Young was punched and he replied in that disingenuous manner he could sometimes employ: 'Was it a blow? Or did he hit the ground with his jaw? Or was it that he hit the corner flag?'

Young himself, when able to speak, said he knew who punched him but he wasn't about to breach any forward code of conduct by naming his attacker.

Colin Meads in his rugby afterlife, speaking at a Skeggs Foundation lunch in Dunedin.

There was no doubting there was a punch and no doubting who the deliverer was. But such things were not talked about publicly then. Thirty years later, various officials would have studied video replays, pronounced importantly there was a case to answer, lawyers would have been assembled and Meads might have found himself missing the match the following week.

Nothing like that happened in 1969. Players' justice prevailed.

Meads himself, in his celebrity afterlife, tells the tale with rough-hewn politically incorrect humour.

'We had this move "Willie Away" . . . a great move. We'd got rid of Wilson so I was allowed to do it. The throw goes to Brian Lochore at the back of the lineout and he catches the ball and it's down to you. This little Welshman was coming round with us and he's not allowed to do that. He's got to go back his side.

'And you're trying to catch a ball, swat a bloody Welshman off behind you; it's damn awkward and frustrating. Nothing more frustrating.

'I always thought of a great Otago man, Kevin Skinner. He said to me at a very young age you never hit a man unless you warn him. So I turned to this Welshman and said, "You do that again and I'll knock your bloody head off." You know what? He didn't believe me.

'It was only five minutes later, we were hot on attack . . . Ken Gray's turn to do the Willie away. I got all excited because I'm going to be outside Ken Gray and you often got the plum if you're outside the next guy. And same result. This bloody little Welsh hooker, swinging on Ken Gray. Ken's trying to catch the ball and swat the little bugger off and same result, he knocked it on. Well, the opportunity was too good. He was only standing half a yard away and I couldn't resist.

'Poor little fellow fell over and you should have heard the Welshmen . . . it was tragic. You go and try and stand among your mates back there and they evaporate and leave you . . . No 5 was getting a fair old hammering.'

Referee Pat Murphy tried to calm the Welshmen and told them, 'Look, I've got it all under control, I saw it all happen. Don't worry, it's all under control. Small problem here and when we get rid of that we'll start the game again.'

Meads continues his story: 'So the poor little fellow got up and fell over again and they brought a stretcher out. This little Welshman was put on the stretcher and taken away and Murphy's about to start the game again and he says, "Penalty the All Blacks." You should have heard the Welsh then. Were they swearing? They were swearing in Welsh. There were some terrible words. Murphy says, "I told you I had it under control. He was offside, penalty the All Blacks. To hell with hitting him, he shouldn't have been offside. That's part of the game." '

WELSH WHEEL OF MISFORTUNE

It was three minutes to go and Wales were ahead 12–10. The Welsh were also doing all the attacking but Doug Bruce had got the ball down to within 30 metres of the Welsh line.

No need to say what year this was, what test this was, what the outcome was.

English schoolteacher Roger Quittenton, refereeing his first big test, gestured towards the touchline for the lineout. He didn't know the score.

'The scoreboard was behind me but I knew it was close and I knew Wales were in front,' he says. 'When the ball went into touch I thought to myself that this lineout could be absolutely critical.'

Quittenton, noted throughout his illustrious test career for not mincing words — and probably thankful he preceded the days when referees' comments could be heard around the world — wasn't happy with the first throw to the lineout by the Welsh hooker, Bobby Windsor.

'So many infringed I couldn't have awarded a penalty to anyone. I said to both sets of forwards, "For Christ's sake fellows, don't fuck about here, throw it in again," ' Quittenton recalls.

Windsor threw it dead straight. Frank Oliver went up for the All Blacks, Geoff Wheel up for Wales. Andy Haden went out for New Zealand.

'Wheel was taller than me,' says Quittenton. 'I didn't know what had happened beyond Wheel and Oliver. Haden's antics were an absolute mystery to me. I didn't know a thing about it. Had I known, or had he materially affected the lineout, I would've penalised him. But I didn't see him; he obviously didn't affect either side trying to gain possession.'

Quittenton immediately penalised Wheel for leaning on Oliver and preventing him from taking the ball. Replacement goalkicker Brian McKechnie moved up and took the ball. The rest, as they say, is history.

Quittenton recalls talking to the Welsh captain, J.P.R. Williams, at the test dinner that night and says Williams told him he was very brave for making the decision, and acknowledged it was the correct one.

Williams told the same thing to New Zealand reporters, though added the International Rugby Board should — as it did later — introduce provision for free kicks for technical offences at lineouts.

That lineout changed Quittenton's life, as it did McKechnie's.

'I have no doubt that it cost me a lot of tests,' he said. 'I was vilified in Wales and told I would never be welcome back there. My name was graven on the hearts of Welshmen as the personification of evil. It affected me at the time because I was young and impressionable, but now I've learnt to live with it and laugh about it.

'Hell, the Welsh should have been thanking me. If it wasn't for me, they wouldn't have been 12–10 up when that lineout started. Remember, I made a cock-up and they got three points out of me they shouldn't have got!'

That occurred in the first half when Bryan Williams late-tackled the Welsh wing, J.J. Williams. Williams had passed the ball to the Welsh centre, Steve Fenwick, who kicked it downfield. Quittenton awarded a penalty to Wales where the ball landed.

'Graham Mourie came up to me and said, "Ref, he didn't kick the ball" and I thought, "Oh shit." I realised I had made a mistake but I couldn't reverse the decision then and Fenwick kicked the penalty goal. That put them up 9–0 but did they thank me later? Did they hell.'

Welsh resentment was not just in Quittenton's imagination. When the All Blacks were again in Wales in 1980, the *South Wales Echo*, the Cardiff afternoon paper, called Quittenton the most hated man in all of Wales.

Quittenton refereed another 17 tests but only one of them, late in his career, in Cardiff.

In command. Roger Quittenton.

SOBERING SLANT ON McKECHNIE GOAL

Somehow the impression has got about that Brian McKechnie was tired and hung over when he took to the field against Wales in 1978 and kicked the memorable goal that won the All Blacks that most controversial of matches.

'Ah, it's been a bit embellished over the years,' McKechnie says with a grin. 'It wasn't like that at all.'

But it's true that the night before the game, for which McKechnie had not been chosen, he and team-mate Lyn Jaffray propped up the bar and had a few beers.

Some background. McKechnie had not even been chosen in the first place for the grand slam All Blacks' 18-match tour. He'd played in the third test against Australia at Eden Park and he was one who paid a price for the 30–16 drubbing.

'The touring team was named the next day and by then I was in New Plymouth for an NPC match,' he says. 'I was in the Southland team's bus when the touring team came over the radio and heard I'd been dropped.'

A couple of weeks later, McKechnie was at home in Invercargill when he had a call from a radio station to say that he'd been named in the team as a replacement for Bevan Wilson, who'd had to withdraw because of injury.

Even then, it was a hard road for this southern man to reach the perfect goalkick.

McKechnie played in the fifth match, against Munster, and like others, suffered because of it. 'Several of us had shockers or Munster just played out of their skins but, anyway, I was in the reserves for the next match, the test against Ireland, then for the following test against Wales I wasn't even in the reserves.'

So the road led to the bar at the Seabank Hotel in Porthcawl, which was a home away from home for so many All Black teams.

It was to the small house bar behind reception that McKechnie and Jaffray adjourned after their meal on the Friday night, there to have a few beers and reflect that after six matches of an 18-match tour, they would both probably end up playing just the midweek matches.

A few other players came and went and some of the accompanying New Zealand journalists were also there.

'At some point Graham Mourie came in and told me I'd better look after myself,' McKechnie recalls, 'saying there was a chance I might be needed. We knew Mark Donaldson had pulled out of the test team because of injury and Dave Loveridge had taken his place but no halfback reserve had been named. We figured if something happened to Trapper [Loveridge], Doug Bruce would go to halfback and I might be needed to be first-five.'

McKechnie doesn't recall precisely when he left the bar, but it wasn't late. Perhaps 10 or 10.30 p.m. is the most common memory among those who were there. 'We'd only had a few drinks, I wasn't roaring drunk or anything. I certainly wasn't in the bar until the early hours of the morning in the way that

**Man for the moment.
Brian McKechnie after the
Welsh test in 1978.**

the story's developed.'

The next morning, coach Jack Gleeson went to McKechnie's room on the first floor of the Seabank. 'You'd better get your gear ready, Colt,' Gleeson told him. 'You're in the reserves.'

The perfectly healthy and not hung-over McKechnie says the late notice of his call-up meant he didn't get wound up by the prospect of the match in the manner players do normally. 'I didn't have much time to think about it and, anyway, I was only in the reserves,' he says.

Reserves then used to sit in the grandstand and, at the Arms Park, that meant being surrounded by Welshmen who weren't afraid to tell the All Blacks their view of the game or incidents therein.

'It was a pretty feisty start to the test and these Welshmen around us were going on at us and a few words were exchanged. Then when Clive Currie went down, the baggageman Graham Short told me I'd better get ready and he and I went down into the tunnel. I was standing there when Clive came off and he looked pretty groggy. But I couldn't go on because he had to be checked by a doctor. It seemed an eternity waiting down there to run on.'

Came the hour, came the man, and came the kick that won the match.

'It's funny, you know,' he says, 'but I didn't even see what happened in the lineout that led to the penalty being awarded. I remember thinking as the game wound down that it could come to a kick to win the match and I was reasonably confident. I'd kicked a couple and I'd just missed with the conversion of Stu Wilson's try.

'When we were given the penalty, I just thought about taking it as quick as I could. I walked up to the mark, Graham handed me the ball, never said a word, and I just kicked it. As soon as I struck it, before I looked up, I knew it was going over. When I turned and raised an arm in the air, I think it was just relief. I'm not normally a showy sort of a person, that's not the sort of thing I do. But it was just relief and I think the significance of the kick hit me then. I remember when I was running back Gary Seear gave me a pat on the back, but for the little time remaining in the match, there was just a determination to keep the ball down their end of the park.'

It was only after the match, when wearing a Welsh jersey — and he can't remember whose it was — he was ushered into a BBC room and saw a recording of the last lineout that he realised what had happened.

'I was quite stunned,' he says, 'then back in the dressing room Andy [Haden] and Frank [Oliver] were talking about it and I heard the full story of how it had happened.'

year since 1905 — was played at St Helen's in Swansea, the Arms Park then not being the sole international venue in Wales. In 1982, 58 years after the test, Nepia was back at St Helen's when the national Maori team played there and the reception from the crowd for Nepia was such that the test could have been just the day before. They have long memories in Wales for their rugby heroes.

If successive All Black teams have felt that Wales was the richest prize, the same has to be said of the Welsh. They had their Five Nations, their triple crowns and grand slams, occasional matches against Australia, South Africa and others, but it was the All Blacks for whom they lay in wait.

One of their loose forwards in the 1935 test against Jack Manchester's All Blacks was Arthur Rees, a no-nonsense sort of a player who later became chief constable of Staffordshire. Years after the 1935 match, he recalled: 'The fixture with the All Blacks on December 21, 1935 was not just a game to me. I felt I had been born and bred for this very day.'

Rees was the Welsh pack leader and he made plain his requirements before the start. 'No rough stuff unless they start it,' he said. 'We want to play rugby. I'll tell you when if they start it and then everybody in — and I mean everybody.'

The game was only a few minutes old and the 'when' happened.

Manchester, a bit rocked by the fiery start to the match by the Welsh forwards, had exhorted his players, according to Rees's memory: 'Come on, New Zealand, get stuck into these Welsh bastards.'

One of the other Welsh loose forwards, Glyn Prosser, a Neath blacksmith who improbably moonlighted as a Sunday School teacher, turned to Rees on overhearing Manchester's entreaty. '*Now*, Mr Rees?' Prosser asked. Rees answered in the affirmative.

'In a flash, eight New Zealanders were either rocking or down,' Rees recalled. 'I connected with a huge sheep farmer, Athol Mahoney, all 17 stone of him, a veritable giant. He recovered just in time to hear Cyril Gadney, the referee, say to me: "What on earth is going on here?"

'I replied, pointing to my friend and enemy, Manchester, "He called us Welsh bastards".'

Gadney responded: 'Well, that's a term of endearment in New Zealand.'

Then they played some football. And what football it was. Rees remembered it as a hard, tough match, with the Welsh playing the best they had ever done, yet still they won by only a point. Nelson Ball, cartoonist Murray's father, scored two tries, the second of them from a loose ball that had spilled after a collision between two Welsh defenders. That was with 10 minutes to go and the Welsh, down to 14 men because their hooker, Don Tarr, had been carried off with a broken neck, seemed beaten. But this was one of the best Welsh teams. The seven Welsh forwards won the ball from a scrum,

Coming through. Captain Wayne Shelford confronts Robert Jones in the first test of the 1988 series. The other All Blacks are John Kirwan and Michael Jones, and on the ground is Welshman Glen Webbe.

18-year-old Haydn Tanner got the ball out to Cliff Jones and then on to Wilfred Wooller, one of the great all-rounders of British sport. Rees said he never saw Wooller run faster. When he was blocked, he chipped infield, missed the bounce over the line but there to claim it was the other Welsh wing, Geoffrey Rees-Jones.

'We had won a splendid, rip-roaring sporting game, never to be forgotten,' Rees said. 'Wales erupted that night; coal output leapt for months; the world was young again.'

There was evidence again after that match how the Welsh, like New Zealanders, invest in rugby a significance beyond the game itself. Writing in the *South Wales Daily News*, columnist 'Old Stager' wrote: 'Wales is proud of this victory. She is particularly proud of

the fact that Welsh peers and Welsh labourers — with all the intervening stratas of society — were united in acclaiming and cheering the Welsh team. It was a victory for Wales in a sense that probably is impossible in any other sphere.'

No one during the carousing into the night in Cardiff could have dared imagine that Wales would have only one more victory in the 20th century against New Zealand. That was in 1953 and, again, the Welsh won the test in the last 10 minutes.

The Welshman who made it happen, Clem Thomas, thought hours before the match that he wouldn't even be playing. Thomas, later a respected journalist and delightful raconteur, took a group of New Zealanders to dinner in Swansea in 1980 and told them

---

CARWYN JAMES — HERO OF THE VALLEYS

One of the great fascinations about sport is the unanswerable question: What if?
Old men who were once boys go to their graves asking themselves that question.

In Wales, the 'what if' is often followed by the rest of the sentence, '. . . Carwyn James had coached Wales in 1972?'

Well, to the eternal regret of every Welshman, he didn't.

James, the inspiring coach of the Lions in New Zealand in 1971, had coached Llanelli to beat the All Blacks 9–3 at Stradey Park on October 31, 1972. It's a day that will live forever in Welsh hearts and minds; it was immortalised in song by the Welsh balladeer Max Boyce.

To one of the favourite sons of Llanelli, Phil Bennett, who played that day, it was, he says with no hesitation, the greatest day of his life.

'Carwyn was incredibly confident,' Bennett recalls. 'Not just in the days before the match against the All Blacks, but from August onwards. We went to London Welsh and they had some great players then and we hammered them. Carwyn said, "Right, that's the start." Then we played the Barbarians and we beat them and Carwyn said, "Right, that's number two" and so on. Everything was a step towards the match against the All Blacks.'

And after the match, and in the days afterwards, when in Boyce's words the pubs ran dry, the Llanelli players were giants in their small land. 'We lived in euphoria,' Bennett says. 'Some of my mates got back to work on the Friday after the match, which was on a Tuesday.'

The test was a month later. 'Wales made Delme Thomas of Llanelli captain and I thought "Yeah, come on,"' says Bennett. 'But, and I shouldn't say this, there was a tiny thing in the back of my mind and in the backs of minds of other players, too. Yes, we'd love to beat the All Blacks playing for Wales but we've beaten them already. If I die tomorrow, we've beaten the All Blacks. That wasn't good, but that's how we felt.'

Wales didn't beat the All Blacks. The score was 19–16 and Bennett missed a 30-metre penalty goal attempt in the last minutes.

**The Welsh master,
Carwyn James.**

Would Wales have won if James had been coach, if the Welsh union hadn't had such a snitcher on him because he was something of a free spirit and didn't toe the party line and, God forbid, because he was successful?

'I don't know,' says Bennett with sorrow in his voice. 'I just don't know. What I do know is that Carwyn was the greatest coach I played under. I was privileged to play for some great coaches and I include Brian Lochore in that, but Carwyn was the greatest, without a doubt. He did small things to make you proud. You'd die for him.'

Bennett related a story that illustrated the special James touch. Two years after the All Blacks' tour, in 1974, Bennett and his wife Pat lost their first child. 'We were devastated,' he says. 'It was the greatest devastation of my life. I was working in the steel mills at the time and Carwyn came to me and said I needed a break, that Pat and I should get away for a while, go to Spain for a week or so. I said to him, "I'm just a steelworker, Jamesy, I just can't go like that and I haven't got the money." Jamesy said not to worry, just go, the club will pay. So Pat and I went to Spain for about 10 days and it was the time we needed, it was just great. When we got back I went to Carwyn and said to him, "Anything you want from me for the rest of your life, just ask."'

On another occasion, James wanted Bennett and some of the other Welsh players to bolster the club's entry in the Snelling sevens, one of the long-standing Welsh sevens tournaments. The players were reluctant because they'd had a hard season but since it was James who asked, they played. They duly won and the bus taking them back to Llanelli stopped on the outskirts by a five-star hotel. James stood up at the front of the bus and told the players to ring their wives and tell them to join them at the hotel at about eight o'clock that night. 'He'd booked rooms for all of us for the night and I only lived five minutes away,' Bennett says. 'We had a great dinner and spent the night in the hotel. The next morning Carwyn took care of the bill. That was Carwyn. He was just such a wonderful man.'

how he nearly never played against Bob Stuart's All Blacks.

These were the days when international teams, the British ones anyway, didn't assemble until the night before the game. Thomas had been in London and on the Friday afternoon was driving west, intending to spend the night at his home in Swansea before joining his team-mates in Cardiff on the Saturday morning. He was driving near Worcester when a woman cyclist seemed to appear out of nowhere and bike and car collided. The woman died later in hospital. Thomas was considerably shaken and phoned a Welsh selector and said he probably couldn't play the next day. He was told to sleep on it and see how he was in the morning. He decided the next day he could still play, though he recalled being still upset

and newspaper reports of the time described him as looking pale.

It didn't affect his play, though. It was eight-all with eight minutes to play when Thomas, a flanker, grabbed the ball in the loose. Blocked, he swivelled and let loose with a huge right-foot centre kick from the left touchline that came down not far out from the All Blacks' goal-line at the River Taff end of the ground. Bob Scott and Ron Jarden turned and ran for it but, as fast as they were, they were not as fast as the Welsh wing, Ken Jones, who had sprinted for Britain at the Olympic Games in 1948 and within a year of the All Black test won the bronze medal in the 220 yards at the Empire Games in Vancouver.

Once again the All Blacks had been beaten in the last minutes,

GETTING THE BETTER OF GARETH

Gareth Edwards agrees with the New Zealand view. Great halfback that he was, Edwards acknowledges that of all the times he and Sid Going opposed each other, Going came out on top.

'Yes, I would say that,' Edwards says after a bit of a pause. 'Mind you, I remember against the All Blacks once thinking that I wouldn't have minded playing with the back row the All Blacks had . . . then Sid might not have come out on top.'

Edwards and Going were opposing halfbacks in seven tests — the two of the Welsh series in 1969, four in the Lions series of 1971 (though Edwards lasted only seven minutes of the first test) and the Welsh test of 1972.

They also opposed each other when the All Blacks played Cardiff in 1972, the fabled Barbarians match of 1973 when Edwards scored the try that's still remembered with dewy eyes as one of the best rugby has seen, and the 1974 unofficial test against Wales when Edwards was captain.

The first All Black halfback Edwards confronted was Chris Laidlaw in 1967, but thereafter it was always Going.

'I played against Chris, Dawie de Villiers and of course any number of European scrumhalves but over that period Sid would have been the most difficult I played against. They were great confrontations.

'Of course I didn't go out on the field with the aim of beating Sid Going. I went out with the aim of beating the All Blacks and I'm sure Sid would have felt the same way. And I'm sure he would also agree that for a scrumhalf to shine, he had to be behind the better pack.

'In 1971, for example, Sid had the benefit of a better pack performance in the second test and I had the benefit in the third and that was the way the results went.'

Edwards says he had the utmost respect for Going, on and off the field. 'As I say, he was the best I played against and, yes, he probably had the edge on me in the games we played. Off the field, he was pretty quiet but we had a few chats and got along fine.'

Enduring foes. Gareth Edwards, this time in 1971, gets ahead of Sid Going. Ian Kirkpatrick is in the background.

KEITH MURDOCH: THE FINAL WORD

The full story of the Keith Murdoch saga of 1972 has never been told and probably never can be. Some of the principals involved have died and it seems improbable that Murdoch, living out his self-imposed exile somewhere in the vastness of Australia, will ever give his version of events.

The outline of the story is clear. Murdoch, after helping the All Blacks beat Wales in December 1972, went to the kitchen of the Angel Hotel in Cardiff late at night in search of food or drink or both. He was confronted by a security guard, Peter Grant, words were spoken and Grant ended the night with a black eye.

The next morning, the All Blacks' manager, Ernie Todd, reprimanded Murdoch and later the same day announced the team, including Murdoch, for the next match. So far so clear, but then the story got murky . . . Fact merged with rumour, speculation and conjecture.

Todd, so it was believed, changed his mind after talks with British officials and sent Murdoch home. Murdoch famously, so it was reported, stood at the door of the team's bus and said, 'Hooray, boys, I'm off.' They were the last words of Keith Murdoch, All Black.

He was escorted from Birmingham to London's Heathrow Airport and there put on a flight to Australia. When it stopped in Singapore, Murdoch disappeared, later surfacing in Australia, where he has been since, aside from a few unannounced visits home.

Todd, who had been ill during the three-month tour but didn't tell the players, died of cancer in November 1974, not quite two years after Murdoch's expulsion. Todd's version of events died with him.

In 1992, 20 years after, I wrote in a book, *Our National Game*, that Todd changed his mind about Murdoch staying on the tour because the chairman of the New Zealand union, Jack Sullivan, told him to. I wrote then: 'Sullivan told Todd to send Murdoch home on the next flight. Todd didn't argue but did ask Sullivan if he was sure. Sullivan affirmed he was.'

My source was impeccable, but must remain anonymous.

Sullivan's reason can now be revealed for the first time. It can now be said that the British officials gave Sullivan an ultimatum: send Murdoch home or we will demand Todd be replaced as manager. If neither happens, the tour is off.

The British officials were led by John Tallent, decorated army officer and schoolmaster, a midfield back for England in the 1930s, a man of just the right background to head the Four Home Unions Committee.

Tallent and Sullivan spoke on the phone about Murdoch first on the Monday after the Welsh match and Tallent said he would cable to Sullivan a full report of the Murdoch incident and the views of his committee. When the promised cable had not arrived by the Wednesday, Sullivan put through a call to Tallent. It was 4 p.m. New Zealand time, pre-dawn in England.

Sullivan had with him the secretary of the New Zealand union, Ray Morgan, and it's understood that Ces Blazey, the deputy chairman, was also in the room at the union's headquarters in the Huddart Parker Building in Wellington.

Morgan was present to record Sullivan's questions to Tallent and Sullivan repeated Tallent's answers so they also could be written down.

Sullivan began by asking Tallent to confirm remarks he had made in the earlier call on the Monday.

Sullivan: Can I quote you to [the NZRFU] Council as saying that the team was undisciplined?

Tallent: Yes.

Sullivan: That if Murdoch did not go home the tour was in jeopardy?

Tallent: Yes.

Sullivan: If Ernie did not make the decision to send Murdoch home he was in jeopardy?

Tallent: Yes.

Tallent added that if Murdoch did not leave the tour, the Four Home Unions would request a change of manager.

Morgan's transcript of the conversation continues: 'Mr Tallent went on to say that the security guard involved in the incident had appeared on television and had said, "Now Murdoch was going home he would not take any civil action."

'Mr Tallent stated that Ernie was a most charming man, well liked, but in his view he felt that Ernie finds it very difficult to discipline the team.'

Sullivan told Tallent he had spoken to Todd and that Todd was upset by press reports about the misbehaviour of the team off the field and he did not accept the behaviour should be criticised.

Morgan's transcript continues:

'Mr Sullivan said "to recap the whole position once more and to confirm the telephone conversation of two days ago, was this the position?"

"a. Unless Murdoch went home, the tour was in jeopardy? Answer — yes.

"b. If Murdoch did not go home the manager was in jeopardy? Answer — yes. They would ask for a replacement of the manager."'

Morgan recorded Tallent as saying that as a result of his conversation with Sullivan, he would not be sending a cable because he did not think it should be put in writing.

Sullivan thanked Tallent for not making public his views and remarked that the public view in New Zealand was that the union council, and he personally, were being accused of overruling the manager to send Murdoch home.

A few hours before the call, Murdoch had left London on Qantas flight 744 for Sydney, where he was due to connect with Qantas flight 368 to Wellington. But when the Sydney-bound aircraft landed in Singapore for refuelling, Murdoch left it.

He checked into the Mandarin Hotel in Singapore as 'Mr Oliver'.

There the trail ended until he resurfaced over the years at various places in the Australian outback, although he made regular trips back to New Zealand and once spent several months working on a farm in east Otago.

The last picture show. This is the last photo of Keith Murdoch taken in Britain in 1972.
Inset: Where it all happened, the Angel Hotel in Cardiff.

once again the whole of Wales rejoiced even though there was a seemingly general acknowledgement that the All Blacks on the whole were the better team.

Wales have not rejoiced since, at least not in the presence of New Zealanders.

Tests in the 1960s were tight affairs and the scores reflected that. It was 6–0 to New Zealand in 1963, a penalty goal from Don Clarke and a dropped goal by Bruce Watt giving the All Blacks their first win on the Arms Park. Four years later, Brian Lochore's unbeaten side swung the ledger the All Blacks' way for the first time when they won 13–6. This test was the first in which the formidable Welsh inside backs Barry John and Gareth Edwards were paired, a test debut preceded by their famous meeting on the training field. 'How do you want it, Barry?' Edwards asked. 'You throw it and I'll catch it,' John replied.

Edwards was in awe of the All Blacks and recalled how hard and uncompromising they were. But there was also some sensitivity for a young lad from the valleys. Edwards recalled being trapped in a ruck alongside the All Black flanker, Graham Williams. 'He grabbed my shirt and pulled me towards him, just underneath him,' Edwards said. '"Get under there kid and keep your head in or you'll get hurt",' Edwards said Williams told him.

France had won the Five Nations, what the British like to call the International Championship, capitals and all, the previous two years, but with the advent of players such as Edwards and John, forwards such as Delme Thomas, Graham Price and Mervyn Davies, and a long-haired fullback better known then as a tennis player, J.P.R. Williams, Wales were on the threshold of another golden era. They won the championship in 1969, losing only to France, and looked forward to touring New Zealand for the first time, confident they would be able to transfer the power of their deeds from the Northern to the Southern Hemisphere.

In this they were mistaken. If Wales felt they were approaching a peak, the All Blacks were already at the summit of their endeavours. Under the coaching of Fred Allen and the captaincy of Brian Lochore, the All Blacks had not lost a test since 1965; they had a settled, winning side, each player confident in the ability of his team-mates. They were the most consistent side in world rugby at the time, as near to unbeatable as any All Black team before or since.

It was a one-sided contest. The first test in Christchurch was won 19–0 — mirroring the Invincibles' score against Wales in 1924 — and the second in Auckland an even more comprehensive All Blacks win, 33–12. It was Wales' heaviest defeat since going down to Scotland 35–10 at Inverleith in Edinburgh in 1924. The match was something of a benefit for the All Blacks fullback, Fergie McCormick, who kicked 24 points, a world record for an individual in a test match at the time.

While New Zealanders wallowed in the victories and wondered at the reputations of some of the Welsh players that had preceded them, for the Welsh the two matches were a lesson that produced benefits two years later, though for the Lions rather than for the Welsh.

It seems ironic for the Welsh that they could be the cornerstone of the Lions successes in New Zealand in 1971 and South Africa in 1974 but could still not beat the All Blacks when wearing the red jerseys of Wales. They tried and failed in 1972, tried and failed in 1978, tried and failed in 1980. They had their chances in the first two of those matches but almost none in the third, the match that was the showpiece of the Welsh union's centenary.

A master of his trade. Andrew Mehrtens against Wales at Wembley in 1997.

Controversy accompanied the All Blacks as it seems to do when in Wales. There was none from the match in 1972, won by the Keith Murdoch try for New Zealand and Joe Karam's boot, but the aftertaste of the match lingers still as Murdoch lives out his days in chosen anonymity somewhere in Australia.

The 1978 match rankles still in Welsh minds. Clem Thomas, the hero of the Welsh win a week before Christmas in 1953, rushed to the BBC outside broadcast van immediately after the match and demanded, in the peremptory manner he could adopt, to see a replay of the lineout that led to Brian McKechnie's winning penalty goal. 'Look,' he said, jabbing a finger at the screen, 'Haden cheated, Oliver cheated, Quittenton was wrong.' They're charges that have echoed down the years, charges that have been disproved, denied but still levelled. But none of the charges have altered the fundamental fact that the All Blacks won the test by 13 points to 12.

It was the last hurrah of the remnants of the great Welsh era. Edwards and John had already gone; others would soon go. By 1980, J.P.R. Williams and players such as Price and Derek Quinnell were still there, but their time had come. The All Blacks won 23–3 and there were grizzles about Nicky Allen, a superb first five-eighth whose career was all too brief, failing to force the ball for his try and Stu Wilson passing illegally off the ground for Hika Reid's try, but the reality was that the Welsh realised the All Blacks were accomplished winners and the score could have been much, much greater.

Wales as a power in rugby was an endangered species.

Wales then were well over their peak and had begun their inexorable slide down the other side. In later matches between the All Blacks and Wales, in a semifinal of the World Cup in 1987, on the tours of 1988 and 1989, in the cup in South Africa in 1995, at Wembley in 1997 and then in Cardiff in 2002, it was a different Wales. Wales as a power in rugby was an endangered species.

There was sadness within Wales itself, but sadness, too, wherever there is appreciation of fine rugby and of a proud rugby nation.

The great Welsh bard, Dylan Thomas, one of the finest writers of the 20th century, was not known as a great rugby man but as a Welshman from Swansea, he must surely have had some passion for the game.

He once wrote a short story called 'Reminiscences of a Childhood'. Reflecting on the way they were, he wrote: 'I do not need to remember a dream. The reality is there. The fine, live people, the spirit of Wales itself.'

The spirit, rugby should like to think, is surely just in abeyance.

LESSONS OF '69

The two-test thumping of Wales by the All Blacks in 1969 was a turning point for British rugby, one of the greats of Welsh rugby, Phil Bennett, firmly believes.

'We went to New Zealand as Five Nations champions,' he says. 'We were passionate Welshmen. We believed rugby was our everything and that we could match anything.

'The results on that tour shook Wales rigid. We had gone out there so confident.'

Led by a 1966 Lion, lock Brian Price, the Welsh squad included older players and a few of whom much more would be heard, men such as Bennett himself (a reserve in the two tests), Gareth Edwards, Barry John, Gerald Davies, Mervyn Davies, John Taylor. All but Bennett returned to New Zealand two years later with the 1971 Lions.

'We were in New Plymouth, I think, when the All Black team for the first test was named,' says Bennett. 'No Waka Nathan, no Kel Tremain. We were amazed. How can you drop these legends?'

In the first test in Christchurch, the All Blacks won 19–0 and the second in Auckland 33–12.

'We were shattered,' Bennett says. 'I remember in Auckland Maurice Richards got a try. He stood up Fergie McCormick to score. It was the only time in the match that he got the ball. The All Blacks were just awesome, no other word for it.'

The Welsh players went home subdued and worried. 'We thought we were the best,' Bennett says, 'but we were shown how good the best could be.'

He says the lessons learnt from the 1969 tour laid the groundwork for the successful visit by the Lions in 1971, the only Lions team to win a series in New Zealand.

'I think that what it taught us most was that whatever we could do in the Five Nations, we had to do better in New Zealand,' he says. 'We knew we had to step up two or three gears to compete against New Zealand. We knew we had to be fitter and faster. It was through that experience in 1969 that Wales and the rest of Britain knew what had to be done in 1971. If we'd been more competitive against the All Blacks in 1969, even taken a test off them, I'm sure the Lions wouldn't have been so successful. The All Blacks did British rugby a favour in 1969, I'm sure of that.'

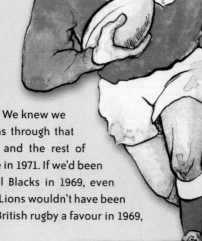

Phil Bennett in Llanelli uniform.

United They Stand

If rugby was the sport of choice in the United States, the Lions wouldn't be the Lions at all. They'd be the British All Stars — because that's what they're intended to be and what they sometimes have in fact been. They're one of the marquee teams in world rugby, rarely seen and valued all the more because of that rarity. Combined teams are unusual in rugby but the might of the world — or as much might as could be mustered — was brought to New Zealand in 1992 to help celebrate the centenary of the New Zealand union.

BRITISH ISLES

Since 1996, New Zealand have played Australia and South Africa at least twice each year. The Australians have been played at least once a year since 1982. Each were once infrequent opponents, especially South Africa, and tours by them to New Zealand or the All Blacks touring were events keenly anticipated, avidly followed and reviewed, sometimes fondly, sometimes less so.

The frequency of contact now, while it may be a commercial imperative, has lessened the attraction. Stadiums are still filled by Australia and South Africa, television viewing figures are presumably high and there is still a great deal of public interest when these old foes meet on home fields or foreign fields.

But some of the attraction has gone. There's no mystique about a South African team whose players, because of the Super 12, are as familiar to New Zealanders as any of the All Blacks. There's little mystery, little wonder about the unknown because most of it is known.

Test buildups are measured in days, even hours, rather than in weeks or even months when Australia or South Africa would come on their long tours and play twice a week through the provinces. It's unlikely small boys, and even big men, anymore lovingly clip stories about the teams out of newspapers and paste them into scrapbooks, decorating the pages with coloured flags or coats of arms they've clipped from match programmes. It's unlikely school classes adopt particular players, compile scrapbooks containing every word written about their designated player and then present them to them at the end of the tour.

Newspapers don't run big photos of the whole team anymore, nor do they reproduce players' autographs, nor do they publish maps of New Zealand with itineraries carefully drawn in.

South Africa and Australia, once the unfamiliar and the infrequent, are now familiar, frequent but fleeting visitors.

Alone of the big tours, the Lions remain as they were. The mystique and the allure remain firmly in place.

In close on 100 years, the Lions or whatever name was used to mean combined British teams have toured New Zealand only 10 times; young New Zealanders have grown up without seeing a Lions team; some great All Blacks have never had the opportunity to play against the Lions.

The first two British teams to play New Zealand were in 1904 and 1908 and neither was remotely representative of the strength

of British rugby at the time. The next, the first of the official British Isles teams, wasn't until 1930 and there wasn't another until 1950 (though there was the small matter of a world war getting in the way). Then not again until 1959, then 1966, 1971, 1977, 1983 and 1993. The Lions are next due in 2005 and though it won't be a tour on the old grand scale of 25 or so matches and four tests, it will still be a tour by today's standards, possibly 10 or 11 games including three tests.

The first British team came to New Zealand in 1888, though that was a purely private venture with the express purpose of making money for its promoters and showing off to the colonials how rugby could be played (they also played Australian rules in Victoria). New Zealand views on what lessons the British brought with them differed.

Tom Ellison, one of the seminal figures of early New Zealand rugby, was sniffily dismissive. 'Beyond learning the minor, though petty and effective, trick of feign passing from Mr [Tommy] Haslam, and learning to disregard the strict laws of offside play as regards forwards in the scrum, I challenge anyone to tell me what else the 1888 side taught us.'

The opposing view came 18 years later from the captain and vice-captain of the Original All Blacks, Dave Gallaher and Billy Stead, who wrote in their book, *The Complete Rugby Footballer*. 'It was left to [Andrew] Stoddart's British team to show Maoriland the finer points of the game and the vast possibilities of combination. The exhibitions of passing which they gave were most fascinating and impressive to the New Zealander, who was not slow to realise the advantages of these methods. One may safely say that, from that season, dates the era of high-class rugby in the colony.'

The 1888 team didn't play a combined New Zealand side — it

Darkie Bedell-Sivright

was four years before the New Zealand union was formed — and the debut of British tests against the All Blacks didn't take place until 1904, when a Scotsman, Darkie Bedell-Sivright (his real given names were David Revell, but he was always referred to by the unflattering Darkie) led a mixed bag of ordinary forwards and sparkling backs. In that at least, it set the tone for Lions tours because if there is one abiding perception of Lions teams in New Zealand, it is that they often had brilliant backs but very seldom had forwards who could contain, let alone dominate, the All Blacks.

For all their lack of real quality, the prospect of the All Blacks — though they hadn't acquired that nickname then — playing a British team created enormous interest throughout New Zealand. The crowds in Wellington when the British team arrived for the only test were said to have been greater than those who lined the streets to see the Duke and Duchess of Cornwall (later King George V and Queen Mary) in 1901.

'They were men from the hills, valley or plain, from provincial township or wayback station,' the *Evening Post* in Wellington recorded, 'farmers, miners, sawmillers, clerks, bank managers, all sorts and conditions of men bent on a pilgrimage to the altar of the deity of rugby. And the pilgrims did their penance right well. Cheerfully submitting to crowded trains and sleeping rooms, blocked gates and long weary waits, such as some of them had never asked themselves to perform before. What need to proclaim the powers of a king to whose court the whole countryside flocked unbidden and came in a solid phalanx to the altar of inter-imperial honours.'

The All Blacks on attack during the only test of the 1904 British tour — and the first test in New Zealand.

The menu for the formal test dinner after the first test to be played in New Zealand.

Adding to the occasion was the fact it was the first test to be played in New Zealand. All previous matches by New Zealand at home had been against Australian state sides. But now, after the first test in Sydney the year before, this was the debut of international rugby in New Zealand.

The All Blacks had assembled at Days Bay across Wellington Harbour from the city earlier in the week and Billy Wallace recalled the launch trip across the harbour on the Saturday. Ferries heading towards Wellington were all full and those going in the opposite direction were empty. One of the latter trailed a huge banner from its mast saying, 'Good luck to our NZ reps'.

New Zealand won 9–3 and according to one of the forwards, Bernard Fanning, it was a great day. 'In the first half the New Zealand backs tried to win but were not perfect on the day,' he wrote. 'The wind was with them but at halftime New Zealand had nothing much to show for it. Then the New Zealand forwards took

charge. They buried the British pack. It was surge, surge, surge all the time . . . forwards won that game if forwards ever won.'

The aftermath was as enthusiastic as the prelude. 'Never have the shifting fortunes of the game been followed with so eager a gaze,' the *Evening Post* said. 'And never in these parts has a result been so awaited even in remote hamlets, with such breathless interest. In Wellington itself the concourse of many thousands have been sufficient testimony that rugby is king.'

If rugby was the king, it was a pretender to the throne that precipitated the next British tour, in 1908. The New Zealand and New South Wales unions were concerned about the beginnings of league and the English union, which then ruled the administrative roost, was alarmed by what it feared was a dilution of amateurism as the two far-off colonies grappled with keeping players from their rival offshoot. So it came up with the idea of another tour but neither Scotland nor Ireland was interested. It was therefore an Anglo-Welsh team that was assembled and it was even less representative of the strength of British rugby than its predecessor had been. The All Blacks won the first and third tests convincingly — the scorelines of 32–5 and 29–0 were thrashings for the time — but the second test in Wellington in dreadful conditions was drawn three-all. The Anglo-Welsh manager, George Harnett, didn't endear himself to New Zealanders when he criticised the play of the wing forward as 'nothing but an obstructionist and always offside'.

The wing forward was the *cause célèbre* between British and New Zealand rugby for the first 30 years of the 20th century. New Zealand had developed the position as a means of getting quicker and more effective possession to the backs. The wing forward put the ball into the scrum and hovered on the outskirts of the scrum while the halfback delivered the ball. The New Zealand argument was that the ball was hooked so quickly in the 2-3-2 scrum formation that the halfback couldn't put the ball in and get behind the scrum in time to receive it. The British view was that the wing forward was nothing more than a cheat, hovering offside and hindering the opponents' forwards and inside backs. One element in the argument was that the laws were framed and policed mainly by the English union and that New Zealand had no ability to influence the lawmaking.

All of this came to a head when the first full British team toured New Zealand in 1930. The manager was a 59-year-old insurance company director, James Baxter — 'Bim' to his friends — who had played rugby for England, had won a silver medal in yachting at the 1908 Olympic Games and had refereed six rugby tests. He was also an England representative on the International Rugby Board. He was a stickler for protocol — each of his players had to buy their own dinner suits so they could dress for dinner on the ship to New Zealand — and for the laws of the game as framed in London. Colonial infractions and inventions were not to be tolerated.

The Lions opened their tour in Wanganui and Baxter was appalled when the local players left the field at halftime for a cup of tea. He was horrified by the play of the local wing forward, or 'rover' as he was called.

A rare souvenir of the British team's tour in 1904.

The Lions opened their tour in Wanganui and Baxter was appalled when the local players left the field at halftime for a cup of tea.

At the aftermatch function, Baxter in his speech called the man that most emotive of sporting words, a cheat. 'I won't say he is on the borderline,' Baxter said, 'he is over it and must be discouraged. He causes irritation to both sets of forwards. I am not speaking of the man playing in the position today, but of a man playing in that position. It is contrary to the spirit of rugby football.'

New Zealand through the 1920s had tried in vain to gain membership of the International Rugby Board and, when spurned, sought an 'imperial conference' at which the laws of rugby, and other matters of mutual interest such as tours, could be discussed. That, too, was spurned. As Baxter made clear, it had no choice but to follow the dictates from London or not play.

'The rules under which we play are laid down by the International Board and, in our opinion, are good enough for the average young man to play under,' he said. 'We don't intend to alter them one jot. Those who don't want to play under them can stay outside.'

Within a year, though, the laws were altered more than a jot.

At the urging of Baxter, the scrum laws were changed to insist that three players had to play in the front row, thus wiping out the New Zealand formation of 2-3-2 and the wing forward.

It wasn't just New Zealanders who were at fault, though. Ted McKenzie, one of the New Zealand selectors and a member of the New Zealand union's management committee, let fly with some retaliation at the test dinner in Auckland.

'I will not pretend our players are perfect,' he said. 'They may on occasions be guilty of lapses . . . But I will say that the British team is a fine enough side to win matches without resorting to obstruction and similar tactics, which may, or may not, be intentional. But I must say that some of the instances of obstruction appeared to have been deliberately studied.'

For all Baxter's fulminating, the Lions were a popular side on and off the field. It still wasn't the best of British because the Four Home Unions Committee had to ask nearly 100 players if they were available until they got the 29 they needed. There were still players of considerable merit, though, especially men such as the England first five-eighth, Roger Spong, Welshman Jack Bassett who could play at fullback or halfback, centres Harry Bowcott of Wales and Carl Aarvold of England. Among the forwards there was none better than the Welsh flanker, Ivor Jones, who ran half the length of the field to set up the Lions' try, scored by wing Jack Morley, that won them the first test.

Although some of the All Blacks were said to be past their best, especially George Nepia, Bert Cooke and Cliff Porter, their best was still too good for the British on the rest of the tour because New Zealand won the remaining three tests, the third by the widest margin, 22–8.

Evidence of the Lions' popularity off the field was provided by Bowcott, who told Welsh journalist Peter Jackson in the late 1990s: 'They worshipped us. Entertainment and hospitality were laid on for us and I can't ever remember having to buy a drink . . . wives would be chasing us and their husbands would be pleased if we looked after them. There was one woman who followed me all over both islands with the permission of her old man. He thought it was an honour and I never abused it. All the fun of the fair!'

The tour was also a decisive one for British Isles rugby. The cumbersome official name, The British Isles Rugby Union Team, was taken over by the simpler Lions, named for the three lions that adorned their blue playing jersey. It was also the end of the blue jerseys because New Zealand changed to white only reluctantly for the series and after they had learnt the British had no alternative. The team that came to New Zealand in 1950 was the first to wear the distinctive scarlet jersey with the crest depicting the four British Isles unions and, as a nod to Ireland, the dark blue socks were given a green turnover. It's only in recent years that, in further acknowledgement of Ireland, the Lions have been decreasingly called 'the British Lions'. Sometimes they've been referred to as the British and Irish Lions, sometimes the British Isles Lions, since British Isles is a geographic not a political description. Common sense dictates they be either the British Isles or the Lions.

The 1950 Lions and their successors in 1959 seemed both to epitomise the general belief that British Isles sides had brilliant backs but forwards who were either not good enough or not cohesive enough to sufficiently control matches against the All Blacks. Certainly the names of players who transcended the years were backs rather than forwards — in 1950 players such as Jack

The first year in which the All Blacks wore white. A lineout in the second test of the 1930 Lions series.

Kyle of Ireland, Ken Jones, Malcolm Thomas, Bleddyn Williams and Jack Matthews of Wales; or in 1959 who's more noted than the red-haired Irish wing, Tony O'Reilly? His fame has grown because of his international business success, but there was no doubting his rugby ability.

The first test in 1950 was drawn and the All Blacks won the other three, most memorably the third test in Wellington 6–3 after the All Blacks had lost two players because of injury (no replacements then) and captain and centre Ron Elvidge returned with a dislocated shoulder and scored the decisive try.

If one player stood out in the 1959 series, it was Don Clarke, the All Black fullback with such a prodigious boot that his kicking prowess sometimes overshadowed the general quality of his play as a fullback. His kicking of six penalties in the first test in Dunedin to beat the Lions' four tries provoked an outcry from British journalists on the tour and raised the spectre of what was then known as the differential penalty (introduced many years later as a free kick). There seemed some justice, from a New Zealand viewpoint at least, in the second test in Wellington when the All Blacks were saved from probable defeat by Clarke diving over for a spectacular try.

The Lions of 1966 were forgettable in the sense of their achievements but still popular off the field, as all their predecessors had been. The All Blacks won each of the four tests well and it was

HEDGING BETS IN 1950

**The naming of All Black teams has seldom been without some form of controversy or attendant drama.
It was certainly so in 1950 when the Lions were in New Zealand and the whole country was desperate to get a win to ease the memories of the six defeats the previous year.**

The first test against the Lions didn't provide it because the match was drawn 9–9 and the selectors, Tom Morrison, Merv Corner and Arthur Marslin, reacted with ruthless haste.

Though there was a fortnight until the second test in Christchurch, the three wise men — the adjective was disputed in some parts of New Zealand — named their next team almost while the first was still in the showers.

They hedged their bets, though, by naming several alternatives, giving no reason for doing so despite the ample time they had.

Vince Bevan of Wellington had played in the first test, but for the second the selectors couldn't for the moment make up their minds between Bevan or a young Taranaki halfback, Bernie Walsh.

Since the weekend between the two tests was the King's Birthday weekend, games on the Saturday and Monday afforded selectors time to have a harder look at their candidates. One was Taranaki against Wanganui, in which Walsh and another test candidate, Peter Henderson, were playing; and the other was a Wellington XV against Manawatu, in which Bevan played.

Morrison and Corner were in Wanganui for the first game, traditionally played in the morning, and drove to Palmerston North to see the second in the afternoon.

Walsh had the good luck to be playing inside George Beatty, who had played in the first test but been replaced by Laurie Haig of Otago in the second test team, but the bad luck to get involved in a collision with one of his wings, Roy Roper. He had to leave the field and have a gash in his chin stitched.

X-rays showed Walsh's jaw had been broken so his chance was gone.

Bevan, by contemporary accounts, didn't have a great game against Manawatu but gained his place in the second test team by default because of Walsh's injury.

Walsh was nevertheless still named in the reserves for the second test, though this was in the days when no replacements were allowed.

The unlucky Walsh and the other reserves still appeared in the official team photo, though curiously they wore plain black jerseys without any silver fern.

New Zealand at the peak of its rugby prowess. This was during the unbeaten reign of Fred Allen as coach and he could command and direct the services of such giants of the game as Colin Meads, Brian Lochore, Waka Nathan, Kel Tremain, Chris Laidlaw, Ian MacRae — they were at the crest of a wave while the Lions at best could just paddle around in the shallows.

They were not helped by having a captain, Mike Campbell-Lamerton, who had been chosen because of his leadership rather than playing abilities, but there were Lions who would loom larger in the future. Willie John McBride made his first appearance in the second test in Wellington; Mike Gibson, regarded as one of the greatest centres to play the game, played in each of the tests and a man who made it his life's work to study New Zealand rugby and adapt the lessons to his homeland, Jim Telfer, was either on the side of the scrum or at No 8 in three of the four tests.

New Zealand couldn't have known it at the time, but in 1966 and on the Lions' next venture, in South Africa in 1968, seeds were sown that would grow into their greatest triumph.

It came in 1971, an unforgettable tour marked by a level of public interest but without the burning intensity of the South African tour of 1956. New Zealand rugby was in something of a state of transition. Allen's rule came to an end at the close of the 1968 season and some players stayed in the game just long enough to go on the grand and fruitless quest to South Africa in 1970. The coach who took them to South Africa, Ivan Vodanovich, was still in

charge in 1971 and as likeable and as knowledgeable as he was, he was not regarded then, and has not been regarded since, as the type of coach who could match the feats of Allen or, as it turned out, the feats of the Lions coach, Carwyn James.

The Four Home Unions chose wisely for 1971. James had never coached Wales but it was a travesty that he had not; in an era in Britain when coaching was only just coming into vogue — captains previously had had to do the job, however well equipped they may or may not have been for it — James was out on his own. He could be a bit of a maverick, though. He didn't care too much for committee thinking and he had no time for the stuffiness of rugby administrators in England, many of whom were old public school types who continued to think the game was the thing and never mind the results. James wanted to win. As a counter to James the Four Home Unions chose as manager a medical doctor, Doug Smith, who had the type of pedigree beloved of the Four Home Unions: university educated, played for Scotland, served in the army. The third critical choice was that of captain and here James held sway. His choice, endorsed by the omnipotent FHU, was John Dawes, then captain of London Welsh and of Wales. Since the Welsh had won the Five Nations grand slam in 1971, since London Welsh included such players as J.P.R. Williams, Gerald Davies, Mike Roberts, Mervyn Davies and John Taylor, and since Wales would provide more players than any other country to the Lions, the choice was a sound one.

When the Lions and All Black test teams were named, any comparison by positions would probably have favoured the Lions. But that may have happened with earlier series, too,

The Boot's test. Don Clarke evades wing Peter Jackson in the first test of the 1959 series, in which Clarke scored 18 points to the Lions' 17.

GARETH HAMSTRUNG

The bus carrying the All Blacks to a test is as silent as the grave. Conversation is absent, words that are spoken are just the bare necessities. Not so for British teams and not so for the Lions.

When the 1971 Lions were on their bus on the short trip from their hotel in the centre of Dunedin to Carisbrook for the first test, they sang. But not just any song. They sang the old spiritual that became an anthem of the civil rights movement of the 1960s, 'We Shall Overcome'.

When they got to the end of the chorus, 'We shall overcome ... someday', the Lions changed the final word to 'today'.

It meant a lot to the Lions, but it had a personal, deeper meaning for halfback Gareth Edwards.

Two days before, when the Lions trained on the sandhills above St Kilda beach, Edwards had injured a hamstring. 'I'd never felt better than when we arrived in Dunedin,' Edwards recalls. 'I knew I was ready and that we were all ready to take it to the All Blacks. We finished off the training on the Thursday with a relay race and I ran the last leg for our team, down a sandhill and onto a rugby ground. About three-quarters of the way through the last leg, I stepped in a hole and felt my hamstring go.'

Edwards told coach Carwyn James who immediately told him to get treatment and tell no one. It was the Lions' big secret.

On the morning of the match, fellow Welshman and reserve halfback Chico Hopkins was warned to be ready. 'I didn't think I could play,' Edwards says. 'I'd learnt in previous matches against the All Blacks that you don't even bother against them unless you're 100 per cent fit and can give it everything. I told Carwyn I didn't think I was right and he said to give it a go.'

So Edwards took the field, as the All Blacks and all of New Zealand expected him to. But seven minutes into the match, Edwards went to drive off the injured leg, felt the pain shoot up it, and knew he couldn't do himself or his team justice.

'It was in the mind more than it was in the muscle,' he says. 'There was just that nagging feeling that I couldn't do my best, I couldn't play instinctively — there was a worry in the back of my mind.'

So off Edwards went and on went Hopkins.

Hopkins played a great game in the Lions win. He was ecstatic but Edwards was miserable.

'It was the lowest point in my rugby life,' he says.

Lions manager Doug Smith, a doctor, told Edwards he thought much of the injury was in his head, a comment that didn't do Edwards' morale a power of good.

'Of course there's a psychological factor when you've got an injury like that, and especially when you're on a mission against the All Blacks. All sorts of things creep into your mind — am I good enough? Am I going to fail at the ultimate challenge?'

Edwards' inside back partner, Barry John, says he was told by Smith to talk to Edwards and to tell him that if he wasn't right, he'd be replaced on the tour.

'I think that was a bit of licence by Barry,' Edwards says. 'There was no talk of a replacement and I was given every chance to come good. I was pretty down when I was feeling the loneliness of the injured player on tour but I knew that with rest and the proper treatment it would come right and it did.

'But I can tell you, playing the remaining tests and being a part of winning the series was a huge relief for me.'

Gareth Edwards

A BRUSH WITH THE ALL BLACKS

Gordon Brown, the popular Scottish lock known wherever he went as 'Broon frae Troon', used to tell of a little ritual he adopted on the morning of the two Lions tests in which he played against the All Blacks in 1971.

'I remember when I was brushing my teeth on the morning of the matches and I'd think, "I wonder how many of them I'll have tonight." '

Brown kept all his teeth, well, most of them, but he did run foul of Peter Whiting in the fourth test, which left Brown on the ground and Whiting upright. But it wasn't Whiting who worried him so much as Colin Meads.

Meads, Brown maintained in his after-dinner speeches, was the most ferocious warrior ever to don an All Black jersey.

'He was like an old, battle-scarred stag,' Brown used to say. 'The monarch of the glen with razor-sharp antlers. He was brutal, really, really brutal. Meads was never that careful what he stood on, and that could be his own team-mates as well as the opposition.' Brown, who played 30 tests for Scotland and nine for the Lions, died from cancer in 2001, aged 53.

THE DAY THE MOUSE ROARED

It was a sparkling Saturday afternoon, June 26, 1971, and it was a quarter of an hour into the first test between the British Isles and New Zealand. The Lions had been unbeaten in their lead-up provincial matches and they were said to have what previous Lions sides didn't have, a formidable forward pack to complement the gifted backs who were the stock in trade of combined British teams.

Anticipation of the test itself, of seeing an All Black team led by the redoubtable Colin Meads for the first time, and of seeing the Lions against the best New Zealand could put on the field, dragged a reported crowd of 45,000 into Carisbrook in Dunedin.

Crowd figures, then as now, were always best guesses and if 45,000 seemed a little on the exaggerated side for one of New Zealand's venerable grounds, there could be no arguing that the place was full.

Neither could there be any arguing that after quarter of an hour, with still no score posted on the old wooden scoreboard at the far end of the famed Carisbrook terrace, thousands of eyes would have been locked on the Lions as they took play down into All Black territory for the first time.

The All Blacks, who'd pretty much controlled play up until then, scrambled their defence. Eyes would have been locked on the All Black No 8, Alan Sutherland from Marlborough, as he scooped up the ball within the All Blacks' in-goal area.

Among the eyes was one pair that belonged to someone who could do something about it: Ian McLauchlan, the Scottish loosehead prop whose technique and strength belied his size and earned him the nickname of Mighty Mouse.

'I remember the ball getting back and Alan picking it up and seeming to take a fortnight to kick it,' McLauchlan recalls. 'I followed up instinctively because I knew there's always a chance of a charge-down or when it's a forward kicking the ball going off the side of the boot.'

McLauchlan went in with arms up, Sutherland kicked and the ball careered into the upraised arms. In such circumstances, it takes a second or two for anyone to work out where the ball has gone. The ball is no longer on its expected track and players get disorientated. McLauchlan seemed to recover first, saw the ball heading for the corner in the damp shadow of the Rose Stand and he chased it and flopped on it.

In the context of the game and of the series, as it turned out, it was a critical try. Within that try seemed to be embodied the fortunes and the quick thinking of the Lions and the ill-luck that dogged the All Blacks. Much of the test had gone the way of the All Blacks. They attacked and attacked again but it was the Lions who won.

'They threw everything at us but the kitchen sink,' Lions lock Willie John McBride remarked in the dressing room. 'Hang on, Willie John,' Irish prop Sean Lynch rejoined, 'I think I got hit by the kitchen sink.'

McLauchlan's try was memorable for the Lions' cause, memorable, too, for McLauchlan.

'Among rugby players in Scotland,' he says, 'the try historically is not all that significant. It's probably been forgotten in Scotland. But it was very significant for the Lions and very special for me — I never scored another one but if I had to score only one try in internationals, I'm glad it was that one.'

The mood in the Lions dressing room at Carisbrook was euphoric, as McLauchlan recalls it, but he felt that mood may have led to the Lions' undoing in the second test in Christchurch, won 22–12 by the All Blacks.

'After that win in Dunedin,' he says, 'some thought we couldn't lose in Christchurch and that of course is why we lost. Defeat just never entered the heads of some of my team-mates and when you get that sort of attitude within a team, it rubs off on the others.'

McLauchlan thinks the Lions actually played better in the second test than they had in the first. 'But so did the All Blacks and the thing that beat us was overconfidence,' he says. 'We could have gone through New Zealand unbeaten if some of the players had been more realistic.'

Despite that self-assuredness among some players, McLauchlan says one of the secrets to the 1971 team's success was the efficient management by men such as manager Doug Smith, coach Carwyn James and captain John Dawes, and the quality of the feeling between players.

'The great thing about Smith, James and Dawes was that they were never over the top with the players,' McLauchlan recalls. 'They never got that excited about anything.

'The management and camaraderie within the team was excellent. We used to have a standing rule on the tour that no one could sit with their fellow countrymen — the different nationalities had to mix in to avoid any possibility of cliques developing and that worked brilliantly. At the beginning, with seven London Welsh players in the squad, some of us thought that would be impossible to achieve but it was done . . . it was remarkable and we've all remained firm friends ever since.'

McLauchlan looks back on 1971 with nothing but the fondest of memories. 'I thought I'd died and gone to heaven,' he says. 'The Lions won a series in New Zealand for the only time, I scored the only try in the first test, we were a good team on and off the field, we met nice people throughout New Zealand, it was impossible to get bored . . . ah, what a tour.'

Gotcha! Ian McLauchlan scores the critical try in the first test of the 1971 series.

especially in 1950. This Lions team was different because with Smith, James and Dawes, allied with hard heads such as McBride and Ian McLauchlan, they believed they could beat the All Blacks. Self-belief at the highest level of sport is a powerful factor and it's one that's often been lacking when visiting rugby teams have had to confront the All Blacks. Opponents have known they're not just facing 15 men on the field, but generations of tradition and heritage. The Lions set that aside. Those Welsh players who had been in New Zealand in 1969 had learnt their lessons well and they had overcome the 'gee whiz'

factor. They also knew they were at least the equal of the players they were opposing.

Gerald Davies, the stylish Welsh wing, summed up the thinking: 'You never beat a New Zealand pack, though you might be the equal of them. One problem we've always had in this country . . . is that somewhere along the line it becomes a mental thing. That's what happened in 1971. We grew in confidence; we came to believe it was possible to beat the All Blacks.'

Before the first test in Dunedin, the most critical, James accurately predicted to his players that the All Blacks would

GOAL THAT STUNNED A NATION

J.P.R. Williams, the Welsh and Lions fullback who sometimes seemed fearless and sometimes had a flair for the dramatic, kicked just one dropped goal in his 62-test career.

For New Zealanders, it could have been the most significant score in Williams' life.

It was in the last test of the 1971 British Isles series. The Lions had won two tests, the All Blacks one. The All Blacks needed to win to square the series; the Lions just had to draw to win it.

After about 15 minutes of the second half, the score was tied at 11–11. The ball went to Williams 45 metres out. He stopped, propped and let rip with a dropkick that may not have got points for style but gained maximum value for accuracy.

Ecstatic, Williams waved to the Lions party in the No 1 stand.

Such a demonstrative gesture was not as common then as it is now and Williams was of the old school, head down and trot back into place. Whether triumph or disaster, he treated them the same.

So what was different this time?

The difference was that Williams before the match had been given some razzing by his team-mates about the lack of a dropped goal in his otherwise considerable repertoire.

Williams himself recalls that this happened in the bus on the way to the ground (British teams, unlike New Zealand, do not usually ride in sombre silence to a test match).

Williams says he told his team-mates in the bus that he would kick a dropped goal. 'This produced a great uproar because I never seemed to have dropped goals as part of my repertoire,' he recalled. 'So it was taken as a bit of a joke. I can't for the life of me think what prompted me to say such a thing.'

Hence the waving to the No 1 stand.

One of Williams' team-mates, prop Ian McLauchlan, recalled it a little differently. He remembered the conversation as being the night before at the Royal International Hotel in Victoria Street in downtown Auckland (a hotel that was often the base for touring teams but is no longer with us).

'A few of us were chatting the night before the match and someone told J.P.R. he couldn't be regarded as the complete fullback until he dropkicked a goal,' McLauchlan recalled. 'So the very next day he goes out

Some joke. J.P.R. Williams shows he does have a dropped goal in his repertoire — fourth test, 1971.

and shows us he could do it.'

The Williams kick took the score to 14–11 but not long after Laurie Mains levelled the scores at 14–14 and the match ended in the draw that's part of rugby history.

It was enough for the Lions to win the series, but not good enough for either Williams or McLauchlan.

'I feel we played better rugby,' Williams says, 'but we just weren't hungry for points. Maybe we believed that winning was just asking too much of ourselves.'

McLauchlan agreed. 'We were the better team but we didn't play better,' he says. 'We should have won that match and the series victory would have been much more emphatic.'

From a New Zealand viewpoint, it was emphatic enough.

Sid Going takes the blindside from a scrum in the third test in 1971. Alex Wyllie had peeled off from No 8 to be in support and Bob Burgess is outside him. The All Black flanker is Ian Kirkpatrick and Lions flanker Derek Quinnell starts moving across.

probably dominate them in the forwards but they could be beaten by strong and unrelenting defence and by accuracy among the backs. It was the way it was. The All Black forwards, led by Meads in his final series, did dominate the Lions and did make all the play in the first half. But the Lions took their chances, none more than when McLauchlan charged down an Alan Sutherland kick to score the only try of the match.

The Lions also had Barry John. They'd had gifted first five-eighths before, but it was John who became the king. He could stand deep and take a lordly overview of a situation before deciding what he'd do next. Sometimes he'd kick for touch, sometimes he'd kick for territory, making the All Black fullback, Fergie McCormick, run hither and yon. John held the string. McCormick was on the end of it. He could glide through gaps that didn't seem to be there. And he could kick goals in a manner that few New Zealanders had seen before.

The All Blacks, through tremendous efforts by the forwards and especially flanker Ian Kirkpatrick, won the second test well but the Lions confessed later — much later — they were not too worried. They felt they'd played badly because after the win in Dunedin they got a wee bit complacent and complacency against any All Black team is a fatal malady. The decisive test was in

Wellington and there the Lions outplayed the All Blacks with John at his most regal, most commanding best. That left a test to play in Auckland and the All Blacks had to win to square the series; the Lions had to only draw to win it. And draw it they did.

The Lions still say that those few months in New Zealand were the greatest in their sporting lives, rivalled only by a similar few months in South Africa in 1974 when the Lions won a series there as well. It was a great period for the Lions but then they had great players to call on. McBride says it was a privilege to play in such teams — 'I just love repeating the names of those backs — Edwards, John, Duckham, Bevan, Gibson, Dawes and J.P.R. Williams — when will we see their like again?'

It's not just McBride who wonders that.

If the 1971 Lions were a great success in terms of their results and in terms of their popularity with the New Zealand public, their 1977 successors were the opposite. Their captain, Phil Bennett, who had replaced John as the Welsh and Lions No 1 first five-eighth, admits that the time he spent in New Zealand was

THE LONELINESS OF A LIONS CAPTAIN

For dreary day after dreary day, Phil Bennett wished he was home. He was in a position to which every British rugby player must aspire, captain of the British Isles, but it was a slow-moving, soul-destroying grind.

It was the 1977 Lions' tour of New Zealand, the worst experience of Bennett's rugby life.

It wasn't just the weather, constant grey skies and rain. It wasn't just some divisions within the Lions party. It wasn't just newspaper coverage that seemed unusually aggressive. It wasn't just the rugby results. It was a combination of all things.

'Without a doubt, it was the worst time of my rugby career,' Bennett says. 'I'd been touring since I was 18, I'd been to different places, I'd been to New Zealand before and it was tremendous . . . but 1977 was just a very, very difficult time.'

'Possibly I shouldn't have gone on the tour.'

Bennett, one of those most likeable of men who will never say a bad word about a team-mate or an opponent and whose passion and love for rugby has been so enduring it should never be questioned, speaks of New Zealand in 1977 with a furrowed brow.

'There were so many things,' he says, his voice dropping as if relating any one of them would be a betrayal of the game.

There was his own loneliness and homesickness. The Welsh are a clannish people and are not exactly the Marco Polos of the rugby world. As captain,

Alone he stands. Phil Bennett and his 1977 Lions.

Bennett felt even more alone and far away.

'When you're sharing a room with a guy, you can have a bit of banter and it's not so bad,' he says. 'But because I was captain I had a room on my own. I was stuck in my room and could hear the wind and rain on the window and I'd be thinking, "It's sunny back home. I could be pushing my son in a park now. I should be pushing my son in a park now." I was very, very homesick.'

There were the newspapers, both New Zealand and British. 'Lions are lousy lovers' was one newspaper billboard. 'Lions wreck hotel' was another. 'There wasn't much truth, if any, attached to these stories but they got to me and they shouldn't have,' Bennett says. 'They got to other players, too. Wives and parents would ring up in the middle of the night because they were worried about what they were hearing.

'There seemed to me a kind of resentment by New Zealand against the Lions, almost as if it was payback for things that had happened in Britain. You were the buggers who got Keith Murdoch sent home, that sort of thing. When I was in New Zealand with Wales in 1969, we had a tremendous welcome wherever we went. But 1977 was just so different.

'I remember in Christchurch after the second test, which we won, two of our players came into the dressing room and they were drenched — their faces were wet, their jerseys were wet. I asked what had happened and one of them said, "This has never happened before — someone threw beer in my face." I asked him if he wanted to get the police involved or something but he said no, just let it lie. I was spat at when I walked off the field. Was this the same New Zealand that had welcomed us previously?'

Things were not all that smooth within the Lions party either. 'Maybe there were too many Welshmen,' says Bennett. 'There were 18 of us. The captain was from Wales and so was the coach. Perhaps that was too many and caused resentment. The weather was a factor, too. I'm not using it as an excuse, but it was the worst winter I've played in and that gets to you, day after day after day.

'A former Lion, a great player, was leading a tour party and writing a newspaper column. He'd written a few things that had annoyed us. He was

drinking in the bar one night with some of our players and when he went to buy a round, one of our players said not to be silly, they could just go to the team room and drink for free.

'So he stupidly went into the team room and walked over and grabbed a beer out of the fridge. The manager [George Burrell] saw it and let rip at him, asking how he could dare intrude on the team after writing the things he had and knowing that the team room was for players alone.

'We were too tense, too wound up.'

Bennett says he and coach John Dawes, who had captained the 1971 Lions, were great friends and former team-mates. But they, too, had a bust-up. 'I had a huge argument with John and that just reflected the siege mentality we were all feeling. It's the tradition on tours that the touring press have a dinner at the end of a tour and they invite the captain and the coach. We went on to Fiji from New Zealand and it was decided to have the dinner there. I wasn't keen on going but I knew the tradition and said I would go. When Dawes heard about it, he accused me of all sorts of things and said I shouldn't associate with them.'

He went anyway.

For all the problems, the Lions could have drawn the series, perhaps even won it, but maybe it was because of the problems that they won only the one test. Any rugby player who's been on tour knows well that what happens off the field can have a marked effect on what happens on it.

'But you know,' says Bennett, 'we could have come away two-two. It's a great regret that we didn't do better. We made a few mistakes in selection; some great Lions weren't chosen. I remember in the first test in Wellington we had a chance of winning. We had a five to two overlap and should have scored but then Grant Batty intercepted and that was it. We won the second, didn't play as well as we should have in the third, and we should have won the fourth. I felt our forwards were better than the All Black pack.

'It's a tour I regret; possibly I shouldn't have gone on it. That lives with you a long time . . . it will never go away. For me, that Lions tour was the biggest disappointment of my career.'

miserably unhappy for him. John Dawes went from being a smiling, affable, winning captain in 1971 to a surly, angry losing coach in 1977. The Lions' manager, George Burrell, had been genial and charming when he managed the Scots to New Zealand in 1975; when he managed the Lions, he became distrustful and moody. Andy Irvine, the brilliant Scottish fullback, says he's in no doubt that the 1977 tour changed Burrell for the rest of his life.

Why? Perhaps it was the incessantly wet weather that got to the Lions, as Bennett says, but it's not like it never rains in Britain and it's not like the All Blacks like training in the rain anymore than anyone else does.

The answer lay with the Lions themselves. They had the winning of the first test in Wellington until an intercept try by Grant Batty, playing in his last test, turned things around. A win then could have made a difference to the outcome. They won the second test and only in the third, when coach Jack Gleeson introduced new players such as Graham Mourie and fullback Bevan Wilson, could the All Blacks be said to have thoroughly deserved their win. The Lions could have won the fourth — the All Blacks were reduced at one point to three-man scrums with Frank Oliver moving from lock to prop. By contrast with the All Blacks' forwards shortcomings, the Lions' strength was their forwards. But they were obsessed with keeping the ball among the forwards and when they should have let the ball out and could have scored, they didn't. There was no better example of that than No 8 Willie Duggan holding the ball in a scrum for a pushover try and ultimately losing possession. The All Blacks were again in a transition period and fortunate to get away with a series win; the Lions had most of the aces in their pack but couldn't deal them.

The Lions of 1983 were captained, as with the 1966 team, by a player whose credentials had more to do with his leadership than his playing ability. Ciaran Fitzgerald of Ireland was a professional soldier whose job was to command. He had as an ally the redoubtable McBride, who managed the team and who, such was the force of his personality, may not have let coach Jim Telfer have as much influence as he should have, though Telfer, ever the diplomat, shies away from any such suggestion.

The fact is the Lions in all probability didn't field their best team in any of the four tests and that's fatal against All Blacks of any era. The All Blacks of 1983 were too good, too strong, too savvy for the Lions. They had speed and finishing ability out wide with Allan Hewson, Stu Wilson and Bernie Fraser; they had ball-winning ability and muscle with a pack that comprised Murray Mexted, Jock Hobbs, Mark Shaw, Andy Haden, Gary Whetton and the veteran front row of John Ashworth, Andy Dalton and Gary Knight. And they had, most crucially of all in the second test in Wellington, Dave Loveridge, a halfback who still deserves to be ranked among the best New Zealand has had. His performance in Wellington, when a freezing southerly whipped up the ground, was the

Take that! Lawrie Knight scores the deciding try in the fourth test of 1977.

COACH DENIED LIONS' SHARE

Scotland's everywhere man, Jim Telfer, was coach of the British Isles when they toured New Zealand in 1983. Telfer, who revelled in the nickname of 'Creamy', had been a flanker for Scotland and the Lions, had coached Scotland and in 1983 was a few steps along the path that led him 20 years later to a position of unassailable eminence in Scottish rugby.

But in 1983 he didn't always get his own way.

The manager of the Lions was the redoubtable Willie John McBride, a man of strong will and with a rugby experience even more noted than Telfer's.

McBride also was a selector.

The first indication that the selection panel (it also comprised captain Ciaran Fitzgerald) was not thinking as one came not long after the team for the first test in Christchurch was named.

Some eyebrows were raised about the selection and none more than at the choice of Welsh halfback Terry Holmes ahead of Scot Roy Laidlaw. There was also some thought that the Scottish flanker, Jim Calder, was more attuned to combating the All Blacks' play than was Peter Winterbottom of England.

But there it was, that was the team.

Russ Thomas, the genial Russ who had been the All Blacks' manager in 1978 and 1979 and who later became chairman of the New Zealand union and of Rugby World Cup, was the NZRFU's liaison man with the Lions.

That traditional role was there as a link between the touring team and the New Zealand union as well as supplying vital local knowledge along the way. Such men, when they did the job well, were indispensable aids to touring teams. And Thomas did the job superbly.

Since the test was in his hometown of Christchurch, he had sought and received permission from McBride to duck off home for a while. The final training had been held, the test team was about to be named, all was well in the Lions' world.

A few hours later, Thomas was driving back across Christchurch from his home in the north of the city to the Russley Hotel out by the airport when he heard the Lions test team on the radio.

Being a keen and dedicated rugby man, he'd already picked his own team, based on the form of what he'd seen in the lead-up matches and of his inside knowledge of the Lions camp.

Arriving back at the Russley, he saw Telfer in the foyer.

'Jim,' Thomas said excitedly, 'I just heard the test team. I got 12 out of 15!'

Telfer, who could look lugubrious, stared back at Thomas: 'Well, Russ,' he said in his soft Borders brogue, 'that's three more than I got.'

The Lions lost the first test 16–12 — and the second, third and fourth as well.

ultimate difference between the two teams. The All Blacks with the wind led 9–0 at halftime. As ever, Wellingtonians wondered whether the lead was enough. With Loveridge, it was. He controlled the game from the base of the scrum in the second half, whether by darting runs down the blindside, flat kicks over the top or by beseeching the forwards to keep the ball in hand. The score at halftime was the score at fulltime.

The All Blacks showed the full measure of their worth, and the relative worth of the Lions, by their 38–6 win in the fourth test.

A decade later, the Lions were in New Zealand again but the tours were not what they were. The 1983 Lions had played 18 matches with a full complement of four tests — historically, Lions played four tests in New Zealand and South Africa because that was the same number of tests the All Blacks or Springboks would play on a full tour of Britain and Ireland.

By 1993, though, the itinerary was only 13 matches and three tests. The new era had arrived.

It was a curious series that the All Blacks won two tests to one but which could so easily have been a second series win for the Lions. Their captain, Gavin Hastings, remains convinced they should have won the first test. With just a few minutes to go, the Lions led 18–17 and had possession. Their No 8, Dean Richards, was penalised at a midfield ruck and Grant Fox, slowly drawing the curtain on his superlative career, kicked the goal that won the match. Hastings says the penalty in that ruck should have been against the All Blacks, not for them. 'If we'd won that match, we'd have won the series,' he says.

It's a good argument because the Lions won the second test, in Wellington, through strong efforts in the forwards, especially by lineout jumpers Martin Bayfield and rookie Martin Johnson. They so dominated the lineouts that All Black Mark Cooksley developed a sudden injury at halftime and was replaced by Robin Brooke. The All Blacks' captain, Sean Fitzpatrick, remembers that test as his worst — it was his fumbling of the ball that led to Rory Underwood scoring the Lions' only try.

Stung by the defeat and hardened by widespread criticism, the All Blacks raced away to win the third test 30–13.

Lions of various tours of New Zealand are united in one belief: to beat the All Blacks in New Zealand, whatever the perceived quality of the All Blacks, everything has to go right, everything has to be planned and executed meticulously. Errors get punished. The remarkable series of 1971 aside, Lions history in New Zealand is littered with punishment.

Frank Bunce scores the All Blacks' only try in the first test against the Lions in 1993. Ieuan Evans has a hand on the ball; Will Carling is concerned but Va'aiga Tuigamala knows it's a try.

FITZY'S MATCH FROM HELL

Sean Fitzpatrick played 92 tests for the All Blacks and prided himself on his consistency. He hesitates about naming a best personal performance, but he has no doubts about his worst.

It was the second test against the British Isles in 1993, a test lost 7–20 by the All Blacks. Not only was it a stinker for Fitzpatrick, it wasn't a memorable performance by the team as a whole either, confirming a general trend that when the leaders in the team don't fire, the whole performance suffers.

'I remember saying to Gavin Hastings after the game, "You watch the country turn against us now," ' Fitzpatrick recalls.

'And they did. Nothing's changed. The All Blacks are always expected to win and when they don't, they get criticised. That feeling in the country was certainly evident after that test.'

Fitzpatrick couldn't remember playing as bad. 'I have no doubt it was my worst game in an All Black jersey,' he says. 'I remember coming away with the ball and dropping it and Rory Underwood ran half the length of the field, scored at the other end of the park. It was one of those days.'

While he finds it easy to pinpoint the game itself, it's less easy to explain why. 'They had not a bad team and we were still developing,' Fitzpatrick says. 'Maybe that was one of the factors. Laurie Mains was into his second year as coach and we were developing as a unit but some way off what we wanted to become. I remember Laurie was quite surprised by the level of criticism we got after that game.

'But I can't say why I in particular didn't play all that well. Perhaps it had something to do with taking my position for granted. Perhaps there wasn't enough of the fear of losing.'

The All Blacks, like after every loss, knew they'd played badly and Fitzpatrick says they didn't need to be told. 'While the criticism was part of being an All Black, we knew we had to regroup, we knew what we had to do — the pressure went on the tight five to perform. The public fingered the tight five, Laurie put the pressure on the tight five, so we knew what we had to do. We wouldn't play like that again.'

And they didn't. The All Blacks had an emphatic 30–13 win in the third test a week later.

It's all over. Sean Fitzpatrick and Gavin Hastings dress up in their opponents' jerseys at the end of the 1993 series.

WORLD XV

It was the year the world came to play at our place. It was the New Zealand union's centenary year of 1992 and, given New Zealand's significant role in world rugby and the underpinning impact of rugby on New Zealand life in general, a bit of a bash was called for.

After all, New Zealand was overdue for some self-indulgence. The 25th anniversary, in 1917, fell during the First World War, and the 50th anniversary, in 1942, during the Second World War. When New Zealanders, All Blacks and other rugby players among them, were dying in their thousands in foreign fields, no one gave celebration a thought.

The 75th anniversary came in 1967 and there was some celebration, but nothing like what was planned for the centenary. Australia played the All Blacks in Wellington and a slap-up dinner was held that night for as many people as could fit into the Wellington Town Hall.

Planning for the centenary began in the late 1980s at the instigation of Peter Wild. He was a character well known and well loved in rugby. He had been a member of the old New Zealand council, he had been the NZRFU's liaison man on several international tours and he had most famously managed the New Zealand Juniors when they beat the All Blacks in 1973. 'Keep your jerseys as souvenirs, boys,' a teary-eyed Wild told the players in their dressing room afterwards. 'Here's the bill,' a gimlet-eyed union secretary, Ray Morgan, told Wild later.

There was no one more ideal than Wild to urge the New Zealand union to start planning its centennial celebrations and no one more fitted to become the quickly formed centennial committee's secretary. His passion was boundless, his love of rugby profound and hadn't his brother, Chief Justice Sir Richard Wild, made the keynote address at the 75th celebrations in 1967?

The committee was no fobbing off exercise. It was high powered. It had a Canterbury luminary, Mervyn Barnett, as chairman, and among his committeemen were the council chairman, Eddie Tonks, former chairmen Ces Blazey, Jack Sullivan and Russ Thomas, plus former All Blacks and long-serving and diligent administrators Bob Stuart and Ivan Vodanovich.

It quickly became evident that no foundation stone was going to be left unturned in marking 100 years of organised rugby in New

Eroni Clarke on his test debut against the
World XV in Wellington in 1992.

Zealand. It was always implicit that some rugby would be played; after all, as the most classic of clichés had it, that was what the game was all about. The question was whether it would be a test against Australia, as it had been in 1967, or some other redoubtable opponent (South Africa, in the political climate of the time, was not a possibility), or whether it would be a festival match with players coming from all of New Zealand's opponents over the years.

What emerged from the committee discussions was that an overseas invitation team would be assembled — called the World XV — and it would play not one, but three matches against the All Blacks, coinciding as closely as possible with the 100th anniversary of the formation of the union on April 16, 1892. The committee also recommended to the union's council — and given the composition of the committee, the recommendation's adoption was a formality — that each of the three matches be given full test status.

This was the tricky bit. Tests or internationals are by definition country against country and the New Zealand union historically had been fastidious about not awarding test status willy-nilly (though it did so against All-America in 1913). It was argued unsuccessfully that the matches would really be festival matches and should not carry the burden of being tests; it was argued successfully that the occasion of the centenary was an auspicious one and that it would lessen the significance if they were not tests.

So tests they became, even if the April dates were indecently early in the season for the new coach, Laurie Mains, and the players he had to choose after seeing them in some of the matches in early season tournaments and in three formal trials in Napier.

While there was some disagreement about the status of the matches, there was none about who would bring the World XVs together — that great man of New Zealand rugby, Brian Lochore, who had captained and coached the All Blacks, became the manager and the two coaches were two unashamed admirers of New Zealand rugby, Ian McGeechan of Scotland and Bob Templeton of Australia.

While Mains watched the trials, and watched in utter despair as his choice of captain, Mike Brewer, was injured in the last of them, Lochore, McGeechan and Templeton ran up phone bills scouring the globe for players. South Africa by then was in the early stages of its post-apartheid era and the government was discreetly asked if South African players would get visas. They would. Indeed, the New Zealand union wasted no time and had already planned the All Blacks would go to South Africa later in the year.

By the second week in April, Mains had his All Blacks — with

Out of our way. Walter Little and Sean Fitzpatrick charge; Naas Botha seems to take evasive action.

Sean Fitzpatrick given the captaincy to begin the most enduring era of any captain — and Lochore, McGeechan and Templeton had their World XV. From the far corners of the world they came — Scotland, England, France, South Africa, Canada, Samoa, Australia, Japan, Argentina. Even though there was none from Ireland, Wales or Fiji, it was still a fair smattering of rugby representation and talent. Any side that could boast players such as Gavin Hastings of Scotland, Jeremy Guscott of England, Tim Horan, Jason Little, Nick Farr-Jones, John Eales and Willie Ofahengaue of Australia, Naas Botha of South Africa, Marc Cecillon and Olivier Roumat of France, was a formidable side.

On the face of it, the All Blacks should have had a decided advantage. They were a national team, united in their upbringing and purpose, and the World XV was a hotchpotch collection of players, albeit talented, brought together just for the occasion. But these were unusual times. The All Blacks of the previous year had ended the World Cup in some disarray and in various stages of disillusionment. Some players didn't want to continue, some players weren't asked to continue and others weren't sure. Mains had a rebuilding task on his hands and little time in which to do it.

The size of the task showed in the first game in Christchurch when the All Blacks were beaten 28–14, suffering from a marked problem of retaining possession. Mains took desperate measures to right the wrongs for the second test, in Wellington, and among others, dropped two of the greatest All Blacks, John Kirwan and Grant Fox. These were tests after all and tests were to be won; there could be no half-measures. The changes worked and the All Blacks won the second test 54–26 and, much more assured, won the third 26–15 in Auckland.

It was a heavy opening diet for a new All Black coach. It was a heavy diet for everyone else who was celebrating the centenary as well. Centenary dinners were held after each of the tests with as many former All Blacks as Peter Wild could find attending the dinner of their choice. It became a week of All Black reunions — the matches became almost secondary to the festivities, except, of course, for those who had to play.

The world has been conquered. Richard Loe, Ant Strachan, Arran Pene and Sean Fitzpatrick at the end of the centenary series.

Welcome to Our World

As rugby has spread its influence and as other countries have learnt of the game's unique appeal, the All Blacks' opponents have come from diverse climes. It hasn't all been a modern phenomenon, either. The All Blacks first played the United States in 1913 — before they'd even played South Africa. But others are of more recent vintage, brought into the test fold by the demands of the World Cup. English was once the language of the scrum, but it's now a polyglot pack.

CANADA

It seems inconsistent and even incongruous that New Zealand rugby had for close on a century gone out of its way to help the development of rugby in Canada, yet the All Blacks have met the Canadians in tests only twice.

And the first one of those was a quarterfinal in the World Cup in 1991 so New Zealand has only once played Canada of its own choosing.

Yet All Black teams have played the stronghold of Canadian rugby, British Columbia, since the Originals' tour of Britain in 1905–06 and indeed, early in the 20th century the New Zealand union had a closer relationship with Canada than it did with South Africa.

The answer lies in the word 'development'. New Zealand was perfectly happy to help Canadian rugby on either end of tours of Britain but was not so keen otherwise.

Until the first test in 1991, played in Lille in the industrial north of France of all places, All Black teams had played various Canadian combinations on 19 occasions. The first two were not in fact in Canada, but in California, when the Originals returned home via North America at the expense of a grateful New Zealand government (or at least at the expense of a grateful premier, Richard Seddon).

Both those games, which were regarded as exhibitions as much for Californians' benefit as for the Canadians, were against the provincial side, British Columbia.

Rugby was first introduced to Canada in the 1860s by English students at McGill University in Montreal but it was in the kinder climate of Vancouver that the game flourished, helped along by a New Zealander, one A. St-G Hammersley, who had migrated to Vancouver in the 1880s.

The All Blacks of 1913 who toured California and played a single test against the United States finished off their tour with two games on the offshore island of Victoria and one in Vancouver.

The Invincibles of 1924–25 played twice in British Columbia, once against Vancouver and once against Victoria. The 1935–36 All Blacks repeated the dose on their way home from Britain while the next All Black team on a major tour, Bob Stuart's side of 1953–54,

played twice in Vancouver and once in Victoria.

The 1963–64 All Blacks also played twice in Vancouver but the 1967 team broke the pattern by playing en route to Britain, once against British Columbia in Vancouver and once against Eastern Canada in Montreal. Ian Kirkpatrick's team of 1972–73 also played in Vancouver on the way to Britain.

The mould was finally broken by Graham Mourie's 1980 team on the way to help spoiling the Welsh Rugby Union's centenary party. They'd played the United States in San Diego, then went north and beat Canada 43–10 in Vancouver. It was the first match between New Zealand and Canada but was not given test status.

Canadian rugby was by then benefiting from a huge injection of government cash into sport in the wake of Canada's failure to win a single gold medal at the Olympics in Montreal. The Canadians became the first Games host nation to suffer such a humiliation and Sport Canada was set up to boost amateur sport.

By the time of the next All Blacks visit there, by Wayne Shelford's team on the way to Wales and Ireland in 1989, the New Zealand connection with Canada was even stronger. The Otago, Waikato and Northland unions had begun the CANZ pre-season series after being locked out of the South Pacific championship and they'd brought Canada and Argentina into their fold. As a result, Otago coach Laurie Mains had been to Canada coaching, as had John Hart, in between national coaching stints, and a former national director of coaching, Bill Freeman.

It was through the CANZ series that the Canadian national team also played in New Zealand.

Shelford's All Blacks, though, did not play against Canada. Their match helped celebrate the centenary of the British Columbia union and while the provincial team was the undoubted strength of Canadian rugby, it didn't make up the whole of the national team.

A New Zealand Development team, coached by the former All Black assistant coach Lane Penn and captained by flanker Kevin Schuler, toured Canada in late 1990 for five matches, each of which was won. They also spread the rugby word a little wider, playing in St John's in Newfoundland, Toronto, Winnipeg and Vancouver.

All this activity in the late 80s and in 1990 gave the All Blacks a greater appreciation of Canadian rugby, not just of the probable strength of the team but also of the difficulties facing the development of the game there. The vast size of the country and the harsh winter climate were real obstacles to Canadian rugby. A traditional Northern Hemisphere season of September to May was played in British Columbia but rugby in the east of Canada was unplayable in the winter months and instead the season there was April to October.

Those New Zealand Development players of 1990 who traipsed from St John's on the eastern seaboard to Vancouver in the west would have well understood the difficulties for the Canadians of establishing a settled national team.

Yet against those odds it was a settled Canada whom the All Blacks confronted in France in 1991. The Canadians had played in the pool based in the south of France and as a result had gone about their business away from the major focus of cup publicity and promotion, which was centred on Britain. They qualified for the quarterfinals by beating Fiji and Romania and lost to France only by six points. They conceded only four tries in pool play, among the best defensive records of the cup thus far (the All Blacks had conceded just three).

They had more than useful players whom the New Zealanders had come to know reasonably well and they bore the characteristics of Canadian rugby: big and fast. Among them were the experienced first five-eighth, Gareth Rees; the captain and goalkicking fullback, Mark Wyatt; a couple of rugged flankers, Gord Mackinnon and Al Charron; and a No 8, Glenn Ennis, who had played a season for Grammar in Auckland. Canada's principal ball-winning lock, Norm Hadley, was, at 2.02 metres and 123 kilograms, the biggest player in the tournament.

The All Blacks, defending cup holders and conquerors of allcomers from 1987 to 1990, were not playing during the cup as they felt they should. Though they'd beaten England in the cup opener, they'd had scratchy wins against the United States and Italy and knew if they

John Kirwan, one of the All Blacks' tryscorers against Canada in the World Cup quarterfinal in France in 1991.

didn't get things together in the quarterfinal, they wouldn't last much longer.

They did look more accomplished against Canada, winning 29–13 and scoring five tries to two, but as it proved, the match was a false dawn for the All Blacks. They trooped off the field to learn that while they'd been playing, Australia had scraped a one-point win in another quarterfinal against Ireland in Dublin, and they'd therefore be meeting the Australians in a semifinal the following weekend.

Co-coaches Alex Wyllie and John Hart expressed themselves happy with the performance and declared themselves to be ready for the rigours to come. But that wasn't to be.

There were a couple of notable statistics in the Canadian match. John Timu played at fullback for the first time since his days at Lindisfarne College in Hawke's Bay and it was captain Gary Whetton's 56th test, one more than the long-established record set by Colin Meads.

It was the next World Cup that led to the All Blacks meeting Canada for the second time, but this was a lead-up test in Auckland rather than the cup itself. It was a far more assertive and authoritative All Black team this time and they won 73–7, showing a brand of rugby and a level of fitness and commitment that they carried through to the cup itself.

While the game reflected the All Blacks' cup preparedness, it also more accurately laid out the gulf between one established rugby country and one developing country. The match was what the All Blacks wanted, but it probably didn't serve the Canadians' interests. They'd been on a

On the cover and on the field. Jeff Wilson features in the 1995 test against Canada at Eden Park.

brief South Pacific tour during which they'd laboured to victory over Fiji, lost to South Island and New Zealand XVs and had just one win in New Zealand, over a North Island XV. They went to the 1991 cup knowing they could be competitive; after Auckland they would have gone to the cup in South Africa knowing they weren't competitive enough.

The Canadian match in 1995 was also notable for being the All Black debut for Andrew Mehrtens. His impact on the match was as profound as the influence he would wield throughout his All Black career. He scored 28 points, which was then a world record for a player making his debut and was also the highest for the All Blacks in a test.

Both marks were eclipsed within a couple of months, but Mehrtens's display signalled to the rugby world what was in store in the succeeding years.

ITALY

Marzio Innocenti was a man of learning from the Italian city of learning, Padua or, as it's rendered in Italian, Padova. Innocenti was a doctor of medicine and the captain of his country at rugby.

He stood under the old grandstand at Carisbrook, dressed in his team's number ones of blazer and tie, his hair still wet from the shower, his feet shuffling in the sawdust that used to cover the warm-up area under the stand.

There was a tear in his eye and a lump in his throat.

Italy had just beaten Fiji in the first World Cup in 1987, but because the Fijians had scored more tries in pool matches than the Italians, it was a farewell speech by Innocenti. He was leading his troops home.

The Italians left behind memories — memories of the superb All Black win against them in the opening match, the match in which John Kirwan scored his end-to-end try and which seemed to set the tone for the cup. That was a memory for New Zealanders to savour.

But there were memories, too, of Innocenti, humble in both defeat and victory, always charming in manner and expressing a gratitude in his halting English for the coming together of the rugby world that few for whom English was their mother tongue could have matched.

We who listened to Innocenti felt humbled.

'You must think what was in our hearts and minds after the All Blacks,' he said. 'I am very proud of my players. I don't know if they're good players, but they're great men.'

He and his team looked around with wide-eyed wonder at the company in which they found themselves. They mixed, he said, with Brian Lochore and Alex Wyllie, two great All Blacks of whom they'd only previously read. At some match or another they came across Murray Mexted and Innocenti, lifting his eyes and looking behind the assembled pressmen, found Graham Mourie, there working for the cup's marketing company.

'And there is Graham Mourie,' he said, 'it is humbling to be in the same place as such men.'

Innocenti was asked what type of reception may await his players in the northern Italian towns such as Padua, Rovigo, Treviso and Venice where rugby is such a passion. He shrugged. 'I don't know,' he said. 'Perhaps they may throw tomatoes.'

Given Italy's entrance onto the world stage, that would have been a waste of good tomatoes.

While rugby had long had a hold in pockets of Italy, it was only the introduction of the World Cup that showed Italy to the rest of the rugby world. That was not necessarily the fault of the Italians. Indeed, they had argued for a cup long before New Zealand and Australia organised the first and, in 1960, the Italians organised a rugby tournament to coincide with the Olympic Games in Rome. New Zealand was invited but declined because of a timing clash with a more formidable and enduring foe, South Africa.

New Zealand's first contact with Italian rugby didn't come until 1977 when Graham Mourie's All Blacks played in Padua on the way to their tour of France and, two years later, they were back again, this time in Rovigo, on the way home from England and Scotland.

The first was against what was styled an Italian President's XV and the second, in 1979, against Italy, but it wasn't deemed to be a test and it's doubtful if the prospect of it being so was ever discussed. Both matches were won by the All Blacks but neither was won with the emphasis and authority that should have been expected of one of the strongest rugby nations against one that could best be described as emerging. It should also be assumed, though, that the All Blacks did not approach either match as they would a France or an England. The 1977 match was a shakedown for the French tour and coach Jack Gleeson indicated what he thought of it by resting captain Graham Mourie and having Bruce Robertson as leader instead (though Mourie went on as a replacement) and also by experimenting for the first time in the All Blacks with having the hooker instead of the wings throw the ball into lineouts. It was pointed out, by the Front Row Club, of course, that its members were more likely to quickly understand the calls without the need to resort to counting their fingers to work out where the ball was intended to go.

The great Welsh coach, Carwyn James, had a love affair with Italy and he was coaching in Rovigo when the All Blacks were there. His observations on Italian rugby laid bare its shortcomings.

'These players need coaching,' he said. 'They need the technique and tactics and certainly, because of the languid, gentle way of living under sunny skies they need to discover the right approach. They play it hard their way but it isn't hard enough.'

James talked about the difficulty of taking the players through the pain barrier. 'When the running began to hurt they discovered psychological ailments. By now I think they have all breached the barrier in Rovigo's premier team except possibly one and, although he is a good player, he will watch the games from the bench until he does.'

By that yardstick alone, the Italians showed themselves to be way behind New Zealand and other countries in preparation and attitude. Club players in New Zealand, never mind provincial or test players, would have first approached the pain barrier at rugby training soon after Charles John Monro got off the boat with an oval ball and persuaded his schoolmates to play rugger.

In such a land of pride, style and learning, though, it should be no surprise that the Italians were quick learners. Within 10 years they played the All Blacks in the first World Cup — that was by invitation so they didn't need to go through a qualifying tournament — and within another decade they had forced their way into the European series, which goes by the official name of The International Championship but which everyone knew as the Five Nations. The Italians, such was their development, forced the Five to become Six.

Italian rugby could have suffered from the size of the loss in Auckland in 1987 in much the same way as Japan suffered in the wake of their thumping by the All Blacks in 1995. That was what Innocenti meant when he said, 'You must think what was in our hearts and in our minds': whether to recover and learn from the defeat, or to slink away demoralised. It was to their credit that they adopted the former course.

By 1991, against an All Black team admittedly older, less fresh and with one or two players who had played a season too long, the Italians were more of a threat than anyone had expected. The All Blacks won 31–21 but it was a hard-fought win with the Italians dominating possession and the game for the last half an hour.

They ambushed the All Blacks. 'They played a better patterned game than we thought,' co-coach Alex Wyllie said. 'Instead of playing as individuals, they worked well as a team and they had a bit of flair.'

New Zealand would not be caught out twice. Four years later, when the first test between the two outside of a World Cup was played, the All Blacks won by the same score as they had in 1987 — 70–6. That match was in Bologna, perhaps better known for its proximity to the Ferrari car plant than for its rugby, and the side coached by Laurie Mains was being headlined as the best team that didn't win the World Cup.

Big try coming up. John Kirwan evades Fabio Gaetaniello and there's more to come as he heads off for his stunning try against Italy in the opening game of the World Cup in 1987.

For all the majesty of the score, though, and for the presence of Jonah Lomu, who was dubbed *Il Colosso* by the Italian press, it was not just the backs of black jerseys that the Italians saw. The All Blacks, fielding a first-choice test team, led only 20–6 at halftime and seemed lucky to have had such a margin.

The meetings between continental Europe's second team — they were third but jumped ahead of Romania — have become more frequent and while the Italians are now better organised and more attuned to the demands of international rugby, they are still some way from the premier league.

There was ample evidence of that at the World Cup in 1999 when the All Blacks beat them 101–3 at Huddersfield, more again at Genoa in 2000 when the score was 59–16 and still more in Hamilton in 2002 when the Italians, coached by then by one of the

greatest of All Blacks, John Kirwan, were beaten 62–10.

The Italians have been called an expressive people and while generalities can both praise and condemn, they're certainly more demonstrative than conservative Anglo-Saxons. They express themselves in their rugby as in other pursuits of life. When the All Blacks were in Genoa in 2000, a print was published to commemorate the event. It showed forward action and a description carried the words: 'A sudden explosion of colours, a chromatic mix that twirls in a whirl, when the bodies clasp and break away and clutch in struggle again . . . and then they invent slalom with their ability to find and penetrate sudden breaches, their strategy abruptly turning into tactics . . .

'With this picture Lovati skilfully interprets the greatness, the physical completeness of rugby: the ultimate result of separate moments when power, intuition and sheer intelligence combine to create what somebody called a metaphor of war. We would rather call it a metaphor of life itself.'

Glen Osborne scores despite the efforts of Cristian Stoica in the pool match against Italy in the 1999 World Cup.

JAPAN

It's necessary to state from the outset the obvious: New Zealand and Japan have met once and once only in a test match. That was at the World Cup in 1995 and the scoreline remains at or near the top of the list that records the biggest hidings in world rugby.

The statistical reckoning depends on what matches are taken into account. In a World Cup sense, the Japanese ironically enough have administered the biggest defeat. They beat Chinese Taipei 155–3 in a cup qualifying match in 2002 and their winning margin equalled the other big thrashing of our times, a 152–0 win by Argentina against Paraguay also in a cup qualifying match in 2002.

In Bloemfontein in 1995 it was New Zealand 145, Japan 17 and how, someone may wonder, amid all the scoring at one end did Japan find the ball and the time to score their 17? What gets lost in any analysis of such a result is the quality of the performance. It is assumed, naturally enough, that one team was very good and that the other was very bad. And when it's added in that Japan have played at each of the World Cups and won only one match — they beat Zimbabwe 52–8 in Belfast in 1991 — it seems confirmed that the match in Bloemfontein in 1995 must have been just a slightly opposed training run for the All Blacks.

But give it some thought and it soon becomes apparent that it takes an exceptional performance by a team to score 145 points in a rugby match, regardless of the opposition. And also irrespective of the opposition, passes still have to stick and kicks still have to succeed.

The size of the scoreline can detract from the quality of the performance rather than reflect it. Only in the context of other matches in 1995 can it be seen just how good those All Blacks were, and how unfortunate they were that for whatever reason — food poisoning, overconfidence after the defeat of England the week before, psyched out by the South African nationalism — they could not beat South Africa in the final.

Rugby is the ultimate team game in which all players are

Cover story. Wayne Shelford was a hit in Japan, too.

Hall of learning. New Zealand Universities players and their Japanese hosts and opponents get together at the end of the pioneering 1936 tour.

utterly interdependent; one weakness can expose the whole. But, conversely, there are players who through their own ability and vision can lift and carry along the rest of his team-mates. Jeff Wilson at his best was a shining example of that. In the game against Japan, two men stood out for their contributions: the irrepressible Marc Ellis with his record six tries (of a staggering 21) and Simon Culhane who, on his debut for the All Blacks, whacked over 20 conversions and scored a try himself.

It was an all-consuming performance by the All Blacks and of a type to which any international team would aspire. Not so much the weight of the scoreline, but the majesty in achieving it.

It cannot sit comfortably in the memory banks of Japanese rugby. Even the first time an All Black team played Japan, in 1987, the score was 106–4

It was an all-consuming performance by the All Blacks and of a type to which any international team would aspire.

and the man who then ruled Japanese rugby with an iron fist, Shiggy Kono, described the result as a national disgrace. The Japanese set great store on such human concepts as pride and face and there was none of either for the Japanese in either of those results.

The match in 1987 was not an official test match, even though both sets of players regarded it as such. The All Blacks were not even a full-strength national team, though they were close to it. It was, in many ways, a curious visit to Japan. It came towards the end of 1987 after the All Blacks had won the first World Cup and the New Zealand union's intention had been to send a team styled as 'a New Zealand XV' or some such. But Kono, who was desperate for rugby in Japan to develop and gain respectability, mounted a persuasive argument in his immaculate Oxford-learned English that it had to be the All Blacks, especially the cup-winning All Blacks, or nothing. He got neither the cup winners nor nothing. Sixteen of the cup squad went plus others who

144

Japan

would later have significant All Black careers such as Mike Brewer and John Schuster.

The team played five matches and their rugby was of a high quality but the tour became more noted for the relationship between the coach, John Hart, and his assistant, Alex Wyllie, and the aspirations of both, than it did for the rugby. It was from this tour that developed the notion that Hart and Wyllie couldn't get on with each other and which led, almost inexorably, to the disaster of the World Cup in 1991 when the pair were co-coaches. That decision reflected more on the administration of New Zealand rugby than it did on the rugby skills or tolerance levels of either coach.

Contact between New Zealand and Japanese rugby has been more enduring than is commonly supposed. The first tour was when New Zealand Universities went there in 1936, the same year that the interisland university match was introduced. They played seven matches and won all but their final 'test' against an All-Japan Student XV, which was drawn.

The New Zealand union mounted its first Japanese venture in 1958 when it sent what was designated a New Zealand Colts team, though the age limit was 23 (rather than 21, which is usually the maximum for colts) and it included eight All Blacks, and a few others who would become so. They won all their matches and so they should have with a side that was captained by Wilson Whineray and included such rugby luminaries as Colin Meads, Pat Walsh, Kevin Briscoe, Kel Tremain and Ross Brown and was coached by Jack Sullivan, a man who rose to the top of each of rugby's three pillars: playing, coaching and administering.

There has been reverse contact, too, at the university level and most notably in 1968 when the Japan national team toured and beat the New Zealand Juniors (under 23) 23–19, a Juniors team that

Six-pack. Marc Ellis heads for another try against Japan in the World Cup pool match in Bloemfontein in 1995. Jeff Wilson's aid seems not to be needed and Japanese Yukio Motoki not to be heeded.

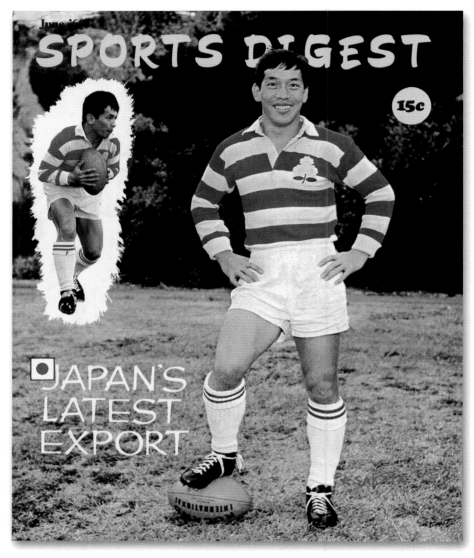

If you can't beat them, join them. Yoshihiro Sakata went from Japan's red and white to Canterbury's red and black.

followed by soccer. Rugby was 13th on the list after Japanese archery and just before handball.

For all that, Japan is fourth in the world in the number of registered players (146,854 according to the same statistics) and top in the number of registered clubs (4502), though a lot of the clubs field just one team.

Rugby was introduced to Japan by British residents there and by Japanese students who had been educated in England. Its origins, therefore, rested as they did in many countries with the well educated and a well-heeled elite. Rugby in Japan, as in other countries and even in England until relatively recent years, has found it difficult to wean itself away from such a privileged birth. Rugby in Japan is likely to remain a minor sport as long as it remains chiefly the preserve of the elite universities and their alumni.

Rugby there also got a kick along in 1923 when the Prince of Wales (later King Edward VIII, who abdicated), took time out from a world tour to play in a university match in Japan. That was the year before he was introduced to the Invincible All Blacks at Twickenham during which he was reported to have had a memorable exchange with Bert Cooke. Given his Japanese experience, it must have been with a background of more rugby knowledge than previously supposed that the future king said to Cooke, 'You're not very big for a rugby player, are you?' To which Cooke was supposed to have replied: 'You're not so bloody big yourself.'

included nine future All Blacks. One of the Japanese wings, Yoshihiro Sakata, stayed behind to study at Canterbury University and played for Canterbury.

These days, mention of rugby and Japan in the same breath conjures up images of company teams and foreign players and cute phrases such as 'the land of the rising sum' and 'a yen for a change in career'. There is a widespread belief in the rest of the rugby world that rugby in Japan is a universally popular sport, held back from real respectability on the world stage only by the stereotypical image of all Japanese being small. (Tell that to some of the sumo wrestlers or tell that to John Kirwan, who reckoned in 1987 he'd never been tackled so hard and so often.)

Japanese statistics, without the interference of rugby wishful thinkers, tell a different story. According to 2001 figures for high school students, baseball was the most popular sport in Japan

ORIGINAL TEXT

The Original All Blacks had a long reach.

When the 1958 New Zealand under 23 team toured Japan, the players would have been surprised to learn that the basis of rugby education in Japan came from the book written after the Originals' tour by its captain and vice-captain, Dave Gallaher and Billy Stead.

Rugby in Japan was first played at Keio University, introduced there by students returning from England, and their only opponents were two teams of mainly British residents formed in Kobe and Yokohama.

The president of the Japanese union when the New Zealand team was there, Shigeru Kayama, told them of the efforts to get rugby started in high schools and at other universities.

Gallaher and Stead's book, *The Complete Rugby Footballer*, was imported from Britain and copies given to three schools.

'With the guide of this book,' Kayama told the New Zealanders, 'the three schools developed their rugby and within 10 to 15 years nearly all the major colleges in Tokyo had adopted this sport.

'The rugby now being played by these teams all originated from the efforts made by the pioneers who learnt their rugby from Gallaher's *Complete Footballer*. Therefore, you will understand our teacher and your teacher is the same.'

ROMANIA

It was, on the face of it, a strange decision by the New Zealand Rugby Union when it initiated contact with Romania in the 1970s. Some of the union's councillors at the time would have struggled, as would have much of the New Zealand population, to pinpoint Romania on a map.

In written mentions at the time, either in newspapers or in correspondence, it was either Romania or 'Rumania', another indication that it was not a country that occupied a high place in the national consciousness.

It was known to be a country with something of a rugby history and had particularly close ties with France, but however strong they may or may not have been, they'd never been to a member country of the International Rugby Board (France did not become a member until 1978).

New Zealand, like the other IRB countries, had a conservative rugby administration. The big eight (New Zealand, Australia, South Africa, the four British countries and Ireland) preferred to play among themselves, with France the only regular outsider.

New Zealand by then had not even agreed to tests against close neighbours Fiji and Samoa; the All Blacks indeed went to Fiji only as an add-on to tours of Australia and had never been to Samoa or any other Pacific nation, and still haven't.

So why this radical departure from the norm to embrace a country such as Romania about which little was known?

The answer seems to have rested firmly with the 1955 All Black prop and long-time national administrator, Ivan Vodanovich. He more than anyone else established contact with the rugby authorities in Bucharest and he more than anyone else persuaded and cajoled the whole of the New Zealand council that it should expand its horizons beyond the traditional.

It was a remarkable feat of persuasion, but Vodanovich was both a persuasive and remarkable man. The ultimate rugby enthusiast, there was nothing he wouldn't do for the game — from playing and coaching it, to sitting around the council table, to supervising the handing out of socks and jerseys to teams.

He never publicly explained his interest in Romania, but it seemed to be a combination of personal interest because of his own ethnic background and just a general desire to spread the rugby word as widely as possible.

His first success was to get the Romanian national team to New Zealand in 1975, a considerable feat since it had never before been outside of eastern Europe. Its players may have wished they'd stayed firmly behind the iron curtain when they got their first taste of New Zealand rugby in Gisborne. This wasn't in the match against Poverty Bay; it was in the hotel corridor barely before they'd had a chance to unpack.

Vodanovich was there as the New Zealand union's liaison man but he made himself their unofficial coach. Vodanovich, who had an infrangible grip, grabbed the Romanian captain, Alexandre Pop, when the players checked into their hotel and told him it was absolutely vital they begin training as soon as possible.

Pop objected with some lame excuse about having been in the air for 30 or so hours.

This to Vodanovich would have been a minor inconvenience. 'Just a couple of scrums, get the kinks out,' he said. While waiting, Vodanovich had the forwards pack down in the corridor, eight of them against one of him and he whacking backs and rumps for emphasis as he instructed them more properly in the black arts of scrummaging.

It was while the Romanians were in New Zealand on their eight-match tour, which culminated in a draw against the New Zealand Juniors captained by Graham Mourie, that plans for the All Blacks to return the visit were discussed.

The manager of the Romanians, Ovidiu Marcu, just happened to also be the secretary-general of the Romanian Rugby Federation, which, from an administrative standpoint, was a happy case of double dipping. Marcu had the rugby say and he had the contacts in Bucharest to gain the necessary government approval, Romania then being under the rule of the communist dictator, Nicolae Ceausescu.

In the cautious language used by rugby administrators, New Zealand said it was hoped a reciprocal visit could be made to Romania, perhaps after the first full stand-alone tour of France, in 1977. The New Zealand union chairman, Jack Sullivan, told Marcu the All Blacks could play two or three matches in Romania before or after France.

As it happened, the All Blacks didn't go to Romania then. They went to Italy instead. The Romanian visit didn't come until four years later when it provided the entrée to the French tour of 1981.

This suited the Romanians because, as Marcu candidly explained, his team in 1977 wouldn't have been capable of matching the All Blacks.

Marcu spoke no English and his words were translated. Perhaps he didn't quite mean matching the All Blacks since no one really expected the

Romanians to do that. What the Romanians wanted to avoid, naturally enough, was being disgraced by their visitors. They certainly weren't.

Romanians as rugby players were almost as much a mystery to the All Blacks of 1981 as the country itself. The All Blacks had not before played in eastern Europe, had never before played in a communist state. Amenities that they and other travellers to places such as Australia and Britain took for granted were either rare or non-existent in Romania. There were no phones in their rooms at

Romania

the Atheneé Palace Hotel, for example, the Bucharest grand dame of hostelries that had fallen on hard times. The flights from Paris to Bucharest and return were on Russian-built Antonov 24s, something like the Fokker Friendships that used to ply New Zealand skies but whose upkeep and service was open to question. When their flight to Bucharest taxied down the runway in Paris, acrid smoke, which seemed to stem from burning oil, drifted through the cabin. Foreboding gave way to black humour and one of the players remarked it was the first flight he had been on in which the aircraft was allowed to smoke before the passengers were.

The All Blacks played a southern Romanian team in the Black Sea port of Constanta before heading for Bucharest, where the test was played at the city's main stadium, 23 August, named for Romania's national day that commemorated the Soviet takeover in 1944.

That was where France beat Romania 18–15 in 1957 before what was held to have been a world record crowd for a rugby international. It's said that 95,000 crammed into the ground — but the rugby was a curtain-raiser to a soccer international. For the All Blacks' match, a crowd of 30,000 showed up.

The Romanians had warmed up for the All Blacks by mounting a brief tour of Britain and Ireland the year before. They'd beaten Munster 32–9 — two years after Munster beat the All Blacks — and also held Ireland to a 13–13 draw. So if they weren't ready, as Marcu had thought, for the All Blacks in 1977, they were certainly ready in 1981.

The All Blacks scrambled out of the match with a 14–6 win. It had been three-all at halftime and only a brief little flurry of scoring

Touchdown. The All Blacks on Romanian soil for the first time.

SECRET AGENT IRIMESCU?

It was a standing joke among the New Zealanders who had close contact with the Romanians in New Zealand in 1975 that one of their party had close connections with the country's communist government.

He was Valeriu Irimescu, a 33-year-old who had played 40 times for Romania. He had originally been named the team's coach but when the team itself was named, he was there as a player and the coach was Petra Cosmanescu.

Irimescu's role on tour was difficult to define. He was neither coach nor player, but was a bit of both. He seemed always to be on the fringes of conversations rather than at the centre of them, living the tour in the shadows instead of in the sunlight.

Irreverent New Zealanders fingered him as the KGB man. He professed not to be able to speak English, yet at times showed remarkable understanding of what was being said in English around him.

Attempts to draw him out were met with an enigmatic smile.

Whatever he was, he could certainly play rugby. His one and only appearance was a cameo role against Marlborough when his side was in some danger of defeat. He went on as a centre, initiated a try the first time he received the ball by flicking a long overhead pass to an unmarked wing. Irimescu then calmly kicked the conversion from the touchline. It was the best individual Romanian performance of the tour.

Six years later when the All Blacks were in Romania, Irimescu was much more in evidence. This time he was the official coach and showed again the depth of his rugby knowledge when his team held the All Blacks to 14–6.

Hang on. Romanian wing Marian Aldea clings to Bernie Fraser during the only test the All Blacks have played against Romania.

between the 63rd and 67th minutes — when Jamie Salmon and Andy Dalton scored tries — came between the All Blacks and embarrassment.

There seemed to be a consensus after the match that if the Romanians had been less cautious with their possession, they could have won the game and left a great black exclamation mark on rugby history. But as with their game in Wellington against the Junior All Blacks, they kicked, kicked and they kicked again — forsaking attacking opportunities with the ball in hand.

It was as well for the All Blacks that they did.

Six years later, the Romanians were back in New Zealand for the first World Cup, though the draw didn't pit them against the all-conquering All Blacks. And two years after that, during the revolution that dismantled communism and rid the country of Ceausescu, rugby along with much of the country suffered.

Several rugby players were killed, among them Romanian international fullback Roducu Durbac, and leisure pursuits such as rugby faded into the background. It's only in more recent years that Romania has begun the long climb back.

The ball's up there somewhere. Gary Whetton, Romanian lock Gheorghe Dumitru, Rod Ketels and others in the test in Bucharest in 1981.

LOCHORE LENDS A HAND

From the perspective of the great changes wrought in rugby over the past seven years, even the year of the first World Cup, in 1987, seems to belong to the age of innocence, a time when the fellowship of the game was the thing. This is not to suggest the freemasonry of rugby was more important than winning or striving to win, because it wasn't. But it seems, looking through the rose-tinted glasses of hindsight and with the mellowness of memory, that it was almost as important.

Would it be likely today, for example, for the coach of one national team at a World Cup to happily and without payment go and assist with the training of one of the other teams? Time, the enmity of opposition, how such a gesture would be perceived, would surely all conspire against such an open-minded and good-hearted gesture.

Yet that was what happened at the first World Cup. All the teams were at the formal and grand opening dinner for the cup in Auckland, sitting within their national groups during the dinner but mingling for a time afterwards, soaking up the novelty of 16 different national teams being in the same place at the same time for the first time in rugby history.

Among them were the Romanians, of the group known as minnows at the cup. Few of them spoke English, few of them moved with the ease and familiarity of those other players who were long used to the social habits of touring.

The Romanian captain, Mircea Paraschiv, had been in New Zealand before, as long ago as 12 years before when he was a young halfback on the tour that culminated in a match against the New Zealand Juniors. He had played for Romania in their only test against the All Blacks, in Bucharest in 1981, and now he was back in New Zealand to lead his country into the promised land of the World Cup.

Having known him in 1975, I sought him out at the Romanian table in the far reaches of the room. We sat and chatted as much as we could with his stilted English and my total lack of Romanian.

'Do you think,' he asked, 'if that great man of New Zealand rugby, Brian Lochore, might be able to help us a little?'

Since Lochore was coach of the All Blacks, favourites for the cup and a realm beyond the immediate dreams of the Romanians, I said I was sure Lochore would happily speak to him and perhaps he should put the question to the great man himself.

I found Lochore amid the throng and asked if he'd mind coming with me to meet the Romanian captain.

Brian Lochore

'Happy to,' he said.

The introductions were made and the pair of them, the big former No 8 and the small present halfback, were left to their conversation.

Lochore, amid the All Blacks' preparations for their opening game against Italy, did find the time to go out to the Romanians' hotel by Avondale racecourse and he worked with them for an hour or so.

To Lochore, it was no big deal. 'I was just happy to help them out if I could,' he said.

To the Romanians, it was one of the greatest things to have happened to their rugby. 'To think that a man such as Brian Lochore found time to teach us,' Paraschiv beamed a few days later.

Lochore wasn't the only All Black coach to help out an opposition team during the first World Cup. Alex Wyllie, who with John Hart was one of Lochore's assistants, also helped out the Italians a few days later after their loss to the All Blacks.

Wyllie took the forwards for a session on a scrum machine at Rugby Park in Christchurch.

It was a typical Wyllie session on the machine. Scrum after scrum after scrum until he was satisfied. Shoulders were tapped, rumps were thumped and backs were slapped as he instructed the sweating, heaving Italians in the proper techniques of scrummaging. 'Lower, lower,' he'd bellow. 'Bend your knees,' he'd exhort. 'Drop your shoulders,' he'd shout.

Eventually, as observers guessed they would, the Italians broke. They'd endured for longer than expected, they'd been willing learners, but enough was enough.

As what turned out to be the last scrum broke up, one Italian lock emerged, his face contorted with effort, his chest heaving, his jersey sodden with sweat. 'Please, Mr Wyllie,' he pleaded, 'not one more!'

Grizz walked away with a smile, satisfied.

UNITED STATES

If one line has been written about rugby in the United States, it must have been written a thousand times: imagine if the Americans ever took rugby seriously.

Californians tried to make it happen in the early years of the 20th century and various other Americans have tried since, especially since the formation of the United States union in 1975.

It is not a sport, though, that sits high in the consciousness of Americans, if it sits at all. It is a sport of sectional interests and foreigners, barely a whisper amid the clamour of the big four of football (American, that is), baseball, basketball and hockey (ice, that is).

Dedicated rugby people have tried to unleash and channel the potential that must lie amid the population of millions and still they're trying, while the rest of the rugby world waits and, if it's got any sense, it would wait in trepidation. If ever the Americans did get a proper hold on rugby, and if it became the football of choice for players, spectators and sponsors, it would be the greatest thing to happen to the game since a bunch of well-educated Brits sat down and agreed handling the ball was all right with them (and that had nothing to do with that Irish bounder, William Webb Ellis).

Imagine. Seven letters that mean dream.

Rugby in the United States was born in the late 19th century and died before the First World War, then was reborn in the 60s and 70s. The All Blacks have played the Americans twice in official test matches, once in the first life and once in the resurrection.

The first is one of the oddities of New Zealand rugby history. At a time when the rugby world was cloistered and conservative, the New Zealand union agreed to dispatch a full-strength team to California and British Columbia in 1913

for a 16-match tour that included one international, against the grandly named All-America. It was not all-America, it was not even all-California, but no one seemed to complain at the time.

It might be said that the New Zealand union had adopted the missionary position. The two great universities on the west coast, the University of California and Stanford University, had for several years been toying with 'the English game' as an alternative to American football, which they felt was showing too much emphasis on commercialism, professionalism and pugilism — and just about every other evil 'ism' they could come up with. Coincidentally, American president Theodore Roosevelt was an ally because he railed against the foul play and intentional brutality of the homegrown version of football that had grown out of rugby.

The two universities formally adopted rugby in 1905–06 and, because of their status as halls of learning, other colleges and high schools in California followed suit. This happily coincided with the return through North America of the Original All Blacks — a trip made at the expense of a grateful New Zealand government — and they played two matches that were little more than exhibitions against British Columbia. One was at Berkeley, Stanford's home, and the other was in San Francisco, both clearly intended to show the locals what rugby was all about. Switching to rugby was one thing; knowing how to play it was quite another. The Originals had also played in New York when they first arrived from Britain, but so few people showed up to watch at Washington Field that it couldn't even be called an exhibition.

OFF TO CALIFORNIA
The New Zealand Rugby Kiwi — 'Now that I've crumpled up the Australian Wallaby, there's nothing left in sight but this Yankee Eagle. I'll just stroll across the paddock and kick some of the starch out of his feathers.'

A presumptuous Kiwi as depicted by a 1913 cartoonist (left) and the reality 78 years later (right) as Va'aiga Tuigamala attacks in the 1991 World Cup match against the United States.

THE SAN FRANCISCO EXAMINER — SPORTS—EDITED BY W. W. NAUGHTON—SPORTS — SUNDAY, NOVEMBER 16, 1913. **83**

NEW ZEALAND SWAMPS AMERICA IN FAREWELL STRUGGLE

U. S. Ruggers Score Three Points on Peart's Field Goal, While South Sea Cracks Chalk Up Fifty-One

LOUIS CASS, the plucky half-back of the All-American team, trying to stop a dribbling rush of the New Zealand forwards. The picture shows the perfect manner in which the All-Blacks spread out when dribbling the ball. Graham, with head down, and Dewar are blocked by Cass, but on the left are Sellars, Downing and Taylor, and on the right Wylie, Cain and Captain McDonald, all ready to carry on the rush.

How the *San Francisco Examiner* recorded the 1913 defeat of All-America.

Californians, or at least some, were enthusiastic once they'd seen the All Blacks play. 'Whether the good old game of rugby football, as it stands or with American improvements, will succeed,' the *San Francisco Chronicle* remarked, 'is a question which is yet to be determined by those learned gentlemen who hold in their hands the destinies of college sports. If a vote had been taken yesterday afternoon on the Berkeley campus, the majority of spectators would have been overwhelmingly in favour of the original game of rugby from which our own game evolved.'

Whatever the early New Zealand influence, UC and Stanford became firmly rugby. Their geographic isolation from the rest of American college sport at the time probably aided them in their bilateral snubbing of the American game.

They were nothing if not enthusiastic and dedicated. They even sent a team dubbed American Universities to New Zealand in 1910 and though they didn't have a win, they did draw with Auckland, the Ranfurly Shield holders, and apparently had a few days intensive coaching from the Originals' captain, Dave Gallaher, who was then the Auckland selector.

The Australians, as recently crowned Olympic gold medalists, visited California in 1909 and again in 1912 and it may have been that latter tour which prompted the New Zealand union to send

such a strong team the following year. The Wallabies lost twice to university teams and beat All-America by the slim scoreline of 12–8 and that may have led the New Zealanders to believe the Americans were stronger than they really were.

So it was, given selection foibles and the ever-ready opinions of the men in the street, a full-strength New Zealand team that took ship to California. They were never tested and most of their games were little more than romps.

The test, as it was designated, was no more rigorous than the other matches. It was won 51–3 (77–3 by today's scoring) and the All Blacks scored 13 tries without barely the hint of a threat to their own line. The *San Francisco Examiner* summed up the match with its headings: 'New Zealand Swamps America in Farewell Struggle. US Ruggers Score Three Points on Peart's Field Goal while South Sea Cracks Chalk Up Fifty-One.'

The field goal was in fact a penalty goal, kicked by Sterling Peart after the Americans' Australian, Danny Carroll, had been tackled without the ball. (Carroll had a remarkable Olympic record as a rugby player. He played in the Australian team that won in 1908, played for the American team that won in 1920 and coached the American team that won the last Olympic rugby tournament, in 1924.)

California dreaming. All Blacks ham it up. Dick Roberts, Tom Lynch, Doolan Downing and Jock McKenzie get alongside a Wild West barmaid.

Tri-star. Terry Wright hares off for one of his three tries against the United States in the 1991 World Cup.

Almost there. Ian Jones caught short against the United States in the 1991 World Cup.

An unidentified New Zealand reporter wrote that some of the All Blacks' play was up with the best that would be seen at home. 'I can say it would have taken another New Zealand team to stop our forwards yesterday,' he wrote. As for the Americans, he thought they should learn the finer points of the game.

Most noticeably, he said, the forwards did not back up the backs. 'This is a necessary attribute to a team as it gives confidence to players when they know they are supported and it also helps to cover up mistakes that would otherwise end in scores by the opposing side.'

The New Zealanders, who were led by one of the Originals, Alex McDonald, who coached the All Blacks on the disastrous tour of South Africa in 1949, may have been so good that unwittingly they did American rugby a disservice rather than the service they thought they were rendering.

A historian, Roberta Park, who was chair of the Department of Physical Education at the University of California in Berkeley, wrote in 1984 that the All Blacks' superiority led to the decline of rugby in California.

'. . . it was the crushing defeats which the Americans experienced at the hands of the All Blacks which contributed to the already growing disaffection that many students and local sports enthusiasts had begun to feel for rugby,' she wrote.

By the First World War, football was reinstated and rugby was on the wane, pockets of resistance lasting long enough for the Olympic victories of 1920 and 1924. Among the resistance was one of the 1913 All Blacks, Jim Wylie, who led a peripatetic life. He began his rugby in Auckland and played for the North Island in 1910, went to Sydney and gained selection in the Wallabies who went to California in 1912, but returned to New Zealand in time to be picked for the All Blacks. After the tour, he stayed at Stanford to study geology and lived the rest of his life in the United States. When Bob Stuart's All Blacks played at Berkeley on their way home from Britain in 1954, Wylie made the ceremonial kickoff.

The All Blacks of 1972–73 also played in the United States, this time in New York against a Metropolitan team, but it wasn't until 1980 that the All Blacks again played a team claiming to be a national side. This was in the reborn phase of American rugby when the team had become known as the Eagles and although the match in San Diego had more legitimate claims to being a test than the one in 1913, it wasn't. It wasn't a test, not because of the quality of either side, but because of the stifling stuffiness of the British Four Home Unions Tours Committee. The All Blacks were on their way to the Welsh centenary tour and the New Zealand union had to receive permission from the Four Home Unions for what were pretentiously called 'deviations' to San Diego and to Vancouver for a match against Canada. A condition with which New Zealand agreed was that neither match be a test.

Perhaps it was as well for the Americans because they were roasted 53–6 by the All Blacks at the Chargers football stadium in San Diego, captain Graham Mourie telling his players to play as if they were playing Wales.

The All Blacks had to wait another 11 years before finally playing their second test against the United States and by the time it was over, some may have wished it wasn't.

It was the All Blacks' second pool match at the 1991 World Cup and the team showed signs even then of a team having gone a year too far. The winning of the first cup in 1987 and the winning streak that followed it were but memories as the All Blacks struggled to find rhythm and pattern.

The All Blacks won handily enough, 46–6, and just about any national team would be proud of such a result, no matter who the opponents, but the All Blacks weren't. The game was played at the Gloucester club's headquarters of Kingsholm, a ground that used to be known as Castle Grim. And grim it was for Gary Whetton's All Blacks as they slumped in their spartan dressing room afterwards, knowing that it was a performance in which there had been no polish.

The Americans played with enthusiasm and no little fire and passion but without the organisation and talent that the All Blacks, even out of sorts All Blacks, could muster. The American attitude seemed summed up by their captain, Kevin Swords, who told his players at the start to look across at their opposites and say to themselves, 'I'm his equal.'

They weren't, but not for want of trying.

Nineteen days later, the once-unbeatable All Blacks were beaten in a semifinal by Australia.

RANJI RULED OUT ON RACE?

**Ranji Wilson was the Waka Nathan or Michael Jones or Josh Kronfeld of his day.
He was a loose forward, he was athletic and skilful, and he was fast.**

His given names were Nathaniel Arthur but because he was of Caribbean ancestry, he was nicknamed Ranji from an early age — Ranji after Kumar Shri Ranjitsinhji, a great England cricketer of the late 19th and early 20th centuries who was also known, for obvious reasons, as Ranji.

Ranji Wilson was a first choice for New Zealand teams when he was at the peak of his powers. And he was at the peak of his powers when the All Blacks team to go to California was chosen. But he wasn't in it.

Before the team was named, he'd played a full season for Wellington and had captained the North Island. He'd played in all three tests by the previous All Black team.

When the All Blacks had left for California, a second-string All Black side played two tests against Australia. Wilson played in both.

Jump a few years to 1919 when the New Zealand Army team, having beaten all challengers in Europe at the end of the war, was preparing to go to South Africa. Wilson had been a member of the army team but was excluded from the tour because of his colour.

Was this also the reason for his mysterious omission from the All Blacks six years previously?

The New Zealand Rugby Museum, not a body given to sensationalism, thought it might have been. It floated the idea in its newsletter of April 1997.

'The lack of comment about Wilson's exclusion . . .' it said, 'gives rise to the suspicion that the racial issue caused him to be discreetly omitted. Enquiries as to the situation on the west coast of America suggest that Wilson's colour would have been a problem in California with separate accommodation and transport from the rest of the side needed.'

**Nathaniel Arthur Wilson,
otherwise known as Ranji.**

The Museum newsletter said the All Blacks did include one Maori, George Sellars, but his complexion could have passed him for a Pakeha. That applied, too, to Billy Stead and Bill Cunningham, who had been in San Francisco with the Originals in 1906. Wilson was of a darker hue.

Would it have been a problem and could this really have been the reason for Wilson's omission — an omission on racial grounds that was echoed later by the non-selection of Maori for tours of South Africa?

There's now no way of knowing.

It's been well enough documented that the United States was not exactly enlightened, in a racial sense, until 50 or 60 years later. The excellent Ken Burns documentary, 'Baseball', which traverses the history of that sport over 18 hours, tells of the separate Negro League because African Americans weren't allowed to play in either the American or National Leagues until Jackie Robinson suited up for the New York Giants in 1947. Even after that, as African Americans gradually took their place, they had to stay in separate hotels to their white team-mates.

There's a hint, too, in an anecdote from one of the Californian papers at the time of the tour. Buried towards the end of a long column about the All Blacks being shown here, there and everywhere in San Francisco, there's a mention of how the team would be entertained by the Reno Press Club at the time of the match against the University of Nevada.

During a discussion at the Press Club about issuing invitations to the team, one member objected on the grounds that they were all blacks.

'I don't give a damn if they are niggers,' was the reported reply. 'They are footballers and they are coming here.'

STRANDED ON THE DOCK OF THE BAY

An All Black manager could surely have no more embarrassing moment, no worse fate, than to lose his team.

That's what nearly happened to the manager of the 1913 All Blacks in California, George Mason.

Their test against All-America was scheduled to begin at 1 p.m. to allow ample time for the players to clean up after the match and get to the wharf to catch the ship that would take them to Vancouver.

Cameramen, called 'moving-pictures men', delayed the start of the game and by the time it finished, time was tight. Still the moving-pictures men wanted their action so Mason hung around and was interviewed while the players headed off for their ship.

The San Francisco mayor, James Rolph, drove Mason down to the wharf to be greeted by the stern of the good ship *Congress* steaming off into the sunset over San Francisco Bay.

Mason appealed to Rolph for help and Rolph appealed to the traffic manager of the Pacific Coast Steamship Company. Back into the car the three piled and according to a contemporary report 'the speed laws were shattered as the machine made a rush' to another wharf further round the bay. There, a launch was commandeered and Mason was sped out in pursuit of the ship.

The chasers were spotted from the *Congress*, the captain hove to and had a Jacob's ladder tossed over the side, and a presumably relieved and embarrassed Mason clambered on board.

There were echoes of this 64 years later when the All Blacks were in France. They were boarding a train for Paris, and French trains do not waste time at stations. The All Blacks and their manager, Ron Don, clambered on and the train started to glide out of the station.

But Don saw to his horror that some of his players hadn't made it and were still standing on the platform. They were in various states of resignation and agitation.

Don shouted, 'Stop the train! Stop the train!'

All Blacks on it, realising what was going on, started to laugh. 'This is not funny,' Don fumed.

Someone pulled or pushed or did whatever was required to an emergency brake and the train shuddered to a halt, bringing forth a posse of French railwaymen demanding to know who had stopped their train and why.

That which had been rent asunder was rejoined in holy cacophony.

Wallabies

SA RUGBY

Under Southern Skies

No New Zealander needs reminding that the All Blacks' most frequent opponents are our old friends and foes, the Australians and the South Africans. They're traditional opponents. Their fortunes have followed the inevitable ups and downs of sport, but their strength in recent years, allied with the strength of the All Blacks, created a new phrase in rugby, 'the Hemisphere gap'. Argentina didn't play the All Blacks until 1976, and didn't meet them in a test until 1985, but there's no denying their merit in the Southern Hemisphere trilogy of opponents.

ARGENTINA

When the All Blacks first went to Argentina, they didn't know much about the rugby there. They'd heard of the _bajada_, the eight-man shove in scrums that was as much an expression of the machismo of Argentine males as it was a muscle ploy to gain a tighthead.

They'd heard, too, of a Latin temperament that was said not to be conducive to good, disciplined rugby, but not much else.

This was in 1976 and the All Blacks' two matches against Argentina were not official tests. The New Zealand team had been chosen from players who had not been in South Africa that year and the New Zealand union decided for this reason the two games would not be tests, as well as the normal qualification for those days that Argentina was not a member of the International Rugby Board.

There were distractions for the All Blacks. They were there not long after a military coup and players heard stories about how the military maintained their hold and some had first-hand knowledge of life under a military dictatorship. Stu Wilson, then at the blossoming of his career, was chased out of an inner-city park while on a run by gun-toting soldiers and Mervyn Jaffray, loose forward and brother of All Black Lyn, was confronted at gunpoint in a bar. One of the journalists with the All Blacks was told from official sources in Buenos Aires the military police were looking for him so he went out into the night with a couple of hulking All Blacks as protection and wearing Andy Haden's blazer as disguise.

The military also had its uses, though. Commercial flights to the up-country city of Cordoba were neither reliable nor cheap, so the Argentine air force put on two venerable DC3s, the aircraft known as the workhorse of the skies. Both aircraft were in military configuration and the players had to sit, backs to the unpadded fuselage, in webbing seats. The pilots, knowing who their passengers were, indulged in a little close formation flying to give them a thrill, flying wing tip to wing tip and turning players even more white than when they started, until manager Ron Don gasped out to desist.

Then there was the rugby. The All Blacks were in Buenos Aires at the start of their tour when a live telecast was beamed in of the Pumas playing Wales — though it was known as a Welsh XV — in Cardiff. Since the All Blacks would be playing the same Pumas in a couple of weeks, minds were concentrated. It was a more valuable lesson than any talk could have been, than any poring over player records and statistics.

The Welsh won by only a point and this was the Welsh team, Gareth Edwards, J.P.R. Williams, Gerald Davies, et al., that was at the peak of its powers. Talk about the Pumas being long on enthusiasm and short on expertise, fun-loving gauchos from the pampas, soon stopped.

Not official tests, but the All Blacks won both their matches against the Pumas — indeed, went through their tour unbeaten — and laid out the template of All Black rugby for the following years. The head triumvirate on that tour, coach Jack Gleeson, manager Ron Don and captain Graham Mourie, were in the same positions on the tour of France the following year, and Gleeson and Mourie were the brains behind the grand slam tour of Britain in 1978. Players developed, too — none more than Wilson, the best wing in the world on his day, and the enigmatic Andy Haden, whom Gleeson compared, after his performance in the second of the 'tests', with Colin Meads at his best.

It was an awakening of learning for New Zealand about rugby in Argentina, and the lessons would be emphasised again and again in the succeeding years. The Pumas, like any national side, have their good years, they have their indifferent years and they have their bad years, except that the Pumas can sometimes have all three in the same year. In 2001, for example, the All Blacks thumped the Pumas in Christchurch 67–19, one of those modern-day matches that serve as warm-ups to 'real' tests. Yet five months later, in Buenos Aires, the All Blacks won by just 24–20 — and were very lucky not to be beaten. There were extenuating circumstances because this was John Mitchell's first, rushed foray into coaching the All Blacks and the players with him were a mixture of those he wanted and some he may not have. But these

Above: The most princely of Pumas, Hugo Porta.

Right: Flying high. Andy Haden seems to be in control ahead of Argentine lock Gustavo Milano in this lineout in 1985 in Buenos Aires. Murray Pierce and Brian McGrattan are the other All Blacks.

were the All Blacks, to whom extenuating circumstances should not apply. However good the Argentines may have been that day, or however lucky, a loss would have been the All Blacks' greatest humiliation and Mitchell, in all probability, would have had the shortest tenure of any All Black coach.

Rugby in Argentina has been a curious beast. It's been played there since late in the 19th century after being introduced by people from Britain who were engaged to establish the Argentina state railway system — Scottish and English engineers and Irish and Welsh navvies. Patagonia in the south of Argentina stretching to the Straits of Magellan was also a magnet for Welsh miners and a strong Welsh influence remains.

Rugby became the preserve of the wealthy, educated classes in Buenos Aires while soccer developed as the sport of the people. The first All Blacks in 1976 were taken to the Hurlingham Club, which could have been in rural Surrey rather than in suburban Buenos Aires, with its hectares of rugby fields, polo grounds, English accents and attitudes. Like rugby in Japan, rugby in Argentina embraced the English ethos of amateurism with a missionary-like zeal and clung to it even longer than England did. It was to Argentine rugby's detriment. Many Argentine players, most notably the outstanding first five-eighth, Diego Dominguez, were told never to darken the Argentine rugby doorstep again after accepting the lure of *lire* in Italy.

Argentine rugby also had problems not of its own making. The distances in the country are vast and therefore costly to traverse, and worthwhile test opponents are time differences away. While the Pumas play neighbours such as Uruguay and Chile regularly, they need to go further afield to find opponents more in their league and the closest of them is South Africa, an eight-hour flight.

Much of the credit for Argentine rugby's development belongs to the South Africans. Isaak van Heerden, who had coached Natal, took up coaching Argentina in the mid-1960s and turned their rugby from a position of hope into one of fulfilment. He persuaded the overlord of South African rugby, Danie Craven, to accept a tour from Argentina and Craven, in a marked contrast to anything he ever offered New Zealand, mapped out what he thought would be a comfortable itinerary for them. To his dismay and van Heerden's delight, the Pumas won 11 of their 16 matches and beat the Junior Springboks. It became their international acceptance.

The first Pumas came to New Zealand in 1979 but, again, not for official tests. The two matches were against what were designated New Zealand teams, and though they had a sprinkling of test players, they were by and large players who had not played earlier that year against France. They were still comfortable enough winners, the first 18–9 and the second 15–6. It gave New Zealand as a whole its first look at Argentine rugby and it was impressive, none more so than their gifted first five-eighth, Hugo Porta, who could run, kick and pass and who could seemingly turn a game all on his own.

It took another six years before New Zealand and Argentina

IN DEFERENCE TO FITZY, PART I . . .

**Dominant players of their eras have often been accused of advising referees, even influencing them —
all in the wider interests of the game, of course.**

Mark Nicholls of the 1920s was said to be adept at keeping referees informed of what was happening, an earlier version perhaps of Andrew Mehrtens.

Colin Meads was a master at helping out referees and Sean Fitzpatrick, too, was seldom averse to giving advice to the man with the whistle.

Fitzpatrick, however, can virtuously claim to have given one referee some

The whistleblower. Brian Campsall signals a try to Josh Kronfeld in the test against Argentina in Hamilton in 1997. Argentine lock German Llanes can do nothing about it.

guidance that benefited the opposition.

It happened at Athletic Park in Wellington in 1997 when the All Blacks were thrashing, humiliating Argentina, who were then coached by Fitzpatrick's old coach, Alex Wyllie.

The score stood at 93–8 and a couple of minutes remained when there was a stoppage in play. The way the All Blacks had been playing, another score seemed almost inevitable and that would have taken it over the hundred.

Referee Brian Campsall of England ordered a scrum but Fitzpatrick, with a jerk of the head in the direction of the main stand, said, 'That's enough, isn't it?'

Campsall, bowing to greater experience, gave a slight nod and blew his whistle to end the game.

Fitzpatrick at the time fobbed off suggestions he'd called for the game to end, saying it was the referee's decision.

But a few years on, Fitzpatrick has come clean.

'What point would it have served to carry on?' he asked. 'We'd won the game and scoring a hundred points against Argentina — a team that had held us to a draw only six years before — wasn't going to do anyone any good. It seemed a good time to end it.'

Wyllie and his Pumas could only have agreed.

The All Blacks have scored hundreds against Italy, Tonga and Japan — but not Argentina.

. . . PART 2

Who said Northern Hemisphere referees don't have a sense of humour and can't enter into the spirit of rugby?

While the All Blacks were romping away against Argentina in Wellington in 1997 towards their 93–8 win, touch judge Tony Spreadbury decided to have a bit of a laugh with his English colleague, referee Brian Campsall.

It was Campsall's first All Black test and he had a respect that was only right and proper for the All Blacks' captain, Sean Fitzpatrick. The latter, of course, had far greater experience in test rugby than the former and Campsall knew his place.

At one point late in the game, the Argentine wing with more bravado than sense, Tomas Solari, decided it was time the All Black captain was roughed up a bit. When the ball was far distant and Campsall's attention was elsewhere, Solari delivered a rapid succession of blows towards the Fitzpatrick frame.

Since Solari was a wing and Fitzpatrick one of the most redoubtable of hard All Black forwards, the impact of the attack, it can be imagined, was not great.

Ineffectual it may have been, but it didn't escape the notice of Spreadbury and he immediately held out his flag, indicating to Campsall he had a report to make.

At the next break in play, Campsall trotted over to Spreadbury and asked what was up. Straight-faced, Spreadbury said, 'Foul play Black No 2, red card.'

Campsall was appalled, his jaw seemed to drop and he responded, 'No 2? Fitzpatrick? Well, I'm not telling him he's off.'

It was only when Spreadbury started to laugh that Campsall realised he'd been had. He was then given the true version of events and the penalty went to the All Blacks.

A laughing matter. Craig Dowd and Tana Umaga like it and so does Sean Fitzpatrick, whose beaming face can be seen beyond referee Brian Campsall.

Argentina

finally met in a test and it was in circumstances, with the best wills in the world, in which the All Blacks could not be at their best. The 1985 tour of Argentina came as a hurriedly arranged replacement for the planned tour of South Africa that had been stopped by an injunction issued by the High Court. The New Zealand union had to accept the injunction and it accepted, too, that it had no time to argue the substantive case in court, so the South African plans were dropped. The same All Blacks who had been chosen for South Africa went instead to Argentina with the exceptions of captain Andy Dalton, midfielder Bill Osborne and prop John Ashworth. Jock Hobbs, who had captained the All Blacks in Fiji the year before, took over as captain.

The first test between the two countries was also the first for Grant Fox, the Auckland first five-eighth and goalkicker who had a profound effect on New Zealand rugby fortunes for the next eight years, rewriting scoring records and generally marshalling one of the finest All Black combinations there has been. But that was in the future. Fox didn't even take the goalkicks in his first test — Kieran Crowley did — but he at least kicked a dropped goal. The All Blacks were far from fine, too, and though they won 33–20, it was only three tries in the last 12 minutes that made it safe for them.

The second test underlined just how strong the Pumas were in the forwards and with Porta behind them, directing and dictating play. Though the All Blacks scored four tries, Porta kicked four penalty goals and three dropped goals to force a 21–21 draw and one of the most notable results in Argentina's rugby history.

While that tour marked the entry of Fox into international rugby, it also marked the end of some illustrious All Black careers — Andy Haden, Murray Mexted and Dave Loveridge, all players dominant in their positions in their day.

Argentina played in the first World Cup in 1987 and met the All Blacks in the last of their pool matches, but it was a different Argentina — and a different New Zealand. Porta's powers were waning and the Pumas had not had a happy time, losing their first pool game to Fiji and only beating Italy. The All Blacks, though, were demonstrably the best-prepared team at the cup and though their 46–15 victory against the Pumas was not as comprehensive as their earlier scores against Italy and Fiji, it was comprehensive enough. All Blacks don't often indulge in revenge, but the win

Where now? David Kirk assesses his options in the World Cup pool match against Argentina in Wellington in 1987. Other All Blacks are test debutants Zinzan Brooke and Bernie McCahill (12) and Craig Green, Andy Earl and John Drake.

must have been sweet anyway for people such as coach Brian Lochore and those players who had been involved in the draw two years before.

By 1989, when the Pumas were again in New Zealand, the All Blacks of that era were at their almost unstoppable best, not having lost a test since 1986 to France in Nantes. Led by Wayne Shelford and with the nucleus of the World Cup team still intact, the Pumas had little show, especially now that Porta had retired. The first test in Dunedin was a 60–9 hammering and the second in Wellington, though won well enough at 49–12, was notable more for the horrific knee injury to the outstanding flanker, Michael Jones.

In the mercurial way that international rugby's cycle turns, it was a different story two years later. By 1991, Shelford had gone and some of the All Blacks played as if they should also have gone. If the coach, Alex Wyllie, had a fault — and of course he did, like anyone else — it was the fault of loyalty. Wyllie became loath to change teams and, indeed, he'd gone through the tour of Australia in 1988 changing the test team only when change was forced upon him by injury or Michael Jones' Sunday absence. The tour of Argentina was part of the buildup towards the 1991 World Cup and it became evident there, and in two matches against Australia, that the All Blacks' magic since 1987 had run its course. Other teams had progressed, the All Blacks had regressed. Both tests in Buenos Aires were won, 28–14 and 36–6, but the power of the All Blacks was not as it had been.

Argentina were no great shakes, either. They, too, went to the World Cup but didn't win a match and they had a horror run through the 90s, a period when they had seven different national coaches, among them Wyllie. Argentina also had four different presidents during the same period, indicative of a series of political crises that mirrored a succession of problems for Argentine rugby, most notably how to react to the International Rugby Board's decision to declare the game open. At first, Argentina held its finger firmly in the dyke and lost players as a result, scattered around the world where they could make money.

It was during this period that Wyllie was at first 'technical advisor' or some other phrase to overcome Argentine sensibilities about foreigners and then officially the coach. It was not a happy time for him in terms of results. It included the 93–8 thumping by the All Blacks at Athletic Park — a match called off early by captain Sean Fitzpatrick to spare Argentina the mortification of having 100 points scored against them. More followed with the second test in Hamilton, 62–10 to the All Blacks.

In a remarkable turnaround, the Pumas performed well in the 1999 World Cup, beating Samoa and Japan in pool play then stunning Ireland in a quarterfinal playoff, leaving them theoretically on the same level as England, Scotland and Wales. This was a team of amateurs who had had three changes of coach

Captain on the charge. Anton Oliver on the burst against Argentina in Christchurch in 2001 with Argentine halfback Augustin Pichot trying to hang on and flanker Rolando Martin wishing he could.

in the two months leading up to the cup.

By 2001, Argentina had caught up with professionalism and of the side beaten in Christchurch, nine of the Pumas were based outside of Argentina. An indication of the insecurity of tenure for international rugby players was that of the All Black side that won narrowly in Buenos Aires in December 2001, only six had played in the win in Christchurch in June. By contrast, 13 of the Pumas played in both matches, including the Bristol-based first five-eighth Felipe Contepomi, whose clearing kick towards the end of the match in Buenos Aires didn't find touch and led directly to the match-winning try by Scott Robertson.

That game was played at the bigger, and grandly named, Estadio Monumental Antonio v Liberti, otherwise known as the River Plate stadium because it is the home ground of the River Plate soccer team. It was an indication of how rugby's popularity in Argentina has grown. The first tests were played at the rundown Ferrocaril Oeste Stadium, then moved to the greater capacity Velez Sarsfield Stadium, then finally the move to the River Plate. Argentina had moved to the big time — the players did, too, that night, but the question of whether they can continue to do so remains.

The stepper. Pita Alatini dances away from Pumas Lisandro Arbizu and Jose Orengo in the 2001 test in Christchurch.

AUSTRALIA

A team of Australian footballers came to New Zealand in 1972, like they'd done many times before and like they would again. Another year, another tour. They were captained by a New Zealander who had made his home in Australia, Greg Davis; coached by a Queenslander, Bob Templeton; and managed by another Queenslander, Joe French.

They were not, to be frank, a very good Australian team. They suffered, like teams before them had and would again, through better players being unavailable because of injuries and other causes.

They lost each of the three tests they played against the All Blacks and they lost other matches besides, even to a combined team from Buller-West Coast. In all, they played 13 matches, won five of them, drew with Bay of Plenty, and lost seven. They were not a successful team on the field. They were so unsuccessful that *Rugby News*, then in its third year of publication, called them the 'Awful Aussies' and the name stuck. In a further search for alliteration, they were also called the 'Woeful Wallabies'.

By the ordinary yardstick that measures the worth of rugby nations, the Australians of 1972 were a forgettable team. That yardstick, to be wielded properly, needs to be applied to the visitors, as it was, but also to the home team. A poor visiting team would be even poorer if it was beaten by a poor All Black team. But the All Blacks who beat the Australians of 1972 were not a poor team, whether by riches of talent or richness of performance.

In August and September of 1972, a long tour of Britain loomed for New Zealand — the last, as it turned out, of those really long tours of around 30 matches and three months away from home, with Christmas spent in captive company in enforced surroundings. All Blacks and waiting-in-the-wings All Blacks wanted to go on that tour so the Australian matches therefore became something of a trial by jury, the jurors being the national selectors, Ivan Vodanovich, Bob Duff and Jack Gleeson, three good men and true. There were also formal trials, two of them, on the Saturday after

the third test against Australia, and there had also been the annual interisland match, played in July before the Australians arrived. There had also been an internal tour by the All Blacks earlier in the year and a tour of Australia by the national under 23 team. All such matches, as well as the haphazardly arranged interprovincial matches around the country between March and the end of September, formed the stages upon which the players performed, hoping to catch the eyes of the selectors.

But it was the matches against Australia that mattered most for only in such a naturally competitive setting of tests, rather than the slightly contrived air of trials, could the real worth of players be judged.

So it was against this background of audition and ambition that the All Blacks beat Australia in each of the three tests, the first in Wellington, the second in Christchurch and the third in Auckland. Only in the second could the Australians be said to have been truly

Expatriate New Zealander Greg Davis, leader of the Australians in 1972.

	AUS	NZ
ROUND 1	6	29
ROUND 2	17	30
ROUND 3	3	38

"HARDLY A WARM-UP FOR THE U.K. BOUTS!"

Wellington cartoonist Nevile Lodge might have been reflecting national feeling with this comment on the 1972 Wallabies.

competitive; they were well beaten in the first and utterly outclassed in the third.

So low was the image in New Zealand of the Wallabies that veteran journalist Terry McLean, writing under the pseudonym of Phil Allan in *Rugby News*, beseeched the New Zealand union to dump Australia as an opponent. McLean's columns as Allan were deliberately provocative; it is unlikely that McLean as himself in the *New Zealand Herald* would have advocated such a short-sighted action.

Among the Australians was another New Zealander. He was Bob Thompson, a hooker from Rotorua via Perth. Nicknamed 'Wallaby Bob', he was also a fine guitarist and singer and if the Wallabies couldn't play rugby all that well, with Thompson as their choir master they could certainly sing. The song of the tour, for it was aired so often, became 'Beautiful Sunday', which had the refrain, 'This is my, my, my beautiful Sunday . . . it is my, my, my beautiful day'. They sang it, as they had many times before, on the Sunday in the Royal International Hotel in Auckland as they waited to go to the airport. It was a beautiful Sunday for the Wallabies because their six weeks of footballing purgatory was about to end.

Few of the names of those Australians stayed long in the memory. Fine men the lot of them, but by the rugby standards New

Zealand demands, their names soon slipped away.

Yet that Australian tour, that desperate experience for Australia as a rugby-playing country, had a significance way beyond the results. In a sense, it represented both the past and the future of Australian rugby.

The elements of the past were the patchy history of Australian rugby, a minor sport played in any seriousness only in two states. No sane person would have questioned, then, before then or since, the competitiveness of the Australian athlete, but rugby suffered from not enough players, not enough depth and not enough footballing nouse. Rugby, or union as the Australians would call it to distinguish it from that other rugby, was the preserve of the private (grammar) schools and the universities and not, as it was in New Zealand, the game of the people. It was what some termed a white collar sport, the 'rah rah boys' as even today they're sometimes known. Of course there had been some fine Australian teams and they'd beaten the All Blacks from time to time, most famously in the early 1930s when the Bledisloe Cup hadn't even had time for its first polish. But generally New Zealanders looked upon Australian teams as ones the All Blacks would beat more often than not.

Another element of the past in 1972 was the monetary power of league over the amateur ethic of rugby. League was the game of the people primarily in Sydney, but also in country areas and Queensland, and it had the money. Rugby would no sooner find and nurture a new star, it seemed, than he would be lost to league. That 1972 Australian team included a man many judges regarded as potentially one of the greatest of Australian players, Russell Fairfax, but he was lost so quickly to league that these days few even remember he was once associated with rugby. The Wallabies' other first five-eighth, Geoff Richardson, also went to league, as did one of their centres, David Burnet.

That was the past.

The elements of the future were represented not so much by the players, though some played a part, but by Templeton and French. They were passionate about rugby and they were sad men when they left Auckland on September 17, 1972. No one likes being laughed at, and the Wallabies were certainly laughed at. No one likes being ridiculed, and the Wallabies were ridiculed. Like the skinny boy in the Mr Atlas ads of long ago who had sand kicked in his face by the muscle-bound bully, Australian rugby decided to do something about it.

On the Electra flight to Nadi for a tour-ending match against Fiji, French and Templeton, one the sage administrator and the other the passionate coach, discussed what could and should be done to get the game both served so dedicatedly to a position in which Australia would at least and at last be on equal terms with New Zealand. It took time; it took Churchillian blood, sweat and tears. It took also the assistance of New Zealand because administrators in Wellington such as Jack Sullivan and Ces Blazey knew only too well that a strong Australia was in their interests. One of the planks on which Australia built its platform for success was for their state teams to have more frequent contact with New Zealand. This was an essential component of the blueprint for the future hatched by French and Templeton initially, and later taken up enthusiastically by others.

In the early days of trans-Tasman rugby, tours of New Zealand by state teams were reasonably frequent and after the First World War, when rugby in Queensland had all but disappeared, it was New South Wales alone that carried the banner for Australian rugby. After 1929 when Queensland re-emerged from its post-war hibernation and until the 60s, visits by state teams to New Zealand were rare. Templeton and French argued that for Australian rugby to improve, there had to be more contact between the two countries. In the following 10 years, Queensland, New South Wales, New South Wales Country and Victoria all toured New Zealand: Queensland on three occasions within eight years of the 1972 nadir and New South Wales twice. They encouraged New Zealand teams to go there and Canterbury and Auckland led the way.

But good things take time. After the tour of New Zealand in 1972, there was even more humiliation for Australian rugby when the Wallabies were beaten in a test in Brisbane in 1973 by Tonga. This was the ultimate embarrassment. This, for the Australians, was enough. A debutant Wallaby that day was Mark Loane, who was to become one of the great Wallabies. He was recently quoted reflecting on the loss to Tonga: 'That was the start of something,' he said. 'We started looking more seriously at things like the scrum and lineout. We always had brilliant backs, but securing possession was the problem.'

As the Australians tried to rediscover themselves, the New Zealand union lent a hand — at one point contributing to the costs of a Wallaby visit to the Northern Hemisphere, an act of generosity with echoes of Anzac fellowship that Australians were reminded of in 2002 during the failed New Zealand attempt to retain sub-hosting rights to the World Cup.

Coincidentally amid this period of Australian planning and striving for a brighter future, the Olympic Games in Montreal came and went without Australia winning a gold medal. This was a major blow to the pride of a nation that revelled in its sporting prowess and it led directly to the federal government setting up the Australian Institute for Sport in Canberra. While that had no immediate bearing on the fortunes of rugby, it widened and helped cement the attitude rugby had already realised, that something had to change if it was to be taken seriously on the world stage. The late 70s and early 80s were times of tremendous change for Australian sport and rugby benefited from it.

In 1978, New Zealand felt the full force of the change when the All Blacks were beaten 30–16 by Australia at Eden Park, a match made more memorable by the four tries scored by No 8 Greg Cornelsen. It was Australia's first defeat of New Zealand since 1964 and, though New Zealanders may not have wanted to know at the time, it was the dawn of the new Australian era, an era in which Australia rose to equal status in the rugby world with those at the top of it.

WALLABIES GET THE JUMP ON RABBITS

Calling New Zealand the All Blacks was, with the benefit of nearly a century of hindsight, self-evident. Calling South Africa the Springboks was obvious since the small antelope-type animal was portrayed on their jerseys before they cast about for a name.

How did Australia become the Wallabies? For a start, because Kangaroos had already been claimed by the first Australian league team.

The name, like those of the All Blacks and the Springboks, originated in Britain where it was evidently *de rigeur* early in the 20th century for sports teams to have nicknames (though the England and Australian cricket teams, far more dominant in the English consciousness than rugby teams, both escaped).

Australia had been playing test rugby for nine years when they went to Britain for the first time, captained by a recently qualified doctor of medicine, Herbert Moran. Though Herbert, he was known wherever he went as Paddy.

'When we arrived at Plymouth a pack of journalists fell upon us,' Moran wrote in his autobiography, *Viewless Winds*, which was more about his life as a surgeon than his brief career as a rugby player.

'They were very anxious to give us some distinctive name but their first suggestion of "Rabbits" we indignantly rejected. It really was going a little too far to palm off on us the name of a pest their ancestors had foisted on our country.'

Waratahs was another suggestion and that was lent credence by the fact the native flower of New South Wales was worn on their hats and coats and on their light blue playing jerseys. But it was rejected on the grounds it was emblematic only of New South Wales rather than the whole of Australia.

The players had a vote and Wallabies won by just a couple of votes.

Australia stuck to the pale blue jerseys until the First World War, and in the first decade after the war rugby in Queensland was in abeyance so New South Wales, still wearing their blue, became the de facto national team. The first appearance of Australia in green jerseys came in the 1929 series when the first full Australian team for 15 years beat the All Blacks in a series 3–0. They switched to gold jerseys in 1961 to avoid a continuing clash with the green of South Africa but reverted to the green for the final test of that year against France. The Australian Rugby Union made the move to gold, with green shorts, permanent in 1962.

One of four. Greg Cornelsen scores at Eden Park in 1978 under the disappointed gaze of Bryan Williams.

Given the background of the lean 70s, it's more understandable why the Australians, when they again beat the All Blacks the following year, paraded the Bledisloe Cup around the Sydney Cricket Ground. The sight of their principal playmaker and goalkicker, Paul McLean, and Loane, who had known the lean days, leading their team-mates in a victory lap appalled and incensed New Zealanders. It was crass, seemed to be the reaction. But for Australians it was a joyful climax to all they had strived for — that one match seemed to be the summit after the long uphill climb since the tour of New Zealand in 1972. Never again, the Australians felt, would they be the whipping boys, and they haven't been.

It needs also to be understood what that victory meant to Australian rugby, not just the players who took the field that day but to the body corporate of Australian rugby. It represented in one sense revenge for the dark days; it represented Australia's first win against the All Blacks in Australia since 1934; it represented a return for the efforts of the past several years and it was simply young Australians celebrating beating the best. New Zealanders may have felt the display was arrogance, but in truth it was also a compliment to New Zealand, to the high esteem in which New Zealand rugby was held. A celebration of victory against a poor side is more muted than one against the best. England's 'victory' lap after losing to the All Blacks in Manchester in 1997 could be seen in a similar light, though it seemed, unfortunately, typically English to glory in a defeat.

What happened in Sydney also served to remind New Zealanders that the outsized piece of silverware called the Bledisloe Cup was something worth having. New Zealand had had it for so

All Black ball — inevitably. Peter Whiting seems to have won another lineout in the first test against the 1972 Australians. Others in the picture are hooker Mick Freney, All Blacks Ian Kirkpatrick, Alan Sutherland and Sam Strahan, Wallaby lock Garrick Fay (upended), Reg Smith, Barry Brown, All Black debutant Alister Scown, Australian captain Greg Davis and halfback Gary Grey.

long it had become part of the rugby furniture, barely noticed when it was there but an instantly noticed gap when it wasn't. It took the Australians to elevate the Bledisloe Cup to a prize worth fighting for and worth marketing to the extent that within 20 years of that Australian victory in Sydney, matches between the two countries 'for the Bledisloe' are the most eagerly awaited, and most feared, of the season.

While state teams saw more action against New Zealand sides, so, too, did trans-Tasman international rugby increase, especially from the early 80s when the two unions decided to play at least one test every year. It's commonly acknowledged on both sides of the Tasman that this increased contact did more for Australian rugby than it did for New Zealand's.

In 100 years of test rugby between the two neighbours and, for the most part, friends, New Zealand had an early ascendancy, maintained that for 70 or so years and then for the past few years the two have been on a par, to put a generous New Zealand interpretation on results.

It is interesting, even comical, to look back on reports of the early matches between New Zealand and Australia and read of almost an Australian resignation that they would always lag behind in rugby. The Sydney *Referee* called New Zealand after the first test in Sydney in 1903 the 'cock of the walk — his view is correct and his pride quite excusable'.

Almost from the first, New Zealand and Australian rugby went their separate ways. In New Zealand, it rapidly became the game of the people and in winter at least, never had — and still doesn't — a serious game to rival it as New Zealand's national game. Although New Zealand rugby went through periods of uncertainty, especially in the 1930s when the distinctive New Zealand style of scrum and a wing forward were banned, the All Blacks were generally winners and, as any sports marketer knows, the crowds follow the winners.

In Australia, rugby struggled to find a place and for years it was little more than a niche sport,

Australia

competing as it did in New South Wales and Queensland against stronger and wealthier league and, in a national sense, competing for the hearts and minds of Australians with the dominant sport in the southern states, Australian rules.

It's a rich irony that if it wasn't for the extraordinary energy and vision of a New Zealander, one Albert Baskerville, rugby could

have been the dominant sport in eastern Australia from the outset. It was Baskerville who, with Originals All Black wing George Smith, organised the first New Zealand league team — dubbed the All Golds — and took them to Sydney on the way to Britain. In Sydney they found rugby players disgruntled by the absence of monetary compensation for time lost from work because of rugby injuries and they signed up one of them, Dally Messenger, to join the All Golds for the rest of their tour. The All Golds played rugby rules against Sydney teams but their visit was the catalyst for the formation of league in Australia — and therein lay many of the future problems for Australian rugby. Generally speaking, the working class in Sydney took to the new game and the private schools and universities players stayed with the old, and that was how it pretty much stayed for the rest of the 20th century.

The next blow to Australian rugby came from its administrators trying to do the right thing by their country but the wrong thing by their game. After the start of the First World War, rugby officials

A marketing era begins. The victory lap that made the Bledisloe Cup a prize worth fighting for. That's Australian coach Dave Brockhoff in the background trying to catch up.

BLEDISLOE — THE MAN BEHIND THE CUP

Rugby history has not treated Viscount Bledisloe kindly. His name is revered, thanks to the cup that's at the centre of a trans-Tasman tug of love, but little is known about the man and even less about his dedication to rugby.

He started out in life as Charles Bathurst and, as Lord Bledisloe, he was Governor-General of New Zealand from 1930 until 1935. He was created Viscount when he returned to Britain, having served his king well.

He served New Zealand well, too, making numerous gifts apart from the cup, the best known of them being the Treaty House at Waitangi. He also had an empathy for the people, volunteering a pay cut during the Depression to match cuts that public servants had to bear.

But rugby history hasn't noted such things. There have been published inferences that he may not have cared, or known, much about rugby and only consented to having his name on a trophy that was introduced soon after Australian rugby emerged from its 1920s slump, when only New South Wales played.

There have also been contradicting stories about whether he ever saw New Zealand and Australia play a test match. One said he was at Eden Park in 1931 for what was purported to be the first cup match; another said he was in Wellington at the time, talking to commercial travellers.

Bledisloe has been painted as a bit of a martinet, nicknamed 'Chattering Charlie' because he was forever badgering newspaper owners about inaccuracies in coverage about him or, even worse, no coverage at all. This penchant was evidently prompted by a Christchurch newspaper, which had run adjacent pictures of Bledisloe and a champion ram and had transposed the captions.

It's time to resurrect the Bledisloe image, give it a bit of gloss after being coated in the dust of history — similar to what happened to the cup itself really.

Bledisloe certainly knew his rugby. There's a small club called Lydney in the west of England near the Welsh border that will attest to that. The very same Bledisloe, or Bathurst as he was then, was elected president by the club in its first year, 1887, when he was 20, and was still president 71 years later when he died, aged 90. Lydney is so close to Wales that the story goes it was once described as being neither Welsh nor English, to which Bledisloe replied it combined the best qualities of both.

Lydney was a tin-mining town and attracted Welshmen, and under Bledisloe's presidency it was said to have been the first English club to adopt the Welsh preference for four three-quarters — English clubs at the time having only three, with the rest of the team in the 'scrimmage'.

Lydney, though a town of only 10,000, continues to thrive in the English

The Bledisloe Cup, the centre of a tug of love.

union's national division three south competition.

As to whether Bledisloe was at Eden Park for the test in 1931, that may be irrelevant. He was certainly at the Wallabies' tour match in Wellington the week before, because there's a photo of him greeting the players before the game.

But the irrelevance centres on whether that 1931 match was really the first match for the Bledisloe Cup. It's commonly supposed it was because that was the year in which it was announced that Bledisloe was presenting the cup. But there was no mention of it in newspaper reports of the game, won by the All Blacks 20–13.

There is a body of evidence to suggest that wasn't the first cup match. The New Zealand union's management committee met on September 23 — 11 days *after* the test — and the minutes record: 'The chairman [Stan Dean] reported that His Excellency the Governor-General had expressed a wish to present a cup for competition between Australia and New Zealand and that after consultation with the New South Wales union, the offer was accepted . . . a letter be sent to the Governor-General thanking him for his generous donation and informing him that the trophy, which will be known as the Bledisloe Cup, will be played for in test matches between the two countries.'

In the following June, nine months after the 1931 test and when the All Blacks were preparing for their first of three tests in Australia, the New Zealand Press Association circulated a story originating from Auckland that reported on the arrival of the cup from England.

The story gave the dimensions of the cup, described what was inscribed on it and recorded it had been designed by Nelson Isaac, the head of the art school at Wellington Technical College, and was made by Walker and Hall in London.

It then said, 'The announcement of the presentation of the cup was made last September. The first game of the first series of matches for it will be played in Sydney on Saturday.'

With the Bledisloe Cup on the sideline for the first time, the Wallabies won that first test 22–17 but the All Blacks won the second in Brisbane 21–3 and then the decider in Sydney, 21–13. Fittingly, New Zealand were managed by the great Billy Wallace, who had been the principal scorer in the All Blacks' first test 29 years before. The start of one era then, the start of another now.

The All Blacks had taken the Bledisloe Cup to Australia with them; now

Australia

they could legitimately take it back again.

The cup had been on the touchline at the Sydney Cricket Ground but the All Blacks had a match to go, against Western Districts, and it wasn't presented to them until the following Friday, at a farewell function in the Hotel Wentworth.

Cup or not, the All Blacks would have been in buoyant mood. The newspaper story that recorded the cup presentation also said the players had had a jolly time the previous night at the Sydney University Sports Union's ball.

'A dozen pretty girls gave them a surprise,' it said. 'The girls were dressed in black football togs, even to the shorts. Their jerseys were buttoned at the side and on the shoulders were large silver buttons. Tiny black caps were perched on the side of their heads. They danced their own creation, the All Black ballet.'

It hasn't been always that Australian rugby has danced to New Zealand's tune.

Bledisloe didn't fade from rugby history once he left New Zealand, either.

He was a regular attender at matches played by Jack Manchester's team in Britain in 1935–36 and had six of the All Blacks to stay with him at his model pig farm at Lydney Park.

The *New Zealand Free Lance* noted in its coverage of the visit: 'The guests were thrilled with the deer in the park and with Lady Bledisloe's own pet one, which comes to her every morning to be fed — tame only to her. Lord Bledisloe took the boys shooting every day and they found him an excellent shot.'

At a farewell function in London for Manchester's team, Bledisloe presented each of the players with an inscribed silver ashtray.

Photo shoot. Viscount Bledisloe takes All Blacks Pat Caughey, Jack Manchester, George Hart and Rusty Page for a spot of pheasant shooting at his Gloucestershire farm in 1935.

turned their energies into a recruiting drive for the armed services. 'Much activity was devoted to the recruiting of members for the Expeditionary Force,' the New South Wales union's annual report for 1915 said. While young men signed up to die on Gallipoli or in France, rugby in Australia effectively shut down. League, however, continued, its officials arguing, as did rugby officials in New Zealand, that it was necessary to continue the sport for the sake of the people still at home. As a consequence, league took an iron and unshakeable grip on the footballing fortunes in the eastern states and rugby, in Queensland in particular, withered and died.

It was left to New South Wales to carry the Australian flag, which they did with some success. The Australian Rugby Union in 1986 retrospectively gave test status to matches played by New South Wales during the 20s. Though 24 of those matches were against the All Blacks, the New Zealand union has never followed suit. The Australians also gave test status to matches between New South Wales and New Zealand Maori.

It says much for the competitiveness and resilience of Australians that when rugby in Queensland was resuscitated and tests were resumed against New Zealand in 1929, the reunified Australians won the series 3–0. They remained the only Australian whitewashers of a full New Zealand team until 1998. They included players of enduring great status in Australian rugby, men such as fullback Alec Ross, centre Cyril Towers, captain and first five-eighth Tom Lawton, halfback Syd Malcolm and Bill Cerutti in the forwards, who throughout his life was known as 'Wild Bill', remembered as one of the toughest forwards to don what was then the green Australian jersey. The

Wallabies also included hooker Eddie Bonis, tough as old leather, who played 12 times against the All Blacks between 1929 and 1938, setting the standards for all All Black and Wallaby hookers who have followed.

The All Blacks in 1929 were in something of a transitional phase after the tour of South Africa the year before and ahead of the first Lions tour of 1930, but they were still a good side and they were still the All Blacks. Any side that included players such as Cliff Porter, Bert Grenside, Charlie Oliver and George Nepia could not be dismissed as a mug side.

For all that success by Australia, and victories in 1932 and 1934, plus the series in New Zealand in 1949 when the real All Blacks were in South Africa, matches against Australia were perceived in New Zealand as the staple fare rather than the feasts of the Lions

Aussie comeback. A scene from the first test in 1929, the first time Australia had fielded a full team against New Zealand since 1914. The Wallabies celebrated their return to full international play with a 9–8 win.

WHEN PINEY CAUGHT CATCHY

If there's one thing guaranteed to wind Australians up, it's to mention Colin Meads and Ken Catchpole in the same sentence.

The one the darling halfback of Australian rugby of the 60s, a player even still referred to occasionally as the greatest. And the other the hard man of New Zealand rugby, the mighty Pinetree.

Catchpole, in the Australian version of events, was the innocent little bloke picked on by the big mean bully.

It happened in the first test in Sydney in 1968. Catchpole, who deserved his reputation as a great player, often ran the ball back into the All Black forwards and on one occasion a ruck formed around him.

Meads grabbed at a Catchpole leg to haul him out of the way. What Meads didn't know was that the other leg was trapped and in the act of pulling Catchpole effectively did the splits, tearing the muscles on the inside of the leg. He was carried off and never played another test.

Australians saw it as a deliberately callous act by Meads. Even as recently as 2002, when the All Blacks were in Sydney, the *Daily Telegraph* devoted a full page to a story by columnist Ray Chesterton, which was headed, 'Why I Loathe the All Blacks.'

In it, Chesterton said of Meads: 'He yanked Catchpole's leg the way a hungry man might pull the breast from the leg of a cooked chicken.'

In 1999 — 31 years after the incident — Catchpole was due to be honoured at one of a series of lunches in Sydney that honour great Australian sports people. Meads was invited but Catchpole urged the organisers not to let him come, fearing what sort of reception he'd get.

The organisers said it would be a chance for Meads to say he was sorry. 'I would be incredibly disappointed if he did,' Catchpole said.

Meads went and he didn't say sorry.

Meads insists he didn't know, couldn't know, that Catchpole's other leg had been trapped and says he would never knowingly injure someone in such a way.

'I was extremely sorry for Catchy for what happened, because you don't like seeing someone get injured, but I'm not apologising for doing what I did,' he says.

Chesterton wrote that the Meads-Catchpole incident, as long ago as it was, 'has come to represent the All Blacks and their public identity to some people as muggers in football boots'.

In a footnote to his story, he said he'd invited many New Zealanders to his home for dinner, but never the same ones.

And never, it is assumed, Colin Meads.

Ken Catchpole is carried from the field in what became his last test.

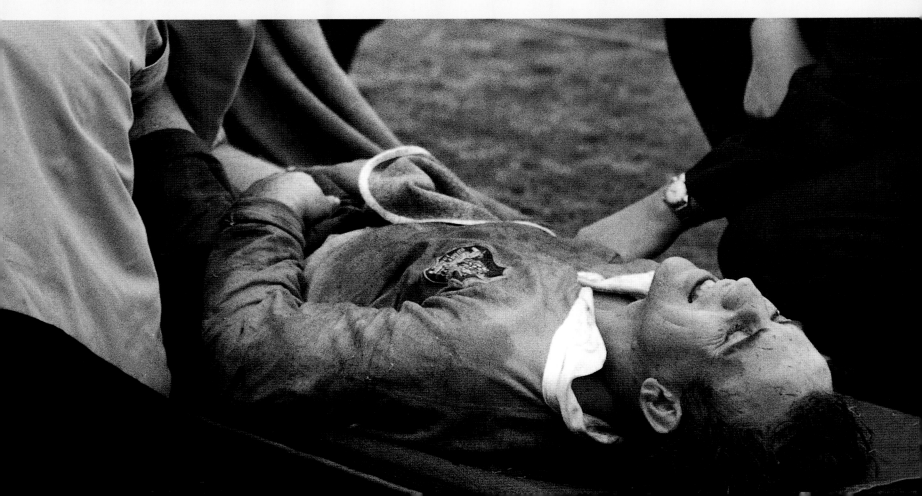

CAMPO '86 — IT WAS THE WORST OF TIMES

If that misunderstood genius of the football field, David Campese, had kept a diary during Australia's tour of New Zealand in 1986, the entry for Saturday, August 23, would have read something like this:

4.10 p.m. Test over. We were robbed. Steve Tuynman scored the try that should have won us the game but that Welshman, Derek Bevan, didn't see it.

4.20 p.m. Dark moods among players. Have shower.

5 p.m. Start to get drunk.

7.30 p.m. Drunk.

It was, recalls Campese, among the most miserable times of his rugby-playing life and was the most frustrating result in which he was involved against the All Blacks.

'We should have won the game,' he says simply. 'Everyone knows that. I know I didn't play all that well and that didn't help my mood. I was drunk by 7.30 — very early I know but very rare for me, too.'

And where did he go to drown such sorrows? Who were his drinking companions in these hours of need?

What's he going to do this time? David Campese against John Kirwan in 1991. The other Wallaby is Rob Egerton.

'Who knows?' he asks. 'Who cares? I didn't.'

It was only a couple of days after that match in Dunedin, won 13–12 by the All Blacks in a reversal of the first test scoreline, that Campese learnt of even more reason for getting drunk.

While he was in the shower at Carisbrook, Wallaby coach Alan Jones evidently told the rest of the players: 'Don't worry, fellows, you played without a fullback today.'

This was only a day or two after Jones of the sharp mind, quick tongue and vast store of knowledge had lauded Campese as the Bradman of rugby, the ultimate sporting praise in an Australian context.

'I was pretty upset about that and Jones gave me a dressing down later but

that was just part of my rugby career,' Campese says now, with a laugh. 'Have a go at Campo seemed to be the order of the day a lot of the time.'

In 1983, when the All Blacks beat Australia in Sydney, Campese had missed a few kicks at goal. After the game, outside one of the dressing rooms in the members' stand at the Sydney Cricket Ground, coach Bob Dwyer said if the Wallabies had had a decent goalkicker, they would have won.

'Yeah, I remember that. That was part and parcel,' Campese says. 'Look, if my name had not been Campese I would have been treated a lot better. If I made a mistake — and of course I did — you'd think the world was about to end but if anyone else made a mistake, it was let's support him and be positive.'

It is, Campese might agree with a sigh, one of the burdens of greatness. Ordinary players make mistakes. The best do not or, at least, should not. And there was no question that he was one of the best; in his prime there was no one to touch him as a wing for his instinctive genius, a flair he feels would probably get knocked out of him today.

'If I was playing today,' he says, 'I wouldn't be enjoying it and I probably wouldn't make any test teams. The game's far too structured for someone like me. You know how people from time to time talk about merging rugby with league — well, what you'd get is almost what's being played now.'

Campese's reign covered almost a generation of All Black wings, from Stu Wilson and Bernie Fraser in the early 1980s to Jonah Lomu in the mid-1990s. 'I think I only played against Jonah the once, when I went on in Sydney in 1995. I tackled him once, too. It's on my resumé: Tackled Jonah Lomu 1995, Sydney Football Stadium. How many CVs do you reckon that's in?'

Australian rugby and Campese grew up almost together. When he began playing in the Australian Capital Territory in the mid to late 70s, Australian rugby was still, in his words, a team of easy-beats. 'Sure we'd have the occasional win, even over the All Blacks, but there was no consistency there,' he says. Through the 80s, the wins became more frequent, especially the grand slam of 1984 (under Jones) and then the World Cup in 1991.

'If I was playing today,' he says, 'I wouldn't be enjoying it and I probably wouldn't make any test teams . . .'

'We have a lot to be thankful to New Zealand for,' he says. 'We learnt so much from playing New Zealand more often; not just the All Blacks, but provincial sides as well. I remember when I first went to New Zealand in 1982 with the Wallabies there was this aura, this mystique about the All Blacks and some people may say that's gone now.

'Well, all I know is that whenever we played New Zealand, it didn't matter which year, you always knew you were going to get the hardest possible game. Look at that team we beat in 1986 in Wellington and then lost to in Dunedin. Baby Blacks? Don't talk about babies. I never played against an All Black team that anyone could say was weak or was not as hard to play against as any other.'

DINING OUT — AUSSIE STYLE

When the Aussies get onto a good thing, they don't let it go.

The day before the Bledisloe Cup test in Sydney in 2002 — the match the Wallabies won with the last-minute penalty goal by Matthew Burke — the well-heeled business people of Sydney went to lunch where one of the hosts was John Eales, in his time the do-anything captain of Australia.

It wasn't just another lunch.

For a start, it was at Aussie Stadium, which used to be known as the Australian Football Stadium.

The diners were taken into the dressing rooms to soak up the remnants of what atmosphere there may have been, then walked down the players' tunnel out onto the ground with the roar of the crowd (via a compact disc) ringing in their ears.

Resplendent in suits, they stood at attention while the national anthem was played — just like the real footy players do.

They then tucked into their lunch. The *pièce de résistance* came from Eales, who invited diners to try their luck (or skill) at kicking a goal from the same approximate distance he'd kicked the winning goal in Wellington against the All Blacks in 2000.

Eales went off first to show how it was done. But oops. It curled to the left. Then a few of the lunch crowd had a go with varying degrees of success.

Eales could hardly believe what he was seeing the following night at Telstra Stadium when Burke placed the ball for the penalty goal to win the match. 'It was unbelievable,' he said. 'It wasn't almost the same spot, it was exactly the same spot.' Well, give or take the Tasman Sea in between.

Burke of course did what most of the diners of the previous day couldn't do. He slotted the goal that kept the Bledisloe Cup in Australia for another year.

Telstra Stadium used to be the Olympic Stadium and used to be Stadium Australia. There was a suggestion to change its name again, this time to Burke's Backyard.

A happy action man, John Eales.

Century in Black

or South Africa, or tours of Britain. It was in 1949 that the Wallabies contributed to a unique day of rugby disaster for New Zealand. September 3, 1939 was the day war in Europe was declared and on the anniversary a decade later, it was a day of national mourning for New Zealand. A home-based All Black team was beaten 11–6 by Australia at Athletic Park and on the same day in Durban, Fred Allen's All Blacks lost the third test to South Africa 9–3. The New Zealand union had decided that the three 1949 matches against Australia would have full test status, even though the country's top 30 players were in South Africa. One of the reasons for the decision was not to deprive test caps to three of the All Blacks, Johnny Smith, Ben Couch and Vince Bevan who were not considered for the South African tour because they were Maori. All three would surely otherwise have gone to South Africa.

That series in 1949 aside, the pattern continued. The All Blacks would go to Australia and win. The Wallabies would come to New Zealand and while they might win a test, the All Blacks would win

Australian captain Tom Lawton clears in the first test in Sydney in 1929, won 9–8 by the Wallabies.

the series. It was a familiar tale, whether the Wallabies were in green or whether, as they have been since 1962, in gold. They made the colour switch, and from white shorts to green, to avoid a colour clash when they were in South Africa in 1961 but they reverted to the green jerseys for their final test of 1961, against France. The decision to adopt the gold jerseys permanently was made in 1962 and the new colours were first paraded in a twin tour with New Zealand, the All Blacks winning two in Australia in May and the Wallabies winning the first in New Zealand in August before losing the second and third.

While the pattern of results was familiar, the Australians had some great players over the years, some of whom the All Blacks would gladly have had and one of whom, halfback Des Connor, they did have. Connor was the incumbent Australian halfback in 1959, but he was from Queensland and the Sydney newspapers constantly called for the selection of an exciting young New South Wales halfback, Ken Catchpole. Connor felt the writing was writ large on the selectors' wall and headed off to New Zealand, partly to pursue his teaching career and partly just to play in a more rugby-orientated environment. By the time

Stand and deliver. Ian MacRae gets the ball away despite attention in the New Zealand union's 75th anniversary test in 1967.

New Zealand and Australia next met, for the twin series in 1962, Connor was the All Blacks' halfback and Catchpole was where the Sydney press wanted him to be.

The Australians had men of talent and men of character. Catchpole is regarded still as one of the finest halfbacks Australia has had and outside him on occasions was Phil Hawthorne, a gifted first five-eighth blessed with the ball-handling skills that seem to come more naturally to Australians than others. In the forward packs of the early 60s were men such as the Thornett brothers, Dick and John, a sort of Ocker equivalent of the Meads duo, durable hooker Peter Johnson and a flanker who would serve Australian rugby for years to come, Peter Crittle.

While the All Blacks never lost in Australia between 1934 and 1979, they sometimes went close. Very close. One such occasion was in the second test of 1968 after the All Blacks had won the first comfortably enough at 27–11. In the second test at Ballymore, though, it looked as if the Australians were going to end the All Blacks' impressive winning sequence of 33 matches and 11 tests

since a 1965 loss to South Africa. With 10 minutes to go, the Wallabies led by four points. With two minutes to go, still they led. But the All Blacks attacked and centre Bill Davis kicked ahead inside the Wallabies' 22. As he went to race after the kick, he was tackled by Australian centre Barry Honan. The referee was a Queenslander, Kevin Crowe, who, some stories have it, was prone to saying 'our ball' when awarding a scrum to Australia. When Davis went down, Crowe gave the All Blacks a penalty try. It seemed, even from a New Zealand perspective, a harsh call. The All Black wing, Grahame Thorne, had also been obstructed in the move by flanker Alan Cardy and there was some confusion then, and there still is, about whether it was that which led to the gift try. Crowe himself didn't help matters by offering both at different times as the reason. Whatever, the All Blacks escaped 19–18.

They also escaped at the same ground six years later, when the second test was drawn 16–16. Coming two years after the 1972 tour, this was an especially meritorious effort by the Australians and showed what they could do with forward commitment. It was the Australian forwards in the second half who dominated possession and so nearly claimed victory against all the odds.

The All Blacks had not been in a happy mood before that test

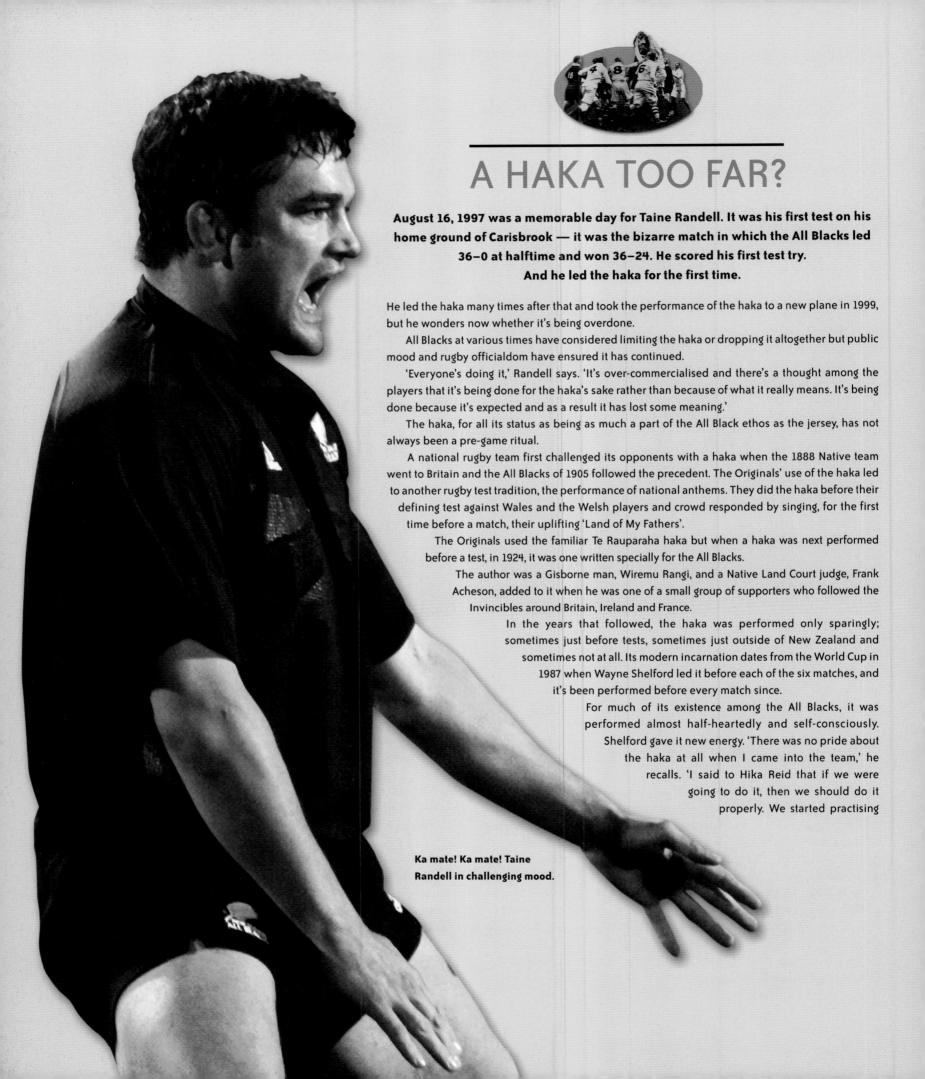

A HAKA TOO FAR?

August 16, 1997 was a memorable day for Taine Randell. It was his first test on his home ground of Carisbrook — it was the bizarre match in which the All Blacks led 36–0 at halftime and won 36–24. He scored his first test try.
And he led the haka for the first time.

He led the haka many times after that and took the performance of the haka to a new plane in 1999, but he wonders now whether it's being overdone.

All Blacks at various times have considered limiting the haka or dropping it altogether but public mood and rugby officialdom have ensured it has continued.

'Everyone's doing it,' Randell says. 'It's over-commercialised and there's a thought among the players that it's being done for the haka's sake rather than because of what it really means. It's being done because it's expected and as a result it has lost some meaning.'

The haka, for all its status as being as much a part of the All Black ethos as the jersey, has not always been a pre-game ritual.

A national rugby team first challenged its opponents with a haka when the 1888 Native team went to Britain and the All Blacks of 1905 followed the precedent. The Originals' use of the haka led to another rugby test tradition, the performance of national anthems. They did the haka before their defining test against Wales and the Welsh players and crowd responded by singing, for the first time before a match, their uplifting 'Land of My Fathers'.

The Originals used the familiar Te Rauparaha haka but when a haka was next performed before a test, in 1924, it was one written specially for the All Blacks.

The author was a Gisborne man, Wiremu Rangi, and a Native Land Court judge, Frank Acheson, added to it when he was one of a small group of supporters who followed the Invincibles around Britain, Ireland and France.

In the years that followed, the haka was performed only sparingly; sometimes just before tests, sometimes just outside of New Zealand and sometimes not at all. Its modern incarnation dates from the World Cup in 1987 when Wayne Shelford led it before each of the six matches, and it's been performed before every match since.

For much of its existence among the All Blacks, it was performed almost half-heartedly and self-consciously. Shelford gave it new energy. 'There was no pride about the haka at all when I came into the team,' he recalls. 'I said to Hika Reid that if we were going to do it, then we should do it properly. We started practising

Ka mate! Ka mate! Taine Randell in challenging mood.

it and put some personality and meaning into it.'

Opponents used to react in different ways. Some watched with amusement; some affected not to notice and nonchalantly threw balls to each other until it was over; some went into a huddle and some ostentatiously got as far away from it as they could.

'Teams don't have to front up to it,' Shelford says. 'They can run away down to the other end of the field if they want to, just like David Campese used to do. I thought it was great when Ireland fronted up to us in 1989. It showed they were not going to back down to us and they played that way, too.'

Another memorable haka confrontation was at Carisbrook in 1998 when Norm Hewitt and England hooker Richard Cockerill went eyeball to eyeball.

The Australians once considered laying a formal complaint to the International Rugby Board about the haka, arguing it gave the All Blacks an unfair advantage. That brought forth a snort from Shelford. 'People are scared we get an edge from it, but the edge is in the game itself.'

After Shelford's era, the All Blacks toured England and Scotland in 1993 and decided they'd do the haka only before the test matches. But when this became known, British rugby authorities pleaded and the players relented.

Three years later, they again decided to limit its use. The test programme that year began with a test against Samoa in Napier and the All Blacks decided to do the haka because of the Polynesian flavour of the night. But they decided against doing it at the next test, against Scotland in Dunedin. They changed their minds only after they learnt the Otago union had arranged to amplify the sound from haka leader Zinzan Brooke so that the scarfies on the terrace could join in.

Randell took over from Brooke as the regular leader the following year and when the New Zealand Rugby Union's apparel contract switched from Canterbury to adidas in 1999, the opportunity was there to develop the haka further. Adidas in a series of television commercials heightened the challenge aspect of the haka, and the All Blacks were given detailed lessons from a kapa haka group on not just the history of the haka itself, but also of the meaning of the gestures and the effects such as the pukana — the dilating of the eyes — and the whetero, the protruding of the tongue.

'At that stage, there was a greater feeling of pride among the players because we knew the background of what we were doing and had a greater understanding of it,' Randell says. It was at this stage that he introduced the cry of 'ka rita', the rallying call to the players to prepare themselves for the haka.

'It was a real challenge then but I think its status has been diminished because everyone does it; it's nothing special anymore, though I know it means a lot to all New Zealanders.'

He says the All Blacks talk still of reducing its frequency.

It's very much a part, though, of the All Blacks' image and has hardly changed from the description given of a haka by botanist Joseph Banks when he accompanied James Cook on the *Endeavour* in 1769: 'In short nothing is omittd which can render a human shape frightful and deformd, which I suppose they think terrible.'

The face of All Black rugby in the late 80s: Wayne Shelford leads the haka.

because they felt the Australian union had forced the champion All Black wing, Grant Batty, out of the test. He had a broken bone in a hand and had been told during the week he could play if the hand was strapped and if the swelling had gone down. He was picked in the team but after an examination by an orthopaedic surgeon, 'Chilla' Wilson, who had captained the Wallabies in New Zealand in 1958, was advised not to play. Then the Australian union stepped in. All Black manager Les Byars was told that he and Batty would have to sign a document indemnifying the Australian union against any medical expenses if Batty played and the injury was aggravated. They refused to sign; coach J.J. Stewart walked out of the meeting and replaced Batty with Auckland wing Jon McLachlan for his one and only test.

It was no big incident, though it cost Batty a test, but it was seen at the time as Australian gamesmanship to rid the All Blacks of a potent player and to gain some sort of psychological ascendancy. Undoubtedly Wilson was right and Batty should not have played; the disagreement was with the way the Australian union went about it. In its way, it was a small sign of things to come in trans-Tasman rugby, of the Australians using every lever they could find to gain an advantage. There would be more such incidents as the rivalry between New Zealand and Australian rugby intensified, as the Australians matched and at times dominated their former masters.

The 1979 match was the turning point in the relationship, a public affirmation that henceforth Australia were here to play. No longer could New Zealand regard Australia with a faintly patronising air, in much the same way as Australia in cricket regarded New Zealand. No longer could it be comfortably and

smugly assumed that the All Blacks would beat Australia much more often than they lost. No longer could New Zealanders find comfort in the belief that All Blacks were inherently better players than the Australians.

Evidence aplenty was waiting around the corner. The Australians won again in 1980, this time winning a series with the culmination a 26–10 hiding of the All Blacks in Sydney, and the All Blacks, not for the first or last time, claiming some nefarious motivation behind a bout of illness in the camp. Series between the two countries from then on were even, hotly contested, fiercely fought. The Australians had players of great gifts, as they always had had, and perhaps none greater than the first five-eighth of the early 80s, Mark Ella. His mother must have known something when she named him because he had the mark of genius. But more than the individual brilliance, the Australians also had organisation, cohesion and the burning will to win that is the abiding characteristic of Australian sport.

They had coaches who were innovative, who thought along different lines to the norm, who could somehow balance the difficult feat of getting the best out of an individual at the same time as getting a collective best out of a group of disparate young men.

It was a far cry from when Ken Catchpole was 21 and captain of the Wallabies and was required also to coach the team. 'Imagine', he once said, 'a 21-year-old of little experience telling 32-year-olds when they had to go to bed.'

Captain Kirk's farewell. David Kirk in his last match for the All Blacks, at Concord Oval in 1987. The Wallabies are Andy McIntyre and Nick Farr-Jones.

HEAD FIRST WAS HOWARD'S WAY

Australian Prime Minister John Howard was ecstatic when the Wallabies beat the All Blacks in Sydney in 2002 through that last-minute penalty goal by Matthew Burke.

Down into the bowels of Telstra Stadium he bowled after the game, his gold Wallaby scarf billowing out behind him. He showered congratulations on the Aussies and headed off to the New Zealand dressing room to offer his sympathies.

There he was met by the All Blacks' manager, Andrew Martin, who courteously ushered him into the inner sanctum and introduced him to the players one by one.

They didn't want to speak to anyone after such a crushing loss, even if he was the Australian prime minister, but they returned Howard's politeness.

(There were exceptions, though. This was when Andrew Mehrtens couldn't contain himself and, unsolicited, told reporters in forthright language what he thought of the referee, André Watson).

The All Black coach, John Mitchell, wasn't there by this time and only a few management people were. Among them was the team's media man, Matt McIlraith, who, dissimilar in most respects to his boss, does share one characteristic: both are bald.

Mitchell and McIlraith were also dressed the same: in the team No 1s of black suit, grey shirt and All Black tie.

As Martin explained it, 'Howard caught Matt's gleaming pate out of the corner of his eye and dropped the hand of the player he was greeting at the time to grasp Matt's hand, put an arm around his shoulders and said, "Bad luck, Coach, well played, though." '

With great aplomb, McIlraith turned to his embracer, muttered, 'Ah, thanks, Prime Minister', and bolted out the door for the refuge of the waiting media throng.

There were coaches such as Dave Brockhoff, he of the innovative bent who originated the Aussie up-the-jumper move with New South Wales Country. This was when a player either literally put the ball up his jumper or more often just held it behind his back and his team-mates ran hither and yon, confusing opponents about where the ball actually was.

The All Blacks in light mood tried some innovation of their own in 1974. An Australian reporter was spied sitting up a tree at one closed All Black training so J.J. Stewart, as innovative and as good at lateral thinking as the best of them, ordered a maul close to the line and had a couple of the hulking forwards pick up halfback Bruce Gemmell and throw him over the forwards to score. The reporter raced off, thinking he'd seen the All Blacks' secret tactic.

The Australians also had thinking coaches such as Bob Dwyer and Alan Jones, each so different in personality but with the common characteristic of putting Australian rugby first. Jones was a great man for the classical allusions. He had reporters scurrying off for dictionaries once when he said his team was like Sisyphus, who in Greek mythology was fated forever to roll a huge stone up a hill in Hades, only to have it roll down again on reaching the top. Another time, before a test against the All Blacks, he said his team was ready to conquer Everest, but he was temporarily lost for words when it was pointed out to him that a New Zealander had got there first. After the World Cup semifinal against France in Sydney in 1987, a match that should live in memories, Jones lamented that his Wallabies had tilted at a rather large windmill.

But neither Jones nor Dwyer, nor others of the modern Australian coaches, have been championing lost causes like Don Quixote did, and the ride on which they have taken Australian rugby has been no bag of bones Rocinante.

Their records, and the records of their players, have been impressive. Two of the first four World Cups makes Australia the envy of the rugby world. Under Jones, the Wallabies won a grand slam in Britain in 1984 — just 12 years after the game in Australia was in tatters.

Their record against New Zealand has been equally impressive. They've had players of the highest calibre, players such as Simon Poidevin, Nick Farr-Jones, Michael Lynagh, John Eales, Matt Burke, David Campese . . . where does such a list stop?

From being opponents New Zealand felt obliged to play regularly, the Australians have represented for the past 10 years the most difficult, the most challenging, the most respected opponents.

Hark back 100 years to when the *Sydney Mail* said after the first test that it seemed hopeless to expect to ever score a substantial victory over New Zealand. '. . . we may never be able to inflict defeat upon them, as they have upon us, we could with, say, annual meetings look forward to considerable improvement in our method of playing rugby.'

Prophetic.

Where the prize is highest.
Sean Fitzpatrick shows off the Bledisloe Cup.

SOUTH AFRICA

When the All Blacks of 1949 lost the third test to the Springboks at Kingsmead in Durban, any hope of squaring the series was gone. They'd lost the first two and, as history records in dark type, they went on to lose the fourth as well. It was a blackwash, though such a hybrid word probably wouldn't have been very fashionable in a South Africa that was then erecting the barriers of apartheid.

The reaction to the third test in Durban was unusually strident, especially in South Africa where it is reasonable to assume a series victory would normally be met with much chauvinistic back-slapping.

The Springboks, rather than being fêted, were criticised; and the All Blacks came under the cosh as well. It was not because of that particular game, though it was evidently a dull affair with penalties determining the outcome of 9–3, but because of what many thought the game was becoming.

The *Natal Mercury* in an editorial was most scathing. 'The third international of the present series between New Zealand and South Africa on Saturday is an event that is best forgotten,' it said. 'It was not sport. It was a facet of nationalism.'

Its point, that the Springboks played to win at all costs and never mind the quality of the rugby, was echoed by other newspapers and by former players.

But that was the same charge levelled at the All Blacks. Boy Louw, a prop who had played 18 times for South Africa, including two victories against New Zealand in 1937, weighed in: 'This team of All Blacks has come here more determined to win the rubber than to play open rugby — the type of rugby I know them to play in New Zealand. They have cramped their true style of game by making it subservient to victory.'

Ah. Win at all costs. Play to win. Win first, entertain second. Music to the ears of any All Black who ever took the field against the Springboks.

And should it have been any different? The editorial writer for the *Natal Mercury* may not necessarily have been well versed in

the titanic intensity of the struggle between New Zealand and South Africa to be acknowledged as the unofficial champion rugby side in the world, but Louw surely would have been. He was, after all, a key member of the side that inflicted a series defeat on New Zealand in 1937 — *in* New Zealand — and thus fuelled the New Zealand resolve to gain vengeance. The fact that the All Blacks of 1949 didn't gain any revenge at all, instead suffered the humiliation of losing all four tests, became just another four logs on the fire of nationalism.

The whole history of rugby between New Zealand and South Africa, then, now and perhaps well into the future, has been about a burning desire to win and only after winning is assured can such luxuries as the ideal of entertainment be indulged in.

In the years before professionalism saw the introduction of the tri-nations and the familiarity of two tests against South Africa each year, supremacy of one side over the other was always sought but seldom attained. Advantage lay usually, though not always, with the home side. The two countries were the dreadnoughts of rugby warfare, lobbing massive salvos at one another, while the other countries were the cruisers to be picked off at will.

In New Zealand in 1921, the first time they'd met, the series was drawn at one test each and one drawn; in 1928 in South Africa it

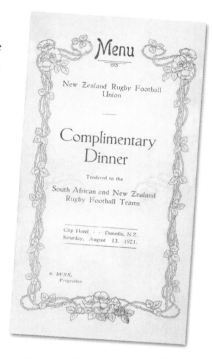

A feast of rugby. An invitation to the first formal dinner to follow a test against South Africa.

was a drawn series again, 2–2. In New Zealand in 1937, the South Africans won 2–1 and it was a standing joke for a generation or two that the Springboks were the best side to leave New Zealand.

Then came the 1949 series and the national blot, followed by the most titanic of struggles, the national crusade of 1956 that saw the All Blacks finally win a series against South Africa for the first time. On to 1960 and it was 2–1 to South Africa, then New Zealand won again at home in 1965, 3–1. In South Africa in 1970, 3–1 to the home side and again the same margin in 1976. In 1981, a series remembered more for the wrong reasons was won by the All Blacks 2–1. The reunification test in 1992 in South Africa was won by the All Blacks and the only other series before professionalism was in the last full year of the pseudo-amateurism, in 1994, when New Zealand won two tests at home and drew the third.

Cars, trams and people — thousands of them — head away from Athletic Park after the second test against South Africa, 1956.

The ledger near as dammit was even, as it pretty much always had been.

New Zealand held sway over every other rugby country but the South Africans. Of course there were losses and sometimes the losses for a time were greater than the wins — against Wales, for example — but in time the proper order of things for New Zealanders was restored except in tests against the Springboks.

It was a canker in the soul of New Zealand rugby, lanced a little by the home series win in 1956, lanced a lot by the away series win 40 years later. Both series victories, in vastly different eras of rugby and of life attitudes, transcended the games themselves. It was not just the All Blacks against the Springboks on green patches of field measuring 100 metres or so by up to 70 metres; it was not just 15 men in black and the other 15 in green, each trying to score more points than the other. It was them against us; it was an earnest pride in something New Zealanders did well against the only country that could do the same thing at least as well, and sometimes a little better, sometimes a little worse (thank God). It was, or so it was perceived, the good guys against the bad guys — the good, of course, being New Zealand. It was

our blokes, all of them normal other than a particular talent for the diversity of skills that rugby demands, against huge forwards and backs who used to keep sending the ball back to them. It was right against might. It was a democratic, egalitarian New Zealand against an undemocratic, racist South Africa.

But mostly it was because New Zealand had beaten everyone else but them. Grown men cursed and cried when the All Blacks returned, and returned again and again, from their various odysseys to South Africa with still the golden fleece not theirs. But they rejoiced and still cried in 1956 when finally the deed was done on home soil — and they laughed to hide the tears when Peter Jones in that genteel age said on state radio that he was 'absolutely buggered'. He was talking for everyone; his relief was everyone's. And they rejoiced and cried again in 1996 when John Hart and Sean Fitzpatrick led the All Blacks to victory in that odd conjunction of test matches, one the finale to the first tri-nations and the next three a separate, or so they said, series. And when the second of those tests was won in Pretoria, and Don Clarke, one of the battlers of long ago, wept with joy amid the concrete confines of Loftus Versfeld, a nation wept with him. At last it was done. Some of the younger players in the All Blacks of 1996 may have wondered what the fuss was all about: they weren't steeped in the history of frustration and anguish; they didn't know the names of the Afrikaans referees who had turned Nelsonian eyes to Springbok errors, names such as Craven and Brand and Geffin and Muller and McCallum and Du Preez and Botha meant nothing; they didn't experience the traumatic times when in the name of the All Blacks playing the Springboks families and friends were split asunder and blood flowed in the streets.

But they knew when they got home. They saw the rejoicing, they saw the tickertape; they heard old men, whom the young could hardly conceive of being young once, too, giving thanks. They saw the tears in the eyes and they heard the heartfelt cry, 'At last we've beaten the bastards.' 'We' was not just the All Blacks; 'we' was a whole country.

It had been a long time coming.

New Zealand rugby knew early the value of rugby in South Africa. Men returned from the Boer War, that ill-fated attempt to impose English rule on the Boers, with tales of the strength of their rugby. Among them was Dave Gallaher, who led the first All Blacks to Britain. Within a couple of years of the Originals' tour, the South Africans went to Britain too and they beat Wales, which the Originals couldn't do, but they lost to Scotland and drew with England. Three years after that, the Springboks beat the British Isles in a three-test series and a year after that, early in 1912, they went back to Britain and beat Scotland, Ireland and Wales.

These results did not escape the notice of rugby administrators in New Zealand. Communications in 1912 were not the swiftest; newspapers came by ships and 'the latest news from home' was generally a couple of months old when it was snapped up; letters took as long; the telegraph was quick but expensive. No radio and John Logie Baird was in his early twenties, thinking about whether

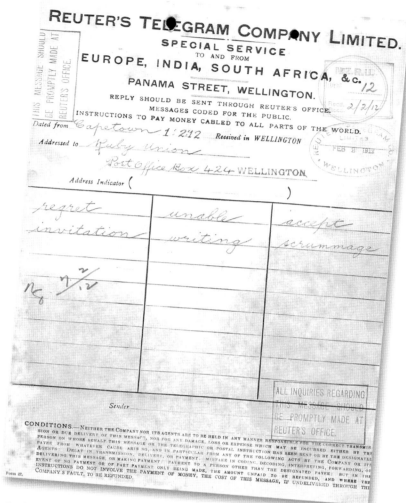

Thanks but no thanks.
South Africa says no to a tour of New Zealand in 1912.

it would ever be possible to transmit pictures over radio waves.

But New Zealand rugby men knew. The rugby world was microscopic and New Zealand needed to play more than just Australia with occasional, and expensive, matches against British teams.

They fired off a letter to the South African Rugby Board in 1911 suggesting that the South Africans send a team to New Zealand in 1912. But nothing ever happens in rugby that quick, not then, not now. Back came a cablegram on its distinctive yellow paper: 'Regret unable accept invitation. Writing.'

By the beginning of February, the writing surfaced in Wellington. It was a letter from the South African board's 33-year-old secretary, Alec Solomon, who had been the board's secretary since 1902. (When it was proposed at a meeting he be the secretary, the 23-year-old accountant stood to protest, whereupon he was kicked under the table and told, 'Sit down, you fool.' He sat and was appointed — rugby politics in action.)

The gist of his letter was that a tour would be difficult to arrange because the South African and New Zealand seasons ran concurrently. 'My board greatly appreciate the compliment paid to them by your invitation,' he said in the polite and precise language of the time, 'but have asked me to point out that as the period covered by your football season corresponds with the season in South Africa, there will always be considerable difficulty in getting a team away to your colony.'

Curiously, New Zealand must have asked about the prospect of a 'Coloured' team touring as well because Solomon added (his capitals): 'With regard to the visit of a coloured team from here my Board has no jurisdiction over the Body you refer to and has no dealings with it in any way.'

A war came and went before New Zealand and South Africa finally met on a rugby field and it was partly because of the war that the South Africans toured New Zealand. Amid the peace celebrations at the end of the First World War and in an effort to keep soldiers occupied while they were waiting for ships home, a series of sports contests involving the three services and the Allied countries were held. Among them was rugby and a New Zealand army team saw off five opponents and lost just once — to Australian Imperial Forces — to win the King's Cup. The New Zealanders had beaten South African Forces at Twickenham and the South African Rugby Board promptly asked the New Zealand team to play in South Africa on the way home. This they did, winning 11 of their 15 matches, which were all against provincial teams. An early sign of things to come was that one of the stars of the army team, loose forward 'Ranji' Wilson, had to pull out of the team for the South African trip because he was of West Indian parentage.

The Springboks' first visit to New Zealand in 1921 was a direct

> **. . . Steel, between rugby seasons, picked up pocket money competing as a professional sprinter.**

result of the army team's tour and the problems explained by Solomon in 1912 had proved not to be as insurmountable as he had thought.

Throughout the drawn series, the South Africans were said to have been overly negative, more concerned with limiting the scoring against them rather than scoring themselves. For all their defensive qualities, one All Black try in the series was still being talked of years later as one of the greatest tries in a test match. It was by the wing, Jack Steel, in the first test in Dunedin. It was five-all in the second half and the All Blacks were on defence. The New Zealand first five-eighth, Ces Badeley, attempted a kick across field in behind the Springbok backs but he sliced the kick.

Mark Nicholls, at second five-eighth and making his test debut, remembered it vividly years later: 'Before the ball landed, Jack Steel ran in and took it on the full (he jumped for it) and immediately swerved out towards the touchline. Gerhard Morkel, the Springbok fullback, didn't get within 15 yards of him. Charlie Meyer, the Springbok second five-eighth, chased Jack every yard of the way to the corner flag, but could not get within tackling distance. Steel ran in right on the corner flag and around, grounding the ball behind the posts.'

Nicholls estimated Steel ran 50 yards, and newspaper reports of the time put the distance variously between 50 and 70. Whatever the distance and given space, Steel would have been too quick for any of the Springboks. Back home on the West Coast, Steel, between rugby seasons, picked up pocket money competing as a professional sprinter.

THE BOKS ARE BORN

The first New Zealand rugby team that went to Britain came home with a new name and so did the first South Africans.

A South African team visited Britain the season after the Original All Blacks and the players sported their recently acquired uniform of myrtle green jerseys with a springbok embroidered on the left breast. The springbok had been chosen by the South African board because, it was said at the time, it was as typical of Africa as the kangaroo was of Australia.

Rugby players weren't the first to use the springbok. A team of athletes and cyclists that went to England in 1894 wore green vests with a springbok monogram.

Anyway, the rugby players arrived at Richmond in south London in 1906 with new jerseys but with no name.

The manager, Cecil Carden, wrote in 1933 that he spoke to the captain, Paul Roos, and vice-captain Paddy Carolin. 'I . . . pointed out that the witty

London press would invent some funny name for us if we did not invent one for ourselves. We thereupon agreed to call ourselves Springboks and to tell pressmen that we desired to be so named. I remember this distinctly, for Paul reminded us that Springbokken was the correct plural. However, the *Daily Mail* after our first practice called us the Springboks, and the name stuck.'

It was the *Daily Mail* that for so many years was wrongly given the credit for also naming the All Blacks on the basis of the mythical tale that the paper's rugby writer, John Buttery, had referred to the team as 'all backs' but an 'l' was inserted by someone in the newspaper office. It's now known that it was a paper in Devon, where the Originals played their first match, which was the first to publicly use the phrase All Blacks.

South Africa

The first test was also remarkable for the omission of halfback Teddy Roberts, generally acknowledged as the finest back in New Zealand when in his prime. His non-selection prompted outrage throughout New Zealand, with people writing letters to editors expressing their disbelief and horror and demanding that the three selectors be sacked. Companies even managed to get the controversy into their newspaper advertisements.

Newspaper writers called it 'sensational' (the *Christchurch Sun*) and 'astonishing' (the *Lyttelton Times*) — the dropping of Wayne Shelford in 1990 was almost nothing by comparison. The Rugby Union and the selectors themselves remained mute.

Things after the first test got curiouser and curiouser. An organisation called the Dominion Sportsmen's Association had gold medals struck for the best forward and back in each test and it asked the selectors to make the choices. The best back in the first test, they decided, was the man who had taken Roberts' position, his provincial team-mate, 'Ginger' Nicholls, a brother of Mark's.

Yet for the second test in Auckland a fortnight later, the selectors dropped Nicholls and brought in Roberts, some newspapers saying they were bowing to public opinion. By the time of the third test in Wellington three weeks later, Roberts was the captain. It represented a remarkable turnaround by the selectors.

The Springboks had won the second test, and the third was a scoreless draw in Wellington in terrible weather conditions and apparently comparable with the 1975 test against Scotland at Eden Park. The *New Zealand Times* had this to say: 'A rugby test was impossible and the strenuous struggle in mud and rain with a

Right: Friends after. All Black captain George Aitken, referee Ted McKenzie and South African captain Boy Morkel. **Below**: Opponents during. Ginger Nicholls breaks from a scrum during the first test in 1921 with Springbok wing Attie van Heerden waiting.

SALTY LOSES OUT TO SEASONED BASIE

When a fullback from Free State, Basie Viviers, was named to lead South Africa to New Zealand in 1956, surprise was widespread.

Though a popular figure, he was said to have been past his best as a rugby player and that for such a critical series, the captain should have been someone more assured of a test place and also in a more appropriate position than fullback from which to lead.

But Viviers was a compromise choice; he was not the first choice of the South African selectors or of the all-powerful manager and coach, Danie Craven.

Journalist Edward Griffiths, for a time the chief executive of the South African Rugby Union, wrote in *The Captains* that the first choice to lead the side was the Springbok lock, Salty du Randt.

But on the last night of trials in Cape Town, du Randt punched the Western Province forward, Jan Pickard, breaking his nose.

Griffiths wrote that accounts of the preceding argument differed, but there was unanimity on the point that du Randt punched Pickard on the nose.

Craven was called to the hotel and organised a team meeting for the next morning. 'Craven started by referring to an unfortunate event that had taken place the previous evening,' Griffiths wrote. 'He then invited du Randt to speak. In scarcely audible tones, head bowed, [he] mumbled an apology and asked to be forgiven.'

Compromise captain Basie Viviers.

As a consequence, du Randt was ruled out of the captaincy and Craven turned instead to Viviers. 'What is done is done,' Craven said. 'Our task is to make the best of the squad that has been chosen.'

Du Randt and Pickard were both in the touring party and, according to Griffiths, the rest of the team was divided between those who sided with du Randt and those who sided with Pickard.

'Viviers, through no fault of his own, found himself caught in the middle, his reputation peppered by crossfire.'

Griffiths said du Randt and Pickard barely spoke to each another during the tour and, to make matters worse, Craven didn't get along with his assistant manager, Dan de Villiers.

Du Randt played in each of the four tests and captained them in the first when Viviers was ill. His sparring partner Pickard played only in the second test.

That wasn't the only time the Springboks in New Zealand didn't get their original choice as captain. The selectors for the tour of 1965 voted 4–1 in favour of Doug Hopwood, a No 8 who captained Western Province.

But the South African board vetoed the decision and the Western Province halfback, Dawie de Villiers, was made captain instead.

No explanation was given, but there was speculation that the change reflected the influence of the Broederbond, the secret society that promoted Afrikanerdom above all else and which was said to have had a profound effect throughout South African white leadership.

When Hopwood died early in 2002, an obituary published in *The Independent* in London said the South African board's vice-president, Kobus Louw, who managed the 1965 team in New Zealand, was the board member who led the opposition to Hopwood being captain.

The players' burden. Would-have-been captain Salty du Randt gives supremo Danie Craven a lift during training in Wellington in 1956.

Follow the leader. Maurice Brownlie leads out the All Blacks for the fourth test against South Africa in 1928. Behind him are Ron Stewart, Bunny Finlayson, Bill Hazlett and Ian Harvey.

slippery ball ended as it should have done. Taking everything into consideration, a score to either side would have been unsatisfactory.'

The only winner, it was reported, was some bright spark who bought the Defence Department's entire surplus stock of soldiers' oilskins, a type of poncho, and sold the lot outside Athletic Park.

There were no illusions even then about the significance of New Zealand and South Africa meeting at rugby. 'The Rugby Football Championship of the World,' the weekly *Free Lance* modestly headlined its review of the tour. The Springboks' manager, Harold Bennett, appeared to agree because he said at a farewell dinner to the team: 'During the last 10 weeks, by your public and in your press, we have been impressed with the fact that we were meeting champions in the New Zealanders; well, we have met them and the result of the test games is one win each with the final match drawn and we make bold to claim that we South Africans are entitled to sit down with the New Zealanders on the top of the pedestal.'

By the time the All Blacks went to South Africa for the first time, they had with them the tag of Invincibles that the team in Britain in 1924–25 had earned. Since the Springboks in 1924 had beaten

the British Isles in a series, the mythical world championship was up for grabs again. But the All Blacks didn't long remain invincible. They lost a couple of early matches and learnt early the peculiar rigours and subterfuges of touring South Africa. Their first loss was to Cape Town Clubs which, before the match, the All Blacks could have been forgiven for thinking was a scratch team of local players there to provide the All Blacks with a warm-up match.

But the team included the recently appointed Springbok captain, Phil Mostert, who had toured New Zealand in 1921, the redoubtable first five-eighth, Bennie Osler, and 10 other internationals. That game was lost and so was the following one, to Transvaal, the South Africans continuing their softening-up process by submitting the All Blacks to a long train journey in between the two. The pattern of All Black tours of South Africa had been set.

Like the 1949 team, the All Blacks had problems with their forwards trying to adapt to the South African scrum formation of 3-4-1 and it was a stupendous effort by them to square the series and to win the fourth test — and win it by dominating play in the forwards. Along the way, though, the All Blacks had been

197

Above: The final act. Bob Duff and Basie Viviers lead out their teams for the fourth test of the 1956 series.

Right: Left arm over. Ron Jarden throws into a lineout in the fourth test of 1956.

DANIE ON ATTACK

Danie Craven, the ruler of South African rugby for the best part of half a century, could be a prickly character. Not for him the pat phrases when being interviewed.

After the Springboks won the second test of the 1956 series in Wellington, a match that was at times violent and always tense, he was approached by an interviewer for South Pacific Films, which had shot a newsreel of the match.

'How do you think the Springboks will go in the third test?' Craven was asked.

'Give us a chance to think about this one first before you ask what's going to happen in the future, surely,' was his terse reply.

Undaunted, the interviewer ploughed on.

'What did you think of the referee today? Did you like the way in which the match was controlled?'

'Yes,' said Craven, fixing a steely glare on the interviewer. 'Why do you ask that question?'

End of questions.

By contrast, the All Black captain, Pat Vincent, was also asked about the referee.

'I think the wind was the referee today,' Vincent replied in his urbane manner. 'That controlled the way the game was played.'

He was known as the Doc or the Boss. Danie Craven.

Collared. All Black hooker Bill Hadley is taken high in the
first test in 1928 in Durban.

thrashed 17–0 in the first test in Durban, a match that for
generations later was fondly remembered as Osler's. Without doubt
the best first five-eighth then playing the game, he scored 14 of the
17 points but it was his tactical running on the blindside, as much
as his kicking, that undid the All Blacks. New Zealand won the
second by a point and were beaten by five points in the third.

New Zealand had a first five-eighth of their own who could
make an impact, too — if only he could get on the field. Mark
Nicholls, who'd made his debut against South Africa in 1921, was
the All Blacks' vice-captain and a tour selector but he hadn't played
in any of the first three tests. Bad blood, it was said, existed
between him and the captain, Maurice Brownlie, stemming from
the Invincibles' tour. Rather than any particular incident leading to
the fallout, it seemed a clash of personalities between the quiet,
conservative Brownlie and the talkative, brash Nicholls.

Before the final test in Cape Town, the All Blacks weren't given
a show. 'If ever a team had their backs to the wall, the All Blacks

have,' the *Cape Argus* said. 'With two tests lost and the narrowest
of victories in one, their form makes it impossible to predict
anything but a South African victory tomorrow.'

The newspaper may not have known it at the time, but Nicholls
had finally been included in the side, but at second five-eighth. The
test came to be called the 'umbrella test' in South Africa because of
the heavy rain throughout, similar in fact to the drawn test of 1921
in Wellington, but it could also be remembered as Nicholls' test.

'We went on to the field with the knowledge that South Africa
thought they could not lose,' Nicholls wrote in his unpublished
autobiography. 'If we had failed, then New Zealand's great name
in the rugby world would have been lowered to second place . . .
this match will always live as an example of what determination
and confidence can achieve with the biggest odds facing a team.

'Our forwards, who played as if inspired, won the match,
because they dominated the play, called the tune while the
Springboks danced to it.'

Nicholls had a profound influence on the match, even before it
began. Brownlie had a habit of liking to play against the wind but
when he'd won the toss, he asked Nicholls' advice. Nicholls, who

CRAVEN FOR HELP IN '49

The All Blacks' manager, Jim Parker, and coach Alex McDonald were so concerned with the play of their forwards in South Africa in 1949 that they cast around for help — and received it from the unlikeliest of sources.

Among those who schooled the All Black pack before the first test in Cape Town was Danie Craven, Springbok selector and de facto coach of the side.

Parker, one of the Invincible All Blacks, explained the problem.

'In our old New Zealand diamond formation (2-3-2) we used to put our main weight on the wedge in the scrum and this was continued when we changed to the 3-4-1 formation,' he said.

'As a consequence, we threw the full weight of heavy locks onto the hooker, thereby restricting his range of movement. The disadvantage was not noticed as long as we played among ourselves but as soon as we reached South Africa we realised things had developed along different, and better, lines.'

Parker and McDonald, one of the Original All Blacks, turned first to the South African union's liaison man with the team, 'Bo' Wintle. He gave the forwards a few pointers and suggested the opposition coach be called in.

Memories differ. Some players recall that Craven's involvement consisted only of explaining interpretations by South African referees at scrum time.

But Craven himself recorded: 'Their scrum was very much below our standards and I found myself in a tight corner when they asked me to assist them. My first inclination was to decline, but I was finally swayed by the fact that rugby is only a game, not a form of war.'

Some with long memories of confrontations between New Zealand and South Africa, especially involving the pugnacious Craven, may beg to differ.

Whatever the efficacy of Craven's assistance, the All Blacks still lost the series 4–0.

Foe but sometime advisor: Danie Craven the dive passer.

said it was the first time Brownlie had asked his advice on anything, advised him to take the wind — and he did. During the match, Nicholls gradually took control — he kicked two penalty goals and a dropped goal and when the weather became even worse in the second half, he took over at first five-eighth, knowing that was where the control should lie.

Mostert was generous towards Nicholls after the test match. If he had played in each test, the All Blacks could have won the series, he said.

But throughout the saga of New Zealand-South Africa rugby, there have always been 'if onlys' and 'could haves'.

If the 1928 series had been won by the All Blacks, as perhaps it may have been if off-field politics hadn't determined selections; if the wise counsel of Philip Nel and Danie Craven hadn't prevailed when the Springboks were in New Zealand in 1937, the All Blacks surely would have won that series as well. And if those two series had been won, would New Zealand have remained as obsessed with beating South Africa as it did? Would the national crusade of 1956 have had the same intensity? Would New Zealand rugby, so at odds with the rest of the country, have been so hellbent on

bringing the Springboks to New Zealand in 1981 when the whole world knew such a tour was dangerous folly?

And since the realms of fantasy have been entered, what would South African rugby have become if there had been no Danie Craven for about 60 years, no Craven who played test matches in three different positions, no Craven who coached, managed and ruled Springbok teams for what seemed like aeons, no Craven who was the voice of South African rugby for half a century, no Craven for whom the means justified the ends as long as the ends were the success of South African rugby?

Craven's first impact on New Zealand was in 1937 when he toured as vice-captain and evidently people laughed when he first played; they laughed not because his shorts were ripped, or so he thought, but because of his dive pass, a method he perfected. But no New Zealanders laughed at him by the end of the tour.

The All Blacks had won the first test in 1937 because the Springboks made a hash of it. Craven and his captain, Nel, were outvoted at a selection meeting. Nel was dropped and Craven was put at first five-eighth. The Springboks played conservative rugby, the type they'd brought with them in 1921, and they were beaten. For the next test, Nel and Craven had their way — Nel was back at lock, Craven was back at halfback and the Springboks won 13–6. By the time of the decider, the Springboks' manager, Percy Day,

Injury break. A knee injury to Springbok flanker Dawie Ackermann early in the second half of the first test in 1956 in Dunedin gives both teams a breather.

IVAN'S TERRIBLE REVENGE

It was a bit of a joke against the All Black coach, Ivan Vodanovich, but he had the last laugh.

But was it really a joke, and did Vodanovich laugh at all?

It was in 1970 in South Africa and the fourth test loomed. The All Blacks could not win the series, but they could still square it. They'd lost the first test, won the second and lost the third.

Vodanovich was preparing for his last throw of the dice.

Just before the All Blacks' second-last tour match, in Potchefstroom, Canterbury players played their joke against Vodanovich.

Prop Alister Hopkinson and flanker Alex Wyllie were lounging about at the foot of the hotel stairs when Vodanovich came hurrying down.

'Grizz stuck a foot out and tripped Ivan, who went hurtling through the swing doors of the dining room and landed on his face,' Hopkinson recalled.

Vodanovich picked himself up, turned to the laughing pair and said, 'Right, there'll be no Canterbury players in the test team.'

A few days later, manager Ron Burk read the fourth test team to reporters. When he'd finished, Gabriel David of the Wellington *Evening Post* said, 'Good joke, Ron, now tell us the real team.'

When Burk, who was ignorant of the Vodanovich statement, replied it was no joke, David then said: 'Then God help you.'

It's hard to believe that Vodanovich, an intensely passionate man who revered the All Black jersey, could have taken his revenge on a couple of pranksters by not picking them or their provincial mates in a test team.

It also has to be understood that Vodanovich did have a sharp sense of humour, sometimes so offbeat that it could be difficult to tell if he was joking. (He once walked into a New Zealand union council meeting and was asked where Ces Blazey was. Vodanovich, dressed impeccably in business suit and NZRFU tie, quick as a flash and with a straight face, responded that he'd last seen Blazey, an arch-conservative, dressed in singlet, shorts and gumboots in the public bar of one of the seedier hotels in Wellington.)

So his statement about no Canterbury players being in the test team had to be a joke. But in the team Burk read out, Canterbury names were noticeably absent.

Wyllie, who had played in the third test, had been replaced by Tom Lister of South Canterbury. Fergie McCormick, everyone's No 1 choice at fullback, had been replaced by Gerald Kember of Wellington.

It's true McCormick had had an injured back, but he had pronounced himself fit for the test. He underwent a fitness test at Ellis Park with Hawke's Bay back Ian MacRae, who'd also been injured, but no one from the team turned up to watch.

'We were as disappointed as hell, astonished and a bit hosed off,' McCormick told his biographer, Alex Veysey. 'Nobody seemed interested whether we'd had a run or not.'

McCormick said there was a split in the touring team as soon as the test team was announced. 'It was a decidedly unhealthy atmosphere, what with mutterings in the corridors, outright angry criticisms in the bedrooms,' he said.

The mood was grim and there was tension in the air when the players next day filed onto the team bus for training.

The joker in the pack, Hopkinson, split the silence by calling out, 'Stand up all the Canterbury guys in the test team.'

Ivan Vodanovich

For a few seconds there was horrified silence. Then the captain, Brian Lochore, started to chuckle, and soon the whole busload joined in. Hopkinson had eased the tension.

The changes wrought by Vodanovich meant that 27 of the 30 players on tour were used in the four tests. It was to no avail. The All Blacks lost the fourth test 20–17.

Hopkinson's breezy humour was not exercised only in moments of tension.

The 1967 All Blacks, like most touring teams, were given a reception by the august British Sportsmen's Club at the Savoy Hotel in London. These functions are attended by the cream of British sporting elite past and present, by the aristocracy and by as many politicians who can find an excuse to absent themselves from Westminster, which is just 10 minutes' walk away.

Such occasions are posh, drawing on the best traditions of British ceremony. They have a scarlet-liveried doorman whose task it is to bark out in a stentorian voice — the job usually goes to former regimental sergeant-majors with famed voices — the name of each guest as he enters the lunch room.

If the doorman doesn't recognise the guest (and they have a great skill in recognising a remarkable number), the guest is required to whisper his name in the doorman's ear.

The All Blacks appeared and the doorman barked out, 'Mr Brian Lochore' and in walked the All Black captain.

'Mr Colin Meads' and so on . . .

At Hopkinson's turn, the doorman inclined his head towards the rough-hewn prop, indicating he needed a whisper.

Deadpan, Hopkinson whispered, 'The name's jockstrap.'

Elaborately, the doorman returned to his full height, looked into the lunch room and continued his announcement: 'Mr Jock Strap!'

had already gone home and the plans laid down for the second test applied for the third. The South Africans won that as well — for the first time, a series between these two countries had a decisive outcome; for the first time, the Springboks had beaten New Zealand in a series. South Africa were the best in the world. It was an outcome that cast a long shadow.

It was in New Zealand minds when the dark days of 1949 came and went and it was in New Zealand minds again in 1956 when the South Africans returned, this time with Craven having the title of manager and the role of coach. He also became, in 1956, the president of the South African Rugby Board. He was the undisputed ruler of Springbok rugby, a position in which he was unassailable for another 30 years.

New Zealanders have been cast as passionless people, slow to show emotion. Anyone who cast New Zealanders thus was not in New Zealand in 1956. Passion, in any case, is not always something that is necessarily on public display. It can be buried deep within but be no less ardent for all that. The New Zealand of 1956 wanted to beat South Africa, had to beat South Africa. We'd won the war, we were a contented nation in peace; a New Zealander had conquered Everest, yet still we hadn't beaten South Africa at rugby, the national passion. Rugby players, especially All Blacks, talk of pressure, they talk of the burdens of public and their own expectations; no All Blacks could surely have been under such pressure as the All Blacks of 1956. It wasn't just a series of four test matches in 1956; it wasn't about being humble in victory or gracious in defeat; it was about winning, about exorcising the demons of the past, about finally doing what New Zealand rugby had not hitherto done.

They were the black and white years with no shades of grey. Reservations about South Africa's racist policies were publicly expressed but not in much volume; all was subjugated to the need to win. New Zealanders knew Maori couldn't tour there in 1928 or 1949 and wouldn't until 1970, but that was there, this was here. Nothing mattered but beating the Springboks.

And they were beaten. Not without concerns, not without travail, not without some heart-stopping moments and not without crisis meetings, but they were beaten. Every ground was packed. Outside every ground, people slept for two or three nights in order not to miss getting tickets. Gates opened early in those days and when they did, people poured in and ran for the prime viewing positions and there parked themselves for the next few hours, anticipating the moment when the All Blacks and South Africans would run onto the field and the mental comfort of a nation was at stake. And, oh yes, the championship of the world.

And we won. There was no more favourite line in 1956. We won. The first test in Dunedin: 10–6. The second test in Wellington: 8–3 to them. One each with two to play. On the Thursday after the second test, the council of the New Zealand union had a special meeting and the selectors were there. Changes were discussed. The selectors came up with a different team. The council approved. No cabinet meeting could have been as critical to the general well being of New Zealand as that council meeting.

The third test in Christchurch: 17–10. The reintroduction of Kevin Skinner at prop was a master stroke. He played both sides; he dealt the blows that needed to be dealt. It was Don Clarke's debut, too. He also dealt the blows that needed to be dealt.

Cheers. Kevin Skinner swigs a lemonade after the third test of 1956 while Bill Clark seems happy enough in his souvenired Springbok jersey.

MURPHY'S LAW CUT SHORT

The replacement of referees in a test match is a rare event. Both times New Zealand have started a test with one referee and finished with another have been against South Africa.

The first was in Christchurch in 1965 in the third test against South Africa when New Zealand's most experienced referee at the time, Pat Murphy of North Auckland, had to quit because of a leg injury. Touch judge Alan Taylor, from Canterbury, replaced him to make his test debut.

The All Blacks were leading 11–5 when Murphy went off and had increased their lead to 16–5 by halftime. But they lost the match 19–16 — a South African victory made famous by lock Tiny Naude kicking the winning penalty goal.

Murphy's injury, and his place in All Blacks test history, later formed a part of Colin Meads' repertoire when he became much in demand as a speaker.

Meads recalls the incident like this:

'Pat Murphy, I think he refereed 13 games, test rugby . . . it's a lot when you only did games at home . . . you didn't go overseas. And out of those 13 games, we won 12 . . . now that's a bloody good referee.

'And the one we lost, he went off at halftime.'

The other match in which the referee was replaced came in much more bizarre circumstances. That was in the tri-nations match in Durban in 2002 when Irish referee David McHugh was attacked by a spectator, Pieter van Zyl.

McHugh had a shoulder dislocated and he was replaced by touch judge Chris White of England.

PREPARATION, PERFORMANCE . . . PERFECT

The All Black coach, John Hart, was in no doubt as to why his team in 1996 was able to do what no New Zealand team before it had been able to do — win a series in South Africa.

Hart had some great All Blacks at his command, but so, too, had there been great All Blacks who had been there before and tried and failed.

The difference in 1996 was threefold, Hart firmly believes.

One was the level of planning and organisation that went into the tour. He and manager Mike Banks went on a reconnaissance trip to South Africa earlier in the year, checking out hotels and other arrangements, ensuring they left as little as possible to chance.

Another reason had nothing to do with Hart, Banks or any of the rugby hierarchy at the time. It was neutral referees. Previous All Black teams, and especially that of 1976, felt they'd been stymied in their ambitions as much by South African referees as they had by their Springbok opponents. By 1996, that factor was out of the equation. Neutral referees in test matches were by then imposed by the International Rugby Board.

And the third reason was Hart's belief, controversial at the time, that he needed a squad of 36 players. It was an unusual squad size but these were unusual circumstances.

The All Blacks' first test in South Africa was the last of the tests in the inaugural tri-nations competition. That was in Cape Town. They also had a mini-tour. Before the Cape Town test, there was a match against a Boland Invitation XV and after Cape Town, there were six matches including three tests.

Under the old order, the All Blacks would have had a squad of 30 and test players would have been expected to double up in midweek matches.

'I knew that for us to have a show of winning the three-test series, we in effect had to have two squads — one for the midweek matches and one for the tests,' Hart says. 'I wrote a paper to the board of the New Zealand Rugby Union early in 1996 suggesting that we take 36. It was a totally new concept and the reaction of the chairman, Richie Guy, was initially one of horror. His objections were not so much the cost involved but the practical, physical things. He thought we'd need two buses, or he thought there would be a split in the whole squad between test players and non-test players. But eventually, and to his credit, he saw the logic of my suggestion: to have a chance, we couldn't have the same guys playing four tests (including Cape Town) as well as the midweekers.'

Cost was also a factor, but this was overcome to a certain extent because some of the midweek players were not then on full All Black contracts.

'It's not even correct to talk of test players and midweek players,' Hart says. 'We were one squad and within it some players played in the tests and some in the other matches. The only time we separated as a squad was for a match in Potchefstroom before the test in Pretoria. I didn't want the test players spending three or four hours in a bus four days before the test so they didn't go.'

Hart's reasons for the success in 1996: organisation, neutral referees and the enlarged squad, were not what he hammered home to the players as they approached the first of the series in Durban. 'We knew we had to win that because it was at sea level and the next two were at altitude,' he says. 'I didn't think we'd be able to come back from a test down. I talked to the players about the wonderful chance they had.

'This is the opportunity of a lifetime,' I told them. 'This is a chance to make history.'

Players, as always, reacted differently. Some, such as Sean Fitzpatrick, Zinzan Brooke and Ian Jones, were steeped in the history of the game and they knew what it would mean to New Zealand to finally win a series in South Africa.

To others, it was just another tour, just another test that had to be won for its own sake.

'Some had barely been born when the All Blacks had last played a series there,' Fitzpatrick says. 'The history meant nothing to them but that didn't mean their resolve was any less than that of the rest of us.'

The Durban test was won 23–19. Then the Pretoria test 33–26. History had been achieved.

Hart remembers the highlights — 'The difference between the two sides was skill really,' he says. 'They had no one like Jeff Wilson or Christian Cullen and the two of them were in superlative form. We had a core of strength, experience and skill throughout our team that was better than what South Africa had.'

Emotion was thick in the air after the Pretoria test. Both Hart and Fitzpatrick recall Don Clarke, a key member of the 1960 team in South Africa, being in tears after the match.

But even then, Fitzpatrick thinks, some of the team didn't really appreciate the significance of what they had achieved. 'It wasn't until we got home that we realised what it really meant to New Zealand and especially to those players who had been there before. It was quite moving.'

Fitzpatrick puts the series win in South Africa higher in his personal memory bank than the World Cup win in 1987.

'In 1987 I don't think anyone knew what to expect about the World Cup,' he says. 'We had a good team and we played better rugby than any of the other countries, but I don't think any of them knew what they were heading into. The World Cup then was like a tour in the old days. I remember Craig Green on the Monday morning after the cup final waiting outside his home in Christchurch at 5.30 in the morning to go to his job as a roofer.

'In South Africa, there was no question what the prize was and we had a pretty amazing team.'

The last of the tests, in Johannesburg, was lost and though it was still a test, it was of no consequence in terms of the series. Hart blames himself for the loss.

'It was one of the biggest mistakes of my coaching career,' he says. 'I got hung up on loyalty to the players who had won the series but I should have made some changes. The test players were drained, physically and emotionally, and some had one foot on the plane home. I should have made some changes.'

Ticker taped. John Hart and Sean Fitzpatrick revel in New Zealand's delight at finally winning a series in South Africa.

The fourth test in Auckland: 11–5. Peter Jones' try, Clarke's kicking, Jones' speech and Craven's 'It's all yours New Zealand.' Blessed words indeed.

New Zealanders, being industrious people, don't like leaving jobs half done. Beating South Africa was only half done. There was a job to be finished and it could only be finished by beating them there. The All Blacks tried in 1960, tried in 1970, tried again in 1976, only to fall each time, only to succumb to the peculiar maladies that seem to inflict themselves upon All Blacks whenever they're in South Africa. Brutal itineraries, inept referees, illnesses, all played their part. But playing the biggest part all the time was a resolve by the South Africans not to lose to New Zealand.

The South African government's insane apartheid policy also played a part, not so much in how the All Blacks played but in how New Zealanders thought of the country. Worldwide awareness of the cruelty of the policy increased through the 1970s as South Africa was banned from all manner of sporting events. However, such was the importance of the game of rugby to the white South African, and such was the importance of South Africa to world rugby, that it continued for a time unhindered, as if rugby could be played in a vacuum not cognisant of everything else around it. While New Zealanders were well aware of the injustices of the system, rugby was of such importance in New Zealand that it unwisely took precedence and the Springboks' visit to New Zealand in 1981 was a tour that should never have been allowed to happen. The rugby, even the outcome, became irrelevant as police fought protesters, as New Zealanders fought New Zealanders, in tandem with every match. No country thereafter could tolerate such disorder and the Springboks went into an imposed isolation.

New Zealand went to South Africa for the first of the post-isolation tests and won that well enough, though it was evident the years of just playing among themselves had had an effect on the way the South Africans played the game. And as welcome as the win was, it was not a series — and New Zealand still had the burning desire to beat them in a series.

The World Cup final in Johannesburg in 1995 came and went, and how galling it was that the All Blacks, acknowledged as the best team at the tournament, lost to South Africa. Would justice never be delivered? But finally it came. The first full year of professionalism in rugby, the first test series in South Africa against the All Blacks in 20 years and, for the first time, neutral referees. The All Blacks coached by John Hart and led by Sean Fitzpatrick played with the ghosts of generations past on their shoulders; when Christian Cullen ran out onto the test fields of Durban and Pretoria, there with him in spirit were men such as Bob Scott and Don Clarke; there with Andrew Mehrtens were men such as Mark Nicholls and Earle Kirton; there with Robin Brooke were men such as Maurice Brownlie and Colin Meads . . . and there with them all rode the hopes of all New Zealanders. And there at the end with them all were the thanks of all New Zealanders.

There with them all were the hopes — and the thanks — of all New Zealanders.
The All Blacks in South Africa in 1996.

TAINE ON PAIN

Migraines are severe, throbbing headaches as anyone who suffers them would unhappily testify. They can be and often are so severe that they are all pervading. The sufferer can think of nothing else, do nothing else, but accept the throbbing pain going on in the head, often concentrated around or behind one eye. They are debilitating.

The pattern of the classic migraine is well established: blurred vision or flashes of light, then 20 or 30 minutes later the pain that can last for several hours. There's no treatment other than aspirin or some other analgesic; the patient has to be patient.

Captain-for-a-time Taine Randell, like thousands of other New Zealanders, is a migraine sufferer. Migraines can strike any time and for Randell they've struck at the most critical of times — during the intensity of rugby tests.

'The first time I had one in a test was in Auckland in 1997 against South Africa,' he says. That was when the All Blacks beat the Springboks 55–35, a previously unimaginable scoreline for a test between such enduring rivals.

'I felt it coming on and I thought "Oh no," ' he says. Randell suffers the classic symptoms, which he describes as like when you look directly at a bright light then look away and the aura of the brightness remains in the vision. 'There's this pinpoint of light with shade all around it and your vision is pretty much stuffed,' he says. 'You can still distinguish outlines, but not details.'

> 'I'd go to the physio and ask for a pill and then just play as best I can . . .'

So how did Randell cope on this and other occasions when a migraine struck when on the test field?

'You just battle on as best you can,' he says. 'You make do. I'd go to the physio and ask for a pill and then just play as best I can until the headache kicks in. That's when the vision clears.'

He suffered a migraine in Cardiff the night before the World Cup playoff match against South Africa in 1999 and again on the field against South Africa in 2000. Three migraines, three South African tests — it's easy to joke Springbok tests give Randell a headache, but it's far from a joke.

'It's hard to pinpoint the cause as anyone who suffers migraines knows,' Randell says, 'but I remember in the 1997 match it came on suddenly after I'd hit my head on someone in a tackle. It was quite a whack so maybe that was what triggered it.

'When it's happened, I've told the other guys that I'll be right in a few minutes and I've avoided lineout calls going to me or cut myself out of moves, that sort of thing. You just have to wait it out then get back into it.'

And, Randell might have added but didn't, get back into it with a blinding headache.

Taine Randell. Behind the smiles there can be pain.

Islands in the Sun

The idyllic image is of palm trees wafting gently in a breeze, the sun beating down on sparkling lagoons and white sandy beaches. But that's for the tourist brochures. The rugby reality is of island peoples steeped in the game and noted for their explosiveness, inventiveness and speed. They're disadvantaged by distance, population and economic base, but collectively they've become a significant force in world rugby.

FIJI

FIJI RUGBY **Fiji for years had been clamouring for an official test against New Zealand. Officially the Fijians were diplomatic; unofficially they were frustrated, as they tried and tried again to get the New Zealand union to agree to their playing the All Blacks.**

They played New Zealand teams it is true, especially at the end of tours of Australia and in one match in Auckland in 1980, but they were not regarded as proper tests. The reason, as advanced by New Zealand, was that Fiji was not a member of the International Rugby Board and tests could be played against only IRB members.

The aberration of the 1913 match against All-America aside, New Zealand at least was consistent in its argument and didn't play tests against anyone else either who wasn't a member of the IRB.

The World Cup changed all that and when Fiji were drawn in the same pool as the All Blacks for the first cup in 1987, New Zealand had no choice in the matter. It was a test, like it or not.

The irony of that first meeting in Christchurch, though, was that the Fijians, at last getting what they had wanted for years, deliberately fielded an understrength team. That was no disrespect for the All Blacks, merely acknowledging the exigencies of the cup. Fiji had, in one of the upsets of the cup, beaten Argentina in their first match, in Hamilton the day after the opening cup match between New Zealand and Italy.

Given that the All Blacks would surely qualify top from the pool, the Fijians figured they would have to beat the Italians in their final pool match to go on to the quarterfinals. They therefore conceded, privately if not publicly, their pool match against New Zealand.

For the game against New Zealand, Fiji made nine changes from the side that had beaten Argentina. True, they had some injury problems and two of the Fijians injured in Hamilton didn't play again in the cup, but the fact remained the Fijians put far from their best team out against New Zealand. It seemed an odd way to treat an opponent they had wanted to meet for years.

To the surprise of no one, probably not even the Fijians, the All Blacks won the match 74–13 and wing Craig Green and fullback John Gallagher each joined the select group of players to have scored four tries in a test.

The best-laid plans of mice and Fijians, however . . . The Fijians also lost the game they had targeted, against Italy, and only made it into the cup quarters because they had scored more tries overall than Italy.

That first test against Fiji had been a long time coming. Fijian rugby had got under way early in the 20th century through the efforts of New Zealand, Australian and British civil servants and traders who were in Fiji, and through the experiences of Fijians who had been sent to New Zealand to get educated and took the game back home with them.

The greatest impetus seemed to have come from a group of New Zealanders who went to Suva in 1913 to build the Grand Pacific Hotel. One of them was a plumber, Paddy Sheehan, who had captained Otago and who was one of those go-ahead chaps who, if nothing had been organised, would set about organising something. He formed the Pacific club in Suva; he became the first president of the Fijian union and got the Fijian government on his side (largely because the influential Fijians had all been educated in New Zealand and knew what Sheehan was talking about).

Fiji's first international contact was when the 1913 All Blacks were returning from their curious tour of California and British Columbia and Sheehan somehow persuaded them, during a stopover in Suva, to play the Pacific club. This they did and the All Blacks won 67–3, though reports about how serious the match may have been have not survived.

Auckland University sent teams to Fiji in 1926 and 1928 and the New Zealand union was persuaded to send a Maori team there in 1938. The results were a bit of an eye-opener for New Zealanders because the Maori won one test, drew one and lost one. This must have left a great impression on the Maori manager, Stan Dean, who was also chairman of the New Zealand union. It was he who gave the Fijians the go-ahead to send a team to New Zealand for the first time in 1939.

The Fijians were a great success in New Zealand. They didn't lose a match, but they were also a very popular side, bringing a

flair to rugby not often seen in New Zealand. Much was made of their smiling faces, their singing, their 'skirts' (*sulus*) and their *cibi*, the Fijian answer to the haka.

The *cibi* (pronounced 'thimbi') was devised especially for the New Zealand tour and it is the one they still perform. The story goes that the captain, George Cakobau (later Fiji's paramount chief and as Governor-General, Ratu Sir George Cakobau), wanted a Fijian response to the haka and he went to Ratu Bola, the high chief of the Navusardave in Bau.

'Ratu Bola gave me a Bauan *cibi* and came down himself and personally taught us at our camp at the old Defence Force hall in Suva,' Cakobau recalled later.

Like the Te Rauparaha haka itself, the *cibi* loses much in translation. In English its first chant goes: 'Make ready, make ready; Oh, oh, oh, oh, oh, oh, oh; make ready, make ready; oh oh . . .' and so on.

The Fijians made ready all right because they remain the only national team to tour New Zealand unbeaten. The New Zealand

union was not so ready, despite Dean's enthusiasm, and contact with Fiji continued to be sporadic.

The Fijians still came to New Zealand every so often but their 'test' was invariably against the Maori. The All Blacks of 1968, 1974 and 1980 tacked Fiji on to tours of Australia, with the 1974 team just scraping home by a point against the Fijian national team on a sweltering afternoon in Suva.

A breakthrough came in 1980 when Fiji played an unofficial test against New Zealand in Auckland. The All Blacks were chosen from players who, for a variety of reasons, had not played against Australia that year. They included the extremes of established All Blacks such as Graham Mourie and Bill Osborne, and the first schoolboy All Black, Craig Wickes. Test or not, the All Blacks were far too strong and won 33–0.

Over you go. Sam Harding gives Norm Maxwell a hand over the goal-line against Fiji in Wellington in 2002.

An All Black team was dispatched solely to Fiji for the first time in 1984 and they won each of their games handsomely. The team was captained by Jock Hobbs and though it was as close to full strength as injuries would allow, the match against Fiji, won 45–0, was still not deemed to be a test.

Even the breakthrough of the World Cup did not mean more tests for New Zealand's next-closest rugby neighbour after Australia. The All Blacks and Fiji didn't meet again for another 10 years, in 1997 — the match at Albany Stadium in which Jeff Wilson scored five tries in the All Blacks' 71–5 win.

Their only meeting since was in Wellington in 2002 when the All Blacks won 68–18.

Fijian rugby, especially in the 1970s and 80s, went through a competitive phase in which the forwards were big and hard, if not all that well versed in tactics, while the backs were fast and eager to throw the ball around. They created problems for their opponents because of their unorthodoxy.

Their style of rugby was ideally suited to the sevens version of the game and the increase in sevens tournaments, plus the International Rugby Board's sanctioning of a world series in sevens, meant that the traditional game in Fiji suffered. That wasn't the sole reason, though. Increased money in rugby elsewhere meant that while other countries could afford to pay players well and run development programmes, the Fijians' small economy couldn't sustain such luxuries. A forward-thinking plan to combine the island nations of Fiji, Samoa and Tonga and to field a Pacific Lions (or something) team, which should have been more competitive than the individual countries on their own, was given the thumbs-down by the IRB.

SAMOA

It was a surprise to the rugby world, even in New Zealand, when Western Samoa beat Wales at the citadel of the Arms Park in Cardiff in their World Cup match in 1991. Being beaten by a team from the South Seas was seen as the nadir of the fortunes of a once powerful rugby country and much was made of how the might of Wales was brought down by people from a tiny island group that most Welshmen would struggle to pinpoint on a map.

New Zealanders should not have been as surprised, though the victory was certainly an upset.

Samoan rugby had developed rapidly over the preceding 20 years, helped along massively by greatly increased migration to New Zealand since independence in 1962.

The surprise was that the rugby world had not taken note of Samoa before 1991.

Samoa's first test was against Fiji in 1924 and there's an oft-told story that the game began in Apia at seven in the morning so the Samoans' regular working day wouldn't be interrupted. Allied with that story is another that the match was won 6–0 by Fiji despite the encumbrance of an ancient tree growing in the middle of the ground.

There wasn't much contact with established rugby countries until nearly 40 years later, however. New Zealand Maori toured there in 1960 and Samoa didn't venture to New Zealand until 1976.

From then, though, rugby took off.

It's Samoa's fate that so many of its best players have played for the All Blacks, starting with the great Bryan Williams who made his sensational debut on the tour of South Africa in 1970. It seemed fitting then that it was Williams, first as technical advisor and then as coach, who took Samoan rugby to another level from the 1980s through the 1990s.

Replacements meet. Walter Little, who went on in the All Blacks' test against Samoa in 1993, meets another reserve, Keneti Sio.

The New Zealand connection, and the reality of dual representation until the International Rugby Board closed that swinging door, has been of inestimable value to Samoan rugby. Frank Bunce, despite his strong blood connections with Niue and what may be termed less strong connections with Samoa, was the rock of the Samoan backline until he took on a similar role with the All Blacks. Michael Jones, among the greatest of All Blacks, played for Samoa before he played for New Zealand, as did centre Alama Ieremia, first five-eighth Stephen Bachop and halfback Ofisa Tonu'u.

The strong Samoan presence in Auckland and Wellington meant their players were being brought up in the New Zealand rugby system, either the formal progression of age grade sides and academies; or the informal, of the week-in, week-out experience of competitive club rugby. It was experience they could never have gained in Samoa and the growing strength of Samoan rugby was demonstrated not just in the quality of their national side, but in New Zealand provincial and national sides.

For all the close links, it wasn't until 1993 that Western Samoa first met the All Blacks in a test. It had to be in Auckland, the biggest Polynesian city in the world, and it was as much a home match for the Samoans as it was for the New Zealanders.

Two Samoans, Jones and wing Vai'iga Tuigamala — three if Bunce is included — were in the All Black team and 13 of the Samoans all played their first-class rugby in New Zealand and a 14th, Mata'afa Keenan, used to.

It was almost, as someone at the time joked, New Zealand against the Rest. This was also at the time that the great All Black wing, John Kirwan, joked that he had been nicknamed Chester by his team-mates — because he was the only white man in the All Black backs.

The All Blacks that year had already dispensed with the Lions and Australia and it would have been a significant falling away of their fortunes if they couldn't have done the same to Samoa. They won 35–13 thanks to the strength of their forwards and also to Grant Fox, who kicked what was then a record seven penalty goals.

No one could know it then, but that was the closest the Samoans would get to New Zealand in a test. They were perceived as considerable threats then but, in the wake of professionalism, have become one of the sides that New Zealand uses as warm-ups for weightier opposition.

When they next met, in the opening test of 1996 and the first night test in New Zealand, the All Blacks won 51–10. It was also the first New Zealand test in Napier and it was Christian Cullen's debut, which he marked by scoring three tries.

It was 71–13 when they next played, in 1999 at Albany, and Jeff Wilson scored four tries. They met again at Albany in 2001 and the All Blacks won 50–6, with first five-eighth Tony Brown scoring

Dual nationalities. Alama Ieremia and John Timu vie for possession in the 1993 test against Samoa. Michael Jones, who like Ieremia played for both countries, is on the left. Sean Fitzpatrick and Ian Jones are also there.

Come and get it. Ron Cribb passes back to his support players as he's grabbed by Fereti Tuilagi during the Samoan test at Albany in 2001.

30 points, equal to the fifth highest total scored in a test.

Professionalism had changed the face of Samoan rugby even more dramatically than it had New Zealand's. In contrast with the 1993 Samoan team, the 2001 team that lost to the All Blacks had just six players who played their first-class rugby in New Zealand. The rest were scattered around England, Italy, Japan and Australia.

The economics of rugby have stalled the great advances Samoa made in the last two decades of amateurism. Samoa has a population of under 200,000 and it, like Tonga and Fiji, simply doesn't have the money to retain and pay the players it needs and neither does it have the money to host tours that would bring it money. It is a vicious circle.

The International Rugby Board both helps and hinders. It acknowledges the problems of small countries and tried to set up a match between the Northern and Southern Hemisphere to raise funds for them. For other reasons, though, it was an unworkable plan but at least, for the IRB, it was the thought that counted. At the same time, though, its harder stance on eligibility means that Samoans who have had All Black careers, players such as

Tuigamala and Tonu'u, can't now return to play for Samoa.

The New Zealand union, conscious of its neighbourly obligations in the South Pacific, does what it can but it's not as overwhelmed with cash as its detractors seem to think and New Zealand has enough problems of its own trying to maintain standards in a rapidly changing rugby world.

Samoans, like Tongans and Fijians, have also had an anecdotal effect of deterring young New Zealanders from starting rugby. The theory at the base of what's known as the 'browning' of New Zealand rugby is that Polynesians, Maori included, mature earlier than Pakehas and therefore at ages of 12 to 14 are much bigger and stronger, and white mothers don't want their sons risking injury against bigger opponents.

Like all theories based on anecdotal evidence, there's probably some truth but equally some exaggeration and oversimplification. An extension of the theory is that Polynesians don't last as long in the game and there is therefore a lack of depth at the higher end of the game, compounded when players go overseas once they know they're not likely to get a contract with the New Zealand union.

As both the Samoan and New Zealand unions know well, it's a simple matter to point out the problems. It's a far trickier exercise to find the solutions, and they remain elusive.

TONGA

It seems to be the unfortunate lot of Tonga, like Samoa, that their best rugby players are snapped up by some other country — usually New Zealand or Australia. The All Blacks and Tongans have met only twice in test matches and on the second occasion, at Albany in 2000, three players who would have qualified for Tonga contributed to the 102–0 damage inflicted by the All Blacks — wings Jonah Lomu and Doug Howlett and second five-eighth Pita Alatini.

Remarkably, Alatini marked his brother Sam in that game — the most assiduous scouring of international rugby records doesn't show any other instance of brothers opposing each other in a test match in the same position.

Though Tonga's rugby ties have historically been closer to Australia than New Zealand, the island kingdom has had similar problems to the two other significant rugby-playing island groups, Samoa and Fiji.

For much of its existence, Tongan rugby has been played in isolation of all but its island neighbours and New Zealand have never played there.

Rugby in Tonga developed early in the 20th century thanks mainly to the Methodist Church and Australian missionaries and early links were forged with especially Fiji, who played Tonga at Nuku'alofa in 1924.

For all its proximity, Tongan rugby was virtually ignored by New Zealand aside from occasional coaching visits until 1960 when the national Maori team first went there and to Samoa, a visit that was repeated in 1973.

But it wasn't until 1969 that Tonga were given permission to tour New Zealand and on that and tours since, they played the All Blacks only the once — at Albany in 2000.

Tonga had much closer links with Australia. The Australians

A century at home. Troy Flavell, Pita Alatini, Anton Oliver and Tana Umaga during the All Blacks' 102–0 defeat of Tonga at Albany in 2000 — their first 100-pointer in New Zealand.

went there with an invitation team in 1954 and to mark the close ties between the two, Tonga went to Australia in 1973 to celebrate Tongan rugby's 50th anniversary. They ended up celebrating more than an anniversary — they also celebrated a test win over the full Australian side, a match that remains one of Australian rugby's most embarrassing moments.

Tonga was one of the invited countries to the first World Cup in New Zealand and Australia in 1987 — losing to Canada, Wales and Ireland — but were beaten by Samoa in qualifying for the 1991 cup. They were back at the cup in South Africa in 1995 and finally met New Zealand for the first time at the cup in 1999.

It was the All Blacks' first match of that campaign and it showed. Though New Zealand won comfortably enough at the Bristol City soccer ground of Ashton Gate by 45–9, it was far from being a vintage All Black performance.

> **While getting thrashed by more than 100 points may not do much for Tongan rugby, it doesn't do much for New Zealand rugby either.**

One of the All Black squad watching from the stand was Alatini, whose father had been one of the veterans of Tongan rugby.

'We didn't really get on top in that game,' he says, 'and they probably got away with a few high shots and it lifted their game.'

Even so, it was only 16–9 at halftime and a flurry of scoring in the second half that allowed the All Blacks a scoreline of something like what they should have expected against a side that should never have tested them. It was a topsy-turvy series of matches for Tonga. They beat Italy 28–25 in their next game but then lost 101–10 to England in their final pool match — a game that became something of a farce after prop Ngalu Ta'u was sent off.

The Tongans, although suffering from a lack of money that became even more pronounced as the established rugby countries started earning even more, knew where they wanted to go and they hired an Invercargill-born coach, Dave Waterston, who had been plying his trade in South Africa.

His and Tongan rugby's vision, though, was not matched by available talent.

After 80-odd years of minimal contact, the All Blacks and Tonga met twice within a few months and, for the All Blacks, with only five matches in between. Once having met for the only time on New Zealand soil, though, Waterston was certainly in no hurry to repeat the experience. More harm than good would have been done by the 102–0 hammering by the first All Black team prepared by coaches Wayne Smith and Tony Gilbert, who had taken over from John Hart after the cup.

Waterston lamented the lack of adequate preparation for the match and he had a point because his players came from all over the globe — from Japan, England, Wales and Tonga.

This was the match in which Howlett made his debut as a replacement and scored a try against his blood brothers within 30 seconds of taking the field.

There's no doubting the rugby talent that comes from Tonga: it's harnessing it that's the problem. The Tongans, like the Samoans, are supporters of the All Blacks but it must be galling for them to see players such as Lomu, Howlett, Isitolo Maka and Alatini playing for the 'other' side, or to see players such as Toutai Kefu and Willie Ofahengaue playing for Australia.

It's as much a socio-economic problem as it is a rugby problem. Their veteran captain, 'Elisi Vunipola, candidly admits that it's difficult to keep young players in Tonga because there's not enough work. Once they're in New Zealand, they qualify for the All Blacks — providing they haven't already played for Tonga — and like the Samoans, they generally choose the better pay and the greater glory of being an All Black.

Under the rugby organisation that used to apply, the All Blacks and Tonga probably still would not have met. The World Cup was one reason they did and the other was a perceived need for warm-up tests for the All Blacks and a commercial requirement that they play a specific number of domestic tests each year.

While getting thrashed by more than 100 points may not do much for Tongan rugby, it doesn't do much for New Zealand rugby either. On balance, though, it's better that two neighbours, so close geographically and in other ways, do play.

The Pacific way. Josh Kronfeld of New Zealand and Elisi Vunipola of Tonga in the 1999 World Cup. Different countries, but both proud of their island heritage.

The New World Order

No one single event has changed rugby as much as the World Cup has. It's led directly to more countries playing the game and it led indirectly to the dropping of the old ways of amateurism. It might be a money tree for the International Rugby Board, but it's the holy grail for those countries which aspire to win it. The All Blacks did so first, in 1987, and since then rugby has been on a four-year cycle. No sooner is a cup finished than the planning for the next one starts.

The first toss. All eyes downwards to see which way the coin has landed before the first World Cup match. David Kirk, touch judge Jim Fleming, referee Bob Fordham, touch judge Kerry Fitzgerald and Italian captain Marzio Innocenti.

A couple of days before the All Blacks played their World Cup semifinal against Wales in Brisbane in 1987, their coach Brian Lochore leaned on a bar in the team's hotel after training and sipped on an orange juice.

The cup was a wonderful thing, he said, but he did have a reservation or two. It had brought the rugby world together like never before and, even a week before the final, it was clear the first World Cup had been a great success.

But, Lochore cautioned, four years might be a bit too often. A cup every six years might have been better. 'I think four years was chosen because the Olympics are every four years and the soccer World Cup is every four years and no one thought of anything different.'

The problem with four years could be that no sooner was one cup finished than countries would be planning for the next. The whole focus would be on the cup and other rugby might suffer. Coaches would be appointed for four-year cycles, countries would map their international programmes around four-year periods with the cup as the ultimate prize.

A few weeks later, with Lochore's All Blacks having won the first cup and with the other 15 countries long gone, the New Zealand union prepared its final report for the International Rugby Board.

It had many recommendations about how it could be done next time. The single most compelling recommendation was that in future, cups should be organised by, and played in, only one country.

The thoughts of wise men have often throughout history been left withering on the vine.

Three cups have been played since and in only one of them, and what could claim to be the most successful, was there a sole host. That was South Africa in 1995. The 1991 cup hosts were nominally England but in the rugby world of politicking and compromising, matches were played throughout the British Isles and France. The 1999 nominal cup hosts were Wales and again the matches were scattered, allied with a bizarre draw that redefined quarters as fifths, around the neighbours who couldn't bear to be left out.

No New Zealander needs reminding of the difficulties, insurmountable in this case, when Australia and New Zealand set out in 1998 to jointly host the 2003 cup only to find the plans end up in acrimonious ruin and for New Zealand to be treated as an errant and naïve schoolboy rather than as one of the few countries in which rugby actually matters.

Lochore's thinking out loud about the four-year cycle proved to be prophetic. The cup dominates thinking and determines the length of players' and coaches' careers. As New Zealand saw in 2002 and as other countries had earlier seen, lesser teams are fielded for otherwise full internationals in the long-term name of preparing for the cup. International programmes are scheduled with the cup in mind; players map out their careers with the cup uppermost as a short-term or long-term goal. The cup, with its fellow traveller, professionalism, brought to an end what might be called the traditional tour. Love affairs with touring teams have been reduced almost to one-night stands.

The advent of the World Cup, as welcome and as successful as it was, and as long sought as it was by some players who had the vision to see, changed rugby forever. The first cup in 1987 came eight years before the International Rugby Board decreed the game open, but that single act had been inevitable for years. Rugby could not sustain a self-indulgent anachronistic adherence to a principle of amateurism. It foundered on the reality that if more was expected of players, if rugby was to become more than a niche sport in most of the countries in which it was played, no longer could players be expected to devote an increasing amount of time to it without being paid. The only surprise about the events of 1995, when the IRB's hand was forced by the grandiose plans of the World Rugby Corporation, was that rugby had been able to hold the reality at bay for so long.

There were ample signs in 1987 when the first cup was played that the amateur days were all but gone. But rugby still had enough Canutes to pretend that the water lapping around their ankles wouldn't soon be up to their knees. There was a bizarre confrontation between the forces of misplaced idealism and pragmatism in Christchurch during the 1987 cup. There had been complaints by some British officials in New Zealand about television commercials that featured, among others, the All Black captain, Andy Dalton. These incensed not just the officials themselves, those responsible for upholding the old order, but also many of the British journalists who felt that New Zealand was cheating. The man charged by the IRB to oversee the cup

Got there! David Kirk scores in the first World Cup final against France.

organisation, John Kendall-Carpenter, a Somerset schoolmaster, challenged the chairman of the New Zealand union, Russ Thomas, over the commercials and charged that they were outside the laws and spirit of the cup. The showdown came at a press conference Thomas convened at his Christchurch office. The two luminaries publicly agreed there was a contradiction between the IRB regulations, which allowed players to appear in commercials in strictly controlled circumstances, and the cup participation agreement, which did not. This disparity was quickly dealt with and the press conference then became almost a slanging match between New Zealand and British journalists, one side arguing the pragmatic view, the other that the old ways were the best and were what made rugby the great game it is.

As trivial as it may have been at the time, it seemed to traverse a watershed for rugby that rugby itself came to grips with only eight years later. The point is made because if the love of (or the need for) money was seen as the root of all evil, then it didn't take long in historical terms for that root to sprout an obsession that now permeates the cup. Even someone with just a superficial knowledge of the events of 2002 that led to New Zealand being dropped as sub-host of the cup in 2003 would know that the base cause was not who flung insults at whom, not who was competent or who was not, not who could trust whom, but about money. Only 15 years separate the first cup and those arguments, but it could have been a couple of lifetimes, such was the difference from when New Zealand and Australia set about persuading the IRB that it should agree to support a cup in the first place, and then set about organising it.

The IRB had to be dragged to the altar for the marriage between rugby and a world tournament. It had spurned previous suitors and the warning of a noted soccer administrator in Britain, Stanley Rous, still echoed in the ears of the Britons who dominated the IRB. Steer clear of the greed and evils of a World Cup, Rous told them. New Zealand and Australia, in their joint report to the board, argued persuasively: 'The World Cup tournament recommended in this report will generate substantial funds which will assist in the development of rugby worldwide and would enable the IRB to fund a secretariat capable of coping with the demands of a rapidly developing sport which requires this form of administrative and organisational support.'

The sweet talkers from New Zealand and Australia got their way and the IRB was still wary when the marriage was consummated in the two countries in May and June 1987, but the fruits of this marriage became so obvious that its reluctance,

EDEN IN PARIS

French inside back Franck Mesnel liked Eden Park so much he formed a company.

Elegant and stylish on and off the field, Mesnel was a member of the Racing Club de France in Paris and he and a friend, Eric Blanc, turned the club into something of a team of eccentrics.

In manner and behaviour, they were more like Oxford or Cambridge undergraduates of the 1930s than they were serious, semi-professional rugby players of the 1980s.

When Racing showed up in 1987 to play Basque, each of the players sported a beret; when they played Brive, they wore blue blazers and when they showed up against the might of Toulouse, they wore bermuda shorts.

It needs to be pointed out this was their attire on the field.

More followed in 1988. In Toulon they wore pink bow ties and back in Toulouse again, they wore black face make-up. Against Beziers, every Racing player sported a false bald head and against Baucau, they wore baggy red and white striped shorts that had been the height of fashion during the French Revolution. During the final against Agen, they wore pink bow ties and quaffed champagne at halftime — and still won.

Mesnel also played in New Zealand on occasions wearing shorts that almost reached his knees, a marked contrast to the tight, high-cut shorts that were worn by his team-mates.

There was a point to all of this. Mesnel developed a high-end men's clothing range and named his company after Eden Park. The company's logo is, appropriately enough, a pink bow tie.

A team-mate of Mesnel's, fullback Serge Blanco, has also found commercial success and fame. His name is attached to a rival clothing range, called simply Blanco, and the logo for it is the apt figure 15. Blanco is also a luxury hotel developer in the south of France.

Putting on the style. The evidence of Franck Mesnel's rugby afterlife.

The New World Order

Player of the day. Michael Jones was the revelation of the first World Cup and was the first to score a try in a cup match.

played their games showed that to them, it was just another tour, albeit a tour of a country where there were other teams as well. New Zealand prepared better than anyone else and, as a result, played better than anyone else.

Brian Lochore as coach and his two selectors, Alex Wyllie and John Hart, were systematic and thorough in their approach. They saw the cup in a way that other countries did not: to win, the All Blacks had to play and win six tests within about a month. They decided on an overall game plan and they chose a squad of 26 players best suited to put that game plan into action. They knew, and told the players, that unlike on a tour, some players may get no games at all. In the event, Frano Botica and Bruce Deans didn't play and neither did Andy Dalton, though that was because of injury. Five others, Kieran Crowley, Terry Wright, Andy Earl, Zinzan Brooke and Mark Brooke-Cowden, played only one.

The All Blacks had a level of fitness — Jim Blair had been introduced as the physical trainer — and a sense of united purpose that no other team had. Through their speed to the loose ball, the tactical sense of Grant Fox and the strength of their forward pack, allied with fast finishers, the All Blacks took the game to another level. New Zealand introduced the World Cup to rugby and the All Blacks first demonstrated how to win it.

The All Blacks also won back the casual supporters of rugby who had tired of the sport because of the New Zealand obsession of playing South Africa when no one else wanted it to. The World Cup, and the manner of the All Blacks' win, plus the imagery of a personable on-field captain, David Kirk, won the uncommitted back to rugby. Lochore says that when the All Blacks left their hotel to go to Eden Park for the final and saw the crowds waiting outside to wish them well, he knew the whole of the country was behind his team for the first time since the events of 1981.

New Zealand not only won the cup in a more complete fashion than any of the subsequent winners, it also set in train a sustained period of excellence for the All Blacks that lasted until 1990. But in that, amid the celebration of continued success, may have lurked the seeds of defeat.

With all the advantages of 20-20 hindsight, some of the All Blacks who attempted to retain the cup in 1991 had gone a season too far. Coach Alex Wyllie has many endearing qualities and among them was a fierce loyalty but, for a coach, loyalty can become a fault. He was loath to change teams unless he was forced to by injury and as 1991 unfolded, and as the All Blacks tripped none too convincingly through Argentina and in home and away matches against Australia, it became apparent that the All Blacks had lost the aura of omnipotence they'd had the previous three years. The players were also burdened by the strange decision by the New Zealand union to appoint John Hart as Wyllie's co-coach. Hart was a fine coach, as he had proved then and would prove again, but the decision to foist him onto Wyllie was redolent more of rugby politics than it was of trying to get the best out of an ageing team. The fact it didn't work had little to do with the personalities of either man, or their relationship.

almost indifference, turned into energetic enthusiasm. Before the World Cup, the IRB was a one-man office in London. It expanded briefly in Bristol then moved holus-bolus to Dublin and had subsidiary companies set up in the tax-friendly Netherlands. It was a remarkable turnaround by the IRB, which now jealously and not always openly protects its most prized property. And were there heartfelt expressions of thanks to New Zealand for showing it the way forwards, for making available such riches to it? New Zealand, in time, became sacrificed on the altar of greed.

Players care little for the machinations of rugby politics and would have known little about what led to the cup first being played. Enough to know that there was a cup. The first one, organised within two years of the IRB giving its approval, came too soon for some countries. The way some chose their squads and

The tight five. The quintet responsible for the All Blacks at the World Cup in 1991: manager John Sturgeon, fitness trainer Jim Blair and the three selectors, Alex Wyllie, Lane Penn and John Hart.

Other teams of lesser import have from time to time experimented with the notion of co-coaches but they don't work because the players need a boss; they need one voice in control, not two, no matter how much in unison the two may be.

The All Black campaign of 1991 began well enough with the 18–12 win against England but faltered along with the other pool wins against the United States and Italy, the quarterfinal victory against Canada and, finally, the semifinal loss in Dublin to Australia. It didn't help, either, that the Australians, who had just beaten Ireland the week before, seemed to be favourites in Dublin while the All Blacks prompted again the stories about unsmiling giants and surly superstars.

It would have been astonishing if the second cup had been anywhere but Britain. Once the Brits on the IRB saw that it not only worked but could make them money, they latched on to it with gusto. As always, there was politicking about who would get what

matches and despite the recommendations of New Zealand, the second cup was spread between not two unions, which New Zealand opposed, but five.

It was in Wellington a year later, in 1992, that the IRB, making a rare foray outside of Britain or Ireland, decided on South Africa hosting the 1995 cup. It seemed a hasty, precipitate step. Nelson Mandela had only just been freed from Robben Island; South Africa never mind the rest of the world couldn't know how smoothly, or roughly, the transition from minority to majority rule would proceed. But rugby wanted South Africa back from its isolation and South Africa wanted to be back. Fears were expressed about widespread violence, about transport and accommodation chaos, about indifference from the majority of the South African population but, in the event, the cup in South Africa went brilliantly from an organisational point of view.

It went brilliantly for New Zealand, too — until the last match. As they had been in 1987, the All Blacks were a level above the opposition and they showed this most graphically with the astonishing semifinal victory against England in Cape Town. The South Africans, by contrast, had progressed with the odd alarm

DAVID DOES DUBLIN

In the storehouse of David Campese's memories, some tries have a much greater significance than others. Some are treasured, perhaps because of the way in which they were executed, perhaps because of their direct impact on the result.

There were two such tries against the All Blacks in Dublin in 1991. It was the World Cup semifinal. The end of dreams of glory for one team, another week's hope for the other.

It was the All Blacks whose dreams ended, the Wallabies whose hopes soared.

And no single player could take greater credit than David Ian Campese, a player of sublime gifts.

The Wallabies scored two tries in their 16–6 victory against the cup holders. The Campese imprimatur was on them both.

The first may still be graven on the minds of New Zealanders who saw it, either at Lansdowne Road or on television.

'Michael Lynagh took the ball up further than he usually did. It was from a lineout, I think,' Campese recalls. 'I came in off my wing, got the ball and just ran on an angle. Because of the angle, I'd beaten Grant Fox and Zinzan Brooke and all I had to do was keep running really. I remember that Phil Kearns was outside me so passing wasn't really an option, so I just kept going.'

The second, the try that sealed the All Blacks' fate, was scored by Tim Horan. 'Lynagh had kicked an up-and-under and Kieran Crowley didn't get to it. The ball was loose and I was going to just kick it ahead but grabbed it instead. John Timu was in front of me and I knew I had to work him . . . I stepped outside, then in, and I could hear Timmy Horan screaming at me for the ball. He sort of came into my line of sight and I just sort of flicked the ball over to him.'

Campese scored eight tries against the All Blacks in his 29 tests against New Zealand, the highest in both respects.

'I think the try I scored in Dublin, for satisfaction and for what it meant in terms of the result for Australia, was probably the one I treasure the most against New Zealand,' Campese says. 'There was another — at the Sydney Cricket Ground in 1984. I was on the right wing and I stepped off my left foot to beat Robbie Deans, I think it must have been. That was more personally satisfying but I think that World Cup semifinal in Dublin was where it mattered the most.'

Where it mattered the most. David Campese scores in John Kirwan's tackle in the World Cup semifinal in 1991.

Above: Bad luck, mate. Words of consolation from Small for Lomu after the final whistle.

Left: Out of my way. Jonah Lomu (left) fends off James Small, with Glen Osborne ready to lend a hand, in the 1995 World Cup final.

along the way and they were only a fingernail away from losing to France in their semifinal. But by the time of the final, things were transformed. Everything seemed to conspire against the All Blacks. There's no doubt they were affected by the food poisoning, whatever its cause. But, equally, the South Africans had clearly studied the All Blacks and worked out how best to contain New Zealand's single most potent weapon, Jonah Lomu. Off the field, it was all South Africa. The day of the final was the day of the Rainbow Nation. The appearance of Mandela in a No 6 Springbok jersey, the overt and raucous nationalism of the crowd, the low flight over Ellis Park by a South African Airways Boeing . . . all helped create a climate that could only benefit South Africa. And maybe there was some truth in a belief that the All Blacks had left a little of themselves at Newlands, and maybe the occasion got to

THE HART BREAK OF '99

As the World Cup semifinal against France in 1999 wound down, as the pendulum swung ever further from likely victory to improbable defeat, John Hart remembers feeling as if a terrible black hole was opening up in front of him.

Gone were his hopes of cup glory — glory not for himself but for his players, for his game, for his country. Gone were his plans for the future and gone, or at least overwhelmed by this one single defeat, was the gloss of his past.

'There was just this feeling of helplessness as the game ran toward its end,' Hart recalls. 'It was just sliding away. Everything seemed to go France's way and none ours. The penalties went to them, the bounce of the ball went their way and they were good enough to capitalise on it all.

'For me, there was just this terrible black hole. It was all finished.'

For nigh on two years afterwards, Hart barely talked about rugby, was rarely seen publicly. For the previous four years, he'd talked rugby every day and had been seen publicly nearly every day.

'It took a while to get over it,' he says now, 'and I'm still very disappointed at the way it all finished.'

In the week between the semifinal and the unwanted playoff match in Cardiff, Hart told his management team that he would not be seeking reappointment. He had decided that much earlier, certainly before the loss to France.

'My contract was up anyway and even if we'd won the World Cup, I wouldn't have wanted to stay on as coach. That part of my life, win or lose, was ending at the World Cup.'

But Hart had formulated plans for the future that had to be scrapped. He had wanted to recommend that two of his assistants, Peter Sloane and Wayne Smith, take over the All Blacks and he said he wanted to still be involved in some role other than coaching.

'I was losing the burning desire to coach but I'd still have liked to be involved in some way with the management of the All Blacks,' he says. 'The management was evolving and I saw a need for a chief executive role with the All Blacks, which would leave the coaches to concentrate purely on getting the right players and getting the best out of them. I guess it was something like what the union tried to do with Andrew Martin as manager but that didn't last.'

(Andrew Martin became the All Blacks' manager early in 2000 with overall authority. The new coaches, Smith and Tony Gilbert, reported to him, but that changed in 2002 when the role changed and John Mitchell assumed overall command, reporting directly to the New Zealand union CEO. Martin left the reduced role and was replaced by Tony Thorpe.)

In the years since the semifinal loss, Hart has offered assistance but his offers have not been taken up. When he first became coach at the end of 1995, he went to Dunedin to meet his predecessor, Laurie Mains, even though it was widely known there was no love lost between the two.

'I felt it was important that I learn as much as I could from Laurie and to his credit, he agreed to help,' Hart says. 'He gave me a very thorough debrief on players and the whole set-up.

The faces of defeat. The All Black management and some squad members at Twickenham, 1999.

New Zealand 31 France 43

'When I left the job after the World Cup, I offered the same assistance to Wayne Smith and Tony Gilbert. I never heard back. I felt disaffected.'

When the pain eased, Hart wrote a paper about how a support group of coaches and others could help the All Black coach, whoever he was, be more successful.

'I suggested people such as Mains, Alex Wyllie, Brian Lochore, myself, Mike Banks or others involved in All Black management could meet every so often and discuss issues or problems with the current All Black coach. There was no question of money other than a few flights perhaps, just an idea to establish a support group that I thought would be to the benefit of the coach and, by extension, to the All Blacks as a whole.

'I didn't hear from the New Zealand union but I did get a call from John Mitchell. He said he thought it was a brilliant idea, but I haven't heard anything about it since.'

Hart says he's not bitter about how his rugby career has turned out, just disappointed with the way it ended.

'I'm pretty proud of the way we managed the All Blacks,' he says. 'We had a good management team and I'm proud of what we and the team achieved. We had some good results, some historic results, but we had some losses and I guess in the end coaches are judged as much by their losses as they are by their wins. I have no problem with that.'

He says he will never reach out for excuses, though the pinpointing of reasons for losses, especially those in 1998 and 1999, can be misinterpreted as excuses.

'In 1998 we'd lost some key players, very critical players such as Sean Fitzpatrick, Frank Bunce, Zinan Brooke; Michael Jones was toward the end of his career . . . you can't lose players of that calibre and think you can just carry on at the same high standard. With the loss of Fitzpatrick we also lost a very experienced leader and it didn't matter how good Taine Randell was, that experience couldn't just be replaced overnight.

'Also in 1998 we were desperately unlucky to have lost a couple of those tests. There was one in which Jeff Wilson scored just inside the dead-ball area but the referee said it was outside. Had we had the benefit then of television replays, the try would have been awarded. There was the try in Durban that James Dalton scored and won the match for South Africa — everyone but the referee knew it wasn't a try. These are not excuses. They're factors in those losses.'

The public reaction to the cup loss in 1999 was intense but Hart says he felt that other than some well-publicised incidents — his being heckled and spat at during a race meeting in Christchurch and an ill-advised magazine cover that treated Hart like a criminal — the public generally had been supportive and understanding.

'There were people on radio saying things they knew nothing about but you expect that and if it wasn't me they had to vent their spleens about, it would have been someone else. But generally I think the public reaction was fair — they were very disappointed the All Blacks didn't win the World Cup and they had every right to be. But I can tell you that no one was anywhere near as disappointed as the players themselves and all of us in the management team. That will stay with us the rest of our lives.'

some of them. Whatever the reason or reasons, it was still a close-run thing. But the All Blacks lost.

It was a new rugby world for the next cup. Professionalism was introduced just a few months after the 1995 final and by 1999, the rugby world was almost unrecognisable from what it had been in 1987. But some things hadn't changed. Wales was supposed to be the host, but that was in name only and in the right to stage opening and closing ceremonies. As in 1991, cup matches were spread around five separate rugby administrations and the cumbersome organisation made a hash of the draw. The fixture list followed no apparent pattern with days on end passing by with no games then a couple of days with a flurry of games. But most bizarre of all was the convoluted system of quarterfinal playoffs. Twenty teams played in 1999 compared with the 16 of the first three cups, and the odd system forced six of the qualifiers into an extra game. Primary school children who know their times table, could have devised a better method.

The All Blacks, as in 1991, had seen better days. The team that had been just about unbeatable in 1996 and 1997 was by 1999 struggling to impose authority in its matches. There were signs for those who had the vision to see when the All Blacks were beaten 28–7 by Australia in Sydney at the end of the tri-nations. New Zealand still had great talent with players such as Jeff Wilson, Christian Cullen and Andrew Mehrtens in the backs and a forward pack that any team would be proud to own, but seemed not to have overcome the losses of key players of the earlier era such as Sean Fitzpatrick, Frank Bunce, Zinzan Brooke and Michael Jones.

Also as in 1991, the All Blacks beat England in pool play, even if the win was achieved from a base of less possession but more savvy about what to do when play broke down. They were scratchy against Tonga, imposing against Italy, scratchy again against Scotland in the quarterfinal, especially after Mehrtens had to leave the field. And then came France.

Hart warned and warned again the players against the dangers of complacency; he warned them about the unpredictability of the French and he told them that, other than Australia, France had beaten the All Blacks more often in recent years than anyone else. He told them to put out of their minds the flattering and deceiving 54–7 win against France in June of that year in the final test at Athletic Park in Wellington.

Any coach would have done the same. Not to have done so would have been too glaring an omission. The players expected to be warned about France — and they were.

So what went wrong? No match could have been more analysed, more pored over, more agonised over, than the semifinal of 1999. How the All Blacks were 17–10 up at halftime and 14 points up with 36 minutes left to play. But how the French conjured up dropped goals, penalty goals and tries in a comeback that plunged New Zealand into a state of rugby despair seldom if ever matched in its proud history.

Any New Zealander with a knowledge of the scriptures could have turned to Exodus 8, verse 8: 'Pharaoh says to Moses, "Entreat the Lord, that he may take away the frogs from me, and from my people."' Any New Zealander with a knowledge of French would have grasped at the winner's language. It was a *coup de foudre*, an overwhelming event, and for New Zealanders anywhere and everywhere, it was a *crève-coeur*, a heartbreak.

It was the day of the Frogs. As in 1995, a team capable of winning the World Cup didn't win it. The greatest rugby country the world had seen again couldn't win the tournament that it introduced to the world.

Within a couple of years, the rugby world's debt to New Zealand for its introduction of the cup, if not for its enduring excellence at the game, was nothing more than an empty, emotional footnote in a chapter of confusion, duplicity and disaster.

It seemed for a time that more words had been written and spoken, many of them in anger, about New Zealand's failure to retain the sub-hosting rights to the 2003 cup than had ever been written or spoken about the All Blacks playing in the four previous cups. The New Zealand union was painted as uncommitted to the cup and incompetent; the Australians were painted as greedy and duplicitous and the International Rugby Board was painted as leaderless, confused and indecisive. Somewhere between all the acrimony, the accusations, the claims and counter-claims, the truth must lie. The report by the retired Chief Justice, Sir Thomas Eichelbaum, couldn't tell the whole story because he could only report and comment on what he was told or what he knew: like a good judge, he could go only on the evidence before him. But even if incomplete, it was damning.

No less damning was the reaction from the IRB, itself far from blameless in the sorry affair. When New Zealand's last-ditch appeal to the IRB's decision-making council failed in April 2002, the IRB had this to say: 'Generous accommodations made by RWCL [Rugby World Cup Ltd] to meet the needs and problems of the NZRFU were repaid with consistent failures and wholly inappropriate behaviour . . .'

Not even when South Africa was being vilified by the rest of the world did the IRB utter such a strong condemnation of one of its members. IRB statements usually toe a soft line, replete with weasel words and milksop phrases. This one was with the gloves off and the sleeves rolled up.

The whole truth may never be known. Even some of the principals involved may not know the whole truth. Some won't want it known.

There was clearly fault in all three key sides: the IRB's (the cup company's) for not being specific early enough about what it really meant by clean grounds, a phrase that had been used as early as the first World Cup but which then didn't include corporate boxes or precincts outside stadiums; Australia's for an apparent unwillingness to negotiate with New Zealand in the latter stages

when it became obvious negotiation and goodwill was sorely needed; New Zealand's for a lack of commitment to the cup, for creating the impression that the NPC was more important than the cup, and for failing to acknowledge until it was too late precisely what was meant by clean grounds. Jointly, the IRB and the NZRFU were at fault for relying on 'an understanding' that 100 per cent clean grounds didn't have to necessarily mean what it said. These, and the ever-present money, were the central issues and when they became mixed with personality differences, dislikes and mistrust, it all became too much.

The central figure as far as the IRB and the cup company was concerned was the chairman of both, Vernon Pugh, a Welsh lawyer who specialised in town planning issues. Towards the end of the saga, he became as scathing towards New Zealand as the New Zealand chairman, Murray McCaw, and chief executive, David Rutherford, had been towards him and the IRB at the time Australia withdrew the sub-hosting offer. At least New Zealand apologised. Pugh never did.

There seemed, amid all the letter-writing, emailing and phone calls from late 2001 until April 2002 when the cup was finally lost, an obsession not so much with the substance of the issues, but with the peripherals, of which the NPC was one. Another was leaks at various times from various bodies that led to at least the IRB and the New Zealand union engaging private detectives in attempts to find sources, which they never did. The leaks themselves led to an obsession with what 'the media' (as rugby puts it) was saying: putting the gloss ahead of the substance. Another was the New Zealand union's engagement of a public relations firm to 'manage' the fallout when first Rutherford and then McCaw left. Quite why it needed to do that when it had its own media department, headed by a former public relations executive, Peter Parussini, was never explained publicly. It at least succeeded in clouding, initially anyway, on a strange night of live television interviews, the circumstances in which Rutherford left and McCaw stood down as chairman to be replaced by Rob Fisher. McCaw received a stronger message, apparently from the Wellington union, a few days later and quit the New Zealand board altogether. Reports months after the dust had settled continued to say about Rutherford that he 'fell on his sword'. If that implies he went voluntarily, it's unlikely to have been the case. Rutherford argued vehemently that he was doing his best for New Zealand rugby and in what he passionately believed. He may have had faults, but he was not a quitter. Rutherford was the first New Zealander to pay the price for losing the cup; subsequently, almost all of the board followed, even though some of its members were guilty only by association.

The Eichelbaum report, and the general debate at the time, was silent about the role of the chief executive who preceded

The New World Order

Rutherford, David Moffett. It was he who began the negotiations with Australia and it was he who took New Zealand through the first year of the host–sub-host arrangement. Anecdotal evidence suggests that the relationship was far from cosy even then.

Another factor in the cup argument that was glossed over was the astounding suggestion that in retaliation for not playing a role as host, the All Blacks would not play in the World Cup in 2003. This was mentioned in the Eichelbaum report but barely remarked upon beyond that. 'On 18 August,' Eichelbaum said, 'Board resolved it was unacceptable for NZRFU to lose money by sub-hosting, and that an "all or nothing" approach was to be taken, *including non-participation in the tournament*.' [The italics were not Eichelbaum's.]

Eichelbaum did not elaborate so it's not known if that threat was ever made to the IRB or to Pugh. But it is known that it was discussed briefly by the New Zealand board.

New Zealand's underlying argument throughout the saga was the need for a 'rugby solution' rather than one based entirely on contracts and who got what amounts of money. New Zealand's long and honourable role in world rugby was used in emotional but unrequited pleas for understanding. Quite how that could be squared against a threat to withdraw the All Blacks from the tournament was never explained.

The reaction by the public, including the provincial rugby unions, to the whole debacle was overwhelmingly damning. The public clamour if the All Black threat had been carried out would have been deafening. It was New Zealand rugby administration's darkest period, darker even than the 1981 Springbok tour or other issues related to playing rugby against South Africa. It was darker, too, than the 1995 split when senior players were on the brink of leaving the establishment to join the World Rugby Corporation. At least then the New Zealand union saved the day. Nothing was saved this time.

One of the great ironies was that after the first cup in 1987 New Zealand argued future cups should be hosted by just one union. In that at least, it finally got its way.

In the firing line. David Rutherford and Murray McCaw during the 2003 World Cup hosting debacle.

THE RELUCTANT SKIPPER

There's no doubt that being the All Black captain is one of the most select jobs in New Zealand sport but one that carries with it the weight of expectation and the burden of responsibility.

Few players will be bold enough, or indiscreet enough, to admit to aspiring to the role but even fewer would reject it given the chance. Some do, though.

The honours board of New Zealand rugby captains echoes greatness down the years . . . from the Originals captain, Dave Gallaher, through to the knighted captains, Wilson Whineray and Brian Lochore, to leaders of men such as Graham Mourie, Wayne Shelford, Sean Fitzpatrick . . . 58 of them in total.

For an All Black, it is the pinnacle appointment.

Taine Randell seemed from his younger days destined to be the captain of the All Blacks. A gifted sportsman and scholar, he was made captain of practically every team he was in. When he was 21 and in his second year as an All Black, he led the midweek All Blacks — but no less All Blacks for that — in South Africa in 1996.

When Sean Fitzpatrick's six-year tenure ended because of injury in 1997 and John Hart made halfback Justin Marshall captain for tests in Britain and Ireland, it seemed only a stopgap measure, a marking of time until Randell was deemed ready to assume the mantle. He was the heir presumptive and, if rugby had been ruled as a monarchy by bloodlines, he would have been the heir apparent.

It came, to the surprise of no one, in 1998. But that was the year of losses. Two wins over an understrength England, then five losses in a row — the worst losing trot by an All Black team save the aberration of 1949 when two separate teams between them lost six.

By the end of 1998, Randell did not want to be captain anymore. The burden was too much. Sport at any level needs to be enjoyed and Randell's enjoyment had soured. He felt he didn't have the support of senior members of the side, all older than him, either on or off the field.

'I was pretty much flummoxed,' Randell says. 'I didn't feel I was secure as an All Black, never mind as captain. I felt it was far too soon for me to be captain. I think some of the older players may have regarded me as a bit of an upstart — I know that if I'd been a senior player and some young guy was brought in as captain I'd regard him in the same way. I could understand the views of guys like Robin Brooke and Ian Jones. I have no doubt that my captaincy was a factor in those losses in 1998.'

So at the end of the season, Randell told John Hart, who had championed the Randell cause, that he did not want to continue as captain and he should look for someone else.

What happened over the following months has never previously been fully told.

Randell sought the assistance of Kevin Roberts, then a New Zealand union board member and the world chief executive of advertising agency Saatchi and Saatchi. Roberts, an enthusiast with a keen intellect and with a vision for rugby that sometimes could outstrip political realities, set much store on the relationship between success in sport and success in business. Put simply, he believed that best practice in business could work in sport and vice versa.

He and Randell had a long conversation, with Randell spilling out his feelings of inferiority and insecurity and Roberts suggesting ways forwards, pointing out positives among the negatives.

'He was fantastic,' Randell says. 'He got out of me what I really wanted to be. It was all about my expectations — I'd been leading the others' expectations whereas it should have been me imposing my expectations on them.'

Hart, meanwhile, had acknowledged Randell's reluctance to remain as captain and started casting around for a new one for the critical role of leading New Zealand in the World Cup in 1999.

'I didn't blame Taine at all,' Hart says. 'I understood perfectly how he felt. I didn't feel the losses of 1998 were his fault but if he wanted out, I had to respect his wishes.'

Hart discussed the captaincy with his closest colleagues, team manager Mike Banks and fellow selectors and coaches Peter Sloane and Gordon Hunter. He also discussed it with, but did not offer it to, Jeff Wilson.

'Taine and I met in Christchurch in May during the Super 12 of 1999 and I told him I hadn't made a decision but that I was looking at Robin Brooke,' Hart says. 'Taine indicated then that he would continue as captain if necessary but that he would rather not.'

Randell's memory of the meeting concurs with Hart's. Randell remembers leaving the meeting thinking that he would not be the captain, and a few days later he said exactly that to *NZ Rugby World* magazine. (In the light of subsequent events that overtook the magazine's production schedule, it had, at the New Zealand union's insistence, to pull out the Randell story.)

In the meantime, and without Randell knowing, Brooke's star had begun to wane. Senior player that he was, he had not played to his highest standards in 1998 and during the Super 12 there were questions about his role in undercurrents within the Auckland Blues that led to the eventual dismissal of their coach, Jed Rowlands.

There was talk, not confirmed by Hart, of other factors influencing the move away from Brooke.

Hart in any case had not discussed the captaincy with Brooke; he'd merely discussed the prospect of Brooke with others.

It was around this time that Anton Oliver, who had leapfrogged into being No 1 hooker after Fitzpatrick's retirement, entered discussions.

A week after the Randell-Hart meeting in Christchurch, Hart was in Wellington when the Hurricanes played the Highlanders in the last round-robin weekend of the Super 12. The coach of the Hurricanes was Frank Oliver, himself a former All Black captain, and Anton's father. On the Friday before the match, in a potentially risky and embarrassing departure from tradition, Frank Oliver went to the hotel of the opposition, the Highlanders.

From a phone in the foyer of what was then the James Cook Centra, Oliver phoned the Highlanders coach, Tony Gilbert, and asked if he could see him. Not about the pending game, but about his son.

The New World Order

Gilbert, knowing that Oliver would have felt uncomfortable in the Highlanders hotel, invited him up to his room. There, the older Oliver said he felt the younger Oliver was not ready to be the All Black captain and he asked Gilbert if he agreed and if he would talk to Anton.

Gilbert agreed.

After the game, in which the Hurricanes beat the Highlanders, Hart went to the Highlanders dressing room and asked Anton Oliver to call him the next morning.

During the New Zealand night, other Super 12 results conspired to summon the Highlanders to Cape Town for a semifinal the following weekend against the Stormers so Gilbert and his Highlanders were up early on the Sunday morning, packing and organising extra gear to be sent from Dunedin.

It was during this maelstrom of activity that Hart phoned Gilbert and asked if Oliver could still call him. Oliver did and told Hart that he felt it was too soon in his All Black career to accept the captaincy.

'Anton told me it was too early and I accepted his reasons,' Hart says. 'I'd also discussed the captaincy with Jeff but had not, despite what's been reported, asked him to be the captain. To say, as it's been said, that Jeff turned it down is wrong. I think both Jeff and I knew that he would not be the ideal captain for a number of reasons. He might have said he would if there was no one else, but only in the manner of trying to help out.'

Wilson confirms he was never asked to be captain and therefore could not have turned it down.

Soon after Oliver's call, Hart phoned Randell and told him that he had decided against Brooke as the captain and he would like Randell to reconsider.

'By Wellington, we'd been through the process that eliminated Brooke,' Hart says, 'but the other players didn't necessarily know that.'

Gilbert, Oliver, Wilson and Randell discussed the captaincy among themselves, Oliver and Wilson telling Randell that if he changed his mind and said yes, he would have their full support.

Randell then went to the hotel where Hart was staying and told him he would agree to being captain again providing he had total backing from Hart and all the players.

The Highlanders left for South Africa soon afterwards and while they were there, they learnt from rugby people with whom they came in contact much more than they had heard in New Zealand about the ructions within the Blues. The Blues had only recently been in South Africa where the story of the dissent within their camp leaked out.

So Randell was captain again through to the end of the World Cup, 1999 ending on an even worse note than 1998.

Randell's dramas with the captaincy were not finished even then. With Hart's departure, Wayne Smith — one of Hart's erstwhile allies — and Gilbert became the All Black coaches. Gilbert says quite frankly that if it had been up to him, he would have retained Randell as captain.

Having been associated with him almost since his earliest days as a student in Dunedin, Gilbert knew Randell well, understood him, and had — and still has — a high regard for both his personal qualities and his leadership abilities.

Smith, though, demurred. This was evidently because of a desire for a fresh broom approach to the All Black hierarchy in the wake of the World Cup, even though Smith himself had been a key member of the previous regime.

Smith opted for the Canterbury captain, Todd Blackadder, whose standing as an uncontroversial and admired player was perhaps greater than his

Coach and captain, John Hart and Taine Randell.

standing as an All Black lock. Smith also knew Blackadder well from their provincial association.

Two and a half years later, though, with another All Black coach, Randell was captain again. Randell had thought his All Black days were over when John Mitchell took over from Smith and Gilbert at the end of 2001. And who could blame him? Mitchell's terse dismissal — 'He's got my number' — when he was questioned about Randell's omission from the team to go to Ireland, Scotland and Argentina could hardly be seen as a ringing endorsement for Randell's future.

While Randell was selected for the All Blacks in 2002, he seemed only on the periphery of the preferred top selection and after recovering from a calf injury, Mitchell and the coaching co-ordinator, Robbie Deans, stated a clear preference for Sam Broomhall of Canterbury as loose forward cover in the test reserves.

Randell began to think about life after rugby and included in those plans was his marriage to his partner from his early university days, Jo Edwards. The wedding was set for a week after the NPC final, which happened also to be the day the All Blacks were scheduled to leave on their whistlestop trip to Europe for tests against England, France and Wales.

Randell did not think he would be part of that tour so the wedding plans went ahead. Mitchell, however, had committed himself to resting key players and the two test captains he had had, Oliver and Reuben Thorne, were both injured.

Mitchell phoned Randell and told him he wanted him to be the captain. Randell, amused, bemused and honoured, said he couldn't. The wedding plans were too far advanced to be altered, he said.

Mitchell went away and thought about it; so did Randell. Each of them separately spoke to the Highlanders coach, Laurie Mains — who had first picked Randell in the All Blacks, in 1995. Mains urged Randell to take the chance he had been offered.

To Mitchell's credit, he made considerable concessions to Randell, and Randell, acknowledging that Mitchell had bent over backwards to help him, knew he had no further choice. Randell assembled with the squad in Auckland on the Monday after the NPC final but was allowed to go to Havelock North during the week for his stag night, returned to Auckland, then back to Havelock for the wedding on the Saturday. He left for Britain on the Sunday, 24 hours after the wedding — and 24 hours after the rest of the squad.

The winners can laugh . . . Sean Fitzpatrick and
Wayne Shelford after the World Cup final in 1987

The Test Programme

Match programmes are the paper markers of the All Blacks' test history. They signpost the matches which were won, those which were drawn and those which were lost. Programmes are an essential part of test match day, and they have been since the first in 1903. Programmes are the only artifacts remaining from some test matches, the only tangible link with the All Blacks' history.

They reflect not just the teams and sometimes the society of the day; they reflect also gradual changes in the arts of the designers and typographers: there were programmes with specially commissioned covers, others with just bland letterpress. There was bold originality and there was tedious repetition. Some programmes have been almost magazines with a range of articles written by an astonishing variety of people; others have been just a basic four pages with teams and advertisements.

Some tests had two programmes — one official and one unofficial (and the All Blacks had letters on their backs instead of numbers to foil the pirates). Some tests had no programmes at all and there are some tests, notably against All-America in 1913, about which it's not known whether there was a programme or not.

Discarded programmes form part of the detritus of test matches, blown hither and yon around an empty ground until the cleaners arrive. But for an increasing number of people in the rugby world, programmes are a collectable item — some people search the world for early test programmes (and some that are not so early. Programmes for the 1957 series in Australia, for example, are among the rarest).

Programme collectors are masters of search and detection techniques — and are willing to spend big money to fill any gaps in their collection.

The programmes represented here are not a complete collection — but they are an extensive and representative look at an essential element of any test match.

A rare breed . . . the little-seen programme for the second test against Australia in 1957.

New Zealand 22, Australia 3
Sydney, August 15, 1903

New Zealand 15, England 0
London, December 2, 1905

Wales 3, New Zealand 0
Cardiff, December 16, 1905

New Zealand 26, Australia 6
Sydney, July 20, 1907

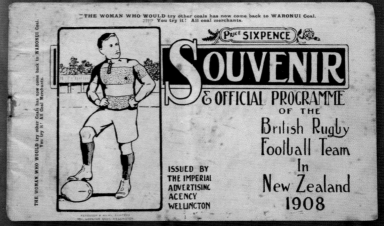

New Zealand 32, Anglo-Welsh 5
Dunedin, June 6, 1908

New Zealand 28, Australia 13
Sydney, July 2, 1910

New Zealand 5, Australia 0
Sydney, July 18, 1914

New Zealand 13, South Africa 5
Dunedin, August 13, 1921

New Zealand 6, Ireland 0
Dublin, November 1, 1924

South Africa 17, New Zealand 0
Durban, June 30, 1928

Australia 17, New Zealand 9
Brisbane, July 20, 1929

New Zealand 15, Great Britain 10
Auckland, July 26, 1930

New Zealand 21, Australia 13
Sydney, July 23, 1932

Wales 13, New Zealand 12
Cardiff, December 21, 1935

South Africa 17, New Zealand 6
Auckland, September 25, 1937

1921–1939

New Zealand 31, Australia 8
Dunedin, September 14, 1946

South Africa 12, New Zealand 6
Johannesburg, August 13, 1949

New Zealand 8, British Isles 0
Christchurch, June 10, 1950

Australia 14, New Zealand 9
Christchurch, September 6, 1952

Wales 13, New Zealand 8
Cardiff, December 19, 1953

France 3, New Zealand 0
Paris, February 27, 1954

New Zealand 11, South Africa 5
Auckland, September 1, 1956

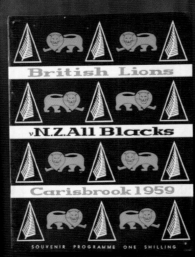

New Zealand 18, British Isles 17
Dunedin, July 18, 1959

New Zealand 11, South Africa 11
Bloemfontein, August 13, 1960

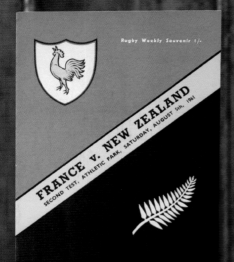

New Zealand 5, France 3
Wellington, August 5, 1961

New Zealand 16, Australia 8
Auckland, September 22, 1962

New Zealand 0, Scotland 0
Edinburgh, January 18, 1964

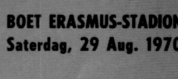

New Zealand 6, South Africa 3
Wellington, July 31, 1965

New Zealand 19, British Isles 6
Christchurch, August 27, 1966

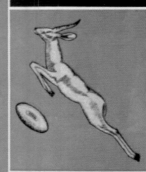

New Zealand 29, Australia 9
Wellington, August 19, 1967

New Zealand 21, France 15
Paris, November 25, 1967

South Africa 14, New Zealand 3
Port Elizabeth, August 29, 1970

New Zealand 22, British Isles 12
Christchurch, July 10, 1971

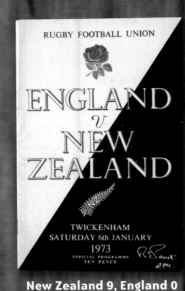

New Zealand 9, England 0
London, January 6, 1973

New Zealand 16, Australia 6
Sydney, June 8, 1974

New Zealand 15, Ireland 6
Dublin, November 23, 1974

New Zealand 15, South Africa 9
Bloemfontein, August 14, 1976

New Zealand 19, British Isles 7
Dunedin, July 30, 1977

New Zealand 10, Ireland 6
Dublin, November 4, 1978

France 24, New Zealand 19
Auckland, July 14, 1979

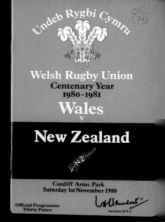

New Zealand 23, Wales 3
Cardiff, November 1, 1980

1971–1980

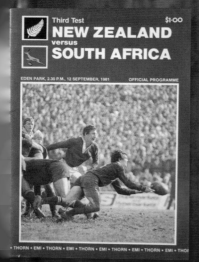

Third Test $1.00
NEW ZEALAND
versus
SOUTH AFRICA

EDEN PARK, 2.30 P.M., 12 SEPTEMBER, 1981   OFFICIAL PROGRAMME

New Zealand 25, South Africa 22
Auckland, September 12, 1981

SOUVENIR
PROGRAMME
2nd Test

BRITISH ISLES

NEW ZEALAND

Athletic Park
Saturday
18th June 1983
Club Competition
Matches

Vol 30, No.13 $1.00

LION BEER

New Zealand 9, British Isles 0
Wellington, June 18, 1983

The Royal Bank
Scotland v New Zealand
INTERNATIONAL

MURRAYFIELD
12th NOVEMBER 1983   PRICE 60p

SCOTTISH RUGBY UNION · OFFICIAL PROGRAMME

New Zealand 25, Scotland 25
Edinburgh, November 12, 1983

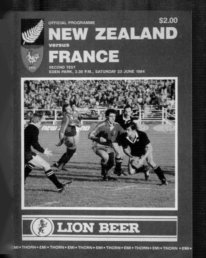

OFFICIAL PROGRAMME $2.00
NEW ZEALAND
versus
FRANCE
SECOND TEST
EDEN PARK, 2.30 P.M., SATURDAY 23 JUNE 1984

LION BEER

New Zealand 31, France 18
Auckland, June 23, 1984

Unión Argentina de Rugby   Unión de Rugby de Nueva Zelanda.

PROGRAMA DE PARTIDOS
CON EL SELECCIONADO DE NUEVA ZELANDA
TEMPORADA INTERNACIONAL 1985

New Zealand 21, Argentina 21
Buenos Aires, November 2, 1985

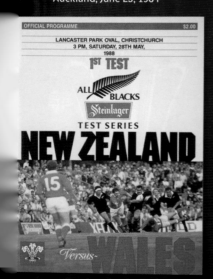

OFFICIAL PROGRAMME $2.00
LANCASTER PARK OVAL, CHRISTCHURCH
3 PM, SATURDAY, 28TH MAY, 1988
1ST TEST
ALL BLACKS
Steinlager
TEST SERIES
NEW ZEALAND
Versus
WALES

New Zealand 52, Wales 3
Christchurch, May 28, 1988

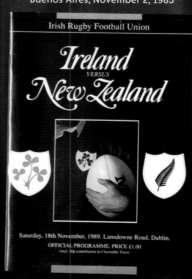

Irish Rugby Football Union

Ireland
VERSUS
New Zealand

Saturday, 18th November, 1989. Lansdowne Road, Dublin.
OFFICIAL PROGRAMME. PRICE £1.00
(incl. 20p contribution to Charitable Trust)

New Zealand 23, Ireland 6
Dublin, November 18, 1989

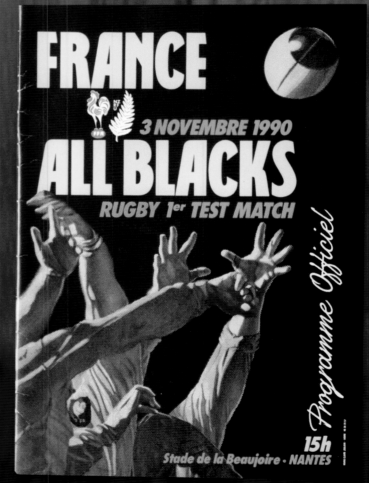

FRANCE
3 NOVEMBRE 1990
ALL BLACKS
RUGBY 1er TEST MATCH

Programme Officiel

15h
Stade de la Beaujoire · NANTES

New Zealand 24, France 3
Nantes, November 3, 1990

1981 – 1990

Australia 16, New Zealand 6
Dublin, October 27, 1991

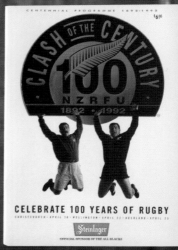

New Zealand 26, World XV 15
Auckland, April 25, 1992

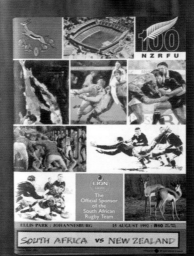

New Zealand 28, Argentina 14
Buenos Aires, July 6, 1991

New Zealand 27, South Africa 24
Johannesburg, August 15, 1992

New Zealand 30, British Isles 1
Auckland, July 3, 1993

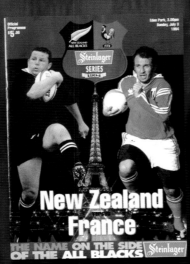

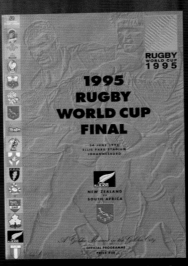

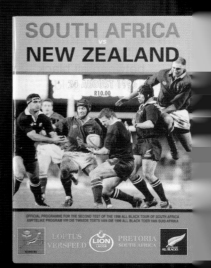

New Zealand 35, Western Samoa 13
Auckland, July 31, 1993

France 23, New Zealand 20
Auckland, July 3, 1994

South Africa 15, New Zealand 12
Johannesburg, June 24, 1995

New Zealand 33, South Africa 2
Pretoria, August 24, 1996

New Zealand 71, Fiji 5
Albany, June 14, 1997

New Zealand 62, Argentina 10
Hamilton, June 28, 1997

New Zealand 40, England 10
Auckland, June 27, 1998

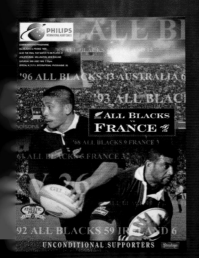

New Zealand 54, France 7
Wellington, June 26, 1999

New Zealand 28, South Africa 0
Dunedin, July 10, 1999

New Zealand 30, Scotland 18
Edinburgh, October 24, 1999

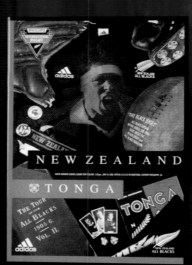

New Zealand 102, Tonga 0
Albany, June 16, 2000

New Zealand 50, Samoa 6
Albany, June 16, 2001

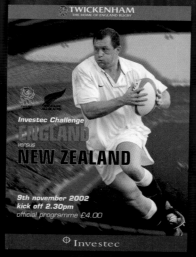

England 31, New Zealand 28
London, November 9, 2002

1997 — 2002

Test Statistics

(complete to April 30, 2003)

New Zealand's test record

Nº	Date	Opponent	Venue	City	NZ score	Opponent	Tries	Cons	Pens	DGs	GMs
1	15.8.1903	Australia	Sydney Cricket Ground	Sydney	22(7)	3(3)	A. Asher* G. Tyler* R. McGregor*	W. Wallace*	W. Wallace		W. Wallace 2
2	13.8.1904	Great Britain	Athletic Park	Wellington	9(3)	3(3)	D. McGregor 2		W. Wallace		
3	2.9.1905	Australia	Tahuna Park	Dunedin	14(3)	3(3)	A. McMinn 2 E. Wrigley T. Cross	A. Francis*			
4	18.11.1905	Scotland	Inverleith	Edinburgh	12(6)	7(7)	G. Smith 2* F. Glasgow* W. Cunningham*				
5	25.11.1905	Ireland	Lansdowne Road	Dublin	15(5)	0	R. Deans 2 A. McDonald	W. Wallace 3			
6	2.12.1905	England	Crystal Palace	London	15(9)	0	D. McGregor 4 F. Newton*				
7	16.12.1905	Wales	Cardiff Arms Park	Cardiff	0	3(3)					
8	1.1.1906	France	Parc des Princes	Paris	38(18)	8(3)	W. Wallace 3 H. Abbott 2* J. Hunter 2 E. Harper 2 F. Glasgow	W. Wallace 2 G. Tyler H. Abbott			
9	20.7.1907	Australia	Sydney Cricket Ground	Sydney	26(13)	6(0)	F. Mitchinson* 3 C. Seeling E. Hughes* A. Francis	W. Wallace 4			
10	3.8.1907	Australia	Brisbane Cricket Ground	Brisbane	14(0)	5(5)	W. Wallace 2 C. Seeling A. Francis	W. Wallace			
11	10.8.1907	Australia	Sydney Cricket Ground	Sydney	5(0)	5(0)	F. Mitchinson	W. Wallace			
12	6.6.1908	Anglo-Welsh	Carisbrook	Dunedin	32(21)	5(0)	F. Mitchinson 2 F. Roberts 2 D. Cameron J. Hunter H. Thomson*	G. Gillett 2 A. Francis F. Roberts	F. Roberts		
13	27.6.1908	Anglo-Welsh	Athletic Park	Wellington	3(0)	3(0)			A. Francis		
14	25.7.1908	Anglo-Welsh	Potter's Park	Auckland	29(12)	0	F. Mitchinson 3 R. Deans A. Francis G. Gillett F. Glasgow H. Hayward* J. Hunter	J. Colman			
15	25.6.1910	Australia	Sydney Cricket Ground	Sydney	6(0)	0	N. Wilson W. Fuller*				
16	27.6.1910	Australia	Sydney Cricket Ground	Sydney	0	11(3)					
17	2.7.1910	Australia	Sydney Cricket Ground	Sydney	28(6)	13(5)	P. Burns 2 L. Stohr 2 A. Paterson F. Mitchinson W. Mitchell H Paton	M. O'Leary 2			
18	6.9.1913	Australia	Athletic Park	Wellington	30(11)	5(5)	T. Lynch 3* R. McKenzie 2* H. Murray* G .Gray R. Roberts*	R. Roberts 3			

Cons — Conversions **Pens** — Penalty goals **DGs** — Dropped goals **GMs** — Goals from a mark **( )** — Halftime score * Debut

New Zealand's test record

Nº	Date	Opponent	Venue	City	NZ score	Opponent	Tries	Cons	Pens	DGs	GMs
19	13.9.1913	Australia	Carisbrook	Dunedin	25(9)	13(8)	C. Brown* W. Cummings* E. Hasell* R. Taylor* N. Wilson	M. O'Leary 3		M. O'Leary	
20	20.9.1913	Australia	Lancaster Park	Christchurch	5(5)	16(5)	A. Fanning*	M. O'Leary			
21	15.11.1913	All-America	Berkeley Field	Berkeley	51(27)	3(3)	R. Roberts 3 R. McKenzie 2 G. Gray 2 H. Murray 2 A. McDonald 2 J. Wylie A. McGregor	J. Graham 4* A. McDonald F. Mitchinson			
22	18.7.1914	Australia	Sydney Sports Ground	Sydney	5(0)	0	J. McNeece	J. Graham			
23	1.8.1914	Australia	Brisbane Cricket Ground	Brisbane	17(9)	0	H. Taylor 3 R. Roberts T. Lynch	E. Roberts			
24	15.8.1914	Australia	Sydney Sports Ground	Sydney	22(3)	7(0)	R. Roberts 2 W. Francis 2 R. McKenzie H. Taylor	R. Roberts E. Roberts			
25	13.8.1921	South Africa	Carisbrook	Dunedin	13(0)	5(5)	M. Belliss* J. Steel* P. Storey*	M. Nicholls 2*			
26	27.8.1921	South Africa	Eden Park	Auckland	5(5)	9(5)	A. McLean*	M. Nicholls			
27	17.9.1921	South Africa	Athletic Park	Wellington	0	0					
28	1.11.1924	Ireland	Lansdowne Road	Dublin	6(0)	0	K. Svenson*		M. Nicholls		
29	29.11.1924	Wales	St Helen's	Swansea	19(11)	0	W. Irvine 2 M. Brownlie K. Svenson	M. Nicholls 2	M. Nicholls		
30	3.1.1925	England	Twickenham	London	17(9)	11(3)	K. Svenson J. Steel M. Brownlie J. Parker	M. Nicholls	M. Nicholls		
31	18.1.1925	France	Stade des Ponts-Jumeaux	Toulouse	30(17)	6(0)	A. Cooke 2 A. White C. Porter* J. Steel K. Svenson W. Irvine J. Richardson	M. Nicholls 3			
32	30.6.1928	South Africa	Kingsmead	Durban	0	17(4)					
33	21.7.1928	South Africa	Ellis Park	Johannesburg	7(3)	6(3)			D. Lindsay	W. Strang	
34	18.8.1928	South Africa	Crusader Ground	Port Elizabeth	6(6)	11(8)	R. Stewart B. Grenside				
35	1.9.1928	South Africa	Newlands	Cape Town	13(6)	5(5)	J. Swain		M. Nicholls 2	M. Nicholls	
36	6.7.1929	Australia	Sydney Cricket Ground	Sydney	8(8)	9(6)	C. Oliver*	G. Nepia	G. Nepia		
37	20.7.1929	Australia	Exhibition Ground	Brisbane	9(3)	17(3)	B. Grenside C. Porter		R. Cundy		
38	27.7.1929	Australia	Sydney Cricket Ground	Sydney	13(13)	15(9)	R. McWilliams J. Stringfellow B. Grenside	H. Lilburne 2			
39	21.6.1930	Great Britain	Carisbrook	Dunedin	3(0)	6(3)	G. Hart*				
40	5.7.1930	Great Britain	Lancaster Park	Christchurch	13(8)	10(5)	G. Hart D. Oliver	M. Nicholls 2			M. Nicholls
41	26.7.1930	Great Britain	Eden Park	Auckland	15(5)	10(5)	H. McLean 2* F. Lucas	W. Strang		M. Nicholls	

New Zealand's test record

№	Date	Opponent	Venue	City	NZ score	Opponent	Tries	Cons	Pens	DGs	GMs
42	9.8.1930	Great Britain	Athletic Park	Wellington	22(6)	8(3)	C. Porter 2 A. Cooke 2 W. Strang W. Batty	W. Strang 2			
43	12.9.1931	Australia	Eden Park	Auckland	20(11)	13(13)	G. Hart N. Ball*	R. Bush*	R. Bush 4		
44	2.7.1932	Australia	Sydney Cricket Ground	Sydney	17(8)	22(5)	G. Bullock-Douglas* J. Hore G. Purdue	H. Pollock 2*		H. Pollock	
45	16.7.1932	Australia	Exhibition Ground	Brisbane	21(12)	3(3)	G. Bullock-Douglas 2 N. Ball J. Page	H. Pollock	A. Collins*	H. Pollock	
46	23.7.1932	Australia	Sydney Cricket Ground	Sydney	21(8)	13(5)	F. Kilby H. McLean F. Solomon J. Manchester B. Palmer	A. Collins 2 H. Pollock			
47	11.8.1934	Australia	Sydney Cricket Ground	Sydney	11(11)	25(6)	J. Hore A. Knight* D. Max	A. Collins			
48	25.8.1934	Australia	Sydney Cricket Ground	Sydney	3(0)	3(3)	J. Hore				
49	23.11.1935	Scotland	Murrayfield	Edinburgh	18(13)	8(3)	H. Caughey 3 W. Hadley	M. Gilbert 3*			
50	7.12.1935	Ireland	Lansdowne Road	Dublin	17(11)	9(6)	N. Mitchell C. Oliver G. Hart	M. Gilbert	M. Gilbert 2		
51	21.12.1935	Wales	Cardiff Arms Park	Cardiff	12(3)	13(0)	N. Ball 2	M. Gilbert		M. Gilbert	
52	4.1.1936	England	Twickenham	London	0	13(6)					
53	5.9.1936	Australia	Athletic Park	Wellington	11(5)	6(6)	G. Hart W. Hadley J. Watt*	H. Pollock			
54	12.9.1936	Australia	Carisbrook	Dunedin	38(11)	13(13)	N. Mitchell 2 G. Hart 2 T. Reid 2 J. Rankin 2 J. Watt	H. Pollock 4	H. Pollock		
55	14.8.1937	South Africa	Athletic Park	Wellington	13(6)	7(3)	J. Dick*		D. Trevathan 2*	D. Trevathan	
56	4.9.1937	South Africa	Lancaster Park	Christchurch	6(6)	13(0)	J. Sullivan 2				
57	25.9.1937	South Africa	Eden Park	Auckland	6(3)	17(8)			D. Trevathan 2		
58	23.7.1938	Australia	Sydney Cricket Ground	Sydney	24(8)	9(3)	C. Saxton 2* J. Sullivan A. Parkhill	J. Taylor 3	J. Taylor 2		
59	6.8.1938	Australia	Exhibition Ground	Brisbane	20(13)	14(3)	W. Phillips H. Milliken A. Bowman N. Mitchell	J. Taylor 2		T. Morrison	
60	13.8.1938	Australia	Sydney Cricket Ground	Sydney	14(6)	6(3)	C. Saxton A. Bowman	J. Taylor	J. Taylor 2		
61	14.9.1946	Australia	Carisbrook	Dunedin	31(13)	8(8)	W. Argus 2* J. Haig* K. Elliott* J. Finlay* J. Smith* R. White*	R. Scott 5*			
62	28.9.1946	Australia	Eden Park	Auckland	14(8)	10(5)	R. Elvidge	R. Scott	R. Scott 3		
63	14.6.1947	Australia	Exhibition Ground	Brisbane	13(8)	5(0)	W. Argus K. Arnold* penalty try	R. Scott 2			
64	28.6.1947	Australia	Sydney Cricket Ground	Sydney	27(11)	14(8)	W. Argus J. Kearney* D. Mason*	R. Scott 3	R. Scott 3 N. Thornton		

New Zealand's test record

Nº	Date	Opponent	Venue	City	NZ score	Opponent	Tries	Cons	Pens	DGs	GMs
65	16.7.1949	South Africa	Newlands	Cape Town	11(11)	15(3)	P. Henderson*	R. Scott	R. Scott	J. Kearney	
66	13.8.1949	South Africa	Ellis Park	Johannesburg	6(3)	12(6)			R. Scott	J. Kearney	
67	3.9.1949	Australia	Athletic Park	Wellington	6(0)	11(11)	G. Moore*		J. Kelly*		
68	3.9.1949	South Africa	Kingsmead	Durban	3(3)	9(6)	M. Goddard*				
69	17.9.1949	South Africa	Crusader Ground	Port Elizabeth	8(3)	11(0)	P. Johnstone R. Elvidge	R. Scott			
70	24.9.1949	Australia	Eden Park	Auckland	9(0)	16(8)	R. Roper*		T. O'Callaghan*	J. Smith	
71	27.5.1950	British Isles	Carisbrook	Dunedin	9(0)	9(3)	R. Roper R. Elvidge		R. Scott		
72	10.6.1950	British Isles	Lancaster Park	Christchurch	8(8)	0(0)	P. Crowley R. Roper	L. Haig*			
73	1.7.1950	British Isles	Athletic Park	Wellington	6(0)	3(3)	R. Elvidge		R. Scott		
74	29.7.1950	British Isles	Eden Park	Auckland	11(8)	8(3)	H. Wilson* P. Henderson	R. Scott		R. Scott	
75	23.6.1951	Australia	Sydney Cricket Ground	Sydney	8(8)	0(0)	K. Skinner	M. Cockerill*	M. Cockerill		
76	7.7.1951	Australia	Sydney Cricket Ground	Sydney	17(9)	11(3)	R. Jarden 2 N. Wilson T. Lynch	M. Cockerill		T. Lynch	
77	21.7.1951	Australia	Brisbane Cricket Ground	Brisbane	16(11)	6(3)	J. Tanner T. Lynch R. Bell* L. Haig	M. Cockerill 2			
78	6.9.1952	Australia	Lancaster Park	Christchurch	9(6)	14(5)	J. Fitzgerald* R. White		R. Bell		
79	13.9.1952	Australia	Athletic Park	Wellington	15(9)	8(3)	J. Hotop C. Robinson		R. Jarden N. Bowden*	J. Hotop	
80	19.12.1953	Wales	Cardiff Arms Park	Cardiff	8(8)	13(5)	W. Clark*	R. Jarden	R. Jarden		
81	9.1.1954	Ireland	Lansdowne Road	Dublin	14(9)	3(0)	W. Clark R. Stuart	R. Scott	R. Scott	R. Scott	
82	30.1.1954	England	Twickenham	London	5(5)	0	N. Dalzell	R. Scott			
83	13.2.1954	Scotland	Murrayfield	Edinburgh	3(0)	0			R. Scott		
84	27.2.1954	France	Colombes Stadium	Paris	0	3(3)					
85	20.8.1955	Australia	Athletic Park	Wellington	16(10)	8(8)	W. Clark I. Vodanovich* R. Jarden	R. Jarden 2	R. Jarden		
86	3.9.1955	Australia	Carisbrook	Dunedin	8(0)	0	R. Jarden	R. Jarden		A. Elsom	
87	17.9.1955	Australia	Eden Park	Auckland	3(0)	8(8)	R. Jarden				
88	14.7.1956	South Africa	Carisbrook	Dunedin	10(10)	6(3)	R. White R. Jarden	R. Jarden 2			
89	4.8.1956	South Africa	Athletic Park	Wellington	3(3)	8(0)	R. Brown				
90	18.8.1956	South Africa	Lancaster Park	Christchurch	17(11)	10(0)	M. Dixon R. Jarden R. White	D. Clarke*	D. Clarke 2		
91	1.9.1956	South Africa	Eden Park	Auckland	11(3)	5(0)	P. Jones	D. Clarke	D. Clarke 2		
92	25.5.1957	Australia	Sydney Cricket Ground	Sydney	25(11)	11(11)	N. MacEwan R. Hemi F. McMullen* P. Walsh	D. Clarke 2	D. Clarke 3		
93	1.6.1957	Australia	Exhibition Ground	Brisbane	22(13)	9(6)	M. Dixon F. McMullen R. Brown C. Meads	D. Clarke 2		R. Brown	D. Clarke
94	23.8.1958	Australia	Athletic Park	Wellington	25(9)	3(0)	W. Whineray 2 P. Walsh 2 D. Graham* F. McMullen P. Jones	D Clarke 2			
95	6.9.1958	Australia	Lancaster Park	Christchurch	3(0)	6(3)	R. Brown				
96	20.9.1958	Australia	Epsom Showgrounds	Auckland	17(6)	8(0)	C. Meads	D. Clarke	D. Clarke 4		
97	18.7.1959	British Isles	Carisbrook	Dunedin	18(6)	17(9)			D. Clarke 6		

New Zealand's test record

Nº	Date	Opponent	Venue	City	NZ score	Opponent	Tries	Cons	Pens	DGs	GMs
98	15.8.1959	British Isles	Athletic Park	Wellington	11(6)	8(0)	R. Caulton 2* D. Clarke	D. Clarke			
99	29.8.1959	British Isles	Lancaster Park	Christchurch	22(14)	8(8)	R. Caulton 2 C. Meads R. Urbahn	D. Clarke 2	D. Clarke	D. Clarke	
100	19.9.1959	British Isles	Eden Park	Auckland	6(3)	9(3)			D. Clarke 2		
101	25.6.1960	South Africa	Ellis Park	Johannesburg	0	13(5)					
102	23.7.1960	South Africa	Newlands	Cape Town	11(3)	3(3)	C. Meads	D. Clarke	D. Clarke	D. Clarke	
103	13.8.1960	South Africa	Free State Stadium	Bloemfontein	11(0)	11(3)	F. McMullen	D. Clarke	D. Clarke 2		
104	27.8.1960	South Africa	Boet Erasmus Stadium	Port Elizabeth	3(3)	8(3)			D. Clarke		
105	22.7.1961	France	Eden Park	Auckland	13(5)	6(6)	D. McKay* T. O'Sullivan	D. Clarke 2		D. Clarke	
106	5.8.1961	France	Athletic Park	Wellington	5(0)	3(0)	K. Tremain	D. Clarke			
107	19.8.1961	France	Lancaster Park	Christchurch	32(13)	3(3)	D. Graham P. Little K. Tremain C. Meads V. Yates	D. Clarke 4	D. Clarke 3		
108	26.5.1962	Australia	Exhibition Ground	Brisbane	20(17)	6(0)	B. Watt 2* N. MacEwan K. Tremain	D. Clarke	D. Clarke	D. Clarke	
109	4.6.1962	Australia	Sydney Cricket Ground	Sydney	14(6)	5(5)	W. Nathan J. Watt	D. Clarke	D. Clarke 2		
110	25.8.1962	Australia	Athletic Park	Wellington	9(3)	9(0)	P. Morrissey*		D. Clarke 2		
111	8.9.1962	Australia	Carisbrook	Dunedin	3(0)	0			D. Clarke		
112	22.9.1962	Australia	Eden Park	Auckland	16(11)	8(0)	P. Morrissey R. Heeps M. Herewini*	D. Clarke 2		M. Herewini	
113	25.5.1963	England	Eden Park	Auckland	21(0)	11(6)	R. Caulton 2 D. Clarke	D. Clarke 3	D. Clarke	D. Clarke	
114	1.6.1963	England	Lancaster Park	Christchurch	9(6)	6(3)	D. McKay P. Walsh				D. Clarke
115	7.12.1963	Ireland	Lansdowne Road	Dublin	6(3)	5(5)	K. Tremain		D. Clarke		
116	21.12.1963	Wales	Cardiff Arms Park	Cardiff	6(3)	0			D. Clarke	B. Watt	
117	4.1.1964	England	Twickenham	London	14(9)	0	R. Caulton C. Meads	D. Clarke	D. Clarke 2		
118	18.1.1964	Scotland	Murrayfield	Edinburgh	0	0					
119	8.2.1964	France	Colombes Stadium	Paris	12(6)	3(3)	R. Caulton K. Gray		M. Herewini	C. Laidlaw*	
120	15.8.1964	Australia	Carisbrook	Dunedin	14(5)	9(3)	B. McLeod*	M. Williment*	M. Williment 2	R. Moreton	
121	22.8.1964	Australia	Lancaster Park	Christchurch	18(10)	3(0)	P. Murdoch* R. Rangi* R. Moreton K. Gray	D. Clarke 3			
122	29.8.1964	Australia	Athletic Park	Wellington	5(0)	20(3)	P. Murdoch	D. Clarke			
123	31.7.1965	South Africa	Athletic Park	Wellington	6(6)	3(0)	W. Birtwistle* K. Tremain				
124	21.8.1965	South Africa	Carisbrook	Dunedin	13(8)	0	K. Tremain B. McLeod R. Rangi	M. Williment 2			
125	4.9.1965	South Africa	Lancaster Park	Christchurch	16(16)	19(5)	K. Tremain R. Rangi R. Moreton	M. Williment 2	M. Williment		
126	18.9.1965	South Africa	Eden Park	Auckland	20(3)	3(0)	I. Smith 2* R. Conway W. Birtwistle K. Gray	F. McCormick*		M. Herewini	
127	16.7.1966	British Isles	Carisbrook	Dunedin	20(8)	3(3)	B. McLeod M. Williment B. Lochore	M. Williment	M. Williment 2	M. Herewini	

New Zealand's test record

№	Date	Opponent	Venue	City	NZ score	Opponent	Tries	Cons	Pens	DGs	GMs
128	6.8.1966	British Isles	Athletic Park	Wellington	16(8)	12(9)	K. Tremain C. Meads A. Steel	M. Williment 2	M. Williment		
129	27.8.1966	British Isles	Lancaster Park	Christchurch	19(6)	6(6)	W. Nathan 2 A. Steel	M. Williment 2	M. Williment 2		
130	10.9.1966	British Isles	Eden Park	Auckland	24(10)	11(8)	W. Nathan M. Dick I. MacRae A. Steel	M. Williment 3	M. Williment	M. Herewini	
131	19.8.1967	Australia	Athletic Park	Wellington	29(9)	9(3)	A. Steel 2 W. Davis* K. Tremain	M. Williment 4	M. Williment 2	M. Herewini	
132	4.11.1967	England	Twickenham	London	23(18)	11(5)	E. Kirton 2* W. Birtwistle C. Laidlaw M. Dick	F. McCormick 4			
133	11.11.1967	Wales	Cardiff Arms Park	Cardiff	13(8)	6(0)	W. Birtwistle W. Davis	F. McCormick 2	F. McCormick		
134	25.11.1967	France	Colombes Stadium	Paris	21(11)	15(9)	S. Going A. Steel I. Kirkpatrick* M. Dick	F. McCormick 3	F. McCormick		
135	2.12.1967	Scotland	Murrayfield	Edinburgh	14(9)	3(3)	I. MacRae W. Davis	F. McCormick	F. McCormick 2		
136	15.6.1968	Australia	Sydney Cricket Ground	Sydney	27(8)	11(0)	I. Kirkpatrick 3 E. Kirton A. Steel C. Laidlaw	F. McCormick 3	F. McCormick		
137	22.6.1968	Australia	Ballymore	Brisbane	19(11)	18(12)	T. Lister G. Thorne penalty try	F. McCormick 2	F. McCormick 2		
138	13.7.1968	France	Lancaster Park	Christchurch	12(3)	9(3)	E. Kirton		F. McCormick 3		
139	27.7.1968	France	Athletic Park	Wellington	9(0)	3(3)			F. McCormick 3		
140	10.8.1968	France	Eden Park	Auckland	19(16)	12(0)	S. Going 2	F. McCormick 2	F. McCormick 2	W. Cottrell	
141	31.5.1969	Wales	Lancaster Park	Christchurch	19(13)	0	M. Dick B. McLeod B. Lochore K. Gray	F. McCormick 2	F. McCormick		
142	14.6.1969	Wales	Eden Park	Auckland	33(14)	12(6)	G. Skudder* I. MacRae I Kirkpatrick	F. McCormick 3	F. McCormick 5	F. McCormick	
143	25.7.1970	South Africa	Loftus Versfeld	Pretoria	6(0)	17(12)	B. Williams*		F. McCormick		
144	8.8.1970	South Africa	Newlands	Cape Town	9(6)	8(0)	C. Laidlaw I. Kirkpatrick		F. McCormick		
145	29.8.1970	South Africa	Boet Erasmus Stadium	Port Elizabeth	3(3)	14(3)			B. Williams		
146	12.9.1970	South Africa	Ellis Park	Johannesburg	17(3)	20(14)	B. Williams	G. Kember*	G. Kember 4		
147	26.6.1971	British Isles	Carisbrook	Dunedin	3(3)	9(3)			F. McCormick		
148	10.7.1971	British Isles	Lancaster Park	Christchurch	22(8)	12(6)	B. Burgess 2 S. Going I. Kirkpatrick penalty try	L. Mains 2*	L. Mains		
149	31.7.1971	British Isles	Athletic Park	Wellington	3(0)	13(13)	L. Mains				
150	14.8.1971	British Isles	Eden Park	Auckland	14(8)	14(8)	W. Cottrell T. Lister	L. Mains	L. Mains 2		
151	19.8.1972	Australia	Athletic Park	Wellington	29(19)	6(0)	J. Dougan* S. Going A. Sutherland B. Williams P. Whiting	T. Morris 3*		T. Morris	

Test Statistics

№	Date	Opponent	Venue	City	NZ score	Opponent	Tries	Cons	Pens	DGs	GMs
152	2.9.1972	Australia	Lancaster Park	Christchurch	30(24)	17(4)	I. Kirkpatrick 2 A. Sutherland P. Whiting B. Williams	T. Morris 2	T. Morris 2		
153	16.9.1972	Australia	Eden Park	Auckland	38(16)	3(0)	I. Kirkpatrick A. Sutherland A. Scown S. Going P. Whiting B. Williams	T. Morris 4	T. Morris 2		
154	2.12.1972	Wales	Cardiff Arms Park	Cardiff	19(13)	16(3)	K. Murdoch		J. Karam 5*		
155	16.12.1972	Scotland	Murrayfield	Edinburgh	14(6)	9(0)	A. Wyllie G. Batty S. Going	J. Karam			
156	6.1.1973	England	Twickenham	London	9(6)	0	I. Kirkpatrick	J. Karam		B. Williams	
157	20.1.1973	Ireland	Lansdowne Road	Dublin	10(6)	10(3)	S. Going A. Wyllie	J. Karam			
158	10.2.1973	France	Parc des Princes	Paris	6(3)	13(10)			J. Karam 2		
159	15.9.1973	England	Eden Park	Auckland	10(10)	16(6)	G. Batty I. Hurst	R. Lendrum*			
160	25.5.1974	Australia	Sydney Cricket Ground	Sydney	11(3)	6(6)	D. Robertson* I. Kirkpatrick		J. Karam		
161	1.6.1974	Australia	Ballymore	Brisbane	16(7)	16(6)	I. Hurst A. Leslie	J. Karam	J. Karam 2		
162	8.6.1974	Australia	Sydney Cricket Ground	Sydney	16(6)	6(0)	I. Kirkpatrick G. Batty I. Stevens	J. Karam 2			
163	23.11.1974	Ireland	Lansdowne Road	Dublin	15(9)	6(3)	J. Karam	J. Karam	J. Karam 3		
164	14.6.1975	Scotland	Eden Park	Auckland	24(6)	0	B. Williams 2 H. Macdonald D. Robertson	J. Karam 4			
165	5.6.1976	Ireland	Athletic Park	Wellington	11(11)	3(0)	B. Robertson I. Kirkpatrick		L. Mains		
166	24.7.1976	South Africa	Kings Park	Durban	7(3)	16(3)	L. Jaffray		B. Williams		
167	14.8.1976	South Africa	Free State Stadium	Bloemfontein	15(12)	9(6)	J. Morgan	S. Going	S. Going 2	D. Bruce	
168	4.9.1976	South Africa	Newlands	Cape Town	10(7)	15(6)	B. Robertson		B. Williams 2		
169	18.9.1976	South Africa	Ellis Park	Johannesburg	14(8)	15(9)	I. Kirkpatrick S. Going		B. Williams	D. Bruce	
170	18.6.1977	British Isles	Athletic Park	Wellington	16(16)	12(12)	S. Going B. Johnstone G. Batty	B. Williams 2			
171	9.7.1977	British Isles	Lancaster Park	Christchurch	9(6)	13(13)			B. Williams 3		
172	30.7.1977	British Isles	Carisbrook	Dunedin	19(10)	7(4)	I. Kirkpatrick A. Haden	B. Wilson*	B. Wilson 2	B. Robertson	
173	13.8.1977	British Isles	Eden Park	Auckland	10(3)	9(9)	L. Knight		B. Wilson 2		
174	11.11.1977	France	Municipal Stadium	Toulouse	13(10)	18(6)	B. Williams		B. McKechnie* B Williams	B. Robertson	
175	19.11.1977	France	Parc des Princes	Paris	15(9)	3(3)	S. Wilson	B. McKechnie	B. McKechnie G. Seear	B. McKechnie	
176	19.8.1978	Australia	Athletic Park	Wellington	13(10)	12(6)	B. Williams		B Wilson 3		
177	26.8.1978	Australia	Lancaster Park	Christchurch	22(9)	6(6)	Mark Taylor G. Seear S. Wilson	B. Wilson 2	B. Wilson	D. Bruce	
178	9.9.1978	Australia	Eden Park	Auckland	16(3)	30(10)	J. Ashworth S. Wilson	B. McKechnie	B. McKechnie 2		
179	4.11.1978	Ireland	Lansdowne Road	Dublin	10(3)	6(3)	A. Dalton			D. Bruce 2	
180	11.11.1978	Wales	Cardiff Arms Park	Cardiff	13(7)	12(12)	S. Wilson		B. McKechnie 3		
181	25.11.1978	England	Twickenham	London	16(10)	6(6)	F. Oliver B. Johnstone	B. McKechnie	B. McKechnie 2		

New Zealand's test record

№	Date	Opponent	Venue	City	NZ score	Opponent	Tries	Cons	Pens	DGs	GMs
182	9.12.1978	Scotland	Murrayfield	Edinburgh	18(9)	9(6)	G. Seear B. Robertson	B. McKechnie 2	B. McKechnie 2		
183	7.7.1979	France	Lancaster Park	Christchurch	23(10)	9(3)	S. Wilson M. Donaldson M. Watts*	B. Wilson	B. Wilson 3		
184	14.7.1979	France	Eden Park	Auckland	19(7)	24(11)	S. Wilson G. Mourie	B. Wilson	B. Wilson 3		
185	28.7.1979	Australia	Sydney Cricket Ground	Sydney	6(6)	12(6)			B. Wilson	Murray Taylor	
186	10.11.1979	Scotland	Murrayfield	Edinburgh	20(4)	6(0)	S. Wilson E. Dunn* D. Loveridge M. Mexted*	R. Wilson 2*			
187	24.11.1979	England	Twickenham	London	10(10)	9(3)	J. Fleming		R. Wilson 2		
188	21.6.1980	Australia	Sydney Cricket Ground	Sydney	9(6)	13(9)			B. Codlin 3*		
189	28.6.1980	Australia	Ballymore	Brisbane	12(6)	9(9)	H. Reid	B. Codlin	B. Codlin 2		
190	12.7.1980	Australia	Sydney Cricket Ground	Sydney	10(3)	26(17)	B. Fraser		B. Codlin 2		
191	1.11.1980	Wales	Cardiff Arms Park	Cardiff	23(11)	3(0)	G. Mourie B. Fraser N. Allen H. Reid	D. Rollerson 2*	D. Rollerson		
192	13.6.1981	Scotland	Carisbrook	Dunedin	11(3)	4(0)	S. Wilson D. Loveridge		A. Hewson*		
193	20.6.1981	Scotland	Eden Park	Auckland	40(10)	15(6)	S. Wilson 3 A. Hewson 2 B. Robertson G. Mourie	A. Hewson 6			
194	15.8.1981	South Africa	Lancaster Park	Christchurch	14(10)	9(3)	D. Rollerson S. Wilson M. Shaw	D. Rollerson			
195	29.8.1981	South Africa	Athletic Park	Wellington	12(3)	24(18)			A. Hewson 4		
196	12.9.1981	South Africa	Eden Park	Auckland	25(16)	22(3)	S. Wilson G. Knight	D. Rollerson	A. Hewson 3 D. Rollerson	D. Rollerson	
197	24.10.1981	Romania	August 23 Stadium	Bucharest	14(3)	6(3)	J. Salmon* A. Dalton		A. Hewson	D. Rollerson	
198	14.11.1981	France	Stadium de Toulouse	Toulouse	13(10)	9(6)	S. Wilson		A. Hewson 2	A. Hewson	
199	21.11.1981	France	Parc des Princes	Paris	18(9)	6(3)	S. Wilson penalty try	A. Hewson 2	A. Hewson 2		
200	14.8.1982	Australia	Lancaster Park	Christchurch	23(19)	16(3)	M. Mexted G. Mourie S. Pokere B. Fraser	A. Hewson 2	A. Hewson		
201	28.8.1982	Australia	Athletic Park	Wellington	16(3)	19(19)	M. Shaw B. Fraser	A. Hewson	A. Hewson 2		
202	11.9.1982	Australia	Eden Park	Auckland	33(12)	18(15)	A. Hewson M. Shaw	A. Hewson 2	A. Hewson 5	A. Hewson W. Smith	
203	4.6.1983	British Isles	Lancaster Park	Christchurch	16(6)	12(9)	M. Shaw		A. Hewson 3	A. Hewson	
204	18.6.1983	British Isles	Athletic Park	Wellington	9(9)	0	D. Loveridge	A. Hewson	A. Hewson		
205	2.7.1983	British Isles	Carisbrook	Dunedin	15(6)	8(4)	S. Wilson	A. Hewson	A. Hewson 3		
206	16.7.1983	British Isles	Eden Park	Auckland	38(16)	6(3)	S. Wilson 3 A. Hewson J. Hobbs A. Haden	A. Hewson 4	A. Hewson 2		
207	20.8.1983	Australia	Sydney Cricket Ground	Sydney	18(12)	8(8)	W. Taylor	A. Hewson	A. Hewson 4		
208	12.11.1983	Scotland	Murrayfield	Edinburgh	25(16)	25(15)	B. Fraser 2 J. Hobbs	R. Deans 2*	R. Deans 3		
209	19.11.1983	England	Twickenham	London	9(3)	15(6)	M. Davie*	R. Deans	R. Deans		
210	16.6.1984	France	Lancaster Park	Christchurch	10(3)	9(3)	W. Taylor		A. Hewson 2		
211	23.6.1984	France	Eden Park	Auckland	31(16)	18(6)	B. Smith A. Dalton W. Taylor	A. Hewson 2	A. Hewson 5		

New Zealand's test record

Nº	Date	Opponent	Venue	City	NZ score	Opponent	Tries	Cons	Pens	DGs	GMs
212	21.7.1984	Australia	Sydney Cricket Ground	Sydney	9(6)	16(9)			A. Hewson 2	A. Hewson	
213	4.8.1984	Australia	Ballymore	Brisbane	19(6)	15(12)	S. Pokere		R. Deans 5		
214	18.8.1984	Australia	Sydney Cricket Ground	Sydney	25(19)	24(15)	M. Clamp A. Stone	R. Deans	R. Deans 5		
215	1.6.1985	England	Lancaster Park	Christchurch	18(12)	13(13)			K Crowley 6*		
216	8.6.1985	England	Athletic Park	Wellington	42(13)	15(9)	C. Green 2 J. Kirwan M. Mexted J. Hobbs M. Shaw	K. Crowley 3	K. Crowley 3	W. Smith	
217	29.6.1985	Australia	Eden Park	Auckland	10(6)	9(3)	C. Green		K. Crowley 2		
218	26.10.1985	Argentina	Ferrocarril Stadium	Buenos Aires	33(15)	20(14)	J. Kirwan 2 J. Hobbs K. Crowley	K. Crowley	K. Crowley 4	G. Fox*	
219	2.11.1985	Argentina	Ferrocarril Stadium	Buenos Aires	21(18)	21(9)	J. Kirwan 2 M. Mexted C. Green	K. Crowley	K. Crowley		
220	28.6.1986	France	Lancaster Park	Christchurch	18(12)	9(6)	M. Brewer*	G. Cooper*	G. Cooper	F. Botica 2* G. Cooper	
221	9.8.1986	Australia	Athletic Park	Wellington	12(0)	13(9)	M. Brooke-Cowden	G. Cooper	G. Cooper 2		
222	23.8.1986	Australia	Carisbrook	Dunedin	13(13)	12(3)	D. Kirk		G. Cooper 2	G. Cooper	
223	6.9.1986	Australia	Eden Park	Auckland	9(6)	22(12)			K. Crowley 3		
224	8.11.1986	France	Stadium de Toulouse	Toulouse	19(6)	7(3)	W. Shelford*		K. Crowley 3	A. Stone K. Crowley	
225	15.11.1986	France	Stade de la Beaujoire	Nantes	3(3)	16(3)			K. Crowley		
226	22.5.1987	Italy	Eden Park	Auckland	70(17)	6(3)	D. Kirk 2 J. Kirwan 2 C. Green 2 M. Jones* W. Taylor S. McDowell J. Stanley A. Whetton penalty try	G. Fox 8	G. Fox 2		
227	27.5.1987	Fiji	Lancaster Park	Christchurch	74(40)	13(3)	C. Green 4 J. Gallagher 4 D. Kirk J. Kirwan A. Whetton penalty try	G. Fox 10	G. Fox 2		
228	1.6.1987	Argentina	Athletic Park	Wellington	46(19)	15(9)	D. Kirk Z. Brooke* J. Stanley A. Earl K. Crowley A. Whetton	G. Fox 2	G. Fox 6		
229	6.6.1987	Scotland	Lancaster Park	Christchurch	30(9)	3(3)	J. Gallagher A. Whetton	G. Fox 2	G. Fox 6		
230	14.6.1987	Wales	Ballymore	Brisbane	49(27)	6(0)	J. Kirwan 2 W. Shelford 2 J. Drake M. Brooke-Cowden J. Stanley A. Whetton	G. Fox 7	G. Fox		
231	20.6.1987	France	Eden Park	Auckland	29(9)	9(0)	D. Kirk J. Kirwan M. Jones	G. Fox	G. Fox 4	G. Fox	

New Zealand's test record

Nº	Date	Opponent	Venue	City	NZ score	Opponent	Tries	Cons	Pens	DGs	GMs
232	25.7.1987	Australia	Concord Oval	Sydney	30(3)	16(6)	S. Fitzpatrick 2 J. Kirwan C. Green	G. Fox	G. Fox 3	G. Fox	
233	28.5.1988	Wales	Lancaster Park	Christchurch	52(24)	3(0)	J. Kirwan 4 T. Wright 2* J. Gallagher B. Deans* W. Shelford G. Whetton	G. Fox 6			
234	11.6.1988	Wales	Eden Park	Auckland	54(21)	9(3)	J. Kirwan 2 T. Wright 2 W. Taylor B. Deans M. Jones S. McDowell	G. Fox 8	G. Fox 2		
235	3.7.1988	Australia	Concord Oval	Sydney	32(14)	7(4)	J. Kirwan 2 S. McDowell A. Whetton J. Schuster*	G. Fox 3	G. Fox 2		
236	16.7.1988	Australia	Ballymore	Brisbane	19(6)	19(16)	M. Jones T. Wright J. Kirwan	G. Fox 2	G. Fox		
237	30.7.1988	Australia	Concord Oval	Sydney	30(12)	9(3)	B. Deans J. Gallagher J. Kirwan	G. Fox 3	G. Fox 4		
238	17.6.1989	France	Lancaster Park	Christchurch	25(18)	17(0)	T. Wright 2 A. Whetton	G. Fox 2	G. Fox 3		
239	1.7.1989	France	Eden Park	Auckland	34(16)	20(13)	J. Stanley B. Deans S. Fitzpatrick A. Whetton	G. Fox 3	G. Fox 4		
240	15.7.1989	Argentina	Carisbrook	Dunedin	60(22)	9(3)	J. Gallagher 3 M. Jones 2 T. Wright 2 J. Kirwan 2 penalty try	G. Fox 7	G. Fox 2		
241	29.7.1989	Argentina	Athletic Park	Wellington	49(15)	12(12)	T. Wright 2 B. Deans 2 J. Gallagher J. Kirwan A. Whetton	G. Fox 6	G. Fox 3		
242	5.8.1989	Australia	Eden Park	Auckland	24(12)	12(6)	J. Gallagher R. Loe	G. Fox 2	G. Fox 4		
243	4.11.1989	Wales	Cardiff Arms Park	Cardiff	34(12)	9(6)	C. Innes 2* G. Bachop* T. Wright	G. Fox 3	G. Fox 4		
244	18.11.1989	Ireland	Lansdowne Road	Dublin	23(13)	6(6)	J. Gallagher T. Wright W. Shelford	G. Fox	G. Fox 3		
245	16.6.1990	Scotland	Carisbrook	Dunedin	31(15)	16(10)	J. Kirwan 2 K. Crowley I. Jones* G. Fox	G. Fox 4	G. Fox		
246	23.6.1990	Scotland	Eden Park	Auckland	21(12)	18(18)	R. Loe	G. Fox	G. Fox 5		
247	21.7.1990	Australia	Lancaster Park	Christchurch	21(10)	6(3)	S. Fitzpatrick K. Crowley C. Innes J. Kirwan	G. Fox	G. Fox		
248	4.8.1990	Australia	Eden Park	Auckland	27(15)	17(7)	S. Fitzpatrick Z. Brooke G. Bachop	G. Fox 3	G. Fox 2	G. Fox	

New Zealand's test record

Nº	Date	Opponent	Venue	City	NZ score	Opponent	Tries	Cons	Pens	DGs	GMs
249	18.8.1990	Australia	Athletic Park	Wellington	9(9)	21(6)			G. Fox 2	G. Fox	
250	3.11.1990	France	Stade de la Beaujoire	Nantes	24(18)	3(3)	C. Innes A. Whetton	G. Fox 2	G. Fox 3	G. Fox	
251	10.11.1990	France	Parc des Princes	Paris	30(15)	12(6)	K. Crowley M. Jones	G. Fox 2	G. Fox 6		
252	6.7.1991	Argentina	Velez Sarsfield Stadium	Buenos Aires	28(12)	14(6)	T. Wright A. Earl	G. Fox	G. Fox 5	K. Crowley	
253	13.7.1991	Argentina	Velez Sarsfield Stadium	Buenos Aires	36(15)	6(3)	Z. Brooke M. Jones J. Kirwan T. Wright	G. Fox 4	G. Fox 4		
254	10.8.1991	Australia	Sydney Football Stadium	Sydney	12(9)	21(9)	I. Jones	G. Fox	G. Fox 2		
255	24.8.1991	Australia	Eden Park	Auckland	6(3)	3(0)			G. Fox 2		
256	3.10.1991	England	Twickenham	London	18(9)	12(12)	M. Jones	G. Fox	G. Fox 4		
257	8.10.1991	United States	Kingsholm	Gloucester	46(20)	6(3)	T. Wright 3 J. Timu A. Earl G. Purvis* V. Tuigamala*	J. Preston 4*	J. Preston 2		
							C. Innes				
258	13.10.1991	Italy	Welford Road	Leicester	31(16)	21(3)	Z. Brooke V. Tuigamala J. Hewett* C. Innes	G. Fox 3	G. Fox 3		
259	20.10.1991	Canada	Stade du Nord	Lille	29(21)	13(3)	J. Timu 2 B. McCahill J. Kirwan Z. Brooke	G. Fox 3	G. Fox		
260	27.10.1991	Australia	Lansdowne Road	Dublin	6(0)	16(13)			G. Fox 2		
261	30.10.1991	Scotland	Cardiff Arms Park	Cardiff	13(6)	6(3)	W. Little		J. Preston 3		
262	18.4.1992	World XV	Lancaster Park	Christchurch	14(3)	28(15)	R. Turner* V. Tuigamala		G. Fox 2		
263	22.4.1992	World XV	Athletic Park	Wellington	54(34)	26(6)	G. Cooper 2 E. Clarke 2* R. Loe 2 V. Tuigamala A. Strachan* A. Pene B. Larsen*	G. Cooper 6 G. Fox			
264	25.4.1992	World XV	Eden Park	Auckland	26(6)	15(9)	A. Pene J. Kirwan R. Loe E. Clarke	G. Cooper 2	G. Cooper 2		
265	30.5.1992	Ireland	Carisbrook	Dunedin	24(18)	21(18)	F. Bunce 2 P. Henderson E. Clarke	G. Cooper 4			
266	6.6.1992	Ireland	Athletic Park	Wellington	59(15)	6(6)	F. Bunce 2 M. Cooper 2* A. Pene 2 J. Kirwan J. Timu E. Clarke A. Strachan I. Jones	M. Cooper 6	M. Cooper		
267	4.7.1992	Australia	Sydney Football Stadium	Sydney	15(12)	16(8)	V. Tuigamala F. Bunce	G. Fox	G. Fox		
268	19.7.1992	Australia	Ballymore	Brisbane	17(7)	19(11)	J. Timu J. Kirwan	G. Fox 2	G. Fox		
269	25.7.1992	Australia	Sydney Football Stadium	Sydney	26(13)	23(13)	W. Little J. Joseph	G. Fox 2	G. Fox 3	G. Fox	

New Zealand's test record

Nº	Date	Opponent	Venue	City	NZ score	Opponent	Tries	Cons	Pens	DGs	GMs
270	15.8.1992	South Africa	Ellis Park	Johannesburg	27(10)	24(0)	Z. Brooke J. Kirwan J. Timu	G. Fox 3	G. Fox 2		
271	12.6.1993	British Isles	Lancaster Park	Christchurch	20(11)	18(9)	F. Bunce		G. Fox 5		
272	26.6.1993	British Isles	Athletic Park	Wellington	7(7)	20(9)	E. Clarke	G. Fox			
273	3.7.1993	British Isles	Eden Park	Auckland	30(14)	13(10)	F. Bunce S. Fitzpatrick J. Preston	G. Fox 3	G. Fox 3		
274	17.7.1993	Australia	Carisbrook	Dunedin	25(9)	10(3)	F. Bunce S. Fitzpatrick		G. Fox 5		
275	31.7.1993	Western Samoa	Eden Park	Auckland	35(22)	13(6)	L. Stensness Z. Brooke	G. Fox 2	G. Fox 7		
276	20.11.1993	Scotland	Murrayfield	Edinburgh	51(22)	15(9)	J. Wilson 3* M. Ellis 2* F. Bunce Z. Brooke	M. Cooper 4 J. Wilson	M. Cooper 2		
277	27.11.1993	England	Twickenham	London	9(0)	15(6)			J. Wilson 3		
278	26.6.1994	France	Lancaster Park	Christchurch	8(3)	22(9)	F. Bunce		M. Cooper		
279	3.7.1994	France	Eden Park	Auckland	20(9)	23(13)	S. Fitzpatrick		M. Cooper 5		
280	9.7.1994	South Africa	Carisbrook	Dunedin	22(12)	14(3)	J. Kirwan	S. Howarth*	S. Howarth 5		
281	23.7.1994	South Africa	Athletic Park	Wellington	13(10)	9(6)	J. Timu Z. Brooke		S. Howarth		
282	6.8.1994	South Africa	Eden Park	Auckland	18(9)	18(12)			S. Howarth 6		
283	17.8.1994	Australia	Sydney Football Stadium	Sydney	16(6)	20(17)	S. Howarth	S. Howarth	S. Howarth 3		
284	22.4.1995	Canada	Eden Park	Auckland	73(30)	7(0)	F. Bunce 2 M. Ellis 2 G. Osborne 2* G. Bachop A. Mehrtens* O. Brown J. Wilson	A. Mehrtens 7	A. Mehrtens 3		
285	27.5.1995	Ireland	Ellis Park	Johannesburg	43(20)	19(12)	J. Lomu 2 F. Bunce J. Kronfeld G. Osborne	A. Mehrtens 3	A. Mehrtens 4		
286	31.5.1995	Wales	Ellis Park	Johannesburg	34(20)	9(6)	W. Little M. Ellis J. Kronfeld	A. Mehrtens 2	A. Mehrtens 4	A. Mehrtens	
287	4.6.1995	Japan	Free State Stadium	Bloemfontein	145(84)	17(3)	M. Ellis 6 E. Rush 3 J. Wilson 3 G. Osborne 2 R. Brooke 2 R. Loe A. Ieremia S. Culhane* C. Dowd P. Henderson	S. Culhane 20			
288	11.6.1995	Scotland	Loftus Versfeld	Pretoria	48(17)	30(9)	W. Little 2 J. Lomu A. Mehrtens F. Bunce S. Fitzpatrick	A. Mehrtens 6	A. Mehrtens 2		
289	18.6.1995	England	Newlands	Cape Town	45(25)	29(3)	J. Lomu 4 J. Kronfeld G. Bachop	A. Mehrtens 3	A. Mehrtens	A. Mehrtens Z. Brooke	
290	24.6.1995	South Africa	Ellis Park	Johannesburg	12(6)	15(9)			A. Mehrtens 3	A. Mehrtens	
291	22.7.1995	Australia	Eden Park	Auckland	28(9)	16(10)	J. Lomu	A. Mehrtens	A. Mehrtens 5	A. Mehrtens 2	

Test Statistics

New Zealand's test record

Nº	Date	Opponent	Venue	City	NZ score	Opponent	Tries	Cons	Pens	DGs	GMs
292	29.7.1995	Australia	Sydney Football Stadium	Sydney	34(12)	23(13)	F. Bunce 2 A. Mehrtens J. Lomu J. Wilson	A. Mehrtens 3	A. Mehrtens		
293	28.10.1995	Italy	Stadio Renato dall'Ara	Bologna	70(20)	6(6)	W. Little 2 J. Lomu 2 M. Jones I. Jones Z. Brooke S. Fitzpatrick E. Rush J. Wilson	S. Culhane 7	S. Culhane 2		
294	11.11.1995	France	Stadium de Toulouse	Toulouse	15(3)	22(17)			S. Culhane 5		
295	18.11.1995	France	Parc des Princes	Paris	37(20)	12(5)	E. Rush G. Osborne I. Jones J. Lomu	S. Culhane	S. Culhane 5		
296	7.6.1996	Western Samoa	McLean Park	Napier	51(27)	10(10)	C. Cullen 3* J. Wilson J. Marshall S. McLeod* O. Brown	A. Mehrtens 5	A. Mehrtens	A. Mehrtens	
297	15.6.1996	Scotland	Carisbrook	Dunedin	62(31)	31(19)	C. Cullen 4 I. Jones J. Lomu Z. Brooke A. Mehrtens J. Marshall	A. Mehrtens 7	A. Mehrtens		
298	22.6.1996	Scotland	Eden Park	Auckland	36(17)	12(7)	J. Kronfeld 2 Z. Brooke M. Jones penalty try	A. Mehrtens 4	A. Mehrtens		
299	6.7.1996	Australia	Athletic Park	Wellington	43(25)	6(6)	M. Jones C. Cullen J. Marshall Z. Brooke J. Wilson J. Lomu	A. Mehrtens 2	A. Mehrtens 3		
300	20.7.1996	South Africa	Lancaster Park	Christchurch	15(6)	11(8)			A. Mehrtens 5		
301	27.7.1996	Australia	Suncorp Stadium	Brisbane	32(9)	25(16)	J. Marshall F. Bunce	A. Mehrtens 2	A. Mehrtens 6		
302	10.8.1996	South Africa	Norwich Park Newlands	Cape Town	29(6)	18(15)	G. Osborne C. Dowd	A. Mehrtens 2	A. Mehrtens 5		
303	17.8.1996	South Africa	Kings Park	Durban	23(15)	19(9)	J. Wilson C. Cullen Z. Brooke	S. Culhane	S. Culhane 2		
304	24.8.1996	South Africa	Loftus Versfeld	Pretoria	33(21)	26(11)	J. Wilson 2 Z. Brooke	S. Culhane 3	S. Culhane J. Preston 2	Z. Brooke	
305	31.8.1996	South Africa	Ellis Park	Johannesburg	22(8)	32(16)	S. Fitzpatrick W. Little J. Marshall	A. Mehrtens 2	A. Mehrtens		
306	14.6.1997	Fiji	North Harbour Stadium	Albany	71(45)	5(5)	J. Wilson 5 C. Cullen 2 M. Jones J. Marshall T. Umaga* C. Riechelmann*	A. Mehrtens 6 C. Cullen 2			

New Zealand's test record

Nº	Date	Opponent	Venue	City	NZ score	Opponent	Tries	Cons	Pens	DGs	GMs
307	21.6.1997	Argentina	Athletic Park	Wellington	93(46)	8(3)	T. Umaga 2 C. Cullen 2 C. Spencer 2* I. Jones J. Marshall J. Kronfeld O. Brown R. Brooke S. Fitzpatrick L. Stensness penalty try	C. Spencer 10	C. Spencer		
308	28.6.1997	Argentina	Rugby Park	Hamilton	62(29)	10(3)	T. Randell O. Brown L. Stensness C. Cullen J. Kronfeld R. Brooke M. Allen T. Umaga C. Spencer	C. Spencer 6 C. Cullen	C. Spencer		
309	5.7.1997	Australia	Lancaster Park	Christchurch	30(23)	13(3)	J. Kronfeld 2 Z. Brooke 2	C. Spencer 2	C. Spencer 2		
310	19.7.1997	South Africa	Ellis Park	Johannesburg	35(19)	32(23)	F. Bunce 2 J. Wilson C. Spencer	C. Spencer 3	C. Spencer 3		
311	26.7.1997	Australia	Melbourne Cricket Ground	Melbourne	33(23)	18(6)	F. Bunce J. Wilson C. Cullen	C. Spencer 3	C. Spencer 4		
312	9.8.1997	South Africa	Eden Park	Auckland	55(23)	35(21)	C. Cullen 2 A. Ieremia C. Spencer J. Marshall T. Randell T. Umaga	C. Spencer 4	C. Spencer 4		
313	16.8.1997	Australia	Carisbrook	Dunedin	36(36)	24(0)	T. Randell C. Cullen J. Marshall	C. Spencer 3	C. Spencer 5		
314	15.11.1997	Ireland	Lansdowne Road	Dublin	63(27)	15(15)	J. Wilson 2 G. Osborne 2 J. Marshall A. Mehrtens A. Ieremia	A. Mehrtens 5	A. Mehrtens 6		
315	22.11.1997	England	Old Trafford	Manchester	25(15)	8(3)	I. Jones J. Wilson T. Randell	A. Mehrtens 2	A. Mehrtens 2		
316	29.11.1997	Wales	Wembley Stadium	London	42(25)	7(0)	C. Cullen 3 T. Randell J. Marshall	A. Mehrtens 4	A. Mehrtens 2	Z. Brooke	
317	6.12.1997	England	Twickenham	London	26(9)	26(23)	A. Mehrtens W. Little	A. Mehrtens 2	A. Mehrtens 4		
318	20.6.1998	England	Carisbrook	Dunedin	64(26)	22(8)	C. Cullen 2 J. Wilson 2 J. Lomu T. Randell 2 M. Mayerhofler* J. Kronfeld	A. Mehrtens 5	A. Mehrtens 3		
319	27.6.1998	England	Eden Park	Auckland	40(14)	10(7)	J. Wilson 2 M. Mayerhofler J. Vidiri* I. Maka* T. Randell	C. Spencer 3 A. Mehrtens 2			

Test Statistics

New Zealand's test record

№	Date	Opponent	Venue	City	NZ score	Opponent	Tries	Cons	Pens	DGs	GMs
320	11.7.1998	Australia	Melbourne Cricket Ground	Melbourne	16(13)	24(15)	J. Kronfeld I. Jones		A. Mehrtens C. Spencer		
321	25.7.1998	South Africa	Athletic Park	Wellington	3(0)	13(3)			A. Mehrtens		
322	1.8.1998	Australia	Jade Stadium	Christchurch	23(3)	27(10)	C. Cullen J. Lomu	A. Mehrtens 2	A. Mehrtens 3		
323	15.8.1998	South Africa	Kings Park	Durban	23(17)	24(5)	J. Marshall T. Randell	A. Mehrtens 2	A. Mehrtens 3		
324	29.8.1998	Australia	Sydney Football Stadium	Sydney	14(11)	19(0)	C. Cullen		A. Mehrtens 2	A. Mehrtens	
325	18.6.1999	Samoa	North Harbour Stadium	Albany	71(31)	13(3)	J. Wilson 4 T. Umaga 2 T. Randell N. Maxwell* J. Lomu	T. Brown 7*	T. Brown 4		
326	26.6.1999	France	Athletic Park	Wellington	54(30)	7(0)	T. Umaga 3 C. Cullen 2 J. Marshall 2	A. Mehrtens 5	A. Mehrtens 3		
327	10.7.1999	South Africa	Carisbrook	Dunedin	28(6)	0	J. Wilson C. Cullen J. Marshall	A. Mehrtens T. Brown	A. Mehrtens 3		
328	24.7.1999	Australia	Eden Park	Auckland	34(22)	15(3)	J. Marshall	A. Mehrtens	A. Mehrtens 9		
329	7.8.1999	South Africa	Loftus Versfeld	Pretoria	34(20)	18(11)	C. Cullen 2		A. Mehrtens 7	J. Wilson	
330	28.8.1999	Australia	Stadium Australia	Sydney	7(7)	28(22)	A. Mehrtens	A. Mehrtens			
331	3.10.1999	Tonga	Ashton Gate	Bristol	45(16)	9(9)	J. Lomu 2 J. Kronfeld B. Kelleher N. Maxwell	A. Mehrtens 4	A. Mehrtens 4		
332	9.10.1999	England	Twickenham	London	30(13)	16(6)	J. Wilson J. Lomu B. Kelleher	A. Mehrtens 3	A. Mehrtens 3		
333	14.10.1999	Italy	Alfred McAlpine Stadium	Huddersfield	101(51)	3(3)	J. Wilson 3 G. Osborne 2 J. Lomu 2 T. Brown D. Mika T. Randell D. Gibson S. Robertson C. Cullen M. Hammett	T. Brown 11	T. Brown 3		
334	24.10.1999	Scotland	Murrayfield	Edinburgh	30(25)	18(3)	T. Umaga 2 J. Wilson J. Lomu	A. Mehrtens 2	A. Mehrtens 2		
335	31.10.1999	France	Twickenham	London	31(17)	43(10)	J. Lomu 2 J. Wilson	A. Mehrtens 2	A. Mehrtens 4		
336	4.11.1999	South Africa	Millennium Stadium	Cardiff	18(12)	22(16)			A. Mehrtens 6		
337	16.6.2000	Tonga	North Harbour Stadium	Albany	102(48)	0	T. Flavell 3* T. Umaga 2 D. Howlett 2* C. Cullen A. Ieremia T. Brown J. Marshall F. Tiatia* J. Kronfeld T. Blackadder M. Hammett	T. Brown 12	T. Brown		

New Zealand's test record

Nº	Date	Opponent	Venue	City	NZ score	Opponent	Tries	Cons	Pens	DGs	GMs
338	24.6.2000	Scotland	Carisbrook	Dunedin	69(26)	20(6)	J. Lomu 3 T. Umaga 2 A. Oliver 2 C. Cullen P. Alatini R. Cribb* T. Flavell	A. Mehrtens 7			
339	1.7.2000	Scotland	Eden Park	Auckland	48(24)	14(0)	T. Umaga 2 C. Cullen M. P. Robinson* A. Ieremia R. Cribb J. Marshall J. Kronfeld	A. Mehrtens 3 T. Brown			
340	15.7.2000	Australia	Stadium Australia	Sydney	39(24)	35(24)	T. Umaga C. Cullen P. Alatini J. Marshall J. Lomu	A. Mehrtens 4	A. Mehrtens 2		
341	22.7.2000	South Africa	Jade Stadium	Christchurch	25(19)	12(12)	C. Cullen 2		A. Mehrtens 3 T. Brown	A. Mehrtens	
342	5.8.2000	Australia	Westpac Trust Stadium	Wellington	23(20)	24(18)	C. Cullen 2	A. Mehrtens 2	A. Mehrtens 3		
343	19.8.2000	South Africa	Ellis Park	Johannesburg	40(27)	46(33)	C. Cullen 2 T. Umaga 2	A. Mehrtens 4	A. Mehrtens 3	A. Mehrtens	
344	11.11.2000	France	Stade de France	Paris	39(15)	26(12)	D. Howlett C. Cullen	A. Mehrtens	A. Mehrtens 9		
345	18.11.2000	France	Stade Velodrome	Marseilles	33(24)	42(26)	J. Marshall D. Howlett G. Slater	A. Mehrtens 3	A. Mehrtens 4		
346	25.11.2000	Italy	Stadio Luigi Ferraris	Genoa	56(27)	19(9)	B. Reihana 2 R. Cribb 2 D. Howlett C. Spencer J. Marshall F. Tiatia	C. Spencer 5	C. Spencer 2		
347	16.6.2001	Samoa	North Harbour Stadium	Albany	50(26)	6(6)	T. Brown 3 N. Maxwell D. Howlett T. Flavell J. Wilson	T. Brown 3	T. Brown 3		
348	23.6.2001	Argentina	Jade Stadium	Christchurch	67(31)	19(14)	L. MacDonald D. Howlett J. Wilson 2 T. Umaga P. Alatini 2 M. Holah T. Randell C. Jack*	A. Mehrtens 3 T. Brown 4	A. Mehrtens		
349	30.6.2001	France	Westpac Trust Stadium	Wellington	37(17)	12(6)	J. Wilson R. Thorne J. Lomu D. Howlett	T. Brown 4	T. Brown 3		
350	21.7.2001	South Africa	Fedsure Stadium	Cape Town	12(12)	3(3)			T. Brown 4		
351	11.8.2001	Australia	Carisbrook	Dunedin	15(5)	23(10)	J. Lomu J. Wilson	A. Mehrtens	T. Brown		
352	25.8.2001	South Africa	Eden Park	Auckland	26(13)	15(9)	P. Alatini penalty try	A. Mehrtens 2	A. Mehrtens 4		
353	1.9.2001	Australia	Stadium Australia	Sydney	26(6)	29(19)	P. Alatini D. Howlett	A. Mehrtens 2	A. Mehrtens 4		

Test Statistics

New Zealand's test record

Nº	Date	Opponent	Venue	City	NZ score	Opponent	Tries	Cons	Pens	DGs	GMs
354	17.11.2001	Ireland	Lansdowne Road	Dublin	40(7)	29(16)	D. Howlett J. Lomu A. Mauger* C. Jack R. Thorne D. Hewett*	A. Mehrtens 5			
355	24.11.2001	Scotland	Murrayfield	Edinburgh	37(9)	6(6)	T. Umaga M. Robinson J. Lomu	A. Mehrtens 2	A. Mehrtens 6		
356	1.12.2001	Argentina	Monumental Stadium	Buenos Aires	24(8)	20(10)	J. Lomu S. Robertson	A. Mehrtens	A. Mehrtens 4		
357	8.6.2002	Italy	Waikato Stadium	Hamilton	64(24)	10(3)	C. Cullen J. Lomu C. Ralph 3 B. Kelleher K. Meeuws D. Hewett J. McDonnell*	A. Mehrtens 8	A. Mehrtens		
358	15.6.2002	Ireland	Carisbrook	Dunedin	15(10)	6(3)	D. Howlett L. MacDonald	A. Mehrtens	A. Mehrtens		
359	22.6.2002	Ireland	Eden Park	Auckland	40(13)	8(3)	L. MacDonald 2 C. Ralph B. Kelleher M. Holah	A. Mehrtens 3	A. Mehrtens 3		
360	29.6.2002	Fiji	Westpac Trust Stadium	Wellington	68(32)	18(6)	C. Cullen 3 D. Howlett L. MacDonald A. Mauger S. Robertson N. Maxwell 2 K. Meeuws 2	A. Mauger 5	A. Mauger		
361	13.7.2002	Australia	Jade Stadium	Christchurch	12(6)	6(3)			A. Mehrtens 4		
362	20.7.2002	South Africa	Westpac Trust Stadium	Wellington	41(21)	20(13)	D. Howlett J. Marshall S. Robertson R. Thorne M Hammett	A. Mehrtens 2	A. Mehrtens 3	A. Mehrtens	
363	3.8.2002	Australia	Telstra Stadium	Sydney	14(3)	16(8)	R. McCaw		A. Mehrtens 3		
364	10.8.2002	South Africa	Absa Stadium	Durban	30(17)	23(17)	L. MacDonald D. Howlett A. Mauger penalty try	A. Mehrtens 2	A. Mehrtens 2		
365	9.11.2002	England	Twickenham	London	28(14)	31(17)	J. Lomu 2 D. Howlett D. Lee*	B. Blair 2 A. Mehrtens 2			
366	16.11.2002	France	Stade de France	Paris	20(10)	20(10)	K. Meeuws T. Umaga	A. Mehrtens 2	A. Mehrtens 2		
367	23.11.2002	Wales	Millennium Stadium	Cardiff	43(9)	17(10)	D. Howlett 2 K. Meeuws R. King	A. Mehrtens 4	A. Mehrtens 5		

All Black tests

	Played	Won	Drawn	Lost	For	Against	Percentage (of wins)
Argentina	11	10	1	–	519	154	91
Australia	116	76	5	35	2096	1449	66
Britain (Lions, Anglo-Welsh etc)	35	26	3	6	527	305	74
Canada	2	2	–	–	102	20	100
England	24	18	1	5	503	295	75
Fiji	3	3	–	–	213	36	100
France	38	27	1	10	815	502	71
Ireland	17	16	1	–	411	152	94
Italy	6	6	–	–	392	65	100
Japan	1	1	–	–	145	17	100
Romania	1	1	–	–	14	6	100
Scotland	24	22	2	–	675	275	91
South Africa	60	31	3	26	934	844	51
Tonga	2	2	–	–	147	9	100
United States	2	2	–	–	97	9	100
Wales	18	15	–	3	473	138	83
Samoa	4	4	–	–	207	42	100
World XV	3	2	–	1	94	69	66
TOTALS	**367**	**264**	**17**	**86**	**8364**	**4387**	**71.9** (average)

Tests year by year

Year	Tests	W	D	L
1903	1	1	0	0
1904	1	1	0	0
1905	5	4	0	1
1906	1	1	0	0
1907	3	2	1	0
1908	3	2	1	0
1910	3	2	0	1
1913	4	3	0	1
1914	3	3	0	0
1921	3	1	1	1
1924	3	3	0	0
1925	1	1	0	0
1928	4	2	0	2
1929	3	0	0	3
1930	4	3	0	1
1931	1	1	0	0
1932	3	2	0	1
1934	2	0	1	1
1935	3	2	0	1
1936	3	2	0	1
1937	3	1	0	2
1938	3	3	0	0
1946	2	2	0	0
1947	2	2	0	0
1949	6	0	0	6
1950	4	3	1	0

Year	Tests	W	D	L
1951	3	3	0	0
1952	2	1	0	1
1953	1	0	0	1
1954	4	3	0	1
1955	3	2	0	1
1956	4	3	0	1
1957	2	2	0	0
1958	3	2	0	1
1959	4	3	0	1
1960	4	1	1	2
1961	3	3	0	0
1962	5	4	1	0
1963	4	4	0	0
1964	6	4	1	1
1965	4	3	0	1
1966	4	4	0	0
1967	5	5	0	0
1968	5	5	0	0
1969	2	2	0	0
1970	4	1	0	3
1971	4	1	1	2
1972	5	5	0	0
1973	4	1	1	2
1974	4	3	1	0
1975	1	1	0	0
1976	5	2	0	3

Year	Tests	W	D	L
1977	6	4	0	2
1978	7	6	0	1
1979	5	3	0	2
1980	4	2	0	2
1981	8	7	0	1
1982	3	2	0	1
1983	7	5	1	1
1984	5	4	0	1
1985	5	4	1	0
1986	6	3	0	3
1987	7	7	0	0
1988	5	4	1	0
1989	7	7	0	0
1990	7	6	0	1
1991	10	8	0	2
1992	9	6	0	3
1993	7	5	0	2
1994	6	2	1	3
1995	12	10	0	2
1996	10	9	0	1
1997	12	11	1	0
1998	7	2	0	5
1999	12	9	0	3
2000	10	7	0	3
2001	7	5	0	2
2002	10	7	1	2

Biggest winning margins

Margin	Score	Against	Where	When
128	145–17	Japan	Bloemfontein	4.6.1995
102	102–0	Tonga	Albany	16.6.2000
98	101–3	Italy	Huddersfield	14.10.1999
85	93–8	Argentina	Wellington	21.6.1997
66	73–7	Canada	Auckland	22.4.1995
66	71–5	Fiji	Albany	14.6.1997
64	70–6	Italy	Auckland	22.5.1987
64	70–6	Italy	Bologna	28.10.1995
61	74–13	Fiji	Christchurch	27.5.1987
58	71–13	Samoa	Albany	18.6.1999
54	64–10	Italy	Hamilton	8.6.2002
53	59–6	Ireland	Wellington	6.6.1992
52	62–10	Argentina	Hamilton	28.6.1997
51	60–9	Argentina	Dunedin	15.7.1989
50	68–18	Fiji	Wellington	29.6.2002

Others

49	69–20	Scotland	Dunedin	24.6.2000
49	52–3	Wales	Christchurch	28.5.1988
48	63–15	Ireland	Dublin	15.11.1997
47	54–7	France	Wellington	26.6.1999
42	64–22	England	Dunedin	20.6.1998
37	43–6	Australia	Wellington	6.7.1996
32	38–6	British Isles	Auckland	16.7.1983
28	28–0	South Africa	Dunedin	10.7.1999

Biggest losing margins

Margin	Score	Against	Where	When
21	7–28	Australia	Sydney	28.8.1999
17	0–17	South Africa	Durban	30.6.1928
16	10–26	Australia	Sydney	12.7.1980
15	5–20	Australia	Wellington	29.8.1964
14	11–25	Australia	Sydney	11.8.1934
14	16–30	Australia	Auckland	9.9.1976
14	14–28	World XV	Christchurch	18.4.1992
14	8–22	France	Christchurch	26.6.1994
13	0–13	England	London	4.1.1936
13	0–13	South Africa	Johannesburg	25.6.1960
13	9–22	Australia	Auckland	6.9.1986
13	3–16	France	Nantes	15.11.1986
13	7–20	British Isles	Wellington	26.6.1993

Behind at halftime and won

1	Scotland	1905	Edinburgh		13	Australia	1968	Brisbane		25	England	1991	London
2	Australia	1907	Brisbane		14	France	1968	Wellington		26	World XV	1992	Auckland
3	South Africa	1921	Dunedin		15	Australia	1974	Sydney		27	Australia	1995	Auckland
4	Australia	1931	Auckland		16	Lions	1977	Auckland		28	Australia	1995	Sydney
5	Australia	1936	Wellington		17	Wales	1978	Cardiff		29	South Africa	1996	Christchurch
6	Australia	1936	Dunedin		18	Australia	1980	Brisbane		30	Australia	1996	Brisbane
7	Lions	1950	Wellington		19	Australia	1982	Auckland		31	South Africa	1996	Cape Town
8	Lions	1959	Dunedin		20	Lions	1983	Christchurch		32	South Africa	1997	Johannesburg
9	France	1961	Auckland		21	Australia	1984	Brisbane		33	Ireland	2001	Dublin
10	England	1963	Auckland		22	England	1985	Christchurch		34	Argentina	2001	Buenos Aires
11	Ireland	1963	Dublin		23	Australia	1987	Sydney		35	Wales	2002	Cardiff
12	Lions	1966	Wellington		24	Scotland	1990	Auckland					

Ahead at halftime and lost

1	Australia	1929	Sydney		12	South Africa	1965	Christchurch
2	Australia	1929	Brisbane		13	England	1973	Auckland
3	Australia	1932	Sydney		14	South Africa	1976	Cape Town
4	Australia	1934	Sydney		15	France	1977	Toulouse
5	Wales	1935	Cardiff		16	Australia	1990	Wellington
6	South Africa	1937	Christchurch		17	Australia	1992	Sydney
7	South Africa	1949	Cape Town		18	South Africa	1998	Durban
8	South Africa	1949	Port Elizabeth		19	Australia	1998	Sydney
9	Australia	1952	Christchurch		20	France	1999	London
10	Wales	1953	Cardiff		21	Australia	2000	Wellington
11	South Africa	1956	Wellington					

Most points in a half

Points	Opponent	Year	Half
84	Japan	1995	1st
61	Japan	1995	2nd
54	Tonga	2000	2nd
53	Italy	1987	2nd
51	Italy	1999	1st
50	Italy	1995	2nd
50	Italy	1999	2nd
48	Tonga	2000	1st
47	Argentina	1997	2nd
46	Argentina	1997	1st
45	Fiji	1997	1st
44	Ireland	1992	2nd
43	Canada	1995	2nd
43	Scotland	2000	2nd
40	Fiji	1987	1st
40	Samoa	1999	2nd
40	Italy	2002	2nd
38	Argentina	1989	2nd
38	England	1998	2nd
36	Australia	1997	1st
36	Ireland	1997	2nd
36	Argentina	2001	2nd
36	Fiji	2002	2nd
34	Fiji	1987	2nd
34	Argentina	1989	2nd
34	World XV	1992	1st
34	Wales	2002	2nd
33	Wales	1988	2nd
33	Argentina	1997	2nd
33	Ireland	2001	2nd
32	South Africa	1997	2nd
32	Fiji	2002	1st
31	Scotland	1995	2nd
31	Scotland	1996	1st, 2nd
31	Samoa	1999	1st
31	Argentina	2001	1st
30	Scotland	1981	2nd
30	Canada	1995	1st
30	France	1999	1st

Test Venues (in order of first use)

Ground	City	Played	Won	Drawn	Lost	All Black wins %
Sydney Cricket Ground	Sydney	28	17	2	9	60.7
Athletic Park	Wellington	42	29	3	10	69
Tahuna Park	Dunedin	1	1			100
Inverleith	Edinburgh	1	1			100
Lansdowne Road	Dublin	12	10	1	1	83.3
Crystal Palace	London	1	1			100
Arms Park	Cardiff	10	7		3	70
Parc des Princes	Paris	6	5		1	83.3
Cricket Ground	Brisbane	3	3			100
Carisbrook	Dunedin	31	27	1	3	86.6
Potter's Park	Auckland	1	1			100
Lancaster Park[1]	Christchurch	40	31		9	76.9
Berkeley Field	Berkeley	1	1			100
Sydney Sportsground	Sydney	2	2			100
Eden Park	Auckland	53	41	2	10	76.9
St Helen's	Swansea	1	1			100
Twickenham	London	15	9	1	5	60
Stade des Ponts-Jumeaux	Toulouse	1	1			100
Kingsmead	Durban	2			2	0
Ellis Park	Johannesburg	12	5		7	41.6
Crusaders Ground	Port Elizabeth	2			2	0
Newlands	Cape Town	8	6		2	75
Exhibition Ground	Brisbane	6	5		1	83.3
Murrayfield	Edinburgh	11	9	2		81.8
Colombes Stadium	Paris	3	2		1	66
Epsom Showgrounds	Auckland	1	1			100
Free State Stadium	Bloemfontein	3	2	1		66
Boet Erasmus	Port Elizabeth	2			2	0
Ballymore	Brisbane	7	4	2	1	57
Loftus Versfeld	Pretoria	4	3		1	75
Kings Park[2]	Durban	4	2		2	50
Municipal Stadium	Toulouse	4	2		2	50
August 23 Stadium	Bucharest	1	1			100
Ferrocarril Stadium	Buenos Aires	2	1	1		50
Stade de la Beaujoire	Nantes	2	1		1	50
Concord Oval	Sydney	3	3			100
Velez Sarsfield Stadium	Buenos Aires	2	2			100
Sydney Football Stadium	Sydney	6	2		4	33
Kingsholm	Gloucester	1	1			100
Welford Road	Leicester	1	1			100
Stade du Nord	Lille	1	1			100
Stadio Renato dall'Ara	Bologna	1	1			100
McLean Park	Napier	1	1			100
Suncorp Stadium	Brisbane	1	1			100
North Harbour Stadium	Albany	4	4			100
Rugby Park[3]	Hamilton	2	2			100
Melbourne Cricket Ground	Melbourne	2	1		1	50
Old Trafford	Manchester	1	1			100
Wembley	London	1	1			100
Stadium Australia[4]	Sydney	4	1		3	25
Ashton Gate	Bristol	1	1			100
McAlpine Stadium	Huddersfield	1	1			100
Millennium Stadium	Cardiff	2	1		1	50
Westpac Trust Stadium	Wellington	4	3		1	66
Stade de France	Paris	2	1	1		50
Stade Velodrome	Marseilles	1			1	0
Stadio Luigi Ferraris	Genoa	1	1			100
Monumental Stadium	Buenos Aires	1	1			100
TOTALS		**367**	**264**	**17**	**86**	**71.9**

[1] Also Jade Stadium [2] Also Absa Stadium [3] Redeveloped as Waikato Stadium [4] Also Telstra Stadium

Night tests

	When	Opponent	Where	Result
1	1994	Australia	Sydney	16–20
2	1995	Ireland	Johannesburg	43–19
3	1995	Wales	Johannesburg	34–9
4	1996	Samoa	Napier	51–10
5	1996	South Africa	Johannesburg	22–32
6	1997	Fiji	Albany	71–5
7	1997	Argentina	Hamilton	62–10
8	1997	South Africa	Johannesburg	35–32
9	1997	Australia	Melbourne	33–18
10	1998	Australia	Melbourne	16–24
11	1998	South Africa	Durban	23–24
12	1998	Australia	Sydney	14–19
13	1999	Samoa	Albany	71–13
14	1999	Australia	Auckland	34–15
15	1999	Australia	Sydney	7–28
16	1999	Scotland	Edinburgh	30–18
17	1999	South Africa	Cardiff	18–22
18	2000	Tonga	Albany	102–0
19	2000	Scotland	Auckland	48–14
20	2000	Australia	Sydney	39–35
21	2000	France	Paris	39–26
22	2000	France	Marseilles	33–42
23	2001	Samoa	Albany	50–6
24	2001	Argentina	Christchurch	67–19
25	2001	France	Wellington	37–12
26	2001	South Africa	Auckland	26–15
27	2001	Australia	Sydney	26–29
28	2001	Argentina	Buenos Aires	24–20
29	2002	Italy	Hamilton	64–10
30	2002	Ireland	Dunedin	15–6
31	2002	Ireland	Auckland	40–8
32	2002	Fiji	Wellington	68–18
33	2002	Australia	Christchurch	12–6
34	2002	South Africa	Wellington	41–20
35	2002	Australia	Sydney	14–16
36	2002	France	Paris	20–20

Winning streaks

17	1965–70
12	1988–90
11	1996–97
10	1987–88
10	1996

Losing streaks

6	1949
5	1998
4	1929–30

Opposition held scoreless

1	Ireland	1905
2	England	1905
3	Anglo-Welsh	1908
4	Australia	1910
5	Australia	1914
6	Australia	1914
7	South Africa	1921 (draw)
8	Ireland	1924
9	Wales	1924
10	Lions	1950
11	Australia	1951
12	England	1954
13	Scotland	1954
14	Australia	1955
15	Australia	1962
16	Wales	1963
17	England	1964
18	Scotland	1964 (draw)
19	South Africa	1965
20	Wales	1969
21	England	1973
22	Scotland	1975
23	Lions	1983
24	South Africa	1999
25	Tonga	2000

All Blacks held scoreless

1	Wales	1905
2	Australia	1910
3	South Africa	1921 (draw)
4	South Africa	1928
5	England	1936
6	France	1954
7	South Africa	1960
8	Scotland	1964 (draw)

Test days

Saturdays	334
Sundays	15
Mondays	4
Tuesdays	1
Wednesdays	6
Thursdays	2
Fridays	5
TOTAL	**367**

Red and yellow cards in tests

		Opponent	Date	Referee	From
Sent Off					
Brownlie	Cyril	England	3.1.1925	Albert Freethy	Wales
Meads	Colin	Scotland	2.12.1967	Kevin Kelleher	Ireland
Yellow cards (temporary suspension)*					
Oliver	Anton	Argentina	23.6.2001	Andrew Cole	Australia
Maxwell	Norm	France	30.6.2001	Allan Lewis	Ireland
Maxwell	Norm	Australia	1.9.2001	Tappe Henning	South Africa
Meeuws	Kees	France	16.11.2002	Scott Young	Australia
Robinson	Mark	France	16.11.2002	Scott Young	Australia
Cullen	Christian	France	16.11.2002	Scott Young	Australia

* the red and yellow card system was introduced Jan 29, 2000

Test All Blacks

Name	DoB	DoD	Province(s)	Position(s)	Years	Tests	Pts
ABBOTT, Harold Louis	17.6.1882	17.1.1972	Taranaki	Wing	1906	1	8
AITKEN, George Gothard	2.7.1898	8.7.1952	Wellington	Centre	1921	2	
ALATINI, Pita Paiva Fimoana	11.3.1976		Otago	Midfield	1999–2001	17	30
ALLEN, Frederick Richard	9.2.1920		Auckland	Five-eighth	1946–47, 49	6	
ALLEN, Mark Richard	27.7.1967		Taranaki, Central Vikings	Prop	1993, 96–97	8	5
ALLEN, Nicholas Houghton	30.8.1958	7.10.1984	Auckland, Counties	First five-eighth	1980	2	4
ALLEY, Geoffrey Thomas	4.2.1903	25.9.1986	Southland, Canterbury	Lock	1928	3	
ANDERSON, Albert	5.2.1961		Canterbury	Lock	1983–85, 87–88	6	
ANDERSON, Brent Leslie	10.3.1960		Wairarapa-Bush	Lock	1986	1	
ARCHER, William Roberts	19.9.1930		Otago, Southland	Five-eighth	1955–57	4	
ARGUS, Walter Garland	29.5.1921		Canterbury	Wing	1946–47	4	12
ARNOLD, Derek Austin	10.1.1951		Canterbury	Second five-eighth	1963–64	4	
ARNOLD, Keith Dawson	1.3.1920		Waikato	Flanker	1947	2	3
ASHBY, David Lloyd	15.2.1931		Southland	Fullback	1958	1	
ASHER, Albert Arapeha	3.12.1879	8.1.1965	Auckland	Wing	1903	1	3
ASHWORTH, Barry Graeme	23.9.1949		Auckland	Flanker	1978	2	
ASHWORTH, John Colin	15.9.1949		Canterbury, Hawke's Bay	Prop	1977–85	24	4
ATKINSON, Henry James	17.7.1888	21.7.1949	West Coast	Lock	1913	1	
AVERY, Henry Esau	3.10.1885	22.3.1961	Wellington	Wing forward	1910	3	
BACHOP, Graeme Thomas Miro	11.6.1967		Canterbury	Halfback	1989–92, 94–95	31	18
BACHOP, Stephen John	2.4.1966		Otago	First five-eighth	1994	5	
BADELEY, Cecil Edward Oliver	7.11.1896	10.11.1986	Auckland	Five-eighth	1920–21, 24	2	
BAIRD, James Alexander Steenson	17.12.1893	7.6.1917	Otago	Centre	1913	1	
BALL, Nelson	11.10.1908	9.5.1986	Wellington	Wing	1931–32, 35–36	5	12
BARRETT, James	8.10.1888	31.8.1971	Auckland	Loose forward	1913	2	
BARRY, Edward Fitzgerald	3.9.1905	12.12.1993	Wellington	Loose forward	1934	1	
BARRY, Liam John	15.3.1971		North Harbour	Flanker	1995	1	
BATTY, Grant Bernard	31.8.1951		Wellington	Wing	1972–77	15	16
BATTY, Walter	1.1.1905	10.5.1979	Auckland	Loose forward	1930–31	4	3
BEATTY, George Edward	29.3.1925		Taranaki	First five-eighth	1950	1	
BELL, Raymond Henry	31.12.1925		Otago	Wing, fullback	1951–52	3	6
BELLISS, Ernest Arthur	1.4.1894	22.4.1974	Wanganui	Wing forward	1921	3	3
BENNET, Robert	23.7.1879	9.4.1962	Otago	Centre	1905	1	
BERGHAN, Trevor	13.7.1914	23.9.1998	Otago	First five-eighth	1938	3	
BERRY, Martin Joseph	13.7.1966		Wairarapa-Bush	Utility back	1986	1	
BERRYMAN, Norman Rangi	15.4.1973		Northland	Centre	1998	1	
BEVAN, Vincent David	24.12.1921	26.5.1996	Wellington	Halfback	1949–50	6	
BIRTWISTLE, William Murray	4.7.1939		Canterbury, Waikato	Wing	1965, 67	7	12
BLACK, John Edwin	25.7.1951		Canterbury	Hooker	1977, 79–80	3	
BLACK, Neville Wyatt	25.4.1925		Auckland	Halfback	1949	1	
BLACK, Robert Stanley	23.8.1893	21.9.1916	Buller	First five-eighth	1914	1	
BLACKADDER, Todd Julian	20.9.1971		Canterbury	Loose forward, lock	1998, 2000	12	5
BLAIR, Ben Austin	26.3.1979		Canterbury	Fullback	2001–02	4	4
BLAKE, Alan Walter	3.11.1922		Wairarapa	Flanker	1949	1	
BLOWERS, Andrew Francis	23.3.1975		Auckland	Flanker	1996–97, 99	11	
BOGGS, Eric George	28.3.1922		Auckland	Wing	1946, 49	2	
BOND, Jack Garth Parker	24.5.1920	29.7.1999	Canterbury	Prop	1949	1	
BOOTH, Ernest Edward	24.2.1876	18.10.1935	Otago	Fullback, threequarter	1906–07	3	
BOROEVICH, Kevin Grant	4.10.1960		Wellington	Prop	1986	3	
BOTICA, Frano Michael	3.8.1963		North Harbour	First five-eighth	1986	7	6
BOWDEN, Noel James Gordon	19.3.1926		Taranaki	Fullback	1952	1	3
BOWERS, Richard Guy	5.11.1932	11.6.2000	Wellington	First five-eighth	1953–54	2	
BOWMAN, Albert William	5.5.1915	20.1.1992	Hawke's Bay	Flanker	1938	3	6
BRAID, Daniel John	13.2.1981		Auckland	Flanker	2002	1	
BRAID, Gary John	25.7.1960		Bay of Plenty	Lock	1983	2	
BREMNER, Selwyn George	2.8.1930		Auckland, Canterbury	Five-eighth	1952, 56	2	
BREWER, Michael Robert	6.11.1964		Otago, Canterbury	Loose forward	1986–95	32	4
BRISCOE, Kevin Charles	20.8.1936		Taranaki	Halfback	1959–60, 62–64	9	

Test Statistics

Test All Blacks

Name	DoB	DoD	Province(s)	Position(s)	Years	Tests	Pts
BROOKE, Robin Matthew	10.12.1966		Auckland	Lock	1992–99	62	20
BROOKE, Zinzan Valentine	14.2.1965		Auckland	Loose forward	1987–97	58	89
BROOKE-COWDEN, Mark	12.6.1963		Auckland	Flanker	1987	4	8
BROOMHALL, Sam Roger	29.7.1976		Canterbury	Loose forward	2002	4	
BROWN, Charles	19.12.1887	2.4.1966	Taranaki	Halfback	1913	2	3
BROWN, Olo Max	24.10.1967		Auckland	Prop	1992–98	56	20
BROWN, Ross Handley	8.9.1934		Taranaki	Five-eighth, centre	1955–59, 61–62	16	12
BROWN, Tony Eion	17.1.1975		Otago	First five-eighth	1999–2001	17	171
BROWNLIE, Cyril James	6.8.1895	7.5.1954	Hawke's Bay	Loose forward	1924–25	3	
BROWNLIE, Maurice John	10.8.1897	21.1.1957	Hawke's Bay	Loose forward	1924–25, 28	8	6
BRUCE, John Alexander	11.11.1887	20.10.1970	Auckland	Loose forward	1913–14	2	
BRUCE, Oliver Douglas	23.5.1947		Canterbury	First five-eighth	1976–78	15	15
BRYERS, Ronald Frederick	14.11.1919	20.8.1987	King Country	Lock	1949	1	
BUDD, Thomas Alfred	1.8.1922	8.3.1989	Southland	Lock	1946, 49	2	
BULLOCK-DOUGLAS, George Arthur Hardy	4.6.1911	24.8.1958	Wanganui	Wing	1932, 34	5	9
BUNCE, Frank Eneri	4.2.1962		North Harbour	Second five-eighth, centre	1992–97	55	96
BURGESS, George Francis	1.11.1876	2.7.1961	Southland	Halfback	1905	1	
BURGESS, Gregory Alexander John	6.7.1953		Auckland	Prop	1981	1	
BURGESS, Robert Edward	26.3.1949		Manawatu	First five-eighth	1971–73	7	6
BURKE, Peter Standish	22.9.1927		Taranaki	Lock	1955, 57	3	
BURNS, Patrick James	10.3.1881	24.2.1943	Canterbury	Halfback, threequarter	1908, 10, 13	5	6
BUSH, Ronald George	3.5.1909	10.5.1996	Otago	Fullback	1931	1	14
BUSH, William Kingita Te Pohe	24.1.1949		Canterbury	Prop	1974–79	11	
BUXTON, John Burns	31.10.1933		Canterbury	Flanker	1955–56	2	
CAIN, Michael Joseph	7.7.1885	27.8.1951	Taranaki	Hooker	1913–14	4	
CALLESEN, John Arthur	24.5.1950		Manawatu	Lock	1974–75	4	
CAMERON, Donald	15.7.1887	25.8.1947	Taranaki	Wing	1908	3	3
CAMERON, Lachlan Murray	12.4.1959		Waikato	Midfield	1979–81	5	
CARLETON, Sydney Russell	22.2.1904	23.10.1973	Canterbury	Utility back	1928	6	
CARRINGTON, Kenneth Roy	3.9.1950		Auckland	Wing	1971	3	
CARTER, Mark Peter	7.11.1968		Auckland	Flanker	1991, 97–98	7	
CASEY, Stephen Timothy	24.12.1882	10.8.1960	Otago	Hooker	1905–08	8	
CASHMORE, Adrian Richard	25.7.1973		Auckland	Fullback, wing	1996–97	2	
CATLEY, Evelyn Haswell	23.9.1915	23.3.1975	Waikato	Hooker	1946–47, 49	7	
CAUGHEY, Thomas Harcourt Clarke	4.7.1911	4.8.1993	Auckland	Wing, midfield	1932, 34–37	9	9
CAULTON, Ralph Walter	10.1.1937		Wellington	Wing	1959–61, 63–64	16	24
CHERRINGTON, Nau Paora	5.3.1924	26.6.1979	North Auckland	Wing	1950–51	1	
CHRISTIAN, Desmond Lawrence	9.9.1923	30.8.1977	Auckland	No 8	1949	1	
CLAMP, Michael	26.12.1961		Wellington	Wing	1984	2	4
CLARK, Donald William	22.2.1940		Otago	Flanker	1964	2	
CLARK, William Henry	16.11.1929		Wellington	Flanker	1953–56	9	9
CLARKE, Adrian Hipkins	23.2.1938		Auckland	Five-eighth	1958–60	3	
CLARKE, Donald Barry	10.11.1933	29.12.2002	Waikato	Fullback	1956–64	31	207
CLARKE, Eroni	31.7.1968		Auckland	Wing, midfield	1992–93, 98	10	25
CLARKE, Ian James	5.3.1931	29.6.1997	Waikato	Prop, No 8	1953–63	24	
CLARKE, Ray Lancelot	7.7.1908	3.6.1972	Taranaki	Lock	1932	2	
COBDEN, Donald Gordon	11.8.1914	11.8.1940	Canterbury	Wing	1937	1	
COCKERILL, Maurice Stanley	8.12.1928		Taranaki	Fullback	1951	3	11
COCKROFT, Eric Arthur Percy	10.9.1890	2.4.1973	South Canterbury	Wing, fullback	1913–14	3	
CODLIN, Brett William	29.11.1956		Counties	Fullback	1980	3	23
COLLINS, Arthur Harold	19.7.1906	11.1.1988	Taranaki	Fullback	1932, 34	3	9
COLLINS, Jerry	4.11.1980		Wellington	No 8	2001	1	
COLLINS, John Law	1.2.1939		Poverty Bay	Second five-eighth	1964–65	3	
COLMAN, John Thomas Henry	14.1.1887	28.9.1965	Taranaki	Utility, wing forward	1907–08	4	2
CONNOR, Desmond Michael	9.9.1935		Auckland	Halfback	1961–64	12	
CONWAY, Richard James	22.4.1935		Otago, Bay of Plenty	Flanker	1959–60, 65	10	3
COOKE, Albert Edward	5.10.1901	29.9.1977	Auckland, Hawke's Bay, Wairarapa, Wellington	Midfield	1924–25, 28, 30	8	12
COOKE, Reuben James	1880	10.5.1940	Canterbury	Loose forward	1903	1	
COOKSLEY, Mark Stephen Bill	11.4.1971		Counties, Waikato	Lock	1992–94, 01	11	

271

Test All Blacks

Name	DoB	DoD	Province(s)	Position(s)	Years	Tests	Pts
COOPER, Gregory John Luke	10.6.1965		Auckland, Otago	Fullback	1986, 92	7	63
COOPER, Matthew James Andrew	10.10.1966		Hawke's Bay, Waikato	Midfield, fullback	1992–94, 96	8	55
CORNER, Mervyn Miles Nelson	5.7.1908	2.2.1992	Auckland	Halfback	1930–31, 34–36	6	
COSSEY, Raymond Reginald	21.1.1935	24.5.1986	Counties	Wing	1958	1	
COTTRELL, Anthony Ian	10.2.1907	10.12.1988	Canterbury	Hooker, prop	1930–32	11	
COTTRELL, Wayne David	30.9.1943		Canterbury	Five-eighth	1968, 1970–71	7	6
COUCH, Manuera Ben Riwai	27.6.1925	3.6.1996	Wairarapa	First five-eighth	1947, 49	3	
COUGHLAN, Thomas Desmond	9.4.1934		South Canterbury	Flanker	1958	1	
CREIGHTON, John Neville	10.3.1937		Canterbury	Hooker	1962	1	
CRIBB, Ronald Te Huia	7.7.1976		North Harbour	No 8	2000–01	15	20
CRICHTON, Scott	18.2.1954		Wellington	Prop	1983	2	
CROSS, Thomas	21.1.1876	?	Canterbury, Wellington	Loose forward	1904–05	2	3
CROWLEY, Kieran James	21.8.1961		Taranaki	Fullback	1983–87, 90, 91	20	105
CROWLEY, Patrick Joseph Bourke	20.10.1923	9.6.1981	Auckland	Flanker	1949–50	6	3
CULHANE, Simon David	10.3.1968		Southland	First five-eighth	1995–96	6	114
CULLEN, Christian Mathias	12.2.1976		Manawatu, Central Vikings, Wellington	Fullback, wing	1996–2002	58	236
CUMMINGS, William	13.3.1889	28.5.1955	Canterbury	Loose forward	1913	2	3
CUNDY, Rawi Tama	15.8.1901	9.2.1955	Wairarapa	Utility back	1929	1	3
CUNNINGHAM, Gary Richard	12.5.1955		Auckland	Wing, midfield	1979–80	5	
CUNNINGHAM, William	8.7.1874	3.9.1927	Auckland	Lock	1905–08	9	3
CUPPLES, Leslie Frank	8.2.1898	10.8.1972	Bay of Plenty	Loose forward	1924–25	2	
CURRIE, Clive James	25.12.1955		Canterbury	Fullback	1978	2	
CUTHILL, John Elliot	24.8.1892	22.4.1970	Otago	Fullback, wing	1913	2	
DALLEY, William Charles	18.11.1901	9.2.1989	Canterbury	Halfback	1924–25, 28	5	
DALTON, Andrew Grant	16.11.1951		Counties	Hooker	1977–85	35	12
DALTON, Douglas	18.1.1913	28.7.1995	Hawke's Bay	Prop, hooker	1935–38	9	
DALTON, Raymond Alfred	14.7.1919	2.2.1997	Wellington, Otago	Prop	1947, 49	2	
DALZELL, George Nelson	26.4.1921	30.4.1989	Canterbury	Lock	1953–54	5	3
DAVIE, Murray Geoffrey	19.9.1955		Canterbury	Prop	1983	1	4
DAVIES, William Anthony	16.9.1939		Auckland, Otago	Fullback, five-eighth	1960, 62	3	
DAVIS, Keith	21.5.1930		Auckland	Halfback	1952–55, 58	10	
DAVIS, Lyndon John	22.12.1943		Canterbury	Halfback	1976–77	3	
DAVIS, William Leslie	15.12.1942		Hawke's Bay	Centre	1967–70	11	9
DEANS, Ian Bruce	25.11.1960		Canterbury	Halfback	1987–89	10	24
DEANS, Robert George	19.2.1884	30.9.1908	Canterbury	Centre	1905–06, 08	5	9
DEANS, Robert Maxwell	4.9.1959		Canterbury	Fullback	1983–84	5	50
DELAMORE, Graham Wallace	3.4.1920		Wellington	Five-eighth	1949	1	
DEVINE, Steven James	12.12.1976		Auckland	Halfback	2002	2	
DEWAR, Henry	13.10.1883	19.8.1915	Taranaki	Loose forward	1913	2	
DIACK, Ernest Sinclair	22.7.1930		Otago	Wing	1959	1	
DICK, John	3.10.1912	29.3.2002	Auckland	Wing	1937–38	3	3
DICK, Malcolm John	3.1.1941		Auckland	Wing	1963–67, 69–70	15	12
DIXON, Maurice James	6.2.1929		Canterbury	Wing	1953–54, 56–57	10	6
DOBSON, Ronald Leslie	26.3.1923	26.10.1994	Auckland	Second five-eighth	1949	1	
DODD, Ernest Henry	21.3.1880	11.9.1918	Wellington	Hooker	1905	1	
DONALD, Andrew John	11.5.1957		Wanganui	Halfback	1983–84	7	
DONALD, James George	4.6.1898	29.8.1981	Wairarapa	Wing forward	1921	2	
DONALD, Quentin	13.3.1900	27.12.1965	Wairarapa	Hooker	1924–25	4	
DONALDSON, Mark William	6.11.1955		Manawatu	Halfback	1977–81	13	4
DOUGAN, John Patrick	22.12.1946		Wellington	First five-eighth	1972–73	2	4
DOWD, Craig William	26.10.1969		Auckland	Prop	1993–2000	60	10
DOWD, Graham William	17.12.1963		North Harbour	Prop	1992	1	
DOWNING, Albert Joseph	12.7.1886	8.8.1915	Auckland	Flanker, lock	1913–14	5	
DRAKE, John Alan	22.1.1959		Auckland	Prop	1986–87	8	4
DUFF, Robert Hamilton	5.8.1925		Canterbury	Lock	1951–52, 55–56	11	
DUGGAN, Rhys John Llewellyn	31.7.1972		Waikato	Halfback	1999	1	
DUNCAN, James	12.11.1869	19.10.1953	Otago	Five-eighth	1903	1	
DUNCAN, Michael Gordon	8.8.1947		Hawke's Bay	Midfield	1971	2	
DUNCAN, William Dow	11.6.1892	14.12.1961	Otago	Hooker	1921	3	

Test Statistics

Test All Blacks

Name	DoB	DoD	Province(s)	Position(s)	Years	Tests	Pts
DUNN, Edward James	19.1.1955		North Auckland	First five-eighth	1979, 81	2	4
DUNN, Ian Thomas Wayne	11.6.1960		North Auckland	First five-eighth	1983	3	
DUNN, John Markham	17.11.1918		Auckland	Wing	1946	1	
EARL, Andrew Thomas	12.9.1961		Canterbury	Utility forward	1986–89, 91–92	13	12
EASTGATE, Barry Peter	10.7.1927		Canterbury	Prop	1952, 54	3	
ELLIOTT, Kenneth George	3.3.1922		Wellington	Lock, No 8	1946	2	3
ELLIS, Marc Christopher Gwynne	8.10.1971		Otago	Utility back	1993, 95	8	55
ELSOM, Allan Edwin George	18.7.1925		Canterbury	Centre	1952–55	6	3
ELVIDGE, Ronald Rutherford	2.3.1923		Otago	Midfield	1946, 49–50	9	12
ERCEG, Charles Percy	28.11.1928		Auckland	Wing	1951–52	4	
EVANS, David Alexander	4.10.1886	12.10.1940	Hawke's Bay	Lock	1910	1	
EVELEIGH, Kevin Alfred	8.11.1947		Manawatu	Flanker	1976–77	4	
FANNING, Alfred Henry Netherwood	31.3.1890	11.3.1963	Canterbury	Lock	1913	1	3
FANNING, Bernard John	11.11.1874	9.7.1946	Canterbury	Lock	1904	2	
FARRELL, Colin Paul	19.3.1956		Auckland	Fullback	1977	2	
FAWCETT, Christopher Louis	28.10.1954		Auckland	Fullback	1976	2	
FEA, William Rognvald	5.10.1898	22.12.1988	Otago	Five-eighth	1921	1	
FEEK, Gregory Edward	20.7.1975		Canterbury	Prop	1999, 2001	10	
FINLAY, Brian Edward Louis	7.11.1927	9.3.1982	Manawatu	Flanker	1959	1	
FINLAY, Jack	31.1.1916	30.6.2001	Manawatu	No 8	1946	1	3
FINLAYSON, Innes	4.7.1899	29.1.1980	North Auckland	Flanker	1928, 30	6	
FITZGERALD, James Train	6.8.1928	13.5.1993	Wellington	Midfield	1952	1	3
FITZPATRICK, Brian Bernard James	5.3.1931		Poverty Bay, Wellington	Second five-eighth	1953–54	3	
FITZPATRICK, Sean Brian Thomas	4.6.1963		Auckland	Hooker	1986–97	92	55
FLAVELL, Troy Vandem	4.11.1976		North Harbour	Lock, flanker	2000–01	15	25
FLEMING, John Kingsley	2.5.1953		Wellington, Waikato	Lock	1979–80	5	4
FLETCHER, Charles John Compton	9.5.1894	9.9.1973	North Auckland	Loose forward	1921	1	
FOGARTY, Richard	12.12.1891	9.9.1980	Taranaki	Flanker, hooker	1921	2	
FORD, Brian Robert	10.7.1951		Marlborough	Wing	1977–79	4	
FORSTER, Stuart Thomas	12.2.1969		Otago	Halfback	1993–95	6	
FOX, Grant James	16.6.1962		Auckland	First five-eighth	1985, 87–93	46	645
FRANCIS, Arthur Reginald Howe	8.6.1882	15.6.1957	Auckland	Loose forward	1905, 07, 08, 10	10	16
FRANCIS, William Charles	4.2.1894	28.11.1981	Wellington	Hooker	1913–14	5	6
FRASER, Bernard Gabriel	21.7.1953		Wellington	Wing	1979–84	23	24
FRAZER, Harry Frederick	21.4.1916		Hawke's Bay	Lock, prop	1946–47, 49	5	
FRYER, Frank Cunningham	2.11.1886	22.9.1958	Canterbury	Wing	1907–08	4	
FULLER, William Bennett	9.4.1883	25.7.1957	Canterbury	Wing, midfield	1910	2	3
FURLONG, Blair Donald Marie	10.3.1945		Hawke's Bay	First five-eighth	1970	1	
GALLAGHER, John Anthony	29.1.1964		Wellington	Fullback	1987–89	18	52
GALLAHER, David	30.10.1873	4.10.1917	Auckland	Wing forward	1903–06	6	
GARD, Philip Charles	20.11.1947	3.6.1990	North Otago	Midfield	1971	1	
GARDINER, Ashley John	10.12.1946		Taranaki	Prop	1974	1	
GEDDES, John Herbert	9.1.1907	16.8.1990	Southland	Wing	1929	1	
GEDDES, William McKail	13.5.1893	1.7.1950	Auckland	First five-eighth	1913	1	
GEMMELL, Bruce McLeod	12.5.1950		Auckland	Halfback	1974	2	
GEORGE, Victor Leslie	5.6.1908	10.8.1996	Southland	Prop	1938	3	
GIBSON, Daryl Peter Earl	2.3.1975		Canterbury	Midfield	1999–2000, 02	19	5
GILBERT, Graham Duncan McMillan	11.3.1911	13.2.2002	West Coast	Fullback	1935–36	4	20
GILLESPIE, Charles Theodore	24.6.1883	22.1.1964	Wellington	Lock	1913	1	
GILLESPIE, William David	6.8.1934		Otago	Flanker	1957	1	
GILLETT, George Arthur	23.4.1877	27.9.1956	Canterbury, Auckland	Wing forward, fullback	1905–08	8	7
GILLIES, Colin Cuthbert	8.10.1912	2.7.1996	Otago	First five-eighth	1936	1	
GILRAY, Colin MacDonald	17.3.1885	15.7.1994	Otago	Wing	1905	1	
GLASGOW, Francis Turnbull	17.8.1880	20.2.1939	Taranaki, Southland	Loose forward	1905–06, 08	6	9
GLENN, William Spiers	21.2.1887	5.10.1953	Taranaki	Loose forward	1904, 06	2	
GODDARD, Maurice Patrick	28.9.1921	19.6.1974	South Canterbury	Centre	1946–47, 49	5	3
GOING, Sidney Milton	19.8.1943		North Auckland	Halfback	1967–77	29	64
GORDON, Steven Bryan	16.5.1967		Waikato	Lock	1993	2	
GRAHAM, David John	1.1.1935		Canterbury	Loose forward	1958, 60–64	22	6
GRAHAM, James Buchan	23.4.1884	15.5.1941	Otago	Loose forward	1913–14	3	10

Test All Blacks

Name	DoB	DoD	Province(s)	Position(s)	Years	Tests	Pts
GRAHAM, Wayne Geoffrey	13.4.1957		Otago	Loose forward	1979	1	
GRANT, Lachlan Ashwell	4.10.1923	27.4.2002	South Canterbury	Flanker, lock	1947, 49, 51	4	
GRAY, George Donaldson	1880	16.4.1961	Canterbury	Five-eighth	1908, 13	3	9
GRAY, Kenneth Francis	24.6.1938	18.11.1992	Wellington	Prop	1963–69	24	12
GRAY, William Ngataiawhio	23.12.1932	10.1.1993	Bay of Plenty	Second five-eighth	1955–57	6	
GREEN, Craig Ivan	23.3.1961		Canterbury	Wing	1983–87	20	44
GRENSIDE, Bertram Arthur	9.4.1899	2.10.1989	Hawke's Bay	Wing	1928–29	6	9
GRIFFITHS, Jack Lester	9.9.1912	13.11.2001	Wellington	Midfield	1934–36, 38	7	
GUY, Richard Alan	6.4.1941		North Auckland	Prop	1971	4	
HADEN, Andrew Maxwell	26.9.1950		Auckland	Lock	1977–85	41	8
HADLEY, Swinbourne	19.9.1904	30.4.1970	Auckland	Hooker	1928	4	
HADLEY, William Edward	11.3.1910	30.9.1992	Auckland	Hooker	1934–36	8	6
HAIG, James Scott	7.12.1924	28.10.1996	Otago	Halfback	1946	2	3
HAIG, Laurence Stokes	18.10.1922	10.7.1992	Otago	First five-eighth	1950–51, 53–54	9	5
HALES, Duncan Alister	22.11.1947		Canterbury	Centre, wing	1972–73	4	
HAMILTON, Donald Cameron	19.1.1883	14.4.1925	Southland	Wing forward	1908	1	
HAMMETT, Mark Garry	13.7.1972		Canterbury	Hooker	1999–2002	20	15
HAMMOND, Ian Arthur	25.10.1925	20.5.1998	Marlborough	Hooker	1952	1	
HARDING, Samuel	1.12.1980		Otago	Flanker	2002	1	
HARPER, Eric Tristram	1.12.1877	30.4.1918	Canterbury	Threequarter	1904, 06	2	6
HARRIS, Perry Colin	11.1.1946		Manawatu	Prop	1976	1	
HART, Augustine Henry	28.3.1897	1.2.1965	Taranaki	Wing	1924	1	
HART, George Fletcher	10.2.1909	3.6.1944	Canterbury	Wing	1930–32, 34–36	11	21
HARVEY, Brett Andrew	6.10.1959		Wairarapa-Bush	Flanker	1986	1	
HARVEY, Ian Hamilton	1.1.1903	22.10.1966	Wairarapa	Lock	1928	1	
HARVEY, Lester Robert	14.4.1919	3.6.1993	Otago	Lock	1949–50	8	
HARVEY, Patrick	3.4.1880	29.10.1949	Canterbury	Halfback	1904	1	
HASELL, Edward William	26.4.1889	7.4.1966	Canterbury	Hooker	1913	2	3
HAYMAN, Carl Joseph	14.11.1979		Otago	Prop	2001, 2002	8	
HAYWARD, Harold Owen	23.5.1883	25.7.1970	Auckland	Loose forward	1908	1	3
HAZLETT, Edward John	21.7.1938		Southland	Prop	1966–67	6	
HAZLETT, William Edgar	8.11.1905	13.4.1978	Southland	Loose forward	1928, 30	8	
HEEPS, Thomas Roderick	7.3.1938	20.11.2002	Wellington	Wing	1962	5	3
HEKE, Wiremu Rika	3.9.1894	30.11.1989	North Auckland	Loose forward	1929	3	
HEMI, Ronald Courtney	15.5.1933	13.9.2000	Waikato	Hooker	1953–57, 59–60	16	3
HENDERSON, Paul William	21.9.1964		Otago, Southland	Flanker	1991–92, 95	7	9
HENDERSON, Peter	18.4.1926		Wanganui	Wing	1949–50	7	6
HEREWINI, MacFarlane Alexander	17.10.1940		Auckland	First five-eighth	1962–67	10	21
HEWETT, David Norman	14.7.1971		Canterbury	Prop	2001–02	10	10
HEWETT, Jason Alexander	17.10.1968		Auckland	Halfback	1991	1	4
HEWITT, Norman Jason	11.11.1968		Hawke's Bay, Southland	Hooker	1995–98	9	
HEWSON, Allan Roy	6.6.1954		Wellington	Fullback	1981–84	19	201
HIGGINSON, Graeme	14.12.1954		Canterbury, Hawke's Bay	Lock	1980–83	6	
HILL, Stanley Frank	9.4.1927		Canterbury	Lock, flanker	1955–59	11	
HINES, Geoffrey Robert	10.10.1960		Waikato	Flanker	1980	1	
HOBBS, Michael James Bowie	15.2.1960		Canterbury	Flanker	1983–86	21	16
HOEFT, Carl Henry	13.11.1974		Otago	Prop	1998–2001	27	
HOLAH, Martin Rowan	10.9.1976		Waikato	Flanker	2001–02	13	5
HOLDER, Edward Catchpole	26.7.1908	2.7.1974	Buller	Wing	1934	1	
HOOK, Llewellyn Simpkin	4.5.1905	4.8.1979	Auckland	Centre, wing, wing fwd	1929	3	
HOOPER, John Alan	10.9.1913	21.4.1976	Canterbury	Second five-eighth	1937–38	3	
HOPKINSON, Alister Ernest	30.5.1941	17.1.1999	Canterbury	Prop	1967–70	9	
HORE, Andrew Keith	13.9.1978		Taranaki	Hooker	2002	2	
HORE, John	9.8.1907	7.7.1979	Otago	Hooker, prop	1930, 32, 34–36	10	9
HORSLEY, Ronald Hugh	4.7.1932		Wellington	Lock	1960	3	
HOTOP, John	7.12.1929		Canterbury	First five-eighth	1952, 55	3	6
HOWARTH, Shane Paul	8.7.1968		Auckland	Fullback	1994	4	54
HOWLETT, Douglas Charles	21.9.1978		Auckland	Wing	2000–02	24	85
HUGHES, Arthur Maitland	11.10.1924		Auckland	Hooker	1949–50	6	
HUGHES, Edward	26.4.1881	1.5.1928	Southland	Hooker	1907–08, 21	6	3

Test Statistics

Test All Blacks

Name	DoB	DoD	Province(s)	Position(s)	Years	Tests	Pts
HUNTER, Bruce Anthony	16.9.1950		Otago	Wing	1971	3	
HUNTER, James	6.3.1879	14.12.1962	Taranaki	Second five-eighth	1905–08	11	12
HURST, Ian Archibald	27.8.1951		Canterbury	Midfield	1973–74	5	8
IEREMIA, Alama	27.10.1970		Wellington	Midfield	1994–97, 99–2000	30	25
IFWERSEN, Karl Donald	6.1.1893	19.5.1967	Auckland	Second five-eighth	1921	1	
INNES, Craig Ross	20.9.1969		Auckland	Centre, wing	1989–91	17	24
INNES, Gordon Donald	8.9.1910	6.11.1992	Canterbury	Second five-eighth	1932	1	
IRVINE, Ian Bruce	6.3.1929		North Auckland	Hooker	1952	1	
IRVINE, John Gilbert	1.7.1888	10.6.1939	Otago	Lock	1914	3	
IRVINE, William Richard	2.12.1898	26.4.1952	Hawke's Bay, Wairarapa	Hooker	1924–25, 30	5	9
IRWIN, Mark William	10.2.1935		Otago	Prop	1955–56, 58–60	7	
JACK, Christopher Raymond	5.9.1978		Canterbury	Lock	2001–02	13	10
JACKSON, Everard Stanley	12.1.1914	20.9.1975	Hawke's Bay	Prop	1936–38	6	
JAFFRAY, John Lyndon	17.4.1950		Otago, South Canterbury	Five-eighth	1972, 75–77, 79	7	4
JARDEN, Ronald Alexander	14.12.1929	18.2.1977	Wellington	Wing	1951–56	16	42
JEFFERD, Andrew Charles Reeves	13.6.1953		East Coast	Second five-eighth	1981	3	
JESSEP, Evan Morgan	11.10.1904	10.1.1983	Wellington	Hooker, prop	1931–32	2	
JOHNSON, Lancelot Matthew	9.8.1897	11.1.1983	Wellington	Five-eighth	1928	4	
JOHNSTON, William	13.9.1881	9.1.1951	Otago	Loose forward	1907	3	
JOHNSTONE, Bradley Ronald	30.7.1950		Auckland	Prop	1976–79	13	8
JOHNSTONE, Peter	9.8.1922	18.10.1997	Otago	Flanker, No 8	1949–51	9	3
JONES, Ian Donald	17.4.1969		North Auckland, North Harbour	Lock	1990–99	79	42
JONES, Michael Niko	8.4.1965		Auckland	Loose forward	1987–98	55	56
JONES, Murray Gordon	26.10.1942	12.2.1975	North Auckland	Prop	1973	1	
JONES, Peter Frederick	24.3.1932	7.6.1994	North Auckland	Loose forward	1954–56, 58–60	11	6
JOSEPH, Howard Thornton	25.8.1949		Canterbury	Centre	1971	2	
JOSEPH, James Whitinui	21.11.1969		Otago	Loose forward	1992–95	20	5
KARAM, Joseph Francis	21.11.1951		Wellington, Horowhenua	Fullback	1972–75	10	65
KATENE, Thomas	14.8.1929	6.6.1992	Wellington	Wing	1955	1	
KEARNEY, James Charles	4.4.1920	1.10.1998	Otago	First five-eighth	1947, 49	4	9
KELLEHER, Byron Terrance	3.12.1976		Otago	Halfback	1999–2002	23	20
KELLY, John Wallace	7.12.1926	29.4.2002	Auckland	Fullback, wing	1949	2	3
KEMBER, Gerald Francis	15.11.1945		Wellington	Fullback	1970	1	14
KETELS, Rodney Clive	11.11.1954		Counties	Prop	1980–81	5	
KIERNAN, Henry Arthur Douglas	24.7.1876	15.1.1947	Auckland	Halfback	1903	1	
KILBY, Francis David	24.4.1906	3.9.1985	Wellington	Halfback	1932, 34	4	3
KILLEEN, Brian Alexander	13.4.1911	9.3.1993	Auckland	Second five-eighth	1936	1	
KING, Regan Matthew	2.10.1980		Waikato	Centre	2002	1	5
KING, Ronald Russell	19.8.1909	10.1.1988	West Coast	Lock	1934–38	13	
KINGSTONE, Charles Napoleon	2.7.1895	6.5.1960	Taranaki	Fullback	1921	3	
KIRK, David Edward	5.10.1960		Otago, Auckland	Halfback	1983–87	17	24
KIRKPATRICK, Ian Andrew	24.5.1946		Canterbury, Poverty Bay	Loose forward	1967–77	39	57
KIRTON, Earle Weston	29.12.1940		Otago	First five-eighth	1967–70	13	12
KIRWAN, John James	16.12.1964		Auckland	Wing	1984–94	63	143
KIVELL, Alfred Louis	12.4.1897	13.2.1987	Taranaki	Loose forward	1929	2	
KNIGHT, Arthur	26.1.1906	26.4.1990	Auckland	Lock	1934	1	3
KNIGHT, Gary Albert	26.8.1951		Manawatu	Prop	1977–86	36	4
KNIGHT, Lawrence Gibb	24.9.1949		Poverty Bay	Loose forward	1977	6	4
KOTEKA, Tohoa Tauroa	30.9.1956		Waikato	Prop	1981–82	2	
KREFT, Anthony John	27.3.1945		Otago	Prop	1968	1	
KRONFELD, Joshua Adrian	20.6.1971		Otago	Flanker	1995–2000	54	70
LAIDLAW, Christopher Robert	16.11.1943		Otago, Canterbury	Halfback	1963–68, 70	20	12
LAIDLAW, Kevin Francis	9.8.1934		Southland	Centre	1960	3	
LAMBERT, Kent King	23.3.1952		Manawatu	Prop	1972–74, 76–77	11	
LAMBOURN, Arthur	11.1.1910	24.9.1999	Wellington	Hooker, prop	1934–38	10	
LARSEN, Blair Peter	20.1.1969		North Harbour	Lock, flanker	1992–96	17	4
LEE, Daniel David	1.2.1976		Otago	Halfback	2002	2	5
LE LIEVRE, Jules Mathew	17.8.1933		Canterbury	Prop	1962	1	
LENDRUM, Robert Noel	22.3.1948		Counties	Fullback	1973	1	2
LESLIE, Andrew Roy	10.11.1944		Wellington	No 8	1974–76	10	4

Test All Blacks

Name	DoB	DoD	Province(s)	Position(s)	Years	Tests	Pts
LEYS, Eric Tiki	25.5.1907	21.1.1989	Wellington	Halfback	1929	1	
LILBURNE, Herbert Theodore	16.3.1908	12.7.1976	Canterbury, Wellington	Five-eighth, fullback	1928–32, 34	10	4
LINDSAY, David Frederick	9.12.1906	7.3.1978	Otago	Fullback	1928	3	3
LINEEN, Terence Raymond	5.1.1936		Auckland	Midfield	1957–60	12	
LISTER, Thomas Norman	27.10.1943		South Canterbury	Flanker	1968–71	8	6
LITTLE, Paul Francis	14.9.1934	7.8.1993	Auckland	Centre	1961–64	10	3
LITTLE, Walter Kenneth	14.10.1969		North Harbour	Five-eighth	1990–96	50	44
LOADER, Colin James	10.3.1931		Wellington	Midfield	1953–54	4	
LOCHORE, Brian James	3.9.1940		Wairarapa, Wairarapa-Bush	Lock, No 8	1963–71	24	6
LOE, Richard Wyllie	6.4.1960		Waikato, Canterbury	Prop	1986–92, 94–95	49	25
LOMU, Jonah Tali	12.5.1975		Counties-Manukau, Wellington	Wing	1994–2002	63	185
LONG, A. J. (Paddy)	?	?	Auckland	Loose forward	1903	1	
LOVERIDGE, David Steven	1.5.1949		Taranaki	Halfback	1978–83, 85	24	12
LOWEN, Keith Ross	14.7.1974		Waikato	Second five-eighth	2002	1	
LUCAS, Frederick William	30.1.1902	17.9.1957	Auckland	Threequarter	1924–25, 28, 30	7	3
LUNN, William Albert	17.9.1926	22.12.1996	Otago	Flanker	1949	2	
LYNCH, Thomas William	20.7.1927		Canterbury	Second five-eighth	1951	3	9
LYNCH, Thomas William	6.3.1892	6.5.1950	South Canterbury	Wing	1913–14	4	12
MACDONALD, Hamish Hugh	11.1.1947		Canterbury, North Auckland	Lock	1972–76	12	4
MACDONALD, Leon Raymond	21.12.1977		Canterbury	Fullback	2000–02	18	30
MacEWAN, Ian Neven	1.5.1934		Wellington	Lock, No 8, Prop	1956–62	20	6
MACKRELL, William Henry Clifton	20.7.1881	15.7.1917	Auckland	Hooker	1906	1	
MACKY, John Victor	3.3.1887	15.9.1951	Auckland	Wing	1913	1	
MACPHERSON, Donald Gregory	23.7.1882	26.11.1956	Otago	Wing	1905	1	
MACPHERSON, Gordon	9.10.1962		Otago	Lock	1986	1	
MacRAE, Ian Robert	6.4.1943		Hawke's Bay	Midfield	1966–70	17	9
MAGUIRE, James Richard	6.2.1886	1.12.1966	Auckland	Hooker	1910	3	
MAHONEY, Atholstan	15.7.1908	13.7.1979	Bush	Loose forward	1935–36	4	
MAINS, Laurence William	16.2.1946		Otago	Fullback	1971, 76	4	21
MAJOR, John	8.8.1940		Taranaki	Hooker	1967	1	
MAKA, Isitolo	25.5.1975		Otago	Loose forward	1998	4	5
MALING, Thomas Simon	3.6.1975		Otago	Lock	2002	7	
MANCHESTER, John Eaton	29.1.1908	6.9.1983	Canterbury	Flanker	1932, 34–36	9	3
MANNIX, Simon James	10.8.1971		Wellington	First five-eighth	1994	1	
MARSHALL, Justin Warren	5.8.1973		Canterbury	Halfback	1995–2002	60	110
MASON, David Frank	21.11.1923	3.7.1981	Wellington	Wing	1947	1	3
MASTERS, Robin Read	19.10.1900	29.8.1967	Canterbury	Lock	1924–25	4	
MATAIRA, Hawea Karepa	3.12.1910	15.11.1979	Hawke's Bay	Loose forward	1934	1	
MATHESON, Jeffrey David	30.3.1948		Otago	Prop	1972	5	
MAUGER, Aaron Joseph Douglas	29.1.1980		Canterbury	Midfield	2001–02	11	28
MAX, Donald Stanfield	7.3.1906	4.3.1972	Nelson	Loose forward, lock	1931, 34	3	3
MAXWELL, Norman Maxwell	5.3.1976		Canterbury	Lock	1999–2002	34	25
MAYERHOFLER, Mark Andrew	8.10.1972		Canterbury	Midfield	1998	6	10
McATAMNEY, Francis Stevens	15.5.1934		Otago	Prop	1956	1	
McCAHILL, Bernard Joseph	28.6.1964		Auckland	Midfield	1987, 89, 91	10	4
McCAW, Richard Hugh	31.12.1980		Canterbury	Flanker	2001–02	9	5
McCAW, William Alexander	26.8.1927		Southland	Loose forward	1951, 53–54	5	
McCOOL, Michael John	15.9.1951		Wairarapa-Bush	Lock	1979	1	
McCORMICK, William Fergus	24.4.1939		Canterbury	Fullback	1965, 67–71	16	121
McCULLOUGH, John Francis	8.1.1936		Taranaki	First five-eighth	1959	3	
McDONALD, Alexander	23.4.1883	4.5.1967	Otago	Loose forward	1905, 08, 13	6	11
McDONNELL, Joseph Michael	1.3.1973		Otago	Prop	2002	8	5
McDOWELL, Steven Clark	27.8.1961		Auckland, Bay of Plenty	Prop	1985–92	46	12
McELDOWNEY, John Thompson	26.10.1947		Taranaki	Prop	1977	2	
McGRATTAN, Brian	31.12.1959		Wellington	Prop	1983, 85, 86	6	
McGREGOR, Alwin John	16.12.1889	15.4.1963	Auckland	Wing	1913	2	3
McGREGOR, Duncan	16.7.1881	11.3.1947	Canterbury, Wellington	Wing	1903–05	4	18
McGREGOR, Neil Perriam	29.12.1901	12.7.1973	Canterbury	Five-eighth	1924–25	2	
McGREGOR, Robert Wylie	31.12.1874	22.11.1925	Auckland	Centre, fullback	1903–04	2	3
McHUGH, Maurice James	19.2.1917		Auckland	Loose forward, lock	1946, 49	3	

Test All Blacks

Name	DoB	DoD	Province(s)	Position(s)	Years	Tests	Pts
McINTOSH, Donald Neil	1.4.1931		Wellington	Flanker	1956–57	4	
McKAY, Donald William	7.8.1937		Auckland	Wing	1961, 63	5	6
McKECHNIE, Brian John	6.11.1953		Southland	Fullback, first five-eighth	1977–79, 81	9	46
McKELLAR, Gerald Forbes	9.1.1884	16.1.1960	Wellington	Loose forward	1910	3	
McKENZIE, Richard John	15.3.1892	25.9.1968	Wellington, Auckland	Five-eighth	1913–14	4	15
McKENZIE, Roderick McCulloch	16.9.1909	24.3.2000	Manawatu	Flanker, lock	1934–38	9	
McLACHLAN, Jon Stanley	23.6.1949		Auckland	Wing	1974	1	
McLAREN, Hugh Campbell	8.6.1926	9.5.1992	Waikato	No 8	1952	1	
McLEAN, Andrew Leslie	31.10.1898	18.1.1964	Bay of Plenty	Flanker	1921	2	3
McLEAN, Hugh Foster	18.7.1907	24.4.1997	Wellington, Auckland	Loose forward	1930, 32, 34–36	9	9
McLEAN, John Kenneth	3.10.1923		King Country, Auckland	Wing	1947, 49	2	
McLEOD, Bruce Edward	30.1.1940	18.5.1996	Counties	Hooker	1964–70	24	12
McLEOD, Scott James	28.2.1973		Waikato	Midfield	1996–98	10	5
McMINN, Archibald Forbes	14.8.1880	23.4.1919	Wairarapa, Manawatu	Loose forward	1903, 05	2	6
McMINN, Francis Alexander	10.11.1874	8.8.1947	Manawatu	Hooker	1904	1	
McMULLEN, Raymond Frank	18.1.1933		Auckland	Wing	1957–60	11	12
McNAB, John Ronald	26.3.1924		Otago	Flanker	1949–50	6	
McNAUGHTON, Alan Murray	20.9.1947		Bay of Plenty	Flanker	1971	3	
McNEECE, James	24.12.1885	21.6.1917	Southland	Forward	1913–14	5	3
McPHAIL, Bruce Eric	26.1.1937		Canterbury	Wing	1959	2	
McRAE, John Alexander	29.4.1914	24.2.1977	Southland	Hooker, prop	1946	2	
McWILLIAMS, Ruben George	12.6.1901	27.1.1984	Auckland	Loose forward	1928–30	10	3
MEADS, Colin Earl	3.6.1936		King Country	Lock, loose forward	1957–71	55	21
MEADS, Stanley Thomas	12.7.1938		King Country	Lock, loose forward	1961–66	15	
MEALAMU, Keven Filipo	20.3.1979		Auckland	Hooker	2002	1	
MEATES, Kevin Francis	20.2.1930		Canterbury	Flanker	1952	2	
MEATES, William Anthony	26.5.1923	1.2.2003	Otago	Wing	1949–50	7	
MEEUWS, Kees Junior	26.7.1974		Otago, Auckland	Prop	1998–2002	24	25
MEHRTENS, Andrew Philip	28.4.1973		Canterbury	First five-eighth	1995–2002	66	932
METCALFE, Thomas Charles	13.5.1909	26.5.1969	Southland	Loose forward, lock	1931–32	2	
MEXTED, Graham George	3.2.1927		Wellington	No 8	1950	1	
MEXTED, Murray Graham	5.9.1953		Wellington	No 8	1979–85	34	16
MIKA, Bradley Moni	2.6.1981		Auckland	Lock	2002	3	
MIKA, Dylan Gabriel	17.4.1972		Auckland	Loose forward	1999	7	5
MILL, James Joseph	19.11.1899	29.3.1950	Hawke's Bay, Wairarapa	Halfback	1924–25, 30	4	
MILLIKEN, Harold Maurice	27.2.1914	10.1.1993	Canterbury	Lock	1938	3	3
MILNER, Henare Pawhara	12.2.1946	2.3.1996	Wanganui	Utility back	1970	1	
MITCHELL, Neville Alfred	22.11.1913	21.5.1981	Southland, Otago	Threequarter	1935–38	8	12
MITCHELL, Terry William	11.9.1950		Canterbury	Wing	1976	1	
MITCHELL, William James	28.11.1890	2.6.1959	Canterbury	Wing	1910	2	3
MITCHINSON, Frank Edwin	3.9.1884	27.3.1978	Wellington	Wing, midfield	1907–08, 10, 13	11	32
MOFFITT, James Edward	3.6.1889	16.3.1964	Wellington	Lock	1921	3	
MOORE, Graham John Tarr	18.3.1923	27.1.1991	Otago	Wing	1949	1	3
MORETON, Raymond Claude	30.1.1942		Canterbury	Midfield	1962, 64–65	7	9
MORGAN, Joseph Edward	7.8.1945	22.12.2002	North Auckland	Second five-eighth	1974, 76	5	4
MORRIS, Trevor James	3.1.1942		Nelson Bays	Fullback	1972	3	33
MORRISON, Terry Geoffrey	16.6.1951		Otago	Wing	1973	1	
MORRISON, Thomas Clarence	28.7.1913	31.8.1985	South Canterbury	Wing	1938	3	4
MORRISSEY, Peter John	18.7.1939		Canterbury	Wing	1962	3	6
MOURIE, Graham Neil Kenneth	8.9.1952		Taranaki	Flanker	1977–82	21	16
MULLER, Brian Leo	11.6.1942		Taranaki	Prop	1967–71	14	
MUMM, William John	26.3.1922	11.12.1993	Buller	Prop	1949	1	
MURDOCH, Keith	9.9.1943		Otago	Prop	1970, 72	3	4
MURDOCH, Peter Henry	17.6.1941	16.10.1995	Auckland	First five-eighth	1964–65	5	6
MURRAY, Harold Vivian	9.2.1888	4.7.1971	Canterbury	Wing forward	1913–14	4	9
MURRAY, Peter Chapman	23.1.1884	6.2.1968	Wanganui	Hooker	1908	1	
MYERS, Richard George	6.7.1950		Waikato	Loose forward	1978	1	
MYNOTT, Harry Jonas	4.6.1876	2.1.1924	Taranaki	First five-eighth	1905–07, 10	8	
NATHAN, Waka Joseph	8.7.1940		Auckland	Flanker	1962–64, 66–67	14	12
NELSON, Keith Alister	26.11.1938		Otago, Auckland	Loose forward	1962	2	

Test All Blacks

Name	DoB	DoD	Province(s)	Position(s)	Years	Tests	Pts
NEPIA, George	25.4.1905	27.8.1986	Hawke's Bay, East Coast	Fullback	1924–25, 29, 30	9	5
NESBIT, Steven Roberto	13.2.1936		Auckland	First five-eighth	1960	2	
NEWTON, Frederick	7.5.1881	10.12.1955	Canterbury	Lock, loose forward	1905–06	3	3
NICHOLLS, Harry Edgar	21.1.1900	1.4.1978	Wellington	Halfback	1921	1	
NICHOLLS, Marcus Frederick	13.7.1901	10.6.1972	Wellington	Five-eighth	1921, 24–25, 28, 30	10	48
NICHOLSON, George William	3.8.1878	13.9.1968	Auckland	Loose forward	1903–04, 07	4	
NORTON, Rangitane Will	30.3.1942		Canterbury	Hooker	1971–77	27	
O'BRIEN, John Gerald	9.12.1889	9.1.1958	Auckland	Fullback	1914	1	
O'CALLAGHAN, Michael William	27.4.1946		Manawatu	Wing	1968	3	
O'CALLAGHAN, Thomas Raymond	19.1.1925		Wellington	Second five-eighth	1949	1	3
O'DONNELL, Desmond Hillary	7.10.1921	18.1.1992	Wellington	Prop	1949	1	
O'HALLORAN, Jason David	28.2.1972		Wellington	Midfield	2000	1	
OLD, Geoffrey Haldane	22.1.1956		Manawatu	Loose forward	1981–82	3	
O'LEARY, Michael Joseph	29.9.1883	12.12.1963	Auckland	Fullback	1910, 13	4	16
OLIVER, Anton David	9.9.1975		Otago	Hooker	1997–2001	39	10
OLIVER, Charles Joshua	1.11.1905	25.9.1977	Canterbury	Midfield	1929, 34–36	7	6
OLIVER, Desmond Oswald	26.10.1930	25.10.1997	Otago	Flanker	1954	2	
OLIVER, Donald Joseph	29.4.1909	25.6.1990	Wellington	Wing	1930	2	3
OLIVER, Francis James	24.12.1948		Southland, Otago, Manawatu	Lock	1976–79, 81	17	4
ORR, Rex William	19.6.1924		Otago	Fullback	1949	1	
OSBORNE, Glen Matthew	27.8.1971		North Harbour	Fullback, wing	1995–97, 99	19	55
OSBORNE, William Michael	24.4.1955		Wanganui	Midfield	1975–78, 80, 82	16	
O'SULLIVAN, James Michael	5.2.1883	21.12.1960	Taranaki	Loose forward	1905, 07	5	
O'SULLIVAN, Terence Patrick Anthony	27.11.1936	25.4.1997	Taranaki	Midfield	1960–62	4	3
PAGE, James Russell	10.5.1908	22.5.1985	Wellington	First five-eighth, centre	1931–32, 34–35	6	3
PALMER, Bertram Pitt	14.11.1901	4.9.1932	Auckland	Hooker, prop	1929, 32	3	3
PARKER, James Hislop	1.2.1897	11.9.1980	Canterbury	Wing forward	1924–25	3	3
PARKHILL, Allan Archibald	22.4.1912	26.8.1986	Otago	No 8	1937–38	6	3
PARKINSON, Ross Michael	30.5.1948		Poverty Bay	Midfield	1972–73	7	
PATERSON, Alexander Marshall	31.10.1885	29.7.1933	Otago	Loose forward	1908, 10	5	3
PATON, Henry	12.2.1881	21.1.1964	Otago	Lock	1910	2	3
PENE, Arran Rewi Brett	26.10.1967		Otago	No 8	1992–94	15	16
PHILLIPS, William John	30.1.1914	10.11.1982	King Country	Wing	1937–38	3	3
PHILPOTT, Shayne	21.9.1965		Canterbury	Utility back	1991	2	
PICKERING, Ernest Arthur Rex	23.11.1936		Waikato	Flanker	1958–59	3	
PIERCE, Murray James	1.11.1957		Wellington	Lock	1985–89	26	
POKERE, Steven Tahurata	11.8.1958		Southland, Auckland	Centre	1981–85	18	8
POLLOCK, Harold Raymond	7.9.1909	10.1.1984	Wellington	Utility back	1932, 36	5	29
PORTER, Clifford Glen	5.5.1899	12.11.1976	Wellington	Wing forward	1925, 29–30	7	12
PRESTON, Jon Paul	15.11.1967		Canterbury, Wellington	Halfback, first five-eighth	1991–93, 96–97	10	34
PROCTER, Albert Charles	22.5.1906	11.10.1989	Otago	Wing	1932	1	
PURDUE, Charles Alfred	10.6.1874	10.10.1941	Southland	Loose forward	1905	1	
PURDUE, Edward	1878	16.7.1939	Southland	Lock	1905	1	
PURDUE, George Bambery	4.5.1909	1.1.1981	Southland	Lock, flanker	1931–32	4	3
PURVIS, Graham Herbert	14.10.1960		Waikato	Prop	1991, 93	2	4
PURVIS, Neil Alexander	31.1.1953		Otago	Wing	1976	1	
QUAID, Charles Edward	17.8.1908	18.2.1984	Otago	Hooker	1938	2	
RALPH, Caleb Stanley	10.9.1977		Auckland, Canterbury	Centre	1998, 2002	8	20
RANBY, Richard Mark	1.6.1977		Waikato	Centre	2001	1	
RANDELL, Taine Cheyenne	5.11.1974		Otago	Loose forward	1997–2002	51	60
RANGI, Ronald Edward	4.2.1941	13.9.1988	Auckland	Centre	1964–66	10	9
RANKIN, John George	14.2.1914	8.12.1989	Canterbury	Flanker	1936–37	3	6
REEDY, William Joseph	1880	1.4.1939	Wellington	Hooker	1908	2	
REID, Alan Robin	12.4.1929	16.11.1994	Waikato	Halfback	1952, 56–57	5	
REID, Hikatarewa Rockcliffe	8.4.1958		Bay of Plenty	Hooker	1980, 85–86	7	8
REID, Keith Howard	25.5.1904	24.5.1972	Wairarapa	Hooker	1929	2	
REID, Sana Torium	22.9.1912	19.3.2003	Hawke's Bay	Lock, flanker	1935–37	9	6
REIHANA, Bruce Trevor	6.4.1976		Waikato	Wing	2000	2	10
RESIDE, Walter Brown	6.10.1905	3.5.1985	Wairarapa	Loose forward	1929	1	
RHIND, Patrick Keith	20.6.1915	10.9.1996	Canterbury	Prop	1946	2	

Test Statistics

Test All Blacks

Name	DoB	DoD	Province(s)	Position(s)	Years	Tests	Pts
RICHARDSON, Johnstone	2.4.1899	28.10.1994	Otago, Southland	Loose forward	1921, 24–25	7	3
RICKIT, Haydn	19.2.1951		Waikato	Lock	1981	2	
RIDLAND, Alexander James	3.3.1882	5.11.1918	Southland	Forward	1910	3	
RIECHELMANN, Charles Calvin	26.4.1972		Auckland	Lock, flanker	1997	6	5
ROBERTS, Edward James	10.5.1891	27.2.1972	Wellington	Halfback	1914, 21	5	4
ROBERTS, Frederick	7.4.1881	21.7.1956	Wellington	Halfback	1905–08, 10	12	11
ROBERTS, Richard William	23.1.1889	8.3.1973	Taranaki	Centre	1913–14	5	29
ROBERTSON, Bruce John	9.4.1952		Counties	Centre	1972–74, 76–81	34	22
ROBERTSON, Duncan John	6.2.1947		Otago	First five-eighth, fullback	1974–77	10	8
ROBERTSON, Scott Maurice	21.8.1974		Canterbury	Flanker, No 8	1998–2002	23	20
ROBILLIARD, Alan Charles	20.12.1903	23.4.1990	Canterbury	Wing	1928	4	
ROBINSON, Charles Edward	5.4.1927	4.3.1983	Southland	Flanker	1951–52	5	3
ROBINSON, Keith John	14.12.1976		Waikato	Lock	2002	3	
ROBINSON, Mark Darren	21.8.1975		North Harbour	Halfback	1998, 2001	3	5
ROBINSON, Mark Powell	17.1.1974		Canterbury	Centre	2000, 2002	9	5
ROLLERSON, Douglas Leslie	14.5.1953		Manawatu	Five-eighth, fullback	1980–81	8	24
ROPER, Roy Alfred	11.8.1923		Taranaki	Threequarter	1949–50	5	9
ROWLEY, Harrison Cotton Banks	15.6.1924	16.12.1956	Wanganui	No 8	1949	1	
RUSH, Eric James	11.2.1965		North Harbour	Wing	1995–96	9	25
RUSH, Xavier Joseph	13.7.1977		Auckland	No 8	1998	1	
RUTLEDGE, Leicester Malcolm	12.4.1952		Southland	Flanker	1978–80	13	
RYAN, James	8.2.1887	17.7.1957	Wellington	Utility back	1910, 14	4	
SADLER, Bernard Sydney	28.7.1914		Wellington	Halfback	1935–36	5	
SALMON, James Lionel Broome	16.10.1959		Wellington	Centre	1981	3	4
SAVAGE, Laurence Theodore	17.2.1928		Canterbury	Halfback	1949	3	
SAXTON, Charles Kesteven	23.5.1913	4.7.2001	South Canterbury	Halfback	1938	3	9
SCHULER, Kevin James	11.3.1967		Manawatu, North Harbour	Loose forward	1990, 92, 95	4	
SCHUSTER, Nesetorio Johnny	17.1.1964		Wellington	Second five-eighth	1988–89	10	4
SCOTT, Robert William Henry	6.2.1921		Auckland	Fullback	1946–47, 49–50, 53–54	17	74
SCOWN, Alistair Ian	21.10.1948		Taranaki	Loose forward	1972	5	4
SCRIMSHAW, George	1.12.1902	13.7.1971	Canterbury	Wing forward	1928	1	
SEEAR, Gary Alan	19.2.1952		Otago	No 8	1977–79	12	11
SEELING, Charles Edward	14.5.1883	29.5.1956	Auckland	Loose forward	1904–08	11	6
SELLARS, George Maurice Victor	16.4.1886	7.6.1917	Auckland	Hooker	1913	2	
SHAW, Mark William	23.5.1956		Manawatu, Hawke's Bay	Flanker	1980–86	30	20
SHELFORD, Frank Nuki Ken	16.5.1955		Bay of Plenty	Flanker	1981, 84	4	
SHELFORD, Wayne Thomas	13.12.1957		North Harbour	No 8	1986–90	22	20
SIDDELLS, Stanley Keith	16.7.1897	3.3.1979	Wellington	Wing	1921	1	
SIMON, Harold James	7.3.1911	1.10.1979	Otago	Halfback	1937	3	
SIMPSON, John George	18.3.1922		Auckland	Prop	1947, 49–50	9	
SIMPSON, Victor Lenard James	26.2.1960		Canterbury	Centre	1985	2	
SIMS, Graham Scott	25.6.1951		Otago	Centre	1972	1	
SKEEN, Jack Robert	23.12.1928	28.9.2001	Auckland	Flanker	1952	1	
SKINNER, Kevin Lawrence	24.11.1927		Otago, Counties	Prop	1949–54, 56	20	3
SKUDDER, George Rupuha	10.2.1948		Waikato	Wing	1969	1	3
SLATER, Gordon Leonard	21.11.1971		Taranaki	Prop	2000	3	5
SLOANE, Peter Henry	10.9.1948		North Auckland	Hooker	1973	1	
SMITH, Alan Edward	10.12.1942		Taranaki	Lock	1969–70	3	
SMITH, Bruce Warwick	4.1.1959		Waikato	Wing	1984	3	4
SMITH, George William	20.9.1874	8.12.1954	Auckland	Threequarter	1905	2	6
SMITH, Ian Stanley Talbot	20.8.1941		Otago, North Otago	Wing	1964–66	9	6
SMITH, John Burns	25.9.1922	3.12.1974	North Auckland	Midfield	1946–47, 49	4	6
SMITH, Ross Mervyn	21.4.1929	2.5.2002	Canterbury	Wing	1955	1	
SMITH, Wayne Ross	19.4.1957		Canterbury	First five–eighth	1980, 82–85	17	6
SMITH, William Ernest	9.3.1881	25.5.1945	Nelson	First five-eighth	1905	1	
SNOW, Eric McDonald	19.4.1898	24.7.1974	Nelson	Loose forward	1929	3	
SOLOMON, Frank	30.5.1906	12.12.1991	Auckland	Wing forward, No 8	1931–32	3	3
SOMERVILLE, Greg Mardon	28.11.1977		Canterbury	Prop	2000–02	22	
SONNTAG, William Theodore Charles	3.6.1894	30.6.1988	Otago	Lock	1929	3	
SO'OIALO, Rodney	3.10.1979		Wellington	Loose forward	2002	1	

Test All Blacks

Name	DoB	DoD	Province(s)	Position(s)	Years	Tests	Pts
SPEIGHT, Michael Wayne	24.2.1962		North Auckland	Lock	1986	1	
SPENCER, Carlos James	14.10.1975		Auckland	First five-eighth	1997–98, 2000, 2002	15	177
SPENCER, John Clarence	27.11.1880	21.5.1936	Wellington	Loose forward	1905, 07	2	
SPIERS, John Edmunde	4.8.1947		Counties	Prop	1979, 81	5	
SPILLANE, Augustine Patrick	10.5.1888	16.9.1974	South Canterbury	Second five-eighth	1913	2	
STANLEY, Joseph Tito	13.4.1957		Auckland	Centre	1986–90	27	16
STEAD, John William	18.9.1877	21.7.1958	Southland	Five-eighth	1904–06, 08	7	
STEEL, Anthony Gordon	31.7.1941		Canterbury	Wing	1966–68	9	21
STEEL, John	10.11.1898	4.8.1941	West Coast	Wing	1921, 24–25	6	9
STEELE, Leo Brian	19.1.1929		Wellington	Halfback	1951	3	
STEERE, Edward Richard George	10.7.1908	1.6.1967	Hawke's Bay	Lock	1930–32	6	
STEINMETZ, Paul Christopher	26.1.1977		Wellington	Second five-eighth	2002	1	
STENSNESS, Lee	24.12.1970		Auckland	Five-eighth	1993, 97	8	15
STEPHENS, Owen George	9.1.1947		Wellington	Wing	1968	1	
STEVENS, Ian Neal	13.4.1948		Wellington	Halfback, first five-eighth	1972–74	3	4
STEWART, Allan James	11.10.1940		Canterbury, South Canterbury	Lock	1963–64	8	
STEWART, James Douglas	3.10.1890	5.5.1973	Auckland	Threequarter	1913	2	
STEWART, Kenneth William	3.1.1953		Southland	Flanker	1973–76, 79, 81	13	
STEWART, Ronald Terowie	12.1.1904	15.12.1982	South Canterbury, Canterbury	Loose forward	1928, 30	5	3
STOHR, Leonard	13.11.1889	25.7.1973	Taranaki	Threequarter	1910	3	6
STONE, Arthur Massey	19.12.1960		Waikato, Bay of Plenty	Midfield	1981, 83–84, 86	9	7
STOREY, Percival Wright	11.2.1897	4.10.1975	South Canterbury	Wing	1921	2	3
STRACHAN, Anthony Duncan	7.6.1966		Auckland, North Harbour	Halfback	1992–93, 95	11	8
STRAHAN, Samuel Cunningham	25.12.1944		Manawatu	Lock	1967–68, 70, 72–73	17	
STRANG, William Archibald	18.10.1906	11.2.1989	South Canterbury	Five-eighth, halfback	1928, 30–31	5	13
STRINGFELLOW, John Clinton	26.2.1905	3.1.1959	Wairarapa	Centre, fullback	1929	2	3
STUART, Kevin Charles	19.9.1928		Canterbury	Fullback	1955	1	
STUART, Robert Charles	28.10.1920		Canterbury	Loose forward	1949, 53–54	7	3
STUART, Robert Locksdale	9.1.1949		Hawke's Bay	Prop	1977	1	
SULLIVAN, John Lorraine	30.3.1915	9.7.1990	Taranaki	Midfield	1937–38	6	9
SUTHERLAND, Alan Richard	4.1.1944		Marlborough	Lock, No 8	1970–73	10	12
SVENSON, Kenneth Sydney	6.12.1898	7.12.1955	Buller, Wellington	Midfield	1924–25	4	12
SWAIN, John Patterson	1902	29.8.1960	Hawke's Bay	Hooker	1928	4	3
TANNER, John Maurice	11.1.1927		Auckland	Midfield	1950–51, 53	5	3
TANNER, Kerry John	25.4.1945		Canterbury	Prop	1974–76	7	
TAYLOR, Glenn Lyndon	23.9.1970		North Auckland	Lock	1996	1	
TAYLOR, Henry Morgan	5.2.1889	20.6.1955	Canterbury	Halfback, threequarter	1913–14	4	12
TAYLOR, John McLeod	12.1.1913	5.5.1979	Otago	Fullback	1937–38	6	24
TAYLOR, Murray Barton	25.8.1956		Waikato	Five-eighth	1979–80	7	3
TAYLOR, Norman Mark	11.1.1951		Bay of Plenty, Hawke's Bay	Midfield, wing	1977–78, 82	9	4
TAYLOR, Reginald	23.3.1889	20.6.1917	Taranaki	Wing forward	1913	2	3
TAYLOR, Warwick Thomas	11.3.1960		Canterbury	Second five-eighth	1983–88	24	20
TETZLAFF, Percy Laurence	14.7.1920		Auckland	Halfback	1947	2	
THIMBLEBY, Neil William	19.6.1939		Hawke's Bay	Prop	1970	1	
THOMAS, Barry Trevor	21.7.1937		Auckland, Wellington	Prop	1962, 64	4	
THOMSON, Hector Douglas	20.2.1881	9.8.1939	Wellington	Wing	1908	1	3
THORNE, Grahame Stuart	25.2.1946		Auckland	Threequarter, midfield	1968–70	10	3
THORNE, Reuben David	2.1.1975		Canterbury	Lock, flanker	1999–2002	27	15
THORNTON, Neville Henry	12.12.1918	12.9.1998	Auckland	No 8	1947, 49	3	3
TIATIA, Filogia Ian	4.6.1971		Wellington	No 8	2000	2	10
TILYARD, James Thomas	27.8.1889	1.11.1966	Wellington	Five-eighth	1913	1	
TIMU, John Kahukura Raymond	8.5.1969		Otago	Wing, fullback	1991–94	26	31
TINDILL, Eric William Thomas	18.12.1910		Wellington	First five-eighth	1936	1	
TONU'U, Ofisa Francis Junior	3.2.1970		Auckland	Halfback	1997–98	5	
TOWNSEND, Lindsay James	3.3.1934		Otago	Halfback	1955	2	
TREMAIN, Kelvin Robin	21.2.1938	2.5.1992	Canterbury, Auckland, Hawke's Bay	Flanker	1959–68	38	27
TREVATHAN, David	6.5.1912	11.4.1986	Otago	First five-eighth	1937	3	16
TUCK, Jack Manson	13.5.1907	23.3.1967	Waikato	Utility back	1929	3	
TUIGAMALA, Va'aiga Lealuga	4.9.1969		Auckland	Wing	1991–93	19	21

Test Statistics

Test All Blacks

Name	DoB	DoD	Province(s)	Position(s)	Years	Tests	Pts
TURNER, Richard Steven	15.3.1968		North Harbour	No 8	1992	2	4
TURTILL, Hubert Sydney	1.2.1880	9.4.1918	Canterbury	Fullback	1905	1	
TWIGDEN, Timothy Moore	14.5.1952		Auckland	Threequarter	1980	2	
TYLER, George Alfred	10.2.1879	15.4.1942	Auckland	Hooker	1903–06	7	5
UDY, Daniel Knight	21.5.1874	29.7.1935	Wairarapa	Hooker	1903	1	
UMAGA, Tana Jonathan Falefasa	27.5.1973		Wellington	Wing, centre	1997, 99–2002	45	120
URBAHN, Roger James	31.7.1934	27.11.1984	Taranaki	Halfback	1959–60	3	3
URLICH, Ronald Anthony	8.2.1944		Auckland	Hooker	1970	2	
UTTLEY, Ian Neil	3.12.1941		Wellington	Centre	1963	2	
VIDIRI, Joeli	23.1.1973		Counties-Manukau	Wing	1998	2	5
VINCENT, Patrick Bernard	6.1.1926	10.4.1983	Canterbury	Halfback	1956	2	
VODANOVICH, Ivan Matthew Henry	8.4.1930	2.9.1995	Wellington	Prop	1955	3	3
WALLACE, William Joseph	2.8.1878	2.3.1972	Wellington	Utility back	1903–08	11	53
WALLER, Dion Alan George	6.1.1974		Wellington	Lock	2001	1	
WALSH, Patrick Timothy	6.5.1936		Counties	Utility back	1955–59, 63	13	12
WARD, Ronald Henry	1.12.1915	1.8.2000	Southland	Flanker	1936–37	3	
WATERMAN, Alfred Clarence	31.12.1903	22.10.1997	North Auckland	Wing	1929	2	
WATKINS, Eric Leslie	18.3.1880	14.8.1949	Wellington	Hooker	1905	1	
WATT, Bruce Alexander	12.3.1939		Canterbury	First five-eighth	1962–64	8	9
WATT, James Michael	5.7.1914	17.9.1988	Otago	Wing	1936	2	6
WATT, James Russell	29.12.1935		Southland, Wellington	Wing	1958, 60–62	9	3
WATTS, Murray Gordon	31.3.1955		Taranaki	Wing	1979–80	5	4
WEBB, Desmond Stanley	10.9.1934		North Auckland	Hooker	1959	1	
WELLS, John	4.1.1908	7.1.1994	Wellington	Flanker	1936	2	
WEST, Alfred Hubert	6.5.1893	7.1.1934	Taranaki	Loose forward	1921	2	
WHETTON, Alan James	15.12.1959		Auckland	Flanker	1984–91	35	40
WHETTON, Gary William	15.12.1959		Auckland	Lock	1981–91	58	4
WHINERAY, Wilson James	10.7.1935		Canterbury, Waikato, Auckland	Prop	1957–65	32	6
WHITE, Andrew	21.3.1894	3.8.1968	Southland	Flanker	1921, 24–25	4	3
WHITE, Hallard Leo	27.3.1929		Auckland	Prop	1953–55	4	
WHITE, Richard Alexander	11.6.1925		Poverty Bay	Lock	1949–56	23	9
WHITE, Roy Maxwell	18.10.1917	19.1.1980	Wellington	Flanker	1946–47	4	3
WHITING, Graham John	4.9.1946		King Country	Prop	1972–73	6	
WHITING, Peter John	6.8.1946		Auckland	Lock	1971–74, 76	20	12
WILLIAMS, Alexander James	30.4.1981		Auckland	Lock	2002	3	
WILLIAMS, Bryan George	3.10.1950		Auckland	Wing, centre	1970–78	38	68
WILLIAMS, Graham Charles	26.1.1945		Wellington	Flanker	1967–68	5	
WILLIAMS, Peter	22.4.1884	30.8.1976	Otago	Hooker	1913	1	
WILLIMENT, Michael	25.2.1940	5.9.1994	Wellington	Fullback	1964–67	9	70
WILLIS, Royce Kevin	28.8.1975		Waikato	Lock	1998–99, 2002	12	
WILLIS, Thomas Eion	20.1.1979		Otago	Hooker	2002	5	
WILLOCKS, Charles	28.6.1919	25.8.1991	Otago	Lock	1946, 49	5	
WILSON, Bevan William	22.3.1956		Otago	Fullback	1977–79	8	55
WILSON, Douglas Dawson	30.1.1931		Canterbury	Five-eighth	1954	2	
WILSON, Hector William	27.1.1924		Otago	Prop	1949–51	5	3
WILSON, Jeffrey William	24.10.1973		Otago	Wing, fullback	1993–99, 2001	60	234
WILSON, Nathaniel Arthur	18.5.1886	11.8.1953	Wellington	Loose forward	1908, 10, 13–14	10	6
WILSON, Norman Leslie	13.12.1922	10.10.2001	Otago	Hooker	1951	3	3
WILSON, Richard George	19.5.1953		Canterbury	Fullback	1979	2	10
WILSON, Stuart Sinclair	22.7.1954		Wellington	Threequarter	1977–83	34	76
WOLFE, Thomas Neil	20.10.1941		Wellington, Taranaki	Five-eighth, centre	1961–63	6	
WOOD, Morris Edwin	9.10.1876	9.8.1956	Wellington, Auckland	Five-eighth	1903–04	2	
WOODCOCK, Tony Dale	27.1.1981		North Harbour	Prop	2002	1	
WOODMAN, Freddy Akehurst	10.2.1958		North Auckland	Wing	1980–81	3	
WRIGHT, Terence John	21.1.1963		Auckland	Wing, fullback	1986–91	30	72
WRIGLEY, Edward	15.6.1886	2.6.1958	Wairarapa	Second five-eighth	1905	1	3
WYLIE, James Thomas	26.10.1887	19.12.1956	Auckland	Loose forward	1913	2	3
WYLLIE, Alexander John	31.8.1944		Canterbury	Loose forward	1970–73	11	8
YATES, Victor Moses	15.6.1939		North Auckland	No 8	1961	3	3
YOUNG, Dennis	1.4.1930		Canterbury	Hooker	1956, 58, 60–64	22	

Points scorers in tests

First name	Surname	Tests	Tries	Cons	Pens	DGs	GMs	Totals
Andrew	Mehrtens	66	7	162	181	10	0	932
Grant	Fox	46	1	118	128	7	0	645
Christian	Cullen	58	46	3	0	0	0	236
Jeff	Wilson	60	44	1	3	1	0	234
Don	Clarke	31	2	33	38	5	2	207
Allan	Hewson	19	4	22	43	4	0	201
Jonah	Lomu	63	37	0	0	0	0	185
Carlos	Spencer	15	6	39	23	0	0	177
Tony	Brown	17	5	43	20	0	0	171
John	Kirwan	63	35	0	0	0	0	143
Fergie	McCormick	16	0	23	24	1	0	121
Tana	Umaga	45	24	0	0	0	0	120
Simon	Culhane	6	1	32	15	0	0	114
Justin	Marshall	60	22	0	0	0	0	110
Kieran	Crowley	19	5	5	23	2	0	105
Frank	Bunce	55	20	0	0	0	0	96
Zinzan	Brooke	58	17	0	0	3	0	89
Doug	Howlett	24	17	0	0	0	0	85
Stu	Wilson	34	19	0	0	0	0	76
Bob	Scott	17	0	16	12	2	0	74
Terry	Wright*	30	18	0	0	0	0	72
Josh	Kronfeld	54	14	0	0	0	0	70
Mick	Williment	9	1	17	11	0	0	70
Bryan	Williams*	38	9	2	9	1	0	68
Joe	Karam	10	1	11	13	0	0	65
Greg	Cooper	7	2	14	7	2	0	63
Taine	Randell	51	12	0	0	0	0	60
Ian	Kirkpatrick	39	16	0	0	0	0	57
Michael	Jones	51	13	0	0	0	0	56
Matthew	Cooper	8	2	10	9	0	0	55
Marc	Ellis	8	11	0	0	0	0	55
Sean	Fitzpatrick	92	12	0	0	0	0	55
Glen	Osborne	19	11	0	0	0	0	55
Bevan	Wilson	8	0	5	15	0	0	55
Shane	Howarth	4	1	2	15	0	0	54
Billy	Wallace	11	5	12	2	0	2	53
John	Gallagher	18	13	0	0	0	0	52
Robbie	Deans	5	0	4	14	0	0	50
Mark	Nicholls	10	0	11	5	2	1	48
Brian	McKechnie	10	0	5	11	1	0	46
Sid	Going	29	10	1	2	0	0	44
Craig	Green	20	11	0	0	0	0	44
Walter	Little	50	9	0	0	0	0	44
Ron	Jarden	16	7	6	3	0	0	42
Ian	Jones	79	9	0	0	0	0	42
Alan	Whetton	35	10	0	0	0	0	40
Jon	Preston	10	1	4	7	0	0	34
Trevor	Morris	3	0	9	4	1	0	33
Frank	Mitchinson	11	10	1	0	0	0	32
John	Timu	26	7	0	0	0	0	31
Pita	Alatini	17	6	0	0	0	0	30
Leon	MacDonald	18	6	0	0	0	0	30
Harold	Pollock	5	0	9	1	2	0	29
Dick	Roberts	5	7	4	0	0	0	29
Aaron	Mauger	10	2	5	1	0	0	28
Kel	Tremain	38	9	0	0	0	0	27
Eroni	Clarke	10	6	0	0	0	0	25
Troy	Flavell	15	5	0	0	0	0	25
Alama	Ieremia	30	5	0	0	0	0	25
Richard	Loe	49	6	0	0	0	0	25
Norm	Maxwell	33	5	0	0	0	0	25

First name	Surname	Tests	Tries	Cons	Pens	DGs	GMs	Totals
Kees	Meeuws	24	5	0	0	0	0	25
Eric	Rush	9	5	0	0	0	0	25
Ralph	Caulton	16	8	0	0	0	0	24
Bruce	Deans	10	6	0	0	0	0	24
Bernie	Fraser	23	6	0	0	0	0	24
Craig	Innes	17	6	0	0	0	0	24
David	Kirk	17	6	0	0	0	0	24
Doug	Rollerson	8	1	4	2	2	0	24
Jack	Taylor	6	0	6	4	0	0	24
Brett	Codlin	3	0	1	7	0	0	23
Bruce	Robertson	34	4	0	0	2	0	22
George	Hart	11	7	0	0	0	0	21
Mac	Herewini	10	1	0	1	5	0	21
Laurie	Mains	4	1	3	4	0	0	21
Colin	Meads	55	7	0	0	0	0	21
Tony	Steel	9	7	0	0	0	0	21
Va'aiga	Tuigamala	19	5	0	0	0	0	21
Robin	Brooke	62	4	0	0	0	0	20
Olo	Brown	56	4	0	0	0	0	20
Ron	Cribb	15	4	0	0	0	0	20
Mike	Gilbert	4	0	5	2	1	0	20
Byron	Kelleher	23	3	0	0	0	0	20
Caleb	Ralph	8	3	0	0	0	0	20
Scott	Robertson	23	4	0	0	0	0	20
Mark	Shaw*	30	5	0	0	0	0	20
Wayne	Shelford	22	5	0	0	0	0	20
Warwick	Taylor	24	5	0	0	0	0	20
Graeme	Bachop	31	4	0	0	0	0	18
Duncan	McGregor	4	6	0	0	0	0	18
Grant	Batty	15	4	0	0	0	0	16
Arthur (Bolla)	Francis	10	3	2	1	0	0	16
Jock	Hobbs	21	4	0	0	0	0	16
Murray	Mexted	34	4	0	0	0	0	16
Graham	Mourie	21	4	0	0	0	0	16
Joe	O'Leary	4	0	6	0	1	0	16
Arran	Pene	15	4	0	0	0	0	16
Joe	Stanley	27	4	0	0	0	0	16
Dave	Trevathan	3	0	0	4	1	0	16
Doug	Bruce	15	0	0	0	5	0	15
Mark	Hammett	20	3	0	0	0	0	15
Jock	McKenzie	4	5	0	0	0	0	15
Lee	Stensness	8	3	0	0	0	0	15
Reuben	Thorne	26	3	0	0	0	0	15
Ron	Bush	1	0	1	4	0	0	14
Gerald	Kember	1	0	1	4	0	0	14
Archie	Strang	5	1	3	0	1	0	13
Wally	Argus	4	4	0	0	0	0	12
Nelson	Ball	5	4	0	0	0	0	12
Bill	Birtwistle	7	4	0	0	0	0	12
Ross	Brown	16	3	0	0	1	0	12
Bert	Cooke	8	4	0	0	0	0	12
Andy	Dalton	35	3	0	0	0	0	12
Malcolm	Dick	15	4	0	0	0	0	12
Andy	Earl	13	3	0	0	0	0	12
Ron	Elvidge	9	4	0	0	0	0	12
Ken	Gray	24	4	0	0	0	0	12
Jimmy	Hunter	11	4	0	0	0	0	12
Earle	Kirton	13	4	0	0	0	0	12
Chris	Laidlaw	20	3	0	0	1	0	12
Dave	Loveridge	24	3	0	0	0	0	12
Tom	Lynch snr	4	4	0	0	0	0	12

Test Statistics

Points scorers in tests

First name	Surname	Tests	Tries	Cons	Pens	DGs	GMs	Totals
Steve	McDowell	46	3	0	0	0	0	12
Bruce	McLeod	24	4	0	0	0	0	12
Frank	McMullen	11	4	0	0	0	0	12
Neville (Brushy)	Mitchell	8	4	0	0	0	0	12
Waka	Nathan	14	4	0	0	0	0	12
Cliff	Porter	7	4	0	0	0	0	12
Alan	Sutherland	10	3	0	0	0	0	12
Kenneth (Snowy)	Svenson	4	4	0	0	0	0	12
Henry	Taylor	4	4	0	0	0	0	12
Pat	Walsh	13	4	0	0	0	0	12
Peter	Whiting	20	3	0	0	0	0	12
Maurice (Snow)	Cockerill	3	0	4	1	0	0	11
Alex	McDonald	6	3	1	0	0	0	11
Fred	Roberts	12	2	1	1	0	0	11
Gary	Seear	12	2	0	1	0	0	11
Craig	Dowd	60	2	0	0	0	0	10
James	Graham	3	0	5	0	0	0	10
Dave	Hewett	10	2	0	0	0	0	10
Marty	Holah	11	1	0	0	0	0	10
Chris	Jack	13	1	0	0	0	0	10
Mark	Mayerhofler	6	2	0	0	0	0	10
Anton	Oliver	39	2	0	0	0	0	10
Bruce	Reihana	2	2	0	0	0	0	10
Filo	Tiatia	2	2	0	0	0	0	10
Richard	Wilson	2	0	2	2	0	0	10
George	Bullock-Douglas	5	3	0	0	0	0	9
Harcourt	Caughey	9	3	0	0	0	0	9
Bill	Clark	9	3	0	0	0	0	9
Arthur	Collins	3	0	3	1	0	0	9
Bill	Davis*	11	3	0	0	0	0	9
Bob	Deans	5	3	0	0	0	0	9
Frank	Glasgow	6	3	0	0	0	0	9
George	Gray	3	3	0	0	0	0	9
Bert	Grenside	6	3	0	0	0	0	9
Paul	Henderson	7	2	0	0	0	0	9
Jack	Hore	10	3	0	0	0	0	9
William (Bull)	Irvine	5	3	0	0	0	0	9
Jim	Kearney	4	1	0	0	2	0	9
Tom	Lynch jnr	3	2	0	0	1	0	9
Ian	MacRae	17	3	0	0	0	0	9
Hugh	McLean	9	3	0	0	0	0	9
Ray	Moreton	7	2	0	0	1	0	9
Harold (Toby)	Murray	4	3	0	0	0	0	9
Ron	Rangi	10	3	0	0	0	0	9
Roy	Roper	5	3	0	0	0	0	9
Charlie	Saxton	3	3	0	0	0	0	9
Jack	Steel	6	3	0	0	0	0	9
Jack	Sullivan	6	3	0	0	0	0	9
Bruce	Watt	8	2	0	0	1	0	9
Richard (Tiny)	White	23	3	0	0	0	0	9
Bunny	Abbott	1	2	1	0	0	0	8
Mark	Brooke-Cowden	4	2	0	0	0	0	8
Andy	Haden	41	2	0	0	0	0	8
Ian	Hurst	5	2	0	0	0	0	8
Brad	Johnstone	13	2	0	0	0	0	8
Steven	Pokere	18	2	0	0	0	0	8
Hika	Reid	7	2	0	0	0	0	8
Duncan	Robertson	10	2	0	0	0	0	8
Ant	Strachan	11	2	0	0	0	0	8
Alex	Wyllie	11	2	0	0	0	0	8
George	Gillett	8	1	2	0	0	0	7
Arthur	Stone	9	1	0	0	1	0	7
Ray	Bell	3	1	0	1	0	0	6

First name	Surname	Tests	Tries	Cons	Pens	DGs	GMs	Totals
Frano	Botica	7	0	0	0	2	0	6
Albert (Snowy)	Bowman	3	2	0	0	0	0	6
Maurice	Brownlie	8	2	0	0	0	0	6
Bob	Burgess	7	2	0	0	0	0	6
Paddy	Burns	5	2	0	0	0	0	6
Wayne	Cottrell	7	1	0	0	1	0	6
Maurie	Dixon	10	2	0	0	0	0	6
William	Francis	5	2	0	0	0	0	6
John	Graham	22	2	0	0	0	0	6
Bill	Hadley	8	2	0	0	0	0	6
Eric	Harper	2	2	0	0	0	0	6
Peter	Henderson	7	2	0	0	0	0	6
John	Hotop	3	1	0	0	1	0	6
Peter	Jones	11	2	0	0	0	0	6
Tom	Lister	8	2	0	0	0	0	6
Brian	Lochore	24	2	0	0	0	0	6
Nev	MacEwan	20	2	0	0	0	0	6
Don	McKay	5	2	0	0	0	0	6
Archie	McMinn	2	2	0	0	0	0	6
Peter	Morrissey	3	2	0	0	0	0	6
Peter	Murdoch	5	2	0	0	0	0	6
Charlie	Oliver	7	2	0	0	0	0	6
John	Rankin	3	2	0	0	0	0	6
Tori	Reid	9	2	0	0	0	0	6
Charlie	Seeling	11	2	0	0	0	0	6
George	Smith	2	2	0	0	0	0	6
Ian	Smith	9	2	0	0	0	0	6
Johnny	Smith	4	1	0	0	1	0	6
Wayne	Smith	17	0	0	0	2	0	6
Leonard	Stohr	3	2	0	0	0	0	6
Jim	Watt	2	2	0	0	0	0	6
Wilson	Whineray	32	2	0	0	0	0	6
Nathaniel (Ranji)	Wilson	10	2	0	0	0	0	6
Mark	Allen	8	1	0	0	0	0	5
Todd	Blackadder	12	1	0	0	0	0	5
Daryl	Gibson	19	1	0	0	0	0	5
Laurie	Haig	9	1	1	0	0	0	5
Jamie	Joseph	20	1	0	0	0	0	5
Regan	King	1	1	0	0	0	0	5
Danny	Lee	2	1	0	0	0	0	5
Isitolo	Maka	4	1	0	0	0	0	5
Richard	McCaw	9	1	0	0	0	0	5
Joe	McDonnell	7	1	0	0	0	0	5
Scott	McLeod	10	1	0	0	0	0	5
Dylan	Mika	7	1	0	0	0	0	5
George	Nepia	9	0	1	1	0	0	5
Charles	Riechelmann	6	1	0	0	0	0	5
Mark D.	Robinson	3	1	0	0	0	0	5
Mark P.	Robinson	9	1	0	0	0	0	5
Gordon	Slater	3	1	0	0	0	0	5
George	Tyler	7	1	1	0	0	0	5
Joeli	Vidiri	2	1	0	0	0	0	5
Nicky	Allen	2	1	0	0	0	0	4
John	Ashworth	24	1	0	0	0	0	4
Ben	Blair	4	0	2	0	0	0	4
Mike	Brewer	32	1	0	0	0	0	4
Mike	Clamp	2	1	0	0	0	0	4
Murray	Davie	1	1	0	0	0	0	4
Mark	Donaldson	13	1	0	0	0	0	4
John	Dougan	2	1	0	0	0	0	4
John	Drake	8	1	0	0	0	0	4
Eddie	Dunn	2	1	0	0	0	0	4
John	Fleming	5	1	0	0	0	0	4

Points scorers in tests

First name	Surname	Tests	Tries	Cons	Pens	DGs	GMs	Totals
Jason	Hewett	1	1	0	0	0	0	4
Lyn	Jaffray	7	1	0	0	0	0	4
Gary	Knight	36	1	0	0	0	0	4
Lawrie	Knight	6	1	0	0	0	0	4
Blair	Larsen	17	1	0	0	0	0	4
Andy	Leslie	10	1	0	0	0	0	4
Herb	Lilburne	10	0	2	0	0	0	4
Hamish	MacDonald	12	1	0	0	0	0	4
Bernie	McCahill	10	1	0	0	0	0	4
Joe	Morgan	5	1	0	0	0	0	4
Tom	Morrison	3	0	0	0	1	0	4
Keith	Murdoch	3	1	0	0	0	0	4
Frank	Oliver	17	1	0	0	0	0	4
Graham	Purvis	2	1	0	0	0	0	4
Teddy	Roberts	5	0	2	0	0	0	4
Jamie	Salmon	3	1	0	0	0	0	4
John	Schuster	10	1	0	0	0	0	4
Alistair	Scown	5	1	0	0	0	0	4
Bruce	Smith	3	1	0	0	0	0	4
Ian	Stevens	3	1	0	0	0	0	4
Mark	Taylor	9	1	0	0	0	0	4
Richard	Turner	2	1	0	0	0	0	4
Murray	Watts	5	1	0	0	0	0	4
Gary	Whetton	58	1	0	0	0	0	4
Keith	Arnold	2	1	0	0	0	0	3
Opai	Asher	1	1	0	0	0	0	3
Walter	Batty	4	1	0	0	0	0	3
Moke	Belliss	3	1	0	0	0	0	3
Noel	Bowden	1	0	0	1	0	0	3
Charles	Brown	2	1	0	0	0	0	3
Donald	Cameron	3	1	0	0	0	0	3
Dick	Conway	10	1	0	0	0	0	3
Tom	Cross	2	1	0	0	0	0	3
Patrick	Crowley	6	1	0	0	0	0	3
William	Cummings	2	1	0	0	0	0	3
Rawi	Cundy	1	0	0	1	0	0	3
Bill	Cunningham	9	1	0	0	0	0	3
Nelson	Dalzell	5	1	0	0	0	0	3
John	Dick	3	1	0	0	0	0	3
Kenneth	Elliott	2	1	0	0	0	0	3
Alan	Elsom	6	0	0	0	1	0	3
Leo	Fanning	1	1	0	0	0	0	3
Jack	Finlay	1	1	0	0	0	0	3
Jim	Fitzgerald	1	1	0	0	0	0	3
William	Fuller	2	1	0	0	0	0	3
Maurie	Goddard	5	1	0	0	0	0	3
Jimmy	Haig	2	1	0	0	0	0	3
Edward	Hasell	2	1	0	0	0	0	3
Harold	Hayward	1	1	0	0	0	0	3
Rod	Heeps	5	1	0	0	0	0	3
Ron	Hemi	16	1	0	0	0	0	3
Edward	Hughes	6	1	0	0	0	0	3
Peter	Johnstone	9	1	0	0	0	0	3
Jack	Kelly	2	0	0	1	0	0	3
Frank	Kilby	4	1	0	0	0	0	3
Arthur	Knight	1	1	0	0	0	0	3
Dave	Lindsay	3	0	0	1	0	0	3
Paul	Little	10	1	0	0	0	0	3
Fred	Lucas	7	1	0	0	0	0	3
Jack	Manchester	9	1	0	0	0	0	3
David	Mason	1	1	0	0	0	0	3
Donald	Max	3	1	0	0	0	0	3
Dick	McGregor	2	1	0	0	0	0	3
Dougie	McGregor	2	1	0	0	0	0	3
Andrew	McLean	2	1	0	0	0	0	3
James	McNeece	5	1	0	0	0	0	3
Ruben	McWilliams	10	1	0	0	0	0	3
Harold	Milliken	3	1	0	0	0	0	3
William	Mitchell	2	1	0	0	0	0	3
Graham	Moore	1	1	0	0	0	0	3
Fred	Newton	3	1	0	0	0	0	3
Tom	O'Callaghan	1	0	0	1	0	0	3
Don	Oliver	2	1	0	0	0	0	3
Terry	O'Sullivan	4	1	0	0	0	0	3
Rusty	Page	6	1	0	0	0	0	3
Bert	Palmer	3	1	0	0	0	0	3
Jim	Parker	3	1	0	0	0	0	3
Allan	Parkhill	6	1	0	0	0	0	3
Sandy	Paterson	5	1	0	0	0	0	3
Henry	Paton	2	1	0	0	0	0	3
Bill	Phillips	3	1	0	0	0	0	3
George	Purdue	4	1	0	0	0	0	3
Jock	Richardson	7	1	0	0	0	0	3
Charles	Robinson	5	1	0	0	0	0	3
Kevin	Skinner	20	1	0	0	0	0	3
George	Skudder	1	1	0	0	0	0	3
Frank	Solomon	3	1	0	0	0	0	3
Ron	Stewart	5	1	0	0	0	0	3
Percy	Storey	2	1	0	0	0	0	3
John	Stringfellow	2	1	0	0	0	0	3
Bob	Stuart	7	1	0	0	0	0	3
John (Tuna)	Swain	4	1	0	0	0	0	3
John	Tanner	5	1	0	0	0	0	3
Murray	Taylor	7	0	0	0	1	0	3
Reg	Taylor	2	1	0	0	0	0	3
Hector	Thomson	1	1	0	0	0	0	3
Grahame	Thorne	10	1	0	0	0	0	3
Neville	Thornton	3	0	0	1	0	0	3
Roger	Urbahn	3	1	0	0	0	0	3
Ivan	Vodanovich	3	1	0	0	0	0	3
Russell	Watt	9	1	0	0	0	0	3
Andrew	White	4	1	0	0	0	0	3
Roy	White	4	1	0	0	0	0	3
Hector	Wilson	5	1	0	0	0	0	3
Norm	Wilson	3	1	0	0	0	0	3
Edgar	Wrigley	1	1	0	0	0	0	3
Jim	Wylie	2	1	0	0	0	0	3
Victor	Yates	3	1	0	0	0	0	3
John	Colman	4	0	1	0	0	0	2
Bob	Lendrum	1	0	1	0	0	0	2
penalty tries			11					45
TOTALS			**1149**	**691**	**686**	**80**	**5**	**8364**

* indicates that in some earlier records, penalty tries were awarded to these players. These have now been deducted from the players' totals and contribute to the sum of the penalty tries shown in the second-last row. One player, Harry Frazer, is thus omitted from the scorers' list because his one try was a penalty try, in the first test against Australia in 1947.

A try was valued at three points from the time of New Zealand's first test, in 1903, until the 151st, against Australia on August 16, 1972, when it became four points. It was increased to five points from July 1, 1992.

A goal from a mark, initially worth four points, was reduced to three in 1905 and it was abolished in 1977.

A dropped goal was valued at four points from the time of New Zealand's first test until 1948, when it was reduced to three points.

Most points by a player in a test

Points	Player	Opponent	Date	Tries	Cons	Pens	DGS
45	Simon Culhane*	Japan	4.6.1995	1	20	0	0
36	Tony Brown	Italy	14.10.1999	1	11	3	0
33	Carlos Spencer*	Argentina	21.6.1997	2	10	1	0
33	Andrew Mehrtens	Ireland	15.11.1997	1	5	6	0
32	Tony Brown	Tonga	16.6.2000	1	12	1	0
30	Marc Ellis	Japan	4.6.1995	6	0	0	0
30	Tony Brown	Samoa	16.6.2001	3	3	3	0
29	Andrew Mehrtens	Australia	24.7.1999	0	1	9	0
29	Andrew Mehrtens	France	11.11.2000	0	1	9	0
28	Andrew Mehrtens*	Canada	22.4.1995	1	7	3	0
26	Grant Fox	Fiji	27.5.1987	0	10	2	0
26	Tony Brown	Samoa	18.6.1999	0	7	4	0
26	Allan Hewson	Australia	11.9.1982	1	2	5	1
25	Grant Fox	Samoa	31.7.1993	0	2	7	0
25	Carlos Spencer	South Africa	9.8.1997	1	4	4	0
25	Jeff Wilson	Fiji	14.6.1997	5	0	0	0
24	Fergie McCormick	Wales	14.6.1969	0	3	5	1
23	Matthew Cooper*	Ireland	6.6.1992	2	6	1	0
23	Andrew Mehrtens	Scotland	11.6.1995	1	6	2	0
23	Andrew Mehrtens	Australia	22.7.1995	0	1	5	2
23	Andrew Mehrtens	Wales	23.11.2002	0	4	5	0
22	Grant Fox	Scotland	6.6.1987	0	2	6	0
22	Grant Fox	Italy	22.5.1987	0	8	2	0
22	Andrew Mehrtens	Scotland	15.6.1996	1	7	1	0
22	Andrew Mehrtens	Australia	27.7.1996	0	2	6	0
22	Grant Fox	Wales	11.6.1988	0	8	2	0
22	Grant Fox	Argentina	1.6.1987	0	2	6	0
22	Grant Fox	France	10.11.1990	0	2	6	0
22	Andrew Mehrtens	Scotland	24.11.2001	0	2	6	0
21	Andrew Mehrtens	South Africa	7.8.1999	0	0	7	0
21	Grant Fox	Argentina	29.7.1989	0	6	3	0
21	Carlos Spencer	Australia	16.8.1997	0	3	5	0
21	Andrew Mehrtens	England	6.12.1997	1	2	4	0
21	Carlos Spencer	Italy	25.11.2000	1	5	2	0
20	Andrew Mehrtens	Tonga	3.10.1999	0	4	4	0
20	Carlos Spencer	Argentina	28.6.1997	1	6	1	0
20	Grant Fox	Argentina	15.7.1989	0	7	2	0
20	Grant Fox	Argentina	13.7.1991	0	4	4	0
20	Allan Hewson	Scotland	20.6.1981	2	6	0	0
20	Greg Cooper	World XV	22.4.1992	2	6	0	0
20	Jonah Lomu	England	18.6.1995	4	0	0	0
20	Simon Culhane	Italy	28.10.1995	0	7	2	0
20	Christian Cullen	Scotland	15.6.1996	4	0	0	0
20	Carlos Spencer	South Africa	19.7.1997	1	3	3	0
20	Jeff Wilson	Samoa	18.6.1999	4	0	0	0
20	Andrew Mehrtens	South Africa	19.8.2000	0	4	3	1

* indicates on debut

Most dropped goals by a player in a test

DGs	Player	Opponent	Where	When
2	Doug Bruce	Ireland	Dublin	1978
2	Frano Botica	France	Christchurch	1986
2	Andrew Mehrtens	Australia	Auckland	1995

Most tries by a player in a test

Tries	Player	Opponent	Where	When
6	Marc Ellis	Japan	Bloemfontein	1995
5	Jeff Wilson	Fiji	Albany	1997
4	Duncan McGregor	England	Crystal Palace	1905
4	Craig Green	Fiji	Christchurch	1987
4	John Gallagher	Fiji	Christchurch	1987
4	John Kirwan	Wales	Christchurch	1988
4	Jonah Lomu	England	Cape Town	1995
4	Christian Cullen	Scotland	Dunedin	1996
4	Jeff Wilson	Samoa	Albany	1999

Most conversions by a player in a test

Cons	Player	Opponent	Where	When
20	Simon Culhane	Japan	Bloemfontein	1995
12	Tony Brown	Tonga	Albany	2000
11	Tony Brown	Italy	Huddersfield	1999
10	Grant Fox	Fiji	Christchurch	1987
10	Carlos Spencer	Argentina	Wellington	1997
8	Grant Fox	Italy	Auckland	1987
8	Grant Fox	Wales	Auckland	1988
8	Andrew Mehrtens	Italy	Hamilton	2002
7	Grant Fox	Wales	Brisbane	1987
7	Grant Fox	Argentina	Dunedin	1989
7	Andrew Mehrtens	Canada	Auckland	1995
7	Simon Culhane	Italy	Bologna	1995
7	Andrew Mehrtens	Scotland	Dunedin	1996
7	Tony Brown	Samoa	Albany	1999
7	Andrew Mehrtens	Scotland	Dunedin	2000

Most penalty goals by a player in a test

Penalties	Player	Opponent	Where	When
9	Andrew Mehrtens	Australia	Auckland	1999
9	Andrew Mehrtens	France	Paris	2000
7	Grant Fox	Samoa	Auckland	1993
7	Andrew Mehrtens	South Africa	Pretoria	1999
6	Don Clarke	British Isles	Dunedin	1959
6	Kieran Crowley	England	Christchurch	1985
6	Grant Fox	Argentina	Wellington	1987
6	Grant Fox	Scotland	Christchurch	1987
6	Grant Fox	France	Paris	1990
6	Shane Howarth	South Africa	Auckland	1994
6	Andrew Mehrtens	Australia	Brisbane	1996
6	Andrew Mehrtens	Ireland	Dublin	1997
6	Andrew Mehrtens	South Africa	Cardiff	1999
6	Andrew Mehrtens	Scotland	Edinburgh	2001

Oldest players

Age	Player	Played	When
40yrs 123days	Ned Hughes	South Africa	27.8.1921
35yrs 305days	Frank Bunce	England	6.12.1997
35yrs 287days	John Ashworth	Australia	29.6.1985
35yrs 226days	Richard Loe	France	18.11.1995
35yrs 136days	Tane Norton	British Isles	13.8.1977
35yrs 72days	Colin Meads	British Isles	14.8.1971
35yrs 54days	Charlie Sonntag	Australia	27.7.1929
35yrs 37days	Andy Haden	Argentina	2.11.1985
35yrs 11days	Gary Knight	Australia	6.9.1986

Youngest players

Age	Player	Played	When
19yrs 45days	Jonah Lomu	France	26.6.1994
19yrs 79days	Edgar Wrigley	Australia	2.9.1905
19yrs 106days	Pat Walsh	Australia	20.8.1955
19yrs 182days	John Kirwan	France	16.6.1984
19yrs 190days	George Nepia	Ireland	1.11.1924
19yrs 211days	William Mitchell	Australia	27.6.1910
19yrs 221days	William Francis	Australia	13.9.1913
19yrs 270days	James Baird	Australia	13.9.1913

Fathers and sons

Braid	Gary	1983
Braid	Daniel	2002
Dalton	Ray	1947
Dalton	Andy	1977–87
Dick	John	1937–38
Dick	Malcolm	1963–70
Irvine	William (Bull)	1924–25, 30
Irvine	Ian	1952
Lynch	Tom	1913–14
Lynch	Tom	1951
Mexted	Graham	1951
Mexted	Murray	1979–85
Purdue	Edward (Pat)	1905
Purdue	George	1931–32
Oliver	Frank	1976–81
Oliver	Anton	1997–2001
Fitzpatrick	Brian	1953–54
Fitzpatrick	Sean	1986–97

Grandfather, grandson

Barry	Ned	1934
Barry	Liam	1995

Brothers

Bachop	Graeme	1989–92, 94–95
Bachop	Stephen	1994
Brooke	Robin	1992–99
Brooke	Zinzan	1987–97
Brownlie	Cyril	1924–25
Brownlie	Maurice	1924–25, 28
Clarke	Don	1956–64
Clarke	Ian	1953, 55–63
Cooper	Greg	1986, 92
Cooper	Matthew	1992–94, 96
Deans	Bruce	1988–89
Deans	Robbie	1983–84
Donald	Jim	1921
Donald	Quentin	1924–25
Dunn	Eddie	1979, 81
Dunn	Ian	1983
Fanning	Alfred	1913
Fanning	Bernard	1903–04
Hadley	Bill	1934–36
Hadley	Swinbourne	1928
Haig	Jimmy	1946
Haig	Laurie	1950–51, 53–54
McMinn	Archie	1903–05
McMinn	Francis (Paddy)	1904
Meads	Colin	1957–71
Meads	Stan	1961–66
Meates	Bill	1949–50
Meates	Kevin	1952
Nicholls	Harry (Ginger)	1921
Nicholls	Mark	1921, 24–25, 28, 30
Purdue	Charles	1905
Purdue	Edward (Pat)	1905
Stuart	Bob	1949, 53–54
Stuart	Kevin	1955
Taylor	Murray	1979–80
Taylor	Warwick	1983–88
Whetton	Alan	1984–91
Whetton	Gary	1981–91

Odd facts

Test All Blacks to be knighted*

Harcourt Caughey, KBE (1972)
Brian Lochore, KNZM (1999)
Colin Meads, DCNZM (2000)
Wilson Whineray, KNZM (1998)

*New Zealand knights were either knights bachelor or knights within one of several British orders of chivalry until May 1996. The New Zealand Order of Merit was then introduced and in May 2000, titles within the order were discontinued. Meads, for example, is a distinguished companion of the order; he previously would have been designated a knight companion.

Rhodes Scholars

George Aitken (1922)
Colin Gilray (1907)
David Kirk (1985)
Chris Laidlaw (1968)

Members of Parliament

Ben Couch (Wairarapa, 1975–84)
Bill Glenn (Rangitikei, 1919–28)
Chris Laidlaw (Wellington Central, 1992–93)
Tony Steel (Hamilton East, 1990–93, 1996–2002)
Grahame Thorne (Onehunga, 1990–93)

Killed in action

First World War (12): John Baird, Bobby Black, 'Norkey' Dewar, Ernest Dodd, 'Doolan' Downing, Dave Gallaher, Eric Harper, Jim McNeece, Jim Ridland, George Sellars, Reg Taylor, 'Jum' Turtill.
Second World War (2): Don Cobden, George Hart.

Test Statistics

Scorers on debut

Surname	First name	Debut date	Opponent	Tries	Cons	PGs	DGs	GMs	Total
Abbott	Harold (Bunny)	1.1.1906	France	2	1				8
Argus	Wally	14.9.1946	Australia	2					6
Asher	Opai	15.8.1903	Australia	1					3
Bachop	Graeme	4.11.1989	Wales	1					4
Ball	Nelson	12.9.1931	Australia	1					3
Bell	Ray	21.7.1951	Australia	1					3
Belliss	Ernest (Moke)	13.8.1921	South Africa	1					3
Birtwistle	Bill	31.7.1965	South Africa	1					3
Botica	Frano	28.6.1986	France				2		6
Bowden	Noel	13.9.1952	Australia			1			3
Brewer	Mike	28.6.1986	France	1					4
Brooke	Zinzan	1.6.1987	Argentina	1					4
Brown	Charles	13.9.1913	Australia	1					3
Brown	Tony	18.6.1999	Samoa		7	4			26
Bullock-Douglas	Arthur	2.7.1932	Australia	1					3
Bush	Ron	12.9.1931	Australia		1	4			14
Caulton	Ralph	15.8.1959	British Isles	2					6
Clark	Bill	19.12.1953	Wales	1					3
Clarke	Don	18.8.1956	South Africa		1	2			8
Clarke	Eroni	22.4.1992	World XV	2					8
Cockerill	Maurice (Snow)	23.6.1951	Australia		1	1			5
Codlin	Brett	27.6.1980	Australia			3			9
Collins	Arthur	16.7.1932	Australia			1			3
Cooper	Greg	28.6.1986	France		1	1	1		8
Cooper	Matthew	6.6.1992	Ireland	2	6	1			23
Crowley	Kieran	1.6.1985	England			6			18
Culhane	Simon	4.6.1995	Japan	1	20				45
Cullen	Christian	7.6.1996	Samoa	3					15
Cummings	William	13.9.1913	Australia	1					3
Cundy	Rawi	20.7.1929	Australia			1			3
Cunningham	Bill	18.11.1905	Scotland	1					3
Davie	Murray	19.11.1983	England	1					4
Davis	Bill	19.8.1967	Australia	1					3
Deans	Bruce	28.5.1988	Wales	1					4
Deans	Robbie	12.11.1983	Scotland		2	3			13
Dick	John	14.8.1937	South Africa	1					3
Dougan	John	19.8.1972	Australia	1					4
Dunn	Eddie	10.11.1979	Scotland	1					4
Elliott	Keith	14.9.1946	Australia	1					3
Ellis	Marc	20.11.1993	Scotland	2					10
Fanning	Alfred	20.9.1913	Australia	1					3
Finlay	Jack	14.9.1946	Australia	1					3
Fitzgerald	Jim	6.9.1952	Australia	1					3
Flavell	Troy	16.6.2000	Tonga	3					15
Fox	Grant	26.10.1985	Argentina				1		3
Francis	Arthur (Bolla)	2.9.1905	Australia		1				2
Fuller	William	25.6.1910	Australia	1					3
Gilbert	Mike	23.11.1935	Scotland		3				6
Glasgow	Frank	18.11.1905	Scotland	1					3
Goddard	Morrie	3.9.1949	South Africa	1					3
Graham	Jim	15.11.1913	United States		4				8
Graham	John	23.8.1958	Australia	1					3
Haig	Jimmy	14.9.1946	Australia	1					3
Haig	Laurie	10.6.1950	British Isles		1				2
Hart	George	21.6.1930	British Isles	1					3
Hayward	Harold (Circus)	25.7.1908	Anglo-Welsh	1					3
Henderson	Peter	16.7.1949	South Africa	1					3
Herewini	Mac	22.9.1962	Australia	1			1		6
Hewett	Dave	17.11.2001	Ireland	1					5

287

Scorers on debut

Surname	First name	Debut date	Opponent	Tries	Cons	PGs	DGs	GMs	Total
Hewett	Jason	13.10.1991	Italy	1					4
Hewson	Alan	13.6.1981	Scotland			1			3
Howarth	Shane	9.7.1994	South Africa		1	5			17
Howlett	Doug	16.6.2000	Tonga	2					10
Hughes	Ned	20.7.1907	Australia	1					3
Innes	Craig	4.11.1989	Wales	2					8
Jack	Chris	23.6.2001	Argentina	1					5
Jones	Ian	16.6.1990	Scotland	1					4
Jones	Michael	22.5.1987	Italy	1					4
Karam	Joe	2.12.1972	Wales			5			15
Kearney	Jim	28.6.1947	Australia	1					3
Kelly	Jack	3.9.1949	Australia			1			3
Kember	Gerald	12.9.1970	South Africa		1	4			14
King	Regan	23.11.2002	Wales	1					5
Kirkpatrick	Ian	25.11.1967	France	1					3
Kirton	Earle	4.11.1967	England	2					6
Knight	Arthur	11.8.1934	Australia	1					3
Laidlaw	Chris	8.2.1964	France				1		3
Larsen	Blair	22.4.1992	World XV	1					4
Lee	Danny	9.11.2002	England	1					5
Lendrum	Bob	15.9.1973	England		1				2
Lynch	Tom	6.9.1913	Australia	3					9
Mains	Laurie	10.7.1971	British Isles		2	1			7
Maka	Isitolo	27.6.1998	England	1					5
Mason	Tim	28.6.1947	Australia	1					3
Mauger	Aaron	17.11.2001	Ireland	1					5
Maxwell	Norman	18.6.1999	Samoa	1					5
Mayerhofler	Mark	20.6.1998	England	1					5
McCormick	Fergie	18.9.1965	South Africa		1				2
McDonnell	Joe	8.6.2002	Italy	1					5
McGregor	Dick	15.8.1903	Australia	1					3
McKay	Don	22.7.1961	France	1					3
McKechnie	Brian	11.11.1977	France			1			3
McKenzie	Richard (Jock)	6.9.1913	Australia	2					6
McLean	Hugh	26.7.1930	British Isles	2					6
McLean	Les	27.8.1921	South Africa	1					3
McLeod	Bruce	15.8.1964	Australia	1					3
McLeod	Scott	7.6.1996	Samoa	1					5
McMullen	Frank	25.5.1957	Australia	1					3
Mehrtens	Andrew	22.4.1995	Canada	1	7	3			28
Mexted	Murray	10.11.1979	Scotland	1					4
Mitchinson	Frank	20.7.1907	Australia	3					9
Moore	Graham	3.9.1949	Australia	1					3
Morris	Trevor	19.8.1972	Australia		3		1		9
Morrissey	John	25.8.1962	Australia	1					3
Murdoch	Peter	22.8.1964	Australia	1					3
Murray	Harold	6.9.1913	Australia	1					3
Newton	Fred	2.12.1905	England	1					3
Nicholls	Mark	13.8.1921	South Africa		2				4
O'Callaghan	Ray	24.9.1949	Australia			1			3
Oliver	Charlie	6.7.1929	Australia	1					3
Osborne	Glen	22.4.1995	Canada	2					10
Pollock	Harold (Bunk)	2.7.1932	Australia		2		1		8
Porter	Cliff	18.1.1925	France	1					3
Preston	Jon	8.10.1991	United States		4	2			14
Purvis	Graham	8.10.1991	United States	1					4
Rangi	Ron	22.8.1964	Australia	1					3
Riechelmann	Charles	14.6.1997	Fiji	1					5
Roberts	Dick	6.9.1913	Australia	1	3				9
Robertson	Duncan	25.5.1974	Australia	1					4
Robinson	Mark P.	1.7.2000	Scotland	1					5

Scorers on debut

Surname	First name	Debut date	Opponent	Tries	Cons	PGs	DGs	GMs	Total
Rollerson	Doug	1.11.1980	Wales		2	1			7
Roper	Roy	24.9.1949	Australia	1					3
Salmon	Jamie	24.10.1981	Romania	1					4
Saxton	Charlie	23.7.1938	Australia	2					6
Schuster	John	3.7.1988	Australia	1					4
Scott	Bob	14.9.1946	Australia		5				10
Shelford	Wayne	8.11.1986	France	1					4
Skudder	George	14.7.1969	Wales	1					3
Smith	George	18.11.1905	Scotland	2					6
Smith	Johnny	14.9.1946	Australia	1					3
Spencer	Carlos	21.6.1997	Argentina	2	10	1			33
Steel	Jack	13.8.1921	South Africa	1					3
Storey	Percy	13.8.1921	South Africa	1					3
Strachan	Ant	22.4.1992	World XV	1					4
Svenson	Kenneth (Snowy)	1.11.1924	Ireland	1					3
Taylor	Reg	13.9.1913	Australia	1					3
Thomson	Hector (Mona)	6.6.1908	Anglo-Welsh	1					3
Tiatia	Filo	16.6.2000	Tonga	1					5
Trevathan	Dave	14.8.1937	South Africa			2	1		10
Tuigamala	Va'aiga	8.10.1991	United States	1					4
Turner	Richard	18.4.1992	World XV	1					4
Tyler	George	15.8.1903	Australia	1					3
Umaga	Tana	14.6.1997	Fiji	1					5
Vidiri	Joeli	27.6.1998	England	1					5
Vodanovich	Ivan	20.8.1955	Australia	1					3
Wallace	Billy	15.8.1903	Australia		1	1		2	13
Watt	Bruce	26.5.1962	Australia	1					3
Watt	Jim	5.9.1936	Australia	1					3
Watts	Murray	7.7.1979	France	1					4
White	Roy	14.9.1946	Australia	1					3
Williams	Bryan	25.7.1970	South Africa	1					3
Williment	Mick	15.8.1964	Australia		1	2			8
Wilson	Bevan	30.7.1977	British Isles		1	2			8
Wilson	Jeff	20.11.1993	Scotland	3	1				17
Wilson	Richard	10.11.1979	Scotland		2				4
Wrigley	Edgar	2.9.1905	Australia	1					3

Most successive tests

63	Sean Fitzpatrick	1986–95
51	Christian Cullen	1996–2000
49	Robin Brooke	1995–99
41	Jeff Wilson	1996–99
40	Gary Whetton	1986–91
38	Ian Kirkpatrick	1968–77
38	Steve McDowell	1987–92
38	Taine Randell	1997–2000
36	Olo Brown	1995–98
35	Ian Jones	1995–98
34	Murray Mexted	1979–85
31	Colin Meads	1962–69
31	Grant Fox	1987–91
30	Frank Bunce	1995–97
28	Craig Dowd	1995–97
28	Ian Jones	1990–93
28	John Kirwan	1985–89
28	Wilson Whineray	1957–64
27	Tane Norton	1971–77
27	Joe Stanley	1986–90
26	Sean Fitzpatrick	1995–97
26	Josh Kronfeld	1996–98
26	Terry Wright	1988–91
25	Frank Bunce	1992–95
25	Bryan Williams	1971–77
24	Don Clarke	1958–64
24	Richard Loe	1988–91
23	Justin Marshall	1995–97
23	Richard (Tiny) White	1949–56
23	Tana Umaga	1999–2001
23	Anton Oliver	1999–2001
22	Andy Haden	1977–80
22	Dave Loveridge	1979–83
21	Kel Tremain	1963–67

Scorers on debut — top scores

Surname	First name	Debut date	Opponent	Tries	Cons	PGs	DGs	GMs	Total
Culhane	Simon	4.6.1995	Japan	1	20				45
Spencer	Carlos	21.6.1997	Argentina	2	10	1			33
Mehrtens	Andrew	22.4.1995	Canada	1	7	3			28
Brown	Tony	18.6.1999	Samoa		7	4			26
Cooper	Matthew	6.6.1992	Ireland	2	6	1			23
Crowley	Kieran	1.6.1985	England			6			18
Wilson	Jeff	20.11.1993	Scotland	3	1				17
Howarth	Shane	9.7.1994	South Africa		1	5			17
Karam	Joe	2.12.1972	Wales			5			15
Flavell	Troy	16.6.2000	Tonga	3					15
Cullen	Christian	7.6.1996	Samoa	3					15
Preston	Jon	8.10.1991	United States			4	2		14
Kember	Gerald	12.9.1970	South Africa		1	4			14
Bush	Ron	12.9.1931	Australia		1	4			14
Wallace	Billy	15.8.1903	Australia		1	1		2	13
Deans	Robbie	12.11.1983	Scotland		2	3			13
Trevathan	Dave	14.8.1937	South Africa			2	1		10
Scott	Bob	14.9.1946	Australia		5				10
Osborne	Glen	22.4.1995	Canada	2					10
Howlett	Doug	16.6.2000	Tonga	2					10
Ellis	Marc	20.11.1993	Scotland	2					10

Most tries on debut

Surname	First name	Debut date	Opponent	Tries
Cullen	Christian	7.6.1996	Samoa	3
Flavell	Troy	16.6.2000	Tonga	3
Lynch	Tom	6.9.1913	Australia	3
Mitchinson	Frank	20.7.1907	Australia	3
Wilson	Jeff	20.11.1993	Scotland	3
Abbott	Harold (Bunny)	1.1.1906	France	2
Argus	Wally	14.9.1946	Australia	2
Caulton	Ralph	15.8.1959	British Isles	2
Clarke	Eroni	22.4.1992	World XV	2
Cooper	Matthew	6.6.1992	Ireland	2
Ellis	Marc	20.11.1993	Scotland	2
Howlett	Doug	16.6.2000	Tonga	2
Innes	Craig	4.11.1989	Wales	2
Kirton	Earle	4.11.1967	England	2
McKenzie	Richard (Jock)	6.9.1913	Australia	2
McLean	Hugh	26.7.1930	British Isles	2
Osborne	Glen	22.4.1995	Canada	2
Saxton	Charlie	23.7.1938	Australia	2
Smith	George	18.11.1905	Scotland	2
Spencer	Carlos	21.6.1997	Argentina	2

94 players have scored one try on debut

Most debut players in one test

Number	Opponent	Venue	Date
15[1]	Australia	Sydney	15.8.1903
15[2]	Australia	Dunedin	14.9.1946
14[3]	South Africa	Dunedin	13.8.1921
13	Australia	Wellington	6.9.1913
13[4]	Australia	Dunedin	13.9.1913
13	South Africa	Durban	30.6.1928
13[5]	Australia	Wellington	3.9.1949
12	Ireland	Dublin	1.11.1924
11	Australia	Sydney	6.7.1929
10	France	Christchurch	28.6.1986
9	Australia	Dunedin	2.9.1905
9	Australia	Sydney	23.6.1951
8	Scotland	Edinburgh	18.11.1905
8	Australia	Auckland	12.9.1931
8	South Africa	Wellington	14.8.1937
8	Australia	Brisbane	14.6.1947

[1] *First test*
[2] *First test after Second World War*
[3] *First test after First World War*
[4,5] *Teams chosen when first-choice team on tour*

Second, third division test players

First name	Surname	Province	Division	When
Mark	Allen	Manawatu	2nd Division	1997
John	Ashworth	Hawke's Bay	2nd Division	1985
Frano	Botica	North Harbour	2nd Division	1986
Mark	Cooksley	Counties	2nd Division	1992, 93
Kieran	Crowley	Taranaki	2nd Division	1985
Simon	Culhane	Southland	2nd Division	1996
Christian	Cullen	Manawatu	2nd Division	1996, 97
Andy	Donald	Wanganui	2nd Div North	1983, 84
Brian	Ford	Marlborough	2nd Div South	1977, 79
Sid	Going	North Auckland	2nd Div North	1977
Geoff	Hines	Waikato	2nd Div North	1980
Andy	Jefferd	East Coast	2nd Div North	1981
Ian	Jones	North Auckland	2nd Division	1993
Ian	Kirkpatrick	Poverty Bay	2nd Div North	1976, 77
Lawrie	Knight	Poverty Bay	2nd Div North	1977
Dave	Loveridge	Taranaki	2nd Div North	1980, 81, 82, 83, 85
Mike	McCool	Wairarapa-Bush	2nd Div North	1979
Graham	Mourie	Taranaki	2nd Div North	1980, 81, 82
Dick	Myers	Waikato	2nd Div North	1978
Bill	Osborne	Wanganui	2nd Div North	1977, 78, 80, 82
Steve	Pokere	Southland	2nd Div South	1982, 83
Mark	Shaw	Hawke's Bay	2nd Division	1986
Wayne	Shelford	North Harbour	2nd Division	1987
Mark	Taylor	Bay of Plenty	2nd Div North	1977
Murray	Taylor	Waikato	2nd Div North	1979, 80
Murray	Watts	Taranaki	2nd Div North	1980

All Black coaches' win records

Name	Years	Tests	Won	Drew	Lost	Percentage of wins
Fred Allen	1966–68	14	14	0	0	100
Ron Bush	1962	2	2	0	0	100
Len Clode	1951	3	3	0	0	100
Dick Everest	1957	2	2	0	0	100
Alex Wyllie	1988–91	29	25	1	3	86.2
Peter Burke	1981–82	11	9	0	2	81.8
Neil McPhail	1961–65	20	16	2	2	80
John Mitchell	2001–02	14	11	1	2	78.5
Brian Lochore	1985–87	18	14	1	3	77.7
Jack Gleeson	1977–78	13	10	0	3	76.9
John Hart	1996–99	41	31	1	9	75.6
Bob Duff	1972–73	8	6	1	1	75
Bryce Rope	1983–84	12	9	1	2	75
Wayne Smith	2000–01	17	12	0	5	70.5
Laurie Mains	1992–95	34	23	1	10	67.6
Tom Morrison	1950, 52, 55–56	12	8	1	3	66.6
Arthur Marslin	1953–54	5	3	0	2	60
Eric Watson	1979–80	9	5	0	4	55.5
Jack Sullivan	1958–60	11	6	1	4	54.5
John Stewart	1974–76	11	6	1	4	54.5
Ivan Vodanovich	1969–71	10	4	1	5	40
Alex McDonald	1949	4	0	0	4	0

The title, role and authority of the All Black coach has varied so much over the years a full definitive list would be foolhardy. This covers coaches only since the All Blacks' tour of South Africa in 1949.

Points tallies by opponent and venue

Argentina

Venue	Played	Won	Drawn	Lost	POINTS FOR						POINTS AGAINST					
					Tries	Cons	Pens	DGs	GMs	Totals	Tries	Cons	Pens	DGs	GMs	Totals
Buenos Aires	5	4	1		16	8	18	2		142	6	2	13	4		81
Dunedin	1	1			10	7	2			60	1	1	1			9
Wellington	3	3			27	18	10			188	3	2	6			35
Hamilton	1	1			9	7	1			62	1	1	1			10
Christchurch	1	1			10	7	1			67	2		3			19
	11	**10**	**1**		**72**	**47**	**32**	**2**		**519**	**13**	**6**	**24**	**4**		**154**

Australia

Venue	Played	Won	Drawn	Lost	POINTS FOR						POINTS AGAINST					
					Tries	Cons	Pens	DGs	GMs	Totals	Tries	Cons	Pens	DGs	GMs	Totals
Auckland	16	12		4	27	19	48	7		304	27	17	22	3		208
Brisbane	16	12	2	2	48	22	22	4	1	286	21	8	31			186
Christchurch	11	7		4	30	15	15	1		196	19	8	11	3		130
Dublin	1			1			2			6	2	1	2			16
Dunedin	11	10		1	35	19	18	3		222	16	10	10	1		115
Melbourne	2	1		1	5	3	6			49	4	2	6			42
Sydney	43	25	2	16	111	61	65	7	2	742	65	36	76	6	1	572
Wellington	16	9	1	6	47	22	23	4		291	20	10	29	1		180
	116	**76**	**5**	**35**	**303**	**161**	**199**	**26**	**3**	**2096**	**174**	**92**	**187**	**14**	**1**	**1449**

British/Irish teams combined

Venue	Played	Won	Drawn	Lost	POINTS FOR						POINTS AGAINST					
					Tries	Cons	Pens	DGs	GMs	Totals	Tries	Cons	Pens	DGs	GMs	Totals
Auckland	9	7	1	1	30	14	12	3		177	11	7	9	1		80
Christchurch	8	7		1	18	9	15	2	1	129	8	3	14	2		79
Dunedin	8	5	1	2	16	7	16	2		119	13	2	6			64
Wellington	10	7	1	2	21	9	5			102	6	4	15	3		82
	35	**26**	**3**	**6**	**85**	**39**	**48**	**7**	**1**	**527**	**38**	**16**	**44**	**6**		**305**

Canada

Venue	Played	Won	Drawn	Lost	POINTS FOR						POINTS AGAINST					
					Tries	Cons	Pens	DGs	GMs	Totals	Tries	Cons	Pens	DGs	GMs	Totals
Lille	1	1			5	3	1			29	2	1	1			13
Auckland	1	1			10	7	3			73	1	1				7
	2	**2**			**15**	**10**	**4**			**102**	**3**	**2**	**1**			**20**

England

Venue	Played	Won	Drawn	Lost	POINTS FOR						POINTS AGAINST					
					Tries	Cons	Pens	DGs	GMs	Totals	Tries	Cons	Pens	DGs	GMs	Totals
Auckland	3	2		1	11	9	1	1		71	5	4	3			37
Cape Town	1	1			6	3	1	2		45	4	3	1			29
Christchurch	2	2			2		6		1	27	3	1	2			19
Dunedin	1	1			9	5	3			64	3	2	1			22
London	15	10	1	4	32	20	22	1		229	15	7	25	5		165
Manchester	1	1			3	2	2			25	1		1			8
Wellington	1	1			6	3	3	1		42	2	2		1		15
	24	**18**	**1**	**5**	**69**	**42**	**38**	**5**	**1**	**503**	**33**	**19**	**33**	**6**		**295**

Fiji

Venue	Played	Won	Drawn	Lost	POINTS FOR						POINTS AGAINST					
					Tries	Cons	Pens	DGs	GMs	Totals	Tries	Cons	Pens	DGs	GMs	Totals
Albany	1	1			11	8				71	1					5
Christchurch	1	1			12	10	2			74	1		3			13
Wellington	1	1			11	5	1			68	2	1	2			18
	3	**3**			**34**	**23**	**3**			**213**	**4**	**1**	**5**			**36**

Points tallies by opponent and venue

France

Venue	Played	Won	Drawn	Lost	POINTS FOR						POINTS AGAINST					
					Tries	Cons	Pens	DGs	GMs	Totals	Tries	Cons	Pens	DGs	GMs	Totals
Auckland	7	5		2	17	11	23	3		165	15	4	11	4		112
Christchurch	7	6		1	15	8	16	3		128	7	4	5	9		78
London	1			1	3	2	4			31	4	4	3	2		43
Marseilles	1			1	3	3	4			33	3	3	5	2		42
Nantes	2	1		1	2	2	4	1		27	2	1	3			19
Paris	11	8	1	2	29	16	30	2		236	12	7	17	2		121
Toulouse	5	3		2	11	3	12	4		90	7	3	7	2		62
Wellington	4	4			12	10	9			105	2	1	5			25
	38	**27**	**1**	**10**	**92**	**55**	**102**	**13**		**815**	**52**	**27**	**56**	**21**		**502**

Ireland

Venue	Played	Won	Drawn	Lost	POINTS FOR						POINTS AGAINST					
					Tries	Cons	Pens	DGs	GMs	Totals	Tries	Cons	Pens	DGs	GMs	Totals
Auckland	1	1			5	3	3			40	1			1		8
Dublin	11	10	1		30	18	17	3		219	8	3	14	2		89
Dunedin	2	2			6	5	1			39	3	3	2	1		27
Wellington	2	2			13	6	2			70	1	1	1			9
Johannesburg	1	1			5	3	4			43	3	2				19
	17	**16**	**1**		**59**	**35**	**27**	**3**		**411**	**16**	**9**	**17**	**4**		**152**

Italy

Venue	Played	Won	Drawn	Lost	POINTS FOR						POINTS AGAINST					
					Tries	Cons	Pens	DGs	GMs	Totals	Tries	Cons	Pens	DGs	GMs	Totals
Auckland	1	1			12	8	2			70			1	1		6
Bologna	1	1			10	7	2			70			2			6
Genoa	1	1			8	5	2			56	2		3			19
Hamilton	1	1			9	8	1			64	1	1	1			10
Huddersfield	1	1			14	11	3			101			1			3
Leicester	1	1			4	3	3			31	2	2	3			21
	6	**6**			**57**	**42**	**13**			**392**	**5**	**3**	**11**	**1**		**65**

Japan

Venue	Played	Won	Drawn	Lost	POINTS FOR						POINTS AGAINST					
					Tries	Cons	Pens	DGs	GMs	Totals	Tries	Cons	Pens	DGs	GMs	Totals
Bloemfontein	1	1			21	20				145	2	2	1			17
	1	**1**			**21**	**20**				**145**	**2**	**2**	**1**			**17**

Romania

Venue	Played	Won	Drawn	Lost	POINTS FOR						POINTS AGAINST					
					Tries	Cons	Pens	DGs	GMs	Totals	Tries	Cons	Pens	DGs	GMs	Totals
Bucharest	1	1			2		1	1		14			1	1		6
	1	**1**			**2**		**1**	**1**		**14**			**1**	**1**		**6**

Scotland

Venue	Played	Won	Drawn	Lost	POINTS FOR						POINTS AGAINST					
					Tries	Cons	Pens	DGs	GMs	Totals	Tries	Cons	Pens	DGs	GMs	Totals
Auckland	5	5			25	19	6			169	7	6	4	1		59
Cardiff	1	1			1		3			13			2			6
Christchurch	1	1			2	2	6			30			1			3
Dunedin	4	4			27	18	3			173	9	6	5	1		71
Edinburgh	12	10	2		36	20	18			242	7	3	15	7		106
Pretoria	1	1			6	6	2			48	3	3	3			30
	24	**22**	**2**		**97**	**65**	**38**			**675**	**26**	**18**	**30**	**9**		**275**

Test Statistics

Points tallies by opponent and venue

South Africa

Venue	Played	Won	Drawn	Lost	POINTS FOR						POINTS AGAINST					
					Tries	Cons	Pens	DGs	GMs	Totals	Tries	Cons	Pens	DGs	GMs	Totals
Auckland	8	5	1	2	18	10	22	2		166	17	11	10	1		124
Bloemfontein	2	1	1		2	2	4	1		26	1	1	5			20
Cape Town	7	5		2	8	4	16	3		95	6	4	11	1		67
Cardiff	1			1			6			18	1	1	3	1		22
Christchurch	6	4		2	13	4	12	1		93	10	7	7	2		74
Dunedin	5	5			12	9	8			86	3	1	4			25
Durban	6	2		4	11	5	8			86	10	6	9	7		108
Johannesburg	10	3		7	17	13	19	5		180	21	15	24	6	1	215
Port Elizabeth	4			4	4	1	2			20	7	4	4	1		44
Pretoria	3	2		1	6	3	11	2		73	7	3	7	1		61
Wellington	8	4	1	3	11	2	11	2		91	7	5	13	4		84
	60	**31**	**3**	**26**	**102**	**53**	**119**	**16**		**934**	**90**	**58**	**97**	**24**	**1**	**844**

Tonga

Venue	Played	Won	Drawn	Lost	POINTS FOR						POINTS AGAINST					
					Tries	Cons	Pens	DGs	GMs	Totals	Tries	Cons	Pens	DGs	GMs	Totals
Albany	1	1			15	12	1			102						
Bristol	1	1			5	4	4			45			3			9
	2	**2**			**20**	**16**	**5**			**147**			**3**			**9**

United States

Venue	Played	Won	Drawn	Lost	POINTS FOR						POINTS AGAINST					
					Tries	Cons	Pens	DGs	GMs	Totals	Tries	Cons	Pens	DGs	GMs	Totals
Gloucester	1	1			8	4	2			46			2			6
San Francisco	1	1			13	6				51			1			3
	2	**2**			**21**	**10**	**2**			**97**			**3**			**9**

Wales

Venue	Played	Won	Drawn	Lost	POINTS FOR						POINTS AGAINST					
					Tries	Cons	Pens	DGs	GMs	Totals	Tries	Cons	Pens	DGs	GMs	Totals
Auckland	2	2			11	11	7	1		87	3	3	1			21
Brisbane	1	1			8	7	1			49	1	1				6
Cardiff	10	7		3	19	13	21	2		171	9	6	15	1		92
Christchurch	2	2			14	8	1			71			1			3
Johannesburg	1	1			3	2	4	1		34			2	1		9
London	1	1			5	4	2	1		42	1	1				7
Swansea	1	1			4	2	1			19						
	18	**15**		**3**	**64**	**47**	**37**	**5**		**473**	**14**	**11**	**19**	**2**		**138**

(Western) Samoa

Venue	Played	Won	Drawn	Lost	POINTS FOR						POINTS AGAINST					
					Tries	Cons	Pens	DGs	GMs	Totals	Tries	Cons	Pens	DGs	GMs	Totals
Albany	2	2			16	10	7			121	1	1	4			19
Auckland	1	1			2	2	7			35	1	1	2			13
Napier	1	1			7	5	1	1		51	1	1	1			10
	4	**4**			**25**	**17**	**15**	**1**		**207**	**3**	**3**	**7**			**42**

World XV

Venue	Played	Won	Drawn	Lost	POINTS FOR						POINTS AGAINST					
					Tries	Cons	Pens	DGs	GMs	Totals	Tries	Cons	Pens	DGs	GMs	Totals
Auckland	1	1			4	2	2			26	1	1	3			15
Christchurch	1			1	2		2			14	3	2	2	2		28
Wellington	1	1			10	7				54	5	3				26
	3	**2**		**1**	**16**	**9**	**4**			**94**	**9**	**6**	**5**	**2**		**69**

Most tests against the All Blacks

First name	Surname	Country	Years	Tests
David	Campese	Australia	82, 83, 84, 86, 87, 88, 89, 90, 91, 92, 93, 94, 95, 96	29
Tim	Horan	Australia	89, 90, 91, 92, 93, 95, 96, 97, 98, 99	23[1]
John	Eales	Australia	91, 92, 94, 95, 96, 97, 98, 2000, 2001	21[2]
Nick	Farr-Jones	Australia	85, 86, 87, 88, 89, 90, 91, 92, 93	21[3]
Phil	Kearns	Australia	89, 90, 91, 92, 93, 94, 95, 98, 99	21[4]
Simon	Poidevin	Australia	80, 82, 83, 84, 85, 86, 88, 89, 91	21
Mark	Andrews	South Africa	94, 95, 96, 97, 98, 99, 2001	19
Jason	Little	Australia	91, 92, 93, 94, 95, 97, 98, 99, 2000	18[5]
Michael	Lynagh	Australia	85, 86, 88, 89, 90, 91, 92	16
Joe	Roff	Australia	95, 96, 97, 98, 99, 2000, 2001	16
David	Wilson	Australia	92, 93, 94, 96, 97, 98, 99, 2000	16
George	Gregan	Australia	94, 96, 97, 98, 99, 2000, 2001, 2002	15
Matthew	Burke	Australia	95, 96, 97, 98, 99, 2001, 2002	14
Viliame	Ofahengaue	Australia	90, 91, 92, 94, 95, 98	14[6]
Joost	van der Westhuizen	South Africa	95, 96, 97, 98, 99, 2000, 2001	14
Andre	Venter	South Africa	96, 97, 98, 99, 2000, 2001	14
Steve	Cutler	Australia	82, 84, 85, 86, 87, 88, 89	13
Ewen	McKenzie	Australia	90, 91, 92, 93, 94, 95, 97	13
Serge	Blanco	France	81, 84, 86, 87, 89, 90	12
Eddie	Bonis	Australia	29, 31, 32, 34, 36, 38	12
Tony	Daly	Australia	89, 90, 91, 92, 93, 94	12
Tim	Gavin	Australia	88, 89, 90, 91, 93, 94, 95, 96	12
Gavin	Hastings	Scotland	87, 90, 91, 92, 93, 95	12[7]
Peter	Johnson	Australia	62, 64, 67, 68	12
Andy	McIntyre	Australia	82, 84, 85, 87, 88, 89	12
John	Thornett	Australia	55, 58, 62, 64	12
Fred	Wood	Australia	07, 10, 13, 14	12

[1]*includes two matches for World XV 1992* [5]*includes one match for World XV 1992*
[2]*includes one match for World XV 1992* [6]*includes two matches for World XV 1992*
[3]*includes two matches for World XV 1992* [7]*includes three matches for World XV 1992, three for British Isles 1993*
[4]*includes three matches for World XV 1992*

All Blacks against All Blacks

First name	Surname	For All Blacks	Opposition	Year
Stephen	Bachop	1992–94	Samoa	1999
Alama	Ieremia	1994–2000	Western Samoa	1993
Evan	Jessop	1931–32	Australia	1934
Jamie	Salmon	1980–81	England	1985
Owen	Stephens	1968	Australia	1974
Ofisa	Tonu'u	1996–98	Western Samoa	1993
Va'aiga	Tuigamala	1989–93	Samoa	1999
Gary	Whetton	1981–91	World XV	1992

Test All Blacks who played tests for others

George	Aitken	Scotland
Graeme	Bachop	Japan
Stephen	Bachop	Western Samoa
Frano	Botica	Croatia
Eroni	Clarke	Western Samoa
Des	Connor	Australia
Matthew	Cooper	Croatia
Colin	Gilray	Scotland
Shane	Howarth	Wales
Alama	Ieremia	Western Samoa
Evan	Jessep	Australia
Michael	Jones	Western Samoa
Jamie	Joseph	Japan
Donald	Macpherson	Scotland
Dylan	Mika	Samoa
Henare	Milner	Singapore
Jamie	Salmon	England
John	Schuster	Western Samoa
Owen	Stephens	Australia
Ofisa	Tonu'u	Western Samoa
Va'aiga	Tuigamala	Samoa
Joeli	Vidiri	Fiji

Most points against the All Blacks

First name	Surname	Country	Years	Tests	Test as replacement	Tries	Cons	Pens	DGs	GMs	Points	Total Points
Matthew	Burke	Australia	95, 96, 97, 98, 99, 2001, 2002	14		6	9	37				159
Michael	Lynagh	Australia	85, 86, 88, 89, 90, 91, 92	16	1		11	35	2			133
Gavin	Hastings	Scotland	87, 90, 91, 93, 95	6			7	12			50	
		British Isles	93	3			1	12			38	
		World XV	92	3	1	1		1			7	95
Christophe	Lamaison	France	99, 2000	4	1	1	9	12	4			71
Joel	Stransky	South Africa	95, 96	6	1		3	14	2			54
Roger	Gould	Australia	80, 82, 84, 85	10		1	7	10	1			51
Hugo	Porta	Argentina	85, 87	3			1	10	4			44
Naas	Botha	South Africa	81, 92	4			7	8	2			44
		World XV	92	2			4	3			17	61
Braam	van Straaten	South Africa	99, 2000, 2001	4			5	10				40
Mark	Ella	Australia	80, 82, 83, 84	10		1	3	8	2			40

Most tries against the All Blacks

Tries	First name	Surname	Country	Years	Tests
8	David	Campese	Australia	82, 83, 84, 86, 87, 88, 89, 90, 91, 92, 93, 94, 95, 96	29
6	Matthew	Burke	Australia	95, 96, 97, 98, 99, 2001–02	14
6	Joost	van der Westhuizen	South Africa	95, 96, 97, 98, 99, 2000–01	14
5	Tim	Horan	Australia	89, 90, 91, 92, 93, 95, 96, 97, 98, 99	21
4	Owen	Bridle	Australia	32, 34, 36	7
4	Greg	Cornelsen	Australia	74, 78, 79, 80	9
4	Colin	Windon	Australia	46, 47, 49, 51, 52	10

Most conversions against the All Blacks

First name	Surname	Country	Years	Cons
Naas	Botha	South Africa	81, 92	11
Michael	Lynagh	Australia	85, 86, 88, 89, 90, 91, 92	11
Matthew	Burke	Australia	95, 96, 97, 98, 99, 2001–02	9
Christophe	Lamaison	France	99, 2000	9
Gavin	Hastings	BI, Scotland	87, 90, 91, 92, 93, 95	8
Roger	Gould	Australia	80, 82, 84, 85	7
Jannie	de Beer	South Africa	1997	5
Alec	Ross	Australia	1929, 31, 32, 34	5
Braam	van Straaten	South Africa	1999, 2000–01	5

Most penalty goals against the All Blacks

First name	Surname	Country	Years	Pens
Michael	Lynagh	Australia	85, 86, 88, 89, 90, 91, 92	35
Matthew	Burke	Australia	95, 96, 97, 98, 99, 2001–02	35
Gavin	Hastings	Scotland, BI, World XV	87, 90, 91, 92, 93, 95	25
Joel	Stransky	South Africa	95, 96	14
Christophe	Lamaison	France	99, 2000	12

Most dropped goals against the All Blacks

First name	Surname	Country	Years	DGs
Hugo	Porta	Argentina	85, 87	4
Jean-Patrick	Lescarboura	France	84, 86	4
Christophe	Lamaison	France	99, 2000	4
Percy	Montgomery	South Africa	97, 98, 99, 2000–01	3
Paul	McLean	Australia	74, 78, 79	3

Seventeen opponents have each scored two dropped goals against NZ

Tests against the All Blacks for three different opponents

First name	Surname	Team	Years
Jeremy	Guscott	England	1991, 95, 99
		World XV	1992
		British Isles	1993
Arthur	Harding	Great Britain	1904
		Wales	1905
		Anglo-Welsh	1908
Gavin	Hastings	Scotland	1987, 90, 91, 93, 95
		World XV	1992
		British Isles	1993

Brother opponents

Beamish	George	British Isles	1930
Beamish	Charles	Ireland	1935
Barnard	Jannie	South Africa	1965
Barnard	Robbie	South Africa	1970
Boniface	André	France	1954, 61, 64
Boniface	Guy	France	1961
Botha	Naas	South Africa	1981, 92
Botha	Darius	South Africa	1981
Boyce	James	Australia	1962, 64
Boyce	Edward	Australia	1962, 64
Brown	Gordon	Scotland, BI	1971, 72, 77
Brown	Peter	Scotland	1964, 72
Burge	Albert	Australia	1907
Burge	Peter	Australia	1907
Calder	Jim	Scotland, BI	1981, 83
Calder	Finlay	Scotland	1987, 90, 91
Cuttita	Marcello	Italy	1987, 91
Cuttita	Massimo	Italy	1991, 95
Ella	Gary	Australia	1982, 88
Ella	Mark	Australia	1980, 82–84
Ford	Eric	Australia	1929
Ford	Jack	Australia	1929
Grant	Derrick	Scotland	1967
Grant	Tom	Scotland	1964
Hastings	Gavin	Scotland	1987, 90–91, 92, 93, 95
Hastings	Scott	Scotland	1990–91, 93, 95–96
Herbert	Anthony	Australia	1990, 92–93
Herbert	Daniel	Australia	1997, 1999–2001
Hewitt	Frank	Ireland	1924
Hewitt	Victor	Ireland	1935
Hewitt	Thomas	Ireland	1924
Honan	Barry	Australia	1968
Honan	Robert	Australia	1964
Jansen	Joggie	South Africa	1970
Jansen	Eben	South Africa	1981

Johnson	Brian	Australia	1952, 55
Johnson	Peter	Australia	1962, 64, 67–68
Lanza	Patrick	Argentina	1985, 87
Lanza	Juan	Argentina	1985, 87
Lawton	Rob	Australia	1988
Lawton	Tom	Australia	1984–88
Louy	Boy	South Africa	1928, 37
Louy	Fanie	South Africa	1937
MacLeod	Kenneth	Scotland	1905
MacLeod	Lewis	Scotland	1905
McLean	Jeff	Australia	1972, 74
McLean	Paul	Australia	1974, 78, 79
McLean	Bill	Australia	1946–47
McLean	Doug	Australia	1934, 36
Milne	Iain	Scotland	1979, 81, 83, 87, 90
Milne	Ken	Scotland, BI	1990, 93, 95
Moriarty	Paul	Wales	1987–88
Moriarty	Richard	Wales	1987
Morkel	Royal	South Africa	1921
Morkel	Harry	South Africa	1921
Osler	Bennie	South Africa	1928
Osler	Stanley	South Africa	1928
Prat	Jean	France	1954
Prat	Maurice	France	1954
Prentice	Clarence	Australia	1914
Prentice	Ward	Australia	1910
Stephenson	George	Ireland	1924
Stephenson	Henry	Ireland	1924
Storey	Geoffrey	Australia	1929
Storey	Keith	Australia	1936
Thornett	John	Australia	1955, 58, 62, 64
Thornett	Dick	Australia	1962
Underwood	Rory	England, BI	1991, 93, 95
Underwood	Tony	England	1993, 95

Father and son opponents

Camberabero	Guy	France	1961
Camberabero	Didier	France, World XV	1987, 90, 92
Cox	Brian	Australia	1952, 55, 57
Cox	Phillip	Australia	1980, 82, 84
Deering	Seamus	Ireland	1935
Deering	Seamus	Ireland	1978
Dourthe	Claude	France	1967, 68, 73
Dourthe	Richard	France	1995, 99, 2000
Du Plessis	Felix	South Africa	1949
Du Plessis	Morne	South Africa	1976
Hewitt	Thomas	Ireland	1924
Hewitt	David	British Isles	1959
McLean	Doug snr	Australia	1905
McLean	Doug jnr	Australia	1934, 36
McLean	Bill	Australia	1946, 47
McLean	Doug jnr	Australia	1934, 36
McLean	Peter	Australia	1978–80
Perrin	Tom	Australia	1931
Perrin	Paul	Australia	1962
Preece	Ivor	British Isles	1950
Preece	Peter	England	1973

Skrela	Jean-Claude	France	1977
Skrela	David	France	2001
Van den Berg	Mauritz	South Africa	1937
Van den Berg	Derek	South Africa	1976
Walker	Alf	South Africa	1921
Walker	Harry	South Africa	1956
Wood	Gordon	British Isles	1959
Wood	Keith	Ireland	1997, 2001–02

Grandfather and grandson opponents

Lawton	Thomas (T.S.)	Australia	1929, 32
Lawton	Tom	Australia	1984–88
Lawton	Rob	Australia	1988
McLean	Doug snr	Australia	1905
McLean	Peter	Australia	1978–80
McLean	Paul	Australia	1974, 78–79
McLean	Jeff	Australia	1972, 74

Provincial representation of test All Blacks

Auckland	137	Bay of Plenty	11
Canterbury	125	Wanganui	8
Wellington	106	King Country	6
Otago	103	Poverty Bay	5
Taranaki	45	Wairarapa-Bush	5
Southland	34	West Coast	4
Waikato	33	Marlborough	3
Hawke's Bay	27	Nelson	3
Northland	23	Buller	2
Manawatu	22	North Otago	2
North Harbour	17	East Coast	2
Wairarapa	15	Horowhenua	1
South Canterbury	14	Nelson Bays	1
Counties-Manukau	14	Bush Districts	1

Widest provincial representation in a test

Number	Provinces	Opponent	Date
13	Auckland, Canterbury, Counties, Hawke's Bay, King Country, North Auckland, Otago, Poverty Bay, South Canterbury, Taranaki, Waikato, Wairarapa, Wellington	Wales	14.6.1969
12	Auckland, Canterbury, Counties, Hawke's Bay, King Country, Manawatu, Otago, Southland, Taranaki, Waikato, Wairarapa, Wellington	England	4.11.1967
12	Auckland, Canterbury, Counties, King Country, Manawatu, Marlborough, Nelson Bays, North Auckland, Otago, Poverty Bay, Taranaki, Wellington	Australia	19.8.1972
12	Auckland, Bay of Plenty, Canterbury, Counties, Manawatu, Otago, Poverty Bay, Southland, Taranaki, Wellington (Hawke's Bay and Wanganui off bench)	France	11.11.1977
11	Nine occasions		
10	Twenty-six occasions		

Most from one province in a test

Players	Reps/subs	Province	Opponents	Date
14	1	Canterbury	Ireland	22.6.2002
13	1	Canterbury	Ireland	15.6.2002
12	1	Canterbury	South Africa	20.7.2002
12		Auckland	Italy	13.10.1991
12		Canterbury	Australia	13.7.2002
11	3	Canterbury	South Africa	10.8.2002
11		Auckland	Argentina	1.6.1987
11		Auckland	Australia	24.8.1991
11		Auckland	England	3.10.1991
10	2	Canterbury	Scotland	24.11.2001
10	1	Auckland	Wales	14.6.1987
10	1	Auckland	Scotland	6.6.1987
10		Auckland	Canada	20.10.1991
10		Auckland	France	20.6.1987
10		Auckland	Australia	25.7.1987
10		Auckland	British Isles	26.6.1993
10		Auckland	Australia	27.10.1991
10		Auckland	Fiji	27.5.1987
10	2	Canterbury	Australia	3.8.2002
10	1	Canterbury	Ireland	17.11.2001
9	2	Auckland	Argentina	29.7.1989
9	1	Auckland	Argentina	15.7.1989
9	1	Auckland	France	3.11.1990
9	1	Auckland	British Isles	3.7.1993
9	1	Canterbury	France	18.11.2000
9	1	Canterbury	Argentina	1.12.2001
9		Auckland	France	1.7.1989
9		Auckland	France	10.11.1990
9		Auckland	Australia	10.8.1991
9		Auckland	Wales	11.6.1988
9		Auckland	British Isles	12.6.1993
9		Auckland	Argentina	13.7.1991
9		Auckland	South Africa	15.8.1992
9		Auckland	Australia	16.7.1988
9		Auckland	France	17.6.1989
9		Auckland	Australia	17.7.1993
9		Auckland	Australia	18.8.1990

Players	Reps/subs	Province	Opponents	Date
9		Auckland	Australia	21.7.1990
9		Auckland	Italy	22.5.1987
9		Auckland	Australia	25.7.1992
9		Auckland	Wales	28.5.1988
9		Auckland	Scotland	30.10.1991
9		Auckland	Australia	30.7.1988
9		Auckland	Australia	4.8.1990
9		Auckland	United States	8.10.1991
9		Canterbury	France	11.11.2000
8	1	Auckland	Samoa	31.7.1993
8		Auckland	Scotland	16.6.1990
8		Auckland	Australia	19.7.1992
8		Auckland	Scotland	23.6.1990
8		Auckland	Australia	3.7.1988
8		Auckland	Australia	4.7.1992
8		Auckland	Australia	5.8.1989
8		Auckland	Ireland	6.6.1992
8		Auckland	Argentina	6.7.1991
7	2	Auckland	Australia	5.7.1997
7	1	Auckland	Argentina	21.6.1997
7	1	Otago	Samoa	18.6.1999
7		Auckland	France	15.11.1986
7		Auckland	Australia	15.8.1903
7		Auckland	Ireland	18.11.1989
7		Auckland	South Africa	19.7.1997
7		Auckland	Australia	23.8.1986
7		Auckland	World XV	25.4.1992
7		Auckland	France	28.6.1986
7		Auckland	Argentina	28.6.1997
7		Auckland	Wales	4.11.1989
7		Auckland	France	8.11.1986
7		Auckland	Australia	9.8.1986
7		Canterbury	Australia	4.8.1984
7		Otago	British Isles	1.7.1950
7		Otago	British Isles	10.6.1950
7		Otago	South Africa	13.8.1949
7		Otago	South Africa	3.9.1949

Referees of All Black tests

Name		Country	Tests
Bevan	D.	Wales	16
Murphy	P.	New Zealand	13
Marshall	P.	Australia	11
Erickson	W.	Australia	10
Fleming	J.	Scotland	10
Morrison	E.	England	9
Pring	J.	New Zealand	8
Fitzgerald	K.	Australia	7
MacNeill	A.	Australia	7
Millar	D.	New Zealand	7
Farquhar	A.	New Zealand	6
Norling	C.	Wales	6
Quittenton	R.	England	6
West	J.	Ireland	6
Byres	R.	Australia	5
Howard	F.	England	5
Stirling	B.	Ireland	5
Young	S.	Australia	5
Anderson	J.	Scotland	4
Burmeister	R.	South Africa	4
Gillies	C.	New Zealand	4
Henning	T.	South Africa	4
Hollander	S.	New Zealand	4
Hosie	A.	Scotland	4
Kaplan	J.	South Africa	4
Neser	V.	South Africa	4
Robin	P.	France	4
Vanderfield	E.	Australia	4
Bezuidenhout	G.	South Africa	3
Burnett	D.	Ireland	3
Cooney	R.	Australia	3
David	I.	Wales	3
Hilditch	S.	Ireland	3
Hourquet	R.	France	3
Mayne	A.	Australia	3
McDavitt	P.	New Zealand	3
McHugh	D.	Ireland	3
Megson	R.	Scotland	3
Parkinson	F.	New Zealand	3
Tindill	E.	New Zealand	3
Watson	A.	South Africa	3
Williams	R.	Ireland	3
Burger	F.	South Africa	2
Campbell	A.	New Zealand	2
Campsall	B.	England	2
Chapman	W.	Australia	2
Cole	A.	Australia	2
Cooper	P.	England	2
Dickinson	S.	Australia	2
Fong	A.	New Zealand	2
Freethy	A.	Wales	2
Fright	W.	New Zealand	2
Gadjovich	G.	Canada	2
Gadney	C.	England	2
Garling	A.	Australia	2
Hofmeyr	E.	South Africa	2
Johnson	J.	England	2
Jones	W.	Wales	2
King	J.	New Zealand	2
Lander	S.	England	2
Martin	N.	Australia	2
Maurette	G.	France	2
McMahon	D.	Scotland	2
Moore	T.	Australia	2
Morgan	C.	Australia	2
Neilson	A.	New Zealand	2
Palmade	F.	France	2
Robbertse	P.	South Africa	2
Sanson	N.	Scotland	2
Strydom	S.	South Africa	2
Taylor	A.	New Zealand	2
Tolhurst	H.	Australia	2
White	C.	England	2
Barnes	P.	Australia	1
Bishop	D.	New Zealand	1
Brown	A.	Australia	1
Brunton	J.	England	1
Burnett	R.	Australia	1
Burrell	R.	Scotland	1
Butt	C.	Australia	1
Cochrane	C.	Australia	1
Collett	C.	Australia	1
Crowe	K.	Australia	1
Dallas	J.	Scotland	1
D'Arcy	D.	Ireland	1
Davies	R.	Wales	1
Dedet	L.	France	1
Deluca	P.	Argentina	1
Domercq	G.	France	1
Doocey	T.	New Zealand	1
Downes	A.	New Zealand	1
Duffy	B.	New Zealand	1
Dume	J.	France	1
Duncan	J.	New Zealand	1
Evans	F.	New Zealand	1
Evans	G.	England	1
Faull	J.	Wales	1
Ferguson	P.	Australia	1
Findlay	J.	Scotland	1
Finlay	A.	Australia	1
Fleury	A.	New Zealand	1
Fordham	R.	Australia	1
Forsyth	R.	New Zealand	1
Frood	J.	New Zealand	1
Gourlay	I.	South Africa	1
Griffiths	A.	New Zealand	1
Haydon	N.	Australia	1
High	C.	England	1
Hill	W.	Australia	1
Hill	E.	New Zealand	1
Irving	A.	Australia	1
Jeffares	R.	Ireland	1
Joseph	M.	Wales	1
Jutge	J.	France	1
Keenan	H.	England	1
Kelleher	K.	Scotland	1
Kennedy	W.	Ireland	1
Kinsey	B.	Australia	1
Larkin	F.	Australia	1
Lewis	A.	Wales	1
Macassey	L.	New Zealand	1
Malan	W.	South Africa	1
Matheson	A.	New Zealand	1
McAuley	C.	New Zealand	1
McCartney	K.	Scotland	1
McKenzie	E.	New Zealand	1
McKenzie	H.	New Zealand	1
McMullen	F.	New Zealand	1
Mene	D.	France	1
Moffitt	J.	New Zealand	1
Nicholson	G.	New Zealand	1
Pauling	T.	Australia	1
Prideaux	L.	England	1
Robson	C.	New Zealand	1
Simpson	R.	New Zealand	1
Sklar	E.	Argentina	1
Slabber	M.	South Africa	1
Spreadbury	A.	England	1
Strasheim	E.	South Africa	1
Sullivan	G.	New Zealand	1
Sutherland	F.	New Zealand	1
Thomas	C.	Wales	1
Thomas	P.	France	1
Thomas	C.	Wales	1
Tierney	A.	Australia	1
Titcomb	M.	England	1
Tomalin	L.	Australia	1
Walsh	L.	New Zealand	1
Waugh	R.	Australia	1
Wilkins	H.	England	1
Williams	J.	New Zealand	1
Williams	N.	Wales	1
Wolstenholme	B.	New Zealand	1
Woolley	A.	South Africa	1
Yemen	R.	Wales	1
Young	J.	Scotland	1

Referee replacements

Name	Opponent	Replacement	Year
Murphy, Pat	South Africa	Taylor, Alan	1965
McHugh, David	South Africa	White, Chris	2002

New Zealand at the World Cup

	1987	1991	1995	1999
Argentina	46–15			
Australia		6–16 (sf)		
Canada		29–13		
England		18–12	45–29 (sf)	30–16
Fiji	74–13			
France	29–9 (f)			31–43 (sf)
Ireland			43–19	
Italy	70–6	31–21		101–3
Japan			145–17	
Scotland	30–3 (qf)	13–6 (po)	48–30 (qf)	30–18 (qf)
South Africa			12–15 (f)	18–22 (po)
Tonga				45–9
United States		46–6		
Wales	49–6 (sf)		34–9	

(sf) – semifinal (f) – final (qf) – quarterfinal (po) – playoff

World Cup match tally

	POINTS FOR					POINTS AGAINST				
	Tries	Cons	Pens	DGs	Total	Tries	Cons	Pens	DGs	Total
Argentina										
Wellington 1987	6	2	6		46	1	1	3		15
Australia										
Dublin 1991			2		6	2	1	2		16
Canada										
Lille 1991	5	3	1		29	2	1	1		13
England										
London 1991	1	1	4		18			3	1	12
Cape Town 1995	6	3	1	2	45	4	3	1		29
London 1999	3	3	3		30	1	1	3		16
Fiji										
Christchurch 1987	12	10	2		74	1		3		13
France										
Auckland 1987	3	1	4	1	29	1	1	1		9
London 1999	3	2	4		31	4	4	3	2	43
Ireland										
Johannesburg 1995	5	3	4		43	3	2			19
Italy										
Auckland 1987	12	8	2		70			1	1	6
Leicester 1991	4	3	3		31	2	2	3		21
Huddersfield 1999	14	11	3		101			1		3
Japan										
Bloemfontein 1995	21	20			145	2	2	1		17
Scotland										
Christchurch 1987	2	2	6		30			1		3
Cardiff 1991	1		3		13			2		6
Pretoria 1995	6	6	2		48	3	3	3		30
Edinburgh 1999	4	2	2		30	2	1	1	1	18
South Africa										
Johannesburg 1995		3		1	12			3	2	15
Cardiff 1999			6		18	1	1	3	2	22
Tonga										
Bristol 1999	5	4	4		45			3		9
United States										
Gloucester 1991	8	4	2		46			2		6
Wales										
Brisbane 1987	8	7	1		49	1	1			6
Johannesburg 1995	3	2	4	1	34			2	1	9
TOTALS	**132**	**97**	**72**	**5**	**1023**	**30**	**24**	**46**	**10**	**356**

All Blacks World Cup summary

Year	P	W	L	POINTS FOR					POINTS AGAINST				
				T	C	P	DG	Total	T	C	P	DG	Total
1987	6	6		43	30	21	1	298	4	3	9	1	52
1991	6	5	1	19	11	15		143	6	4	13	1	74
1995	6	5	1	41	37	12	4	327	12	10	10	3	119
1999	6	4	2	29	22	22		255	8	7	14	5	111
	24	**20**	**4**	**132**	**100**	**70**	**5**	**1023**	**30**	**24**	**46**	**10**	**356**

Bibliography

Those monumental tomes produced by the indefatigable Rod Chester and Neville McMillan, *Men In Black* (Hodder Moa Beckett), *The Encylopedia of New Zealand Rugby* (Hodder Moa Beckett) and *Centenary* (Moa Publications), have become standard reference works for anyone interested in or fascinated by more than just the present in New Zealand rugby. They were my constant companions. Complementing them have been various editions of the *Rugby Almanack* (Hodder Moa Beckett), which first appeared under the editorship of Arthur Carman in 1935 and is now jointly edited by Clive Akers and Geoff Miller. The excellent new version of the *South African Rugby Annual* (MWP Media), edited by Andy Colquhoun, and various editions of the old *Rothmans Rugby Union Yearbook*, now the *International Rugby Yearbook* (IRB) edited by Mike Cleary and John Griffiths, provided answers when questions were posed. Useful too was *The Complete Who's Who of International Rugby* (Blandford Press) compiled by Terry Godwin.

Wallaby Gold (Random House), written by Peter Jenkins, contains wonderful Australian material, as does *The Wallabies* (GAP Publishing) and both provided excellent background on our friends across the Tasman. What they did for Australian rugby, *Welsh International Matches 1881–2000* (Mainstream), compiled by Howard Evans, did for Welsh rugby. Would that all rugby-playing countries had such complete records.

Contemporary newspaper accounts of matches, tours and players were frequently consulted and, fortunately, these are all hardbound in scrapbooks dating from the tour by South Africa in 1921. These were meticulously compiled by Henry Magnusson, first of Wellington and then of Auckland, and form a unique record of New Zealand test rugby. These scrapbooks, which include clippings from New Zealand and overseas newspapers and tour ephemera such as tickets, programmes and autographs, were supplemented by the excellent series of articles written during the Originals' tour by the team's vice-captain, Billy Stead, for the *Southland Times*.

The Captains (Jonathan Ball Publishers), written by a former chief executive of the South African Rugby Union, Edward Griffiths, gave unusual insights into the personalities and politics of rugby in South Africa, and Ivor Difford's extensive work, *The History of South African Rugby Football* (Specialty Press), was a help with the early days of rugby there.

Background information on that infrequently seen team, the British Isles, came from Clem Thomas' work, *The History of the British Lions* (Mainstream), and *1950 — The Year of the Lions*, written and published by Des Williams of Hamilton. *Lions of Wales* (Mainstream) written by Peter Jackson, and *Willie John* (Gill and Macmillan), written by Willie John McBride and Edmund van Esbeck, also provided useful information.

Gordon Slatter's *On the Ball* (Whitcombe and Tombs), a book ahead of its time when it was published in 1970, provided contexts and background, Keith Quinn's *The Encyclopedia of World Rugby* (Shoal Bay Press) was a valuable aid and *Rugby* (Hamlyn) by Chris Rea was useful for background information on the roots of lesser known rugby countries.

Newspapers and rugby magazines in various countries were also consulted.

Once again, it was comforting to return to John Mulgan's *Report On Experience* (Oxford University Press, 1947), from which I have borrowed the quotation on the back cover.

Index

301

Index